From Norway to Newport...

Flavors of the Fjords

⌘ ⌘ ⌘ ⌘

Norwegian Holiday Cookbook

"My task which I am trying to achieve is, by the power of the written word, to make you hear, to make you feel--it is, before all, to make you see. That--and no more, and it is everything."
Joseph Conrad

"...let it be our pride that we ourselves may put meaning into our lives, and sometimes a significance that transcends death. If a man is fortunate he will, before he dies, gather up as much as he can of his civilized heritage and transmit it to his children."
Will and Ariel Durant

Five-year old Andrew Henson presses his mother, Karen, for more information after she tells him a story about his Norwegian ancestors.

"I'm sorry Andrew, that's all we know about them."

"But why Mother? Didn't they know I would want to know about them?"

From Norway to Newport...

FLAVORS
of the
FJORDS

Norwegian
Holiday
Cookbook

Faith Cottrell Raymond Connors
Tracy Daniel Connors
Tove Johansen Halvorsen
Bjørn Fladvad Johansen

The BelleAire Press
Crofton, Maryland

Subscription Notice

This BelleAire Press publication is updated on a periodic basis with supplements to reflect important changes in the subject matter. If you purchased this book directly from BelleAire Press, we have already recorded your subscription for this update service.

If, however, you purchased *Flavors* from a bookstore or other source and wish to receive (1) the current update at no additional charge, and (2) future updates and revised, or related volumes with a 30-day examination review, please send or fax your name, organization (if applicable), and address to:

Supplement Department
The BelleAire Press
P.O. Box 8424
Crofton, Maryland 21114
1-301-464-4789 FAX

This publication is designed to provide accurate and authoritative information in regard to the subject matter covered. It is sold with the understanding that the publisher is not engaged in rendering professional services. If expert assistance is required, the services of a competent professional person should be sought. From a Declaration of Principles jointly adopted by a Committee of the American Bar Association and a Committee of Publishers.

The authors and editors who prepared this book have tried to make all the contents as accurate and as correct as possible. Ingredients, preparation, photographs, and text have all been carefully checked and cross-checked. However, due to the variability of local products, variations in preparation, and personal skill, neither the authors nor BelleAire Press assumes any responsibility for any adverse outcomes, or for damages or other losses incurred that result from the material presented herein. **Readers working with kitchen equipment and appliances must always be alert to their safety, as well as that of others in the area, and to the proper preparation of food. Particular care must be taken when working with hot pans and cooking oils.**

Library of Congress Cataloging-in-Publication Data

Flavors of the Fjords: The Norwegian Holiday Cookbook/Faith Cottrell Raymond Connors, Tracy Daniel Connors, Tove Johansen Halvorsen, and Bjørn Fladvad Johansen.
p. cm.
Includes bibliographical references, glossary and index.
ISBN 0-9640138-0-0
Library of Congress Catalog Card Number: 95-75924
I. Connors, Connors, Halvorsen, Johansen
Printed in the United States of America

In Loving Memory
of

Anna Fladvad Johansen

Marie Theresa Fladvad Cottrell

Marie Theresa Cottrell Raymond

Nina Johansen,

our grandmothers and our mothers.

About the Authors

Faith Cottrell Raymond Connors

Faith Connors is an Associate Professor at the University of Maryland, serving as the Extension Agent 4-H for Charles County, Maryland. She manages one of the state's largest 4-H programs which assist youth in leadership and life skills development. The Charles County 4-H program includes nearly 600 youth and 300 adult leaders. Her education includes: Master of Arts in Teaching degree, Jacksonville University, 1980; and the Bachelor of Science in Education degree, University of Connecticut; 1961. She attended the University of Oslo, International Summer School in 1960, and has completed other graduate level studies at Bowie State University and the University of Maryland. In 1992 she received the National Achievement in Service Award from the National Association of Extension Agents 4-H, and has served as Vice President of the Maryland Association of Extension 4-H Agents. In 1993, she served as member of the U.S. Department of Agriculture Extension Service 4-H National Visual Metaphors Conference and the National 4-H Work Force Preparedness Program Design Conference to design a new national model. She has an extensive background in foods and nutrition and serves on various state planning and curriculum committees.

Tracy Daniel Connors

For over thirty years, Tracy Connors has filled senior management and leadership positions in business, government and philanthropic organizations, with particular emphasis on public and Congressional affairs, business information services, management of advanced technology development or application programs, and electronic publishing.

As a Captain in the Naval Reserve, he has accepted numerous special active duty assignments for the Navy since 1986, including: Director, Congressional Relations & Public Affairs, Naval Sea Systems Command; Total Quality Leadership Public Affairs Officer, Office of the Chief of Naval Operations; Deputy Director, Command Excellence & Leader Development Division, Navy Military Personnel Command, Washington, DC; Public Affairs Officer, Naval District Washington; and, Director, Congressional and Public Affairs, Space and Naval Warfare Systems Command; and, the U.S. Commission on Roles and Missions.

Since 1984 he has visited Norway ten times on business or Navy duties. His NATO operational experience, includes numerous exercises in Norway during which he served in senior public information positions .

His civilian positions have included service as Administrative Assistant to Congressman Charles E. Bennett; Manager, Corporate Communications, Gould Electronics Defense Business Section; Vice President, Taft Corporation; and, Director of Satellite Learning Services for the U.S. Chamber of Commerce.

As an editor, he has published seven reference works in communications and management of nonprofit organizations--Wiley, McGraw-Hill, AMACOM, and Longman. For the last 15 years, the most comprehensive management texts for nonprofit organizations in print have been those he published.

He attended Jacksonville University, and received a Bachelor's degree from the University of Florida, and a Master of Arts degree from the University of Rhode Island.

Tove Johansen Halvorsen

Tove Halvorsen was born and educated in Oslo, Norway where she graduated from the Fagerborg Gymnasium, majoring in English. After starting her business career with positions in Copenhagen and Oslo, at the age of 24 she left Norway for what she intended to be a one year stay in the United States. During that year she met her husband to be, and the one year extended to 25 years.

She has lived in New York, Vermont, Maine, and Wisconsin. In 1981 she returned to Norway to live and to resume her career with an Oslo Marine Insurance Broker firm. She divides her time between business, family, and several hobbies, including travel in Europe and the United States, and cooking. Of her three children, two live in the United States, and one lives in Norway. She hopes *Flavors of the Fjords* "will be like a window to the readers," a window through which they can catch a glimpse of her beloved country.

Bjørn Fladvad Johansen

After graduating from the College of Economics, Bjørn Johansen served in a Norwegian brigade as a component of the British Army on the Rhine in Germany. Following military service, he entered the insurance business and completed the Higher Insurance Examination. In 1958 he joined the Gjensidige ("The Mutual") to develop and expand its business operations. In 1961 he was appointed manager and a member of the management board of directors, and was placed in charge of all insurance and reinsurance activities for the company. During his career, he was a member of many insurance liaison committees between Nordic countries. In addition, he was a board member or chairman of many profit and nonprofit organizations operating in Nordic countries. From 1975 until his retirement, he was a member of the board for insurance companies operating in London, Paris, New York, and Bermuda. He is an avid stamp collector and gardener (ecological vegetables).

Contributing Editor

Ruth Knighton Miller

A home economist and nutrition educator, Ruth Miller taught food science and food economics at the University of Maryland for eleven years. Currently, she is a University Extension Agent for Southern Maryland. She received her Bachelor of Science degree from the University of Massachusetts, and her Master of Science degree from the University of Maryland. She is the author of seven cookbooks, in addition to her contributions to Flavors of the Fjords.

Acknowledgements

We wish to thank the many relatives and friends who helped in preparing the book. Special thanks to family members includes:

Anne Opdøl Arnesen
Anne Cottrell Barker (deceased)
Samuel Middleton Cottrell Barker
Miriam Faith Connors
Lars Opdøl Flatvad
Randi Johanne Flatvad
Karen Connors Henson
Kari Johansen
Ingrid E. Opdøl
Virginia Barker Tate

We also want to express our appreciation to the following friends and colleagues who have provided invaluable assistance and support throughout the many years it has taken to prepare this unique book:

Jerry Kashtan
Dr. Frances B. Kinne
Ruth Knighton Miller
David Patterson, U.S. Department of State
Per André Ragdem
Per Ragdem
Reidun Ragdem
William A. Sherman

In addition, many organizations have been most generous with their resources and support, including:

Bowie Public Library, Bowie, Maryland
Brumunddal Bibliotek, Brumunddal, Norway
Bymuseum (Oslo City Museum), Oslo, Norway
Jamestown Historical Society, Jamestown, Rhode Island
Kristiansund Folk Bibliotek, Kristiansund, Norway
Leikvin Bygdemuseum, Grøa, Norway
Newport Historical Society, Newport, Rhode Island
Norsk Folkemuseum, Oslo, Norway
Norwegian Embassy, Washington, D.C.
Norwegian State Archives, Hamar, Norway
PC Outfitters, Ijamsville, Maryland
People's Library, Newport, Rhode Island
Redwood Library, Newport, Rhode Island
Romfo Kyrkje, Romfo, Norway
Statsarkivet, Oslo, Norway
Sunndal Reiselivslag (Travel Association), Sunndalsøra, Norway
Sunndalsøra Bibliotek, Sunndalsøra, Norway

Table of Contents
Innhold

Preface 1
The Story Behind "From Norway to Newport..." 1
The Faded Yellow Cookbook 2
Norwegian Holiday Traditions 23
The Fladvad and Bjørke Families 45
Flatvad & Bjørke 54
The Cottrells of Newport 99
Cakes and Cookies 159
Arendalskaker 160
Amerikansk kake 160
Berlinerkranser I 161
Berlinerkranser II 162
Biskopskake 162
Bløtkake I 163
Bløtkake II 163
Bordstabel-bakkels 164
Almond Paste or Mandelrøre 164
Clabbered Cream 165
Diagonaler 166
Eggedosis 166
Egg Nog 166
Frugtkage 167
Eplekake I 167
Eplekake II 167
Marie Theresa Cottrell Raymond's Dutch Apple Cake 168
Fruktkake 169
Flatbrød 169
Fyrstekake 170
Gjærbakst 171
Gjærbakst med Eple 171
Gudbrandsdaler 172
Hjortetakk 173
Guldkake 173
Honningkake 174
Hveteboller 175
Jødekaker 176
Julekake 177
Kaffebrød 178
Karamellpudding 179
Kardemommemuffins 180
Kassandrakaker 181
King Haakon's Coffee Cake 181
Kongevifter 182
Korintkake 183
Kransekake I 184
Kransekake II 185
Kringle I 186
Kringle II 186
Kringle III 187
Krumkake 189
Krydderkake I 190

Krydderkake II 191
Kvæfjordkake 191
Linser 192
Mandelflarn 193
Mandelkake 193
Mandelkake med Krem 194
Marabukaker 195
Mandelstenger 195
Mor Monsen's Kake I 196
Mor Monsen's Kaker II 197
Munker I 198
Munker II 199
Norsk kake 200
Norwegian Spice Loaf 201
Norwegian Pancakes 202
Pepperkake 202
Pepperkake 203
Peppernøtter 204
Pleskener 205
Potetlefse 206
Pritsar 207
Rømmegrøt 208
Rømmebrød 209
Rosett-Bakkels 210
Rullekake 211
Sandkaker I 212
Sandkaker II 213
Sandkaker III 213
Sandkaker IV 214
Sandkake 214
Sandnøtter I 215
Sandnøtter II 215
Sjokoladekuler 216
Sitronkake 216
Skillingsboller 217
Smørkranser 218
Smørpletter 219
Smør-Krem 219
Smultringer 220
Sølvkake 221
Sukkerbrød 223
Sukkerbrød 224
Tebrød 225
Tosca kake I 226
Tosca kake II 226
Tyske skiver 227
Vanilla Custard Filling 228
Vaniljeboller 229
Waffles 230
Fløtelapper I 230
Fløtelapper II 230

The Diary of Datter Olise 231
Letters from Christian and Jeanne Willumsen 241
Glossary of Norwegian-English Foods, Cooking and Family Life 261
Bibliography 307
Index 310

Preface
The Story Behind "From Norway to Newport..."

The day the United States put a man on the moon for the first time in 1969, I watched the incredible event on television well into the wee hours of the morning. Sitting in the living room of her vacation home in Jamestown, Rhode Island with me was my mother-in-law, Marie Theresa Cottrell Raymond. The rest of the family gave up and went to bed before the now immortal words were spoken from the moon to signal a giant step for mankind.

"Petie," as she was called by the family, was a highly intelligent, interesting woman who had curtailed a promising business career in New York to devote her attention to her children, a son, William Raymond, III and a daughter, Faith Cottrell Raymond. She awed me with her ability to complete the New York Times cross-word puzzle quickly and completely, every morning.

I had known her for eight years, but that early morning visit was the closest conversation we ever had. During the lulls in space activity, we talked about many things, including her youth in Newport, just across Narragansett Bay. She had lived in Stamford, Connecticut for many years after she married, but Newport was always home to her. She told me about her mother, Marie Theresa Fladvad Cottrell, who came on a

"visit" to the United States from Norway in 1894 and married a Newport merchant, Charles Middleton Cottrell. Petie considered herself a Norwegian-American.

Six months later, Petie died—too quickly—after a very short final struggle with the cancer she had fought so bravely for years. There was so much I wish I had taken time to say. Then, it was too late.

Some weeks later, Faith and I were given the first of many boxes of Petie's "things," an eclectic assortment of photographs and mementoes stretching back over her entire life. "Mother never threw anything away," Faith explained as we looked at the jumbled boxes in great dismay. Sorting them was too painful. We put them in the attic and basement for years. Finally, in the late Seventies, we began to sort through the "collection." Much of it we determined was not worth saving. However, we kept all photographs, letters, postcards, and mementoes in good condition. [We may have the only dance card left from the Graduation Ball for the Class of 1923 from Rogers High

At left, Marie Theresa Cottrell Raymond, in about 1924, a fun-loving "flapper" starting her business career in New York. Below, with her daughter, Faith Cottrell Raymond Connors in 1962 at her home in Westport, Connecticut.

School in Newport.] There were letters in bundles, old 616-size Brownie negatives, buttons, snap shots and portraits, and on the bottom, the yellowed little book.

There was much more. Many of the items kept by Petie had belonged to her mother, Marie Theresa Fladvad Cottrell. There were many photographs, from snapshots of the family in Newport to studio portraits taken in Norway and Newport. Many of these were of Marie's sisters from Christiania (now Oslo) who visited her often in Newport.

Charles Middleton Cottrell   *Marie Theresa Fladvad Cottrell*

The Faded Yellow Cookbook

Marie's Manuscript Cookbook didn't look like much at first glance, simply a yellowed little 19th century manuscript note book. In fact, it looked a lot like an ancient college "test book."

When we took a closer look at it, we found it was written in a beautiful, flowing script--in Norwegian. A few sessions with a Norwegian dictionary helped us determine that it had been Faith's grandmother's manuscript cookbook.

The faded cover was marked simply, "Marie T. Fladvad," and below that "Mrs. Cottrell." It was Marie's handwritten manuscript cookbook of Norwegian desserts, soups, puddings, and geles. Further review showed the booklet contained recipes written by three different individuals. In addition to

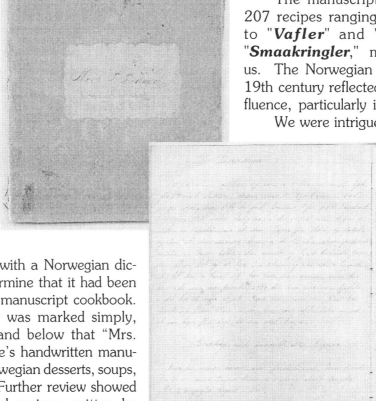

Marie, we believe one of the the other authors was Marie's mother, Oline Bjerke (or Bjørke) Fladvad. The identity of the third hand which added some recipes in the very back of the book, may never be known.

The initial sessions with a Norwegian dictionary have stretched into years of steady discovery as Marie Fladvad Cottrell's cookbook gave up its secrets. And, its "secrets" included more than just the wonderful aroma of cardamom flavored holiday cookies. Eventually, the discovery of **Bestemor's** cookbook would send us back to Norway to locate distant relatives and to rediscover Marie's heritage.

The manuscript cookbook includes 207 recipes ranging from "***Kavringer***" to "***Vafler***" and "***Brunekager***" to "***Smaakringler***," many of them new to us. The Norwegian language of the late 19th century reflected a strong Danish influence, particularly in the spelling.

We were intrigued by the recipes and were determined to try them ourselves. That became a challenge which is not fully resolved to this day. First, there was the problem of translating the 19th century Norwegian text. With the invaluable help of Tove Johansen Halvorsen, Marie's great niece, the recipes were translated. Next the

The "mystery" photograph of Flatvad that sent the authors to Norway to find the family farm. Found in Marie Cottrell's scrapbook after her death, it had been sent to her by her brother-in-law, Chris Willumsen, in 1945. A small "X" marks the farm where her father, Tron Fladvad was born and raised.

problem of ingredient measures presented itself. From many sources we compiled the present day equivalents of the **gamle Norske mål**--traditional Norwegian measures.

The final problem was nutritional--many of the recipes were heavy on butter fat, lard, and other ingredients high in cholesterol. The challenge then was to develop recipes which retained the taste and consistency of the traditional recipe, but which were considerably reduced in fat calories.

Unraveling the Puzzles

As work and correspondence continued on Marie's Manuscript Cookbook, we continued to collect, sort, and organize the contents of the boxes Petie had kept for so long. As we did so, we felt ourselves begin to feel the tugs and pulls of interest and intrigue from Marie's experiences and the story of her life before and after she left Christiania (Oslo) for Newport in 1895.

Early in the process, we were helped immeasurably by the letters and research of Christian Willumsen, Marie's brother-in-law, husband of her younger sister, Jeanne. It was obvious that "Kiss" had devoted a great deal of time over many years to lay the foundations for the Fladvad family history.

His letters to Marie show him to be a warm,

Roald Amundsen, the Norwegian explorer who discovered the South Pole, with Marie's sisters Otilie (left) and Olise (right) during a trans-Atlantic voyage in 1907.

loving, and highly observant man, who took a great interest in her welfare. His annotated geneology was the foundation on which the Norwegian history chapters were based. Later, the efforts of Bjørn Fladvad Johansen, were invaluable in adding a wealth of new information, resolving contradictions, and providing a better understanding of the history and times through which the Fladvad family lived.

The wealth of photographs Petie had saved led us to begin adding captions and explanatory information. Eventually, these needed to be organized and to have additional background provided to explain more fully their significance. For example, the autographed snapshots of Norwegian explorer Roald Amundsen required more information on his life and achievements.

The answer to one question inevitably led to another. For example, if we know that Marie returned with her sisters from Norway in October, 1907, how long was her visit?

One of the old books kept by Marie Cottrell Raymond was a yellowed copy of *Synnøve Solbakken* by Björnstjerne Björnson. We noted an annotation on its title page that Marie had purchased the book in Oslo and mailed it to Charlie as a Christmas present in 1906—"Charles M. Cottrell Xmas 1906 Christiania Marie." [Incidentally, Faith and I spent some memorable hours during Christmas, 1993 reading *Synnöve Solbakken* aloud to each other during the holidays. We felt we were somehow much closer to the spirit of Christmas 1906.]

The Sunndalen near Flatvad *(lower right), a contemporary view approximating the family snapshot which sent the authors to Norway to find the family's ancestral home.*

Flatvad, the family's ancestral home for hundreds of years.

Obviously, Marie was in Norway in December, 1906. Later, we discovered Charlie's anguished letter to his daughter Margaret indicating that Marie was still in Norway and had been gone for many months. When the information was finally in place, it showed that Marie had stayed in Norway from May, 1906 until October, 1907—a year and a half. What could explain such a long, drawn out visit? Did she return for health reasons (asthma), as some family information suggests, to visit her family, or to deal with marital stresses? Questions, then answers, led to more questions.

Over the years, a much clearer picture developed of Marie's life and history—a life time "polaroid" taking years to "develop" before it finally become a sharp image. Even so, there is much tantalizing detail missing from our understanding of Marie's life and experiences. Over time we know the story will continue to gain focus and clarity.

The wild, beautiful Driva River near Flatvad.

Marie & Charlie

The story as it has unfolded over the years is poignant. Contrary to popular belief, not every Norwegian-American moved to the mid-West to carve out a farm. Indeed, contrary to myth, not everyone lived "happily ever after" once they arrived in the New World. The story of Marie Theresa Fladvad was, on balance, a happy story. However, it is hard to find evidence that her marriage was of a "story book" quality. What we did learn about her life and times was fascinating.

In 1895, on her way to California to establish a stitchery school, Marie Theresa Fladvad stopped in Boston, Massachusetts to see a friend, Eleanor Mack. Marie never made it to California. Instead, through Mrs. Mack, she met and married in 1895 Charles Middleton Cottrell, a Newport businessman and member of a solid Irish-American family. Her intended visit became a new life in America. The marriage produced four beautiful daughters, but some key members of the Cottrell family never really accepted Marie.

When Charlie's health deteriorated in the late teens, he placed himself in the care of his domineering sister, Harriet, who attempted to control Marie and her daughters. Harriet offered to let Marie return to the fine Cottrell home on Pelham Street. However, this time Marie and her daughters could live in the basement—and Marie could support herself and her children by becoming the family cook.

Undaunted, Marie marched down to the local bank, borrowed the major sum (in 1916) of $10,000 and bought two adjacent houses on Bellevue Avenue. Until her daughters were adults and began to help out, she was self-supporting and very much a part of Newport city life. She was very active in the Newport Chamber of Commerce, helping to raise funds to build the Viking Hotel. She became a Suffragette and attended meetings and rallies with Mrs. Vanderbilt. From that time on she made her own way in the world.

All her life she was known for her cooking as well as her encyclopedic knowledge of opera. Periodically she and her sisters would return to Norway to see family and familiar scenes. They traveled with Roald Amundsen, the famous Norwegian explorer. Heretofore unpublished and autographed photographs of Amundsen traveling with the Marie and her sisters are included, as well as his "calling card," with a note on the back intimating a five year relationship with the Fladvad sisters.

Trying to discover and understand Marie's life and times became a passionate commitment, to ourselves, to our children, and to our grandchildren, Andrew, Catherine, and Marie (named for her great grandmothers and born 100 years after her great-great grandmother's arrival in the United States). The years moved by rapidly as we devoted as much time as we could from our own hectic schedules to continue the research and writing.

During the Christmas holidays of 1992 we took stock of where we stood on the project. We had come a long way to be sure, but there was so much yet unknown. For example, we had an old copy of a photograph taken in the 1940s in the Sunndalen of the Flatvad farm. There were no directions, just an "X" over a farm to mark the location of this almost (to us) mystical ancestral home of the Fladvad family. Where exactly was the farm? Who lived there now? At the time the picture was taken it was still owned by family members. Were they still there? Could we find it? Would it be possible to meet them and to introduce ourselves? What would their reaction be to these Americans suddenly showing up on their doorstep with an old photograph? There were so many questions, and far fewer answers.

We made some decisions.

We would go to Norway to learn what we could and to see Tove Halvorsen and Bjørn Johansen, Faith's cousins. I had been there many times since the early 1980s to participate in NATO exercises as part of my Navy duties. Of course, this left time for just a few "flying visits" as I came back through Oslo's Fornebu airport enroute home. Faith had not been back since 1960 when she attended the International Summer School at the University of Oslo. Since then her beloved Tante Jeanne Willumsen had died.

We decided also to make a serious personal commitment to publish our work in a book to share with others. This soon took us down the desktop publishing road and into a computer based typesetting system which could help us include the massive amount of imagery we had in mind. The text was vital of course, but we believed strongly that the photographs we had uncovered during our research and those we planned to take ourselves would add immeasurably to your understanding of the story, the people, the times, and the land about which the story revolves.

MEMORABLE MILESTONES...

FROM NORWAY TO NEWPORT

From then until now, the pace picked up rapidly until, compared to previous years, it became almost breakneck. Our trips to Norway and to Newport since 1992 were the turning points in our decades long quest to assemble Marie's story and to understand her life and times.

Our journeys have been exciting and passionately interesting. In addition, they have given us wonderful memories, new friends we plan to keep, and renewed ties with family we treasure. We thought you might be interested in sharing a few of the highlights from our travels.

The Sunndal looking west towards Sunndalsøra near Flatvad.

Finding Flatvad

In 1993, we flew to Olso. After a brief initial stay, we started out to find Flatvad. It required a long, cross-country drive from Oslo, across the Gudbrandsdal, over the Dovrefjell, and down the Sunndal to Sunndalsøra, as its name explains, the southern-most town on the Sunndalfjord. It was then early October, and we were racing the weather predictions for an early snow.

As we drove through the Sunndalen, we were impressed by its rugged beauty. The winding road shifted up and down the side of the mountains as we left Oppdal, then descended to the valley floor where it paralleled the meanderings of the Driva River.

Many of the farm buildings we could see from the road were quite old, yet well cared for. We knew what we were looking for, we just didn't know where it was. We kept comparing the old snapshot we had brought with us to the profiles of the cliffs above us. Several times we thought we were close to the "X" over Flatvad on the photograph, then the road would make another curve and we would shake our heads: "Well, maybe around the next bend."

We had left Oslo with no exact idea of where to find Flatvad, but we knew it was in the Sunndal and not too far from the locations on the map for Flatvad, Bjørnhjell, and Hoås. We checked out each farm house, looking for something that would resemble something in the photograph. Our problem was that many of the farm houses were of the same general design. To us, many of them looked the same, a long, two-story, single gable house with grey, board-and-batten siding (covering the original logs from which they were constructed). Later, we would find that we had driven right by the ancestral home.

When we pulled into Sunndalsøra, like the old homily says, we knew we had gone too far. Finding Flatvad might be harder than we expected.

We drove through the town to the banks of the fjord, then turned around. If we could find the **Rådhus** (city hall), perhaps we could get a better map.

As we pulled up in front of the Rådhus, we changed our minds. The **bibliotek** (library) was right next to the city hall. Surely it would have more information.

Entering the modern, well appointed library, we approached the busy librarian, Bodil Sunde. Explaining as best we could our attempt to find Flatvad, she brought us some appropriate reference books, then asked us if we could wait a few minutes. Of course we could, we had traveled many thousands of miles and a wait of a few more minutes would not be a problem.

Soon, she returned to explain that she had called Flatvad and talked to Faith's cousins, whom we had never met. In a fortunate stroke of luck, they were in town on errands, she said. If we could wait a few more minutes, they would come to the library to meet us. The next fifteen minutes seemed like hours. When Anne Opdøl Arnesen and her husband, Knut, arrived we knew them immediately—the family resemblence was unmistakable.

Their welcome was warm and sunny. Soon, we were clustered around the circular library table reviewing the various photographs of family members we had brought with us. Anne and Faith had never met, but they shared warm memories of many relatives they had known and loved.

Then Knut and Anne shared a special look, one which couples who have been married for a long time develop, a special form of nonverbal communication. Knut invited us to Flatvad for coffee. We accepted immediately, although in some respects we were in a daze.

We had come all the way from the United States to try and find Flatvad. After driving for two days up the Gudbrandsdal, across the Dovrefjell, and down the Sunndalen, we had come to the library with just an optimistic hope that we might somehow be directed to find Flatvad. Obtaining a photograph was our goal. Now, in the short space of an hour, we had not only located Flatvad, but we had met and gotten to know relatives whose hospitality we were about to enjoy.

With mutual feelings of "we don't believe this is really happening," Faith and I followed the Arnesen's Volvo back to Flatvad. We had driven right past it on the way into Sunndalsøra. Soon, we were around their table sipping coffee and sharing family memories and photographs with their son, Lars and his wife, Randi. Significantly, Lars had adopted Flatvad as his new surname. Later in the book you will learn how and why the family refers to itself as "Fladvad," while the farm is called, "Flatvad."

Our Norwegian is limited, but their English was much better. We spent many wonderful hours with them on a subsequent visit in 1994. All are very special and precious to us. However, the two

Oslo's Grand Hotel on Karl Johan. Even today it's hard not to look for the distinguished old gentleman in the frock coat.

hours of our first visit with them remains one of our fondest memories. We had found Flatvad. We were visiting Marie's father's ancestral home. Incredibly, the Fladvad family was still there. And, we had met relatives whose warmth and welcome was as astonishing as it was treasured by us. We can only hope and wish for those readers who are exploring their Norwegian family roots that they are as fortunate as we were in finding and reestablishing the special relationships that once existed between family members.

Ibsen and the Grand Cafe

Marie Fladvad thought a lot of Henrik Ibsen, the internationally acclaimed Norwegian playwright and author. We found three photographs of him in her letters and documents. Certainly many of the dramatic themes around which he developed his plays were close to her heart. Ibsen's characters are commonplace, even prosaic. In the course of the plot, they are stripped of their various disguises and forced to acknowledge their true selves.

Marie was excruciatingly honest, and probably felt some empathy with Ibsen's characters, particularly Nora Helmer in *A Doll's House*. Nora is trapped in a stifling relationship with her husband, Torvald and three children. As the plot unfolds, Nora becomes disillusioned about her husband, a hollow fraud. The play concludes with Nora choosing independence from a weak, hypocritical husband.

Henrik Ibsen, Norway's most famous playwright. One of three photographs of him found with Marie Fladvad Cottrell's effects after her death.

Later in her own life, Marie would be forced to make a remarkably similar decision. When her husband, Charles Cottrell's health deteriorated, he finally decided to place himself in the care and control of his domineering older sister, Harriet. "Aunt Hattie" then gave Marie, married to Charlie for over twenty years and with four beautiful daughters, an ultimatum. Marie could live in the basement of their Greek Revival home on Pelham Street, and be the cook.

Like Nora, Marie chose independence and self sufficiency. It promised to be a road with more uncertainty, but it offered self respect and pride. Unlike Nora, Marie did not abandon her children. Instead, she worked very hard to provide for them until they were adults.

At the time Ibsen lived in Christiania (Oslo), Marie's parents, Tron and Oline Bjerke Fladvad were living there as well. They arrived in the city about 1884. Marie lived with them until 1895 when she left Norway for Newport, Rhode Island. They lived in an apartment building on Holbergsgate, near the present SAS hotel, not far from the city center of Oslo, Karl Johans Gate. One of the most prominent landmarks along Karl Johan is the Grand Hotel. Even then it was the center of things in downtown Oslo.

As we entered the crowded Grand Cafe in October, 1993, we could not help remembering the ties to this room shared by Henrik Ibsen and Marie Fladvad. He came here most days to take his coffee and to visit with well wishers. Marie and her family lived only blocks away and surely came here as well. Did she ever see him here? Chances are that she did. The fact that she kept so many of his photographs provides a clue to her feelings about him.

We were heading back home the next day, but we were trying to squeeze in just a few more

Tron and Oline Fladvad with their children in Kristiansund. Teenaged Anna (center rear) stands next to Marie (right rear).

hours with special people. We had shared a memorable lunch with cousin, Ingrid Opdøl. Then, we linked up with Tove Halvorsen for several delightful hours of just strolling around downtown Oslo, taking in the crowds and browsing through stores. Now, to conclude the afternoon, we went to the Grand Cafe for **kaffe med krem, og Napoleans-kaker**, a delicious dessert of wafers and vanilla custard.

As we enjoyed a memorable visit over the next hour, our eyes moved back and forth across the animated diners there with us in the Grand Cafe. What were we looking for? Somehow, as improbable as it seems, we were hoping to catch a glimpse of an old, bearded man in a frock coat having coffee with a beautiful young woman of about thirty. Perhaps she would be telling him about her broken engagement with a doctor and of her plans to visit America.

Look as we did, we didn't see either one of them. But we felt their presence.

Off to Kristiansund

As we prepared to leave Flatvad after a wonderful visit with the family, Lars Flatvad insisted on calling ahead to Kristiansund to let other members of the family know we were coming. We tried to discourage him because we did not want to be an imposition. Lars would not be dissuaded and made the call as we drove the circuitous route from Sunndalsøra to Kristiansund.

The next morning we were warmly welcomed and assisted by the staff of the Kristiansund Folk Bibliotek with documents and photographs of old Kristiansund, most never before published. At midday, we drove the short distance to the Fladvad **gård** (farm) on the outskirts of the city to have

kaffe with them. It was a delightful visit during which we learned a great deal of "oral history" about the family in the 19th century, and later, about the trials they faced during the German occupation of Kristiansund during World War II.

The Kristiansund visit was another "breakthrough" for Flavors. As a result, we were able to understand and chronicle the many years Tron and Oline spent there, years during which Marie became a young adult.

Thanks to the assistance offered by the Bibliotek and by the Fladvad family in Kristiansund, we learned that although he first leased farm land, in 1880, Tron became a **gårdbruker**, a farm owner and manager, and purchased four farms in and around Kristiansund, one of them near the present location of Kristiansund's **Rådhus**, or city hall.

The records noted that in 1884 Tron and Oline left Kristiansund and moved to Olso. Thanks to Marius Fladvad, we learned that Tron used his knowledge of boats and sailing to carry out the move. Over coffee with his brother, Odd, sister-in-law, Oddrun, and his wife, Henny, Marius related that Tron loaded his family, his belongings, and his cattle aboard his ship and sailed around the Southern coast of Norway and up the Oslo fjord to reach their new home. At the time, he was 53 years old and Oline was 45. Anna was 22, and Marie was 18.

Another fascinating coincidence revealed itself to us in Kristiansund. In her later years Marie had been quite actively involved in the Newport Rhode Island Chamber of Commerce. The Chamber sent her several letters of appreciation for her

efforts to support the major fund raising drive which led to the construction of Newport's Viking Hotel. She provided the hospitality cooking—cookies and cakes. But where had she learned those skills? Was there some experience in her background that might account for some of her well developed abilities as a cook and caterer?

We found what could be part of the answer in a faded clipping which fell out of an envelope being examined by a kind and patient librarian at the folk bibliotek. The headline mentioned "Marit Flatvad." We were intrigued. Following Tove's translation, and further discussions with Bjørn Johansen and Lars Flatvad, we determined that she was probably not a direct relative. However, her husband did have ties close enough to the farm to assume its name as his own.

What was particularly interesting to us in light of Marie's well developed cooking and hospitality skills was the fact that Marit Flatvad established and managed for many years Norway's first real **kaffestue** ("coffee house"). She was described as both "pleasant" and "temperamental" in newspaper accounts written about her and her role as Kristiansund's **kafevertinne** ("coffee hostess").

She operated the coffee house in Loenneehengarden from about 1880 until after 1900. Tron and Oline were there during this period and Marie was old enough to work outside the home, as had her mother at that age.

Marit Kårbø Fladvad was born in 1833 in Lesja, in the Romsdal valley to the east of Kristiansund. She met and married Lars Olsen Flatvad, who was a farmer and businessman in the town. However, the newspaper later concluded that it

Kristiansund today. *Tron and Oline Fladvad lived there for many years before moving to Christiania (Oslo).*

The Dovrefjell, Norway's high mountain plateau between Dombas and Opdal.

was Marit who was probably "the real leader" of their business enterprises. She was called a "business genius" and an extremely clever human being.

Weary, hungry Krisitiansund fishermen at four and five o'clock in the morning would be welcomed at Marit's **kaffestue** which was open and doing a brisk business. They looked forward to the delicious aroma of her coffee and her famous specialty, **skillingskaker**, a large bun with raisins and coarse sugar on top. She would top them with butter and lots of **gamelost**, a pungent cheese made from goat's milk.

She was a "popular and original character in town," the newspaper reported. She dressed in a short, gray skirt with a checkered apron. She wore a knitted scarf around her waist and around her head. Her hands, the report noted, were usually placed at the hips and she looked very strict. She was active politically and was a "liberal."

When Marit Flatvad died on February 14, 1912, Kristiansund lost one of its "most popular and exceptional figures."

Marie Theresa, was fifteen in 1880, old enough to help Marit in the **kaffestue**. We be-

lieve it is possible that she helped out in the **kaffestue**, learning important business skills in the process. [It is even more probable that she obtained additional education and training at a home economics school in Oslo following their relocation there in about 1884.]

Nearly 40 years later, she would need these skills when she would be forced to support herself and her four daughters in Newport, Rhode Island. Drawing upon her experience and using the example set by colorful, independent, entrepreneurial Marit Flatvad, Marie would establish a boarding house business in Newport. She was active in its all-male Chamber of Commerce, which commended her for her service as hospitality chairperson during efforts in the 1920s to raise money to build the Viking Hotel.

Oslo's Genealogical Center

Bjørn Johansen took us to visit Norway's impressive state archive building in West Oslo. It led to a major breakthrough. There we found several key documents about Tron and Oline. One of them, the 1870 census sheet for section number 586 in Kristiansund provided a great deal of important information about the family. For example, it notes that Tron Fladvad was the **Jorebruger**, (farmer), and that he was born in 1827 in Sunndalen. Oline is listed as his wife, born in 1837 in Hedemarken (Furness, near Hamar). Daughters Anna and Marie were born in Kolvereid in 1861 and 1865 respectively. Son Ole was born in Kolvereid in 1863. Sons Frederick and Theodor were born in Kristiansund in 1868 and 1870 respectively.

In addition to family members, the census notes others living on the **gård**. Elen Gjekling, for example, was a servant from Sunndal. Others were helping Tron farm land, including: John Hansen, Ingebrikt Aas, and Thor Rasmusjin.

The Royal Road across the Dovrefjell

Before the carriage track was built at the bottom of the valley in 1820, the old road to Nidaros (Trondheim) crossed the mountains from the settlement of Dovre, Gautstigen, since the Middle Ages. From Dovre to Hjerkinn, the Royal Road passed the farms at Tofte, then crossed the Hardbakken and descended to Fokstugu. Norwegian kings since Harald Håfagre used the road, first on horseback, then after 1704, in carriages.

It was a dangerous journey. Travelers erected a stone altar to give them a place to kneel and pray for a safe journey. A rock heap at the highest point on the road near Hardbakken, remains from the time when travelers would throw a stone on the pile to bring them good luck.

In May, 1994, we returned to Norway to continue our research and to accept a very thoughtful invitation to visit Flatvad for several days. We had just completed the trip up the Gudbrandsdal from Oslo. After leaving Dombås, the road climbed quickly with switchbacks to several thousand feet above the town, then struck out North towards Trondheim. We were on our way to Flatvad in the

Marie Fladvad Cottrell

Sunndalen.

It was early Spring in the Gudbrandsdal. On the Dovrefjell's high mountain plateau, the season was poised somewhere between Winter and Spring. The sun was bright, but the wind was still "crisp." The trees would not see leaves for several more weeks. Looking for the right angle for the photograph to illustrate Oline's trip from Furnes to Kolvereid, we pulled over at a scenic point. The two lane road for miles ahead and behind us was empty. It seemed like we were the only humans at what looked like the top of the world, a giant basin of red-brown lichens, boulders, and stunted trees rimmed by snow capped mountains.

Slinging the camera over my head, I moved away from the car toward a tree-rock combination that looked promising. Stepping off the gravel, I was surprised by the sponginess of the lichen ground cover. It was like walking on a soft, but springy mattress. Reaching the tree, I took several shots then realized that the best angle would be from ground level. Reaching down, I tested the surface, expecting it to be wet. It wasn't. It was dry and warm. Cautiously, I stooped on one knee, then slowly, the other. I still expected the ground to be wet and I didn't want to wear wet or soiled clothes to our reunion at Flatvad.

I continued my descent to ground level. Still dry. Soon, I was lying in what my rifle instructor of many years past would call the "prone position." Squeezing off several shots with my camera, I began to relax and enjoy the moment.

The next few minutes stand out to this day. There I was lying on my stomach in the middle of a huge mountain basin on a soft, warm blanket of lichens listening to the much cooler wind whistle above me. Time seemed to stand still. It was a truly perfect few minutes. Everything was, well, just perfect.

A contemporary view of Marie's former home on Catherine Street in Newport. It was here she told a lie—to save a man's life. Clement Moore, the author of "A Visit from St. Nicholas," lived next door.

Thousands of pilgrims had struggled by this spot enroute to the cathedral in Trondheim. Faith was waiting patiently in the car (writing notes from the historical marker by the roadside). But for those few moments I was the first, and the only person in that strangely beautiful and barren world of lichens, rocks, stunted trees, and stark mountains. Who knows, perhaps some of those pilgrims, like me, had found a cathedral of another kind on their way to Nidaros.

Understanding Marie Fladvad

I learned about Marie Fladvad Cottrell soon after Faith and I were married. First, I heard the tender stories from Faith about how her Norwegian grandmother (**Bestemor** Marie, although the family called her "Monnie," pron. "Money") had often stayed with her daughters and their families for extended periods. How when Faith was born Marie had washed the entire room down with soap and water, including the ceiling. How Faith had rarely taken a nap or gone to bed without Marie

being there by her side, holding her hand as she went to sleep. How devastated Faith had been when Marie had died suddenly after a very short illness.

As a young girl, family recollections indicate that Marie had rheumatic fever. Although she lived into her Eighties, she was always extra careful about her health. She made a special effort to develop and stick to a healthy diet. A hard worker, when she was tired or under the weather, her daughters would try to see that she got her rest.

Her daughter, Eleanor ("Ellie") related many times the story of how, when they were living at 23 Catherine Street in Newport, Aunt Hattie came to the door unannounced and demanded to see Marie. Ellie "stood her down" saying: "My mother is resting upstairs. She is not well." Ellie was always proud that she had sent Hattie packing. It says a lot about how protective Marie's daughters were of her, and of their feelings about their father's domineering sister.

As the years passed and we continued to work on putting this book together, it became the longest single project on which we had worked as a couple (with the exception of raising our two grown daughters, a project we know to be a "work in progress" that will continue for many decades to come).

Aside from the wonderful smells and tastes warming our kitchen and our insides, I remember asking myself one long afternoon as I was slowly scanning photographs into the computer's memory: what was it about this subject and Marie herself that had such a grip on our interest and energies? True, it was a fascinating story with great emotional and even historical aspects, but could that totally acccount for the "fixation," that went far beyond the foods and recipes we were preparing to share with readers.

At some point we realized that a substantial part of our continuing interest in the subject was Marie herself. We were fascinated and frankly, inspired, by her strength of character and her determination in life. Time and again, as her story slowly revealed itself, we were impressed by her creativity, innovation, and resiliency in dealing with the many challenges life put in her path. Marie showed great resourcefulness in providing for herself and her children despite enormous challenges.

She was, and is, an inspiration to us and to those who knew her in life.

In 1990 a period of Navy duty provided a more "scientific" explanation for us about Marie's "strength of character."

As a Naval Reserve Officer, it has been my privilege to be asked to serve in a variety of active duty assignments over the years. In that instance, as Deputy Director of the Navy's Command Excellence and Leader Development Division in its Bureau of Naval Personnel.

One of our primary objectives was to incorporate into Navy training those principles and approaches to what is now known as inspirational or transformational leadership. It included awareness that today's high rate of organizational change required a new awareness and understanding of leaders as "change agents."

"Core values" is an increasingly popular term in management these days. In general, core values refers to those basic principles strongly held to the extent that they motivate and guide basic behavior and decision making.

Management and leadership authorities now realize that instilling and fostering strong, positive core values also encourages similar behavior.

Core values are generally grouped within six broad areas, including: integrity, dedication, loyalty, concern for people, tradition, and patriotism. Of course, few individuals operate with this "full complement" of values categories.

In particular, we focused on ways to not only improve basic leadership training throughout the Navy, but on ways to incorporate and emphasize core values in all training programs, regardless of whether they dealt exclusively with leadership training or not. Many aspects of behavior can be explained in terms of core values--that the individual is "operationalizing" or acting upon those fundamental principles they hold and value. Inculcating or strengthening selected core values helps create the necessary foundation for positive behavior. Of course, this approach still needs more attention and

Based almost entirely on her personal integrity, *a Newport bank loaned Marie $10,000 to "go into real estate." This house at 59 Bellevue Avenue, Newport, was the home she purchased when she began to make her own way in the world.*

development, but it does offer us fasinating insights into non-intrusive behavior reinforcement.

For me it provided an important insight into our quest to learn as much as possible about Marie's life and times. After studying her life for many years, we are still impressed by the depth and strength of her "core values," terms unknown in her day. To her, it was just the way she was raised. To us, it explained so much about her strength and determination.

Honesty means free from fraud or deception, truthful, real, genuine, reputable, respectable, good, worthy, and marked by integrity. Integrity is a firm adherence to a moral code or set of values.

Integrity was fundamental to Marie, the cornerstone of her outlook on life. In fact, the very reason she decided to visit America was related to integrity. She was engaged to a doctor in Christiania. She later explained to her daughters that he told her an untruth. The engagement was ended, and she decided to leave the country. To her, people of character did not lie, and they owned up to mistakes, no coverups.

Marie herself did tell a lie--once.

Late one evening in the mid-Teens, when she was living on Catherine Street with her daughters, they heard a frantic pounding on the door. Opening it cautiously, she was faced with a very frightened, frantic man--a man she knew even though he was far from his own neighborhood.

"Mrs. Cottrell, there's a mob after me," the man gasped, out of breath.

"Come inside," she commanded, and found him a place to hide in the basement. Moments later, came more pounding on the door. When she opened it, she saw in the flickering lanterns the angry profiles of the crowd.

"We're looking for a man," they shouted, "have you seen him?"

With a straight face, Marie answered, "Of course not. I have four little children asleep upstairs, please don't frighten them."

Her commanding presence, what family members remember as "the look," had a calming effect. The mob quieted down and began moving back down the walkway to Catherine Street.

Later, when they had left and things were quiet, she escorted the very grateful man out the back door. Marie had told a lie--and saved a life.

In Marie's values structure, integrity meant to stand up for your colleagues and those for whom

you are responsible (subordinates). When the frightened mob victim placed himself in her care, he knew she would try to help him.

Integrity is the foundation for trust. When Charlie's health required that he be hospitalized, he chose to place himself in his sister's control. Marie needed to find a way to support her girls. Marching down to the bank, she borrowed $10,000, a very tidy sum in the Teens. Her integrity was persuasive, even for bankers.

Another form of integrity was at work when Marie refused to discuss "disagreeable things." Despite all of the hurt and pain she had suffered, her family could not remember a single instance in which she said anything negative about Charlie Cottrell. Even when he died, and she was not invited by the family to his funeral or mentioned in his obituary, Marie held a "memorial service" of her own with a friend. She was genuinely grief stricken at his passing.

Monnie was a dear person, but firm. She never thought of herself as a victim, by any stretch of the imagination. She was not melancholy or a dreamer. She possessed a stoic and dignified quality the likes of which we shall probably never see again.

When the family remembers Monnie, the words "love," "respect," and "strength" are words grandchildren still use to describe her character. The words "definite" and "consistent" are terms they attribute to her parenting skills and the way she raised her daughters.

"I imagine it might seem strange to the reader of the future," a granddaughter explained, "for Monnie to be so generous and forgiving after being put through such degradation. But that is just the point. She was the strong one, able to rise above the fray with total dignity, thereby giving her children the greatest gift of all," she concluded.

As you read the chapters that follow, we believe you will be impressed, as we have been, by Marie's exceptional complement of core values. To us, they explain the reasons behind many of the decisions and choices she made. Taken together, they should inspire us in our own lives. To complete our emphasis on the importance of core values in understanding Marie Fladvad Cottrell, we have provided a brief review of them starting on page 303.

We believe we live in a frightening, uncertain world. However, when we really look back and consider the concerns and uncertainties of earlier periods, we can better appreciate many of the securities that we enjoy today. Improvements in medical science, for example. Marie endured many miscarriages before her daughters were born. She lost twin boys shortly after their birth. And, Charlie's health problems resulted in the end of her marriage. Today, much could be done for them.

Education, we should understand, Will and Ariel Durant pointed out in their synthesis work, *The Lessons of History*, is not "the painful accumulation of facts and dates and reigns, nor merely the necessary preparation of the individual to earn his keep in the world, but as the transmission of our mental, moral, technical, and aesthetic heritage as fully as possible to as many as possible, for the enlargement of man's understanding, control, embellishment, and enjoyment of life."

That heritage, they reminded us, gets richer generation by generation. Each of us inherits a richer heritage than our parents.

"History," in its essence, is the creation and recording of that heritage. Progress, according to the Durants, was the "increasing abundance, preservation, transmission, and use" of history. For those who study history, this "heritage" is not intended solely as a "warning reminder of man's follies and crimes, but also as an encouraging remembrance of generative souls…"

Marie Fladvad Cottrell was a "generative soul," who epitomized the Durants' definition of "immortality" as the selective survival of creative minds. Almost half a century after her death, her creative mind and strength of character are remembered and used to educate the young in her expanding family. We hope that in some small way this work gives her and the values and strengths she lived by some measure of immortality.

So too, did she fit the definition of "resilient man" the Durants described. When change or developments limit personal growth or happiness, the "resilient man picks up his tools and his arts, and moves on, taking his memories with him…and builds somewhere another home." Struggling to overcome prejudice and exploitation, Marie built a new life in a new country. She set a lasting example of "grace under pressure," and a fierce self-determination that retains its ability to inspire us to this day.

The Durants concluded their lifetime quest together by pointing out that the historian will not mourn "because he can see no meaning in human existence except that which man puts into it; let it be our pride that we ourselves may put meaning into our lives, and sometimes a significance that transcends death. If a man is fortunate he will, before he dies, gather up as much as he can of his civilized heritage and transmit it to his children."

Through her strength of character and independence, Marie gave her life special meaning to her family and friends. We have tried to take to heart the Durant's advice and to gather up as much as we could of her "civilized heritage" and to transmit it to her children—and yours.

We believe her story is a significant addition to the "civilized heritage" brought to our country by Marie Fladvad and hundreds of thousands of other Norwegian-Americans--and indeed, by all of our ancestors that arrived in this country from other lands. We hope you enjoy your journey **From Norway to Newport** as much as we did. We encourage you to take a similar journey in the footsteps of your ancestors. You will learn much about them to admire and respect, even as you better appreciate your own richer heritage--made so by their contributions.

Tracy D. Connors
Bowie, Maryland
June, 1995

About the Book

Flavors of the Fjords includes recipes for over 100 holiday cookies, cakes and breads, toppings, and puddings, all interwoven with fascinating bits of Norwegian social history, including explanations of Norwegian Holiday traditions and customs, many of them kept alive to this day by millions of Norwegian-American families.

We believe the book itself will appeal to millions of Norwegian-Americans who will delight in reliving their culinary cultural heritage. These dishes reflect authentic cooking of the old country, and those flavors, uniquely Norwegian, brought to America by nearly one million Norwegian immigrants. The recipes have been modified to take advantage of today's healthier alternatives, while retaining mouth-watering taste and consistency.

"From Norway to Newport..." is the first Norwegian holiday cookbook, and includes many cookie and cake recipes never seen in "American" or "Scandinavian" cookbooks.

Lavishly illustrated, it offers over 300 photographs illustrating life in Norway and Newport, R.I.--then and now-- from period portraits and views of the late 19th and early 20th century, including antique post cards, to the present day. Unpublished photographs selected from the authors' private collection (including an autographed picture of Roald Amundsen, who discovered the South Pole), and contemporary Norwegian and Newport scenes are included.

The photographs and illustrations benefit from the 8 1/2 x 11 page format which allows the reader to appreciate details often lost in "smaller works."

It makes interesting reading beyond its recipes. In addition to over 100 tasty recipes, we included several entire chapters outlining the life and times of the Fladvad and Bjørke families--from the challenges of life on the farm in Norway, to surviving as a "businesswoman" in Newport, R.I.

Interesting and poignant family recollections shed light on life in Newport, Rhode Island at the turn of the century. All was not "Bellevue Avenue high life."

One chapter traces the history of the Fladvad and Bjørke family farms in Central and Western Norway from 1400-1900, using information obtained from Norwegian archives. Fascinating glimpses of life and customs in Norway since written records were first kept are revealed. We know of no other work which follows the life and times of a typical Norwegian family as far back as recorded history allows.

In addition, we incorporated an unusual section of letters and photographs from family members describing the trials of life in German-occupied Norway during World War II.

Tove Johansen Halvorsen prepared an 1,800-word Norwegian-English glossary, with useful terms for foods and cooking, but also family, kinship, and home. We believe the Glossary will help readers who wish to translate their family Norwegian recipes.

Recipes are complete and easy to make. Step by step directions on large pages make it easy to keep your place.

Traditional recipes, many reworked to use today's healthier ingredients, while retaining original flavor and consistency--were selected for taste and for ease of preparation.

About Norway

Total area

150,000 square miles (324,220 square kilometers), or slightly larger than New Mexico.

Population of Major Cities

Capital, Oslo (467,000)
Bergen (216,000)
Trondheim (139,600)
Stavanger (99,800)

Climate

Temperate along its coast, modified by the North Atlantic Current, a branch of the Gulf Stream. Much colder in the interior. Rainy year-round on the west coast.

Terrain

Glaciated, mostly high plateaus and rugged mountains broken by fertile valleys. Norway coastline is deeply indented by fjords. Norway has one of the longest and most rugged coastlines in the world. Arctic tundra prevails in its northern-most regions.

Land use

Arable land (3%); permanent crops (0%); meadows and pastures (1%); forest and woodland (27%); other (70%).

Population

4,300,000 in 1992 with a growth rate of about 0.5%.

Birth rate

14 births/1,000 population in 1992.

Net migration rate

2 migrants/1,000 population in 1992.

Life expectancy at birth

74 years male, 81 years female in 1992.

Religion

Evangelical Lutheran (87.8%), other Protestant and Roman Catholic (3.8%); none (3.2%), unknown (5.2%).

Labor force

2,167,000 with 34.7% in services, 18% in commerce, 16.6% mining and manufacturing, 7.2% in transportation, 7.2% construction, 7.5% banking and financial services, 6.4% agriculture, forestry, and fishing.

Government

Long-form name: Kingdom of Norway
Type: Hereditary constitutional monarchy

Independence

October 26, 1905 from Sweden.

Constitution

May 17, 1814, modified in 1884.

National holiday

Constitution Day, 17 May (1814).

Dependent areas

Bouvet Island, Jan Mayen, Svalbard.

Legal system

Mix of customary law, civil law system, and common law traditions. Supreme court renders advisory opinions to legislature when asked.

Executive branch

Monarch, prime minister, State Council (cabinet).

Legislative branch

Storting or **Stortinget**, unicameral Parliament, consisting of the **Lagting** (Upper Chamber), and the **Odelsting** (Lower Chamber).

Judicial branch

Høyesterett (Supreme Court)

Leaders

Chief of State, King Harald V (born February 21, 1937). Heir Apparent Crown Prince Haakon Magnus (born July 20, 1973). Prime Minister, Gro Harlem Brundtland (Labor) since November, 1990.

Economy

Norway is a prosperous capitalist nation with the resources to finance extensive welfare measures. Since 1975 exploitation of large crude oil and natural gas reserves has helped achieve an average annual growth of about 4%. Its industries include: petroleum and gas, food processing, shipbuilding, pulp and paper products, metals, chemicals, timber, mining, textiles, and fishing.

Agriculture accounts for over 3% of Norway's GNP and nearly 7% of its labor force. Norway is among the world's top ten fishing nations. Its livestock output exceeds the value of its crops.

Over half of its food must be imported.

People

Ethnically, Norwegians are predominantly Germanic, although in the far north there are communities of Sami (Lapps) who came to the area more than 10,000 years ago, probably from central Asia. In recent years, Norway has become home to increasing numbers of immigrants, foreign workers, and asylum-seekers from various parts of the world. Immigrants now total nearly 150,000; some 5,000 obtained Norwegian citizenship in 1991.

Although the Evangelical Lutheran Church is the state church, Norway has complete religious freedom. Education is free through the university level and is compulsory from ages 7 to 16. At least 12 months of military service and training are required of every eligible male. Norway's health system includes free hospital care, physician's compensation, cash benefits during illness and pregnancy, and other medical and dental plans. There is a public pension system.

Norway is in the top rank of nations in the number of books printed per capita, even though Norwegian is one of the world's smallest language groups. Norway's most famous writer is the dramatist Henrik Ibsen. Artists Edvard Munch and Christian Krogh were contemporaries of Ibsen. Munch drew part of his inspiration from Europe and in turn exercised a strong influence on later European expressionists. Sculptor Gustav Vigeland has a permanent exhibition in the Vigeland Sculpture Park in Oslo. Musical development since Grieg has followed either native folk themes, or more recently, international trends.

Brief History

The Viking period (9th to 11th centuries) was one of national unification and expansion. The Norwegian royal line died out in 1387, and the country entered a period of union with Denmark. By 1586, Norway had become part of the Danish Kingdom. In 1814, as a result of the Napoleonic wars, Norway was separated from Denmark and combined with Sweden. The union persisted until 1905, when Sweden recognized Norwegian independence.

The Norwegian Government offered the throne of Norway to Danish Prince Carl in 1905. After a plebiscite approving the establishment of a monarchy, the parliament unanimously elected him king. He took the name of Haakon VII, after the kings of independent Norway. Haakon died

in 1957 and was succeeded by his son, Olav V, who died in January 1991. Upon Olav's death, his son Harald was crowned as King Harald V. Norway was a non-belligerent during World War I, but as a result of the German invasion and occupation during World War II, Norwegians generally became skeptical of the concept of neutrality and turned instead to collective security. Norway was one of the signers of the North Atlantic Treaty in 1949 and was a founding member of the United Nations. The first UN General Secretary, Trygve Lie, was a Norwegian.

Government Overview

The functions of the king are mainly ceremonial, but he has influence as the symbol of national unity. Although the 1814 constitution grants important executive powers to the king, these are almost always exercised by the Council of Ministers in the name of the king (King's Council). The Council of Ministers consists of the prime minister--chosen by the political parties represented in the **Storting** (parliament)--and other ministers.

The 165 members of the Storting are elected from 18 fylker (counties) for 4-year terms according to a complicated system of proportional representation. After elections, the Storting divides into two chambers, the **Odelsting** and the **Lagting**, which meet separately or jointly depending on the legislative issue under consideration.

The special High Court of the Realm hears impeachment cases; the regular courts include the Supreme Court (17 permanent judges and a president), courts of appeal, city and county courts, the labor court, and conciliation councils. Judges attached to regular courts are appointed by the king in council after nomination by the Ministry of Justice.

Each **fylke** is headed by a governor appointed by the king in council, with one governor exercising authority in both Oslo and the adjacent county of Akershus.

Economy

Norway is one of the world's richest countries. It has an important stake in promoting a liberal environment for foreign trade. Its large shipping fleet is one of the most modern among maritime nations. Metals, pulp and paper products, chemicals, shipbuilding, and fishing are the most significant traditional industries.

Norway's emergence as a major oil and gas producer in the mid-1970s transformed the economy. Large sums of investment capital poured into the offshore oil sector, leading to greater increases in Norwegian production costs and wages than in the rest of Western Europe up to the time of the global recovery of the mid-1980s. The influx of oil revenue also permitted Norway to expand an already extensive social welfare system.

High oil prices in the 1983-85 period led to significant increases in consumer spending, wages, and inflation. The subsequent decline in oil prices since 1985 has sharply reduced tax revenues and required a tightening of both the government budget and private sector demand. As a result, the non-oil economy showed almost no growth during 1986-88, and the current account went into deficit. As oil prices recovered sharply in 1990 following the Persian Gulf crisis, the 1990 current account posted a large surplus which continued into 1991.

Norway's exports have continued to grow every year, largely because of favorable world demand. Moreover, the flight of Norwegian-owned ships from the country's traditional register ended in 1987, as the government established an international register, replete with tax breaks and relief from national crewmember requirements. At the same time, a drop in private consumption has helped to reduce Norway's imports.

Norway continues to adapt its economic policy to international developments, notably the emerging European Community (EC) single market. Norway and the other European Free Trade Association (EFTA) members are in the process of concluding an economic cooperation agreement with the EC under the framework of the European Economic Area (EEA). This agreement, which promotes free trade, is being designed to limit the distortive impact of the EC single market on commodity trade and the movements of labor and capital.

On EC membership, Norway voted in November, 1994 not to join the EC.

Energy Resources

Offshore hydrocarbons were discovered in the 1960s, and development began in the 1970s. The growth of the petroleum sector has contributed significantly in recent years to Norwegian economic vitality. Current petroleum production capacity is over 2 million barrels per day.

Hydropower provides nearly all of Norway's electricity, and all of the gas and most of the oil produced were exported. Production is expected to increase significantly as new fields are developed.

Although not a major energy supplier to the world, Norway provides about 40% of Western Europe's crude oil requirements and 16% of gas requirements. In 1991, Norwegian oil and gas exports accounted for 44% of total merchandise exports. In addition, offshore exploration and production have stimulated onshore economic activities. Foreign companies, including many American ones, participate actively in the petroleum sector.

Foreign Relations

Norway supports international cooperation and the peaceful settlement of disputes, recognizing the need for maintaining a strong national defense through collective security. Accordingly, the cornerstones of Norwegian policy are active membership in NATO and support for the United Nations and its specialized agencies.

Norway also pursues a policy of economic, social, and cultural cooperation with other Nordic countries (Denmark, Sweden, Finland, and Iceland) through the Nordic Council.

Faith Raymond Connors (upper left) attended the University of Oslo Summer School in 1960. King Olav (right) hosted a reception at **Oscarshall Slott**, *his summer home overlooking the Oslo Fjord on Bygdøy.*

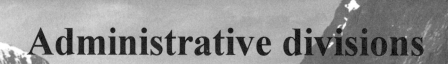

Administrative divisions

19 provinces or **fylker** (plural), **fylke** (singular), including:
Akershus
Aust-Agder
  Risør
  Arendal
  Grimstad
Buskerud
  Ringerike
  Drammen
  Kongsberg
Finnmark
  Hammerfest
  Vardø
  Vadsø
Hedmark
  Hamar
  Kongsvinger
Hordaland
  Bergen
Møre og Romsdal
  Alesund
  Kristiansund

  Molde
  Sunndalsøra
Nordland
  Bodø
  Narvik
Nord-Trondelag
  Steinkjer
  Namsos
Oppland
  Lillehammer
  Gjøvik
Oslo
  Oslo
Ostfold
  Halden
  Sarpsborg
  Fredrikstad
  Moss
Rogaland
  Eigersund
  Haugesund
  Sandnes
  Stavanger

Sogn og Fjordane
  Flora
Sør-Trøndelag
  Trondheim
Telemark
  Notodden
  Porsgrunn
  Skien
Troms
  Harstad
  Tromsø
Vest-Agder
  Farsund
  Flekkefjord
  Kristiansand
  Mandal
Vestfold
  Holmestrand
  Horten
  Larvik
  Sandefjord
  Stavern
  Tønsberg

NORWEGIAN HOLIDAY TRADITIONS

Syttendemai
Independence Day Celebration

Juletid
Christmas Time in Norway

by
Tracy Connors
Faith Connors
Tove Halvorsen

Norwegians especially enjoy two major holidays each year. One commemorates their struggle to regain independence as a nation, the other celebrates the Christmas season. Both are family-oriented, combining national festivities and warm, convivial times with their immediate and extended families.

On May 16th of each year, the pace in Oslo begins to quicken. An international capital of nearly half a million people, Oslo bustles year round. However, on the 16th of May, the city begins to change. At first the casual visitor might suppose it is due to the arrival of Spring. Winter is over, the trees are glowing with a fresh, brilliant green. Mornings are cool enough for **vinter klærne** (winter clothes), however, sweaters and windbreakers are off by midday when a few bare arms are seen. Sunrise is at 6:30 a.m., but dawn

*Bakery windows are filled with **kransekake**–"crown cakes"–some over 18-inches high and made of concentric rings of **mandle masse** (almond paste) dough. Each ring is drizzled with white icing neatly looped to simulate snow. Every cake is covered with red, white, and blue Norwegian flags.*

occurred two hours earlier. Twilight lasts until 11 p.m. In a few weeks, it will be daylight almost 24 hours a day.

Suddenly, taxi cabs sprout Norwegian flags from their "For Hire" lights on top. Store displays–from hardware to clothing—are bedecked with red, white, and blue ribbons and rosettes.

On the streets, horns suddenly begin honking for no apparent reason. Their drivers don't seem to be upset, in fact, many are smiling.

Sidewalks are filled with shoppers chatting pleasantly and looking cheerful. They are filling their shopping bags with bread from the bakery, sweet delicacies from the **konditori** (the bakery specializing in confectioneries), and vegetables from the **grønsakshandel** (green grocer). From the size of their bags, a great deal of cooking—

As **Syttendemai** *festivities begin in Oslo on the morning of May 17, marching groups convene, each wearing the uniform of the school it represents.* **Musikkorps** *(school bands) arrive downtown, form up, play several numbers, then march off to assemble nearby for the parade which starts at 10:00 o'clock. Crowds grow to 5 and 6 people deep along Karl Johan. The street is alive with movement. (right) King Harald, Queen Sonja, and Princess Martha Louise acknowledge the enthusiastic cheers and salutes during the Children's Parade past* **Slottet**.

and eating–will go on tomorrow.

The city doesn't really settle down during that short night. A surprisingly large number of people are still strolling along the sidewalks when darkness falls at about 11 p.m. Open apartment windows convey frequent laughter and animated discussions in lilting, musical Norwegian. Finally, the city settles down only to begin waking again as dawn arrives at 4:30 a.m.

Constitution Day

For much of its history, Norway's destiny was determined by either Denmark or Sweden. One result of the Napoleonic Wars in 1813, was the transfer of Norway from Danish to Swedish control. After Napoleon's defeat at Leipzig, King Carl Johan of Sweden declared war on Denmark, and eventually took Norway away from the Danes. However, the Swedish diplomats had not consulted the Norwegians about the arrangement. They did not want to be a part of Sweden.

Leaders from throughout Norway gathered at Eidsvoll, a small town about an hour's drive north of Oslo, and prepared their own Constitution. They even elected the Danish Prince Christian Fredrik as King of Norway. A short war between Norway and Sweden delayed full independence for nearly a century, however the Swedish government did accept the Norwegian Constitution, which gave the Norwegians the right to have their own **Storting** (Parliament). The union with Sweden lasted until 1905.

On May 17, 1829, the Norwegians were celebrating what they had come to call Constitution Day. The Swedish authorities were upset. They considered May 17th to be a day of rebellion. In their view, November 4th, the day the union with Sweden was established, was a more appropriate national holiday.

The Swedish governor sent in troops to disperse holiday revelers in the square. Later, it was known as the Battle of Market Square. The "battle" had two important results. From then on, Norway's governors would be Norwegian. Also, May 17th was firmly established as Norway's national day of celebration–**syttendemai**–the 17th of May.

Bunad

On the morning of May 17th, another major change may be observed in Oslo. Instead of wearing contemporary clothing, many of the women are dressed in a basic combination of long skirt, white blouse, and trim vest–their *bunad*, or national costume.

The variety of color combinations and lavish decoration is astonishing. Most skirts and vests are trimmed and ornamented with detailed embroidery obviously requiring untold hours of effort with needle and thread, stitch by careful stitch. Brilliantly polished silver belts and jewelry complement the colorful embroidery and weaving.

One piece of jewelry is worn by all the women. While it varies greatly in size and design, all the women wear the Norwegian *sølje* pin at the top of their blouses between the collar points. Many pins flash and sparkle with numerous, tiny, concave silver ornaments. These are independently attached to swing freely, catching the sun and reflecting its rays briefly to dazzle the observer and highlight the wearer. One *bunad* would be a cultural feast, however each year on the morning of May 17th, the streets are thronged with women wearing the bunad traditional to their native town or valley or one to which they feel most closely attached. Many of the men are wearing their bunad too, but it is the women who stand out.

Syttendemaitog

After enjoying a big *frokost* (breakfast), of eggs, herring, cheeses, coffee and whole wheat bread, Norwegians walk downtown toward Oslo's sentrum. In somewhat less than a mile, Karl Johans Gate, the city's tree-lined thoroughfare, links *Slottet* (the palace), with the *Storting* (Norwegian Parliament). Karl Johan plus several blocks along its length make up the heart of downtown Oslo.

Karl Johan passes to the north of the Storting, and takes on a new character when it becomes a pedestrian mall stretching to Oslo's *Domkirke* (cathedral) four city blocks later.

At 8:00 a.m., crowds are already gathering around the Storting to hear brief concerts by local school bands, and to watch spirited folk dancing by groups wearing

Children from an Oslo elementary school lead their school band up the hill to march past the palace and cheer the Norwegian Royal Family.

First comes the honor guard of students *carrying the school banner, followed by other marchers waving large national flags. The flags are followed by the **musik korps** (school band). They are a happy, cheering group. Scores of spectators on the curb call out to friends and relatives marching in the parade, waving and cheering.*

bunad from all over Norway. The dancers are celebrating their heritage and having a joyous time.

Small groups in national costume, many including radiantly healthy children dressed in their **bunad** riding in strollers pushed by their parents, move slowly down Karl Johan toward the palace. Hours before the **barnetog** (children's parade), people start their own parades; groups laughing and talking walk slowly toward Slottet, being observed and appreciated by their countrymen standing patiently along the sidewalks.

High school seniors soon to face their comprehensive examinations prior to graduation are dressed in red "coveralls" with iron-on patches, numbers and slogans. They cavort among the crowds. Many of them toss their calling cards in the air to be caught or picked up by younger children following behind. The calling cards have humorous

sayings and are eagerly sought by the younger children who collect them immediately whereever they have fallen.

A roll of drums and the clop of horses hooves on the cobblestones behind the **Storting** at precisely ten o'clock signal the start of the official parade. The Oslo Police Department band leads off with mounted patrolmen maneuvering their horses close to the curbs. This encourages the crowds to move back onto the sidewalk–a subtle, but very effective way to create a clear line of march for the parade of bands to come.

The police band is followed by the first of what will be hundreds of bands and marching groups from schools throughout the greater Oslo region. Similar parades and celebrations are being held all over Norway in cities and towns large and small.

Most band members sport medals won in music competitions. The entire front of many a uniform is covered with medals won in music competitions.

Arriving At Slottet

With a Lincolnesque flavor, Norway's Independence Day parade is a parade "of the children, by the children, and for the children." On they come, one band after another, group after group of marchers, child after child dressed in **bunad**, flags flying over all, proceeding down Karl Johan, and up the hill to **Slottet**. [Note: the letters "et," at the end of the word **slottet** replace the English definite article "the." Thus, **et slott**, a castle. **Slottet**, the castle. **Flere slott**, several castles.]

Turning left as they enter the palace grounds, the seemingly endless parade of people and flags flows up the hill in a clockwise motion.

Viewed from atop Karl Johan, the fluttering red, white, and blue flags move steadily through the cheering people creating in effect a colorful national artery. Of course, in a way, with the music rising and the surging procession, it may be just that: enthusiastic and patriotic young people marching toward the slottet are the life's blood of the nation, they are Norway's future.

On top of the hill, in front of the palace, each band pauses briefly, in order to give the group ahead of them enough time to pass in front of the palace. Then, leading off with a rattle of drums, they step out smartly to pass in review of the King's balcony.

King Harald and Queen Sonja salute the flags dipped in their honor. Behind the marching bands, the flag-waving students don't bother to "get in step." They are too busy cheering as Queen Sonja waves to them and King Harald doffs his black satin hat in a grand gesture.

As the bands complete their pass in review,

*After the **Syttendemaitog** (parade), Norwegian families enjoy **Middag**, followed by coffee and **Syttende-maikake**.*

the tired but happy marchers parade rapidly down the hill toward their dispersal point where buses will take them back to their neighborhoods, foot-weary, but triumphant. However, in many ways, **syttendemai** is just beginning.

Middag

After the parades, it's time for family. Throughout the country, tables are being set for a hearty syttendemai luncheon. Families are gathering for **middag**, the noon meal. A typical menu will include: a smørbord of luncheon food, such as yeast rolls, sliced meats, and a **syttendemai** cake, frosted in red and white.

For the next hour or so, there is plenty to eat and lots of animated conversation in Norwegian, unless there are American family members present, in which case, both Norwegian and English are spoken. In many neighborhoods, the local school will have a **syttendemai tog** of its own, the **musikkorps** following the national flags around the neighborhood. Residents interrupt **middag** (lunch time) conversation to rush to their balconies and cheer the local **musikkorps**. Every balcony and flag pole flies Norwegian flags.

After the local parade has passed, the noon meal concludes with coffee and **Syttende-maikake**, resplendent with red, white, and blue icing topped with small Norwegian flags. Often, another branch of the family hosts an evening meal. This allows members of several families to visit with different groups of relatives.

After a long, busy day of parades and reunions, Norwegians go home–pleasantly fatigued and already looking forward to next year.

Christmas In Norway

Christmas is the most treasured holiday for all Norwegians, wherever

Christmas Cookies

Norwegian Christmas cookies will add an extra special touch to your holiday celebrations. Choose a recipe from our collection of traditional Norwegian Christmas cookies to start your holiday baking. Bake them ahead of time, and freeze them or store them in tin boxes in a cool spot.

The traditional Norwegian Christmas cookies are:

Berlinerkranser
Fattigmann
Pepperkaker
Sandkaker
Serinakaker
Sirupsnipper
Smørpletter

Why are seven kinds of butter cookies baked and stored in tins until Christmas Eve? Perhaps there is a long history behind the custom, going back to Viking times when our Norwegian ancestors followed the four phases of the moon, seven days in each. During the seven days between Christmas and New Year, guests visiting in Norwegian homes are served these seven varieties of cookies.

Berlinerkranser are Christmas wreaths with a delicate buttery flavor. While Berlinerkranser may sound like German cookies, the recipe for these delightful wreath-shaped cookies is traditional Norwegian. These little cookie wreaths are made by hand-rolling the dough into pencil-thin strips. Wreaths are formed by looping the ends. The Norwegians decorate Berlinerkranser with coarse granulated sugar which makes them sparkle.

Fattigmann, full of eggs and cream, are referred to as "Poor Man's" cookies, Tove suggests with a smile, because "after you make them, you are sure to be poor."

In medieval times, cooks used pepper and ginger together. **Pepperkaker** get their "zip" from white pepper which gives them a delicate, but zesty taste. Black pepper can be used but the result will be a bolder taste–plus dark specks in your cookies.

Sandkaker are tart-shaped butter cookies that may be filled with fresh berries or whipped cream.

Serinakaker are studded with almonds.

Sirupsnipper not only smell good while they are baking, but their combination of ginger and molasses make them mild but full of flavor.

Smørpletter, butter dots, are an "ice box cookie." Perhaps the earliest "slice and bake," this buttery cookie dough can be made and chilled days before baking.

they may be, from the **gård** (farm) in Sunndal to a condominium in Oslo overlooking the fjord.

As Christmas approaches, even Norwegian ships signal their participation: in harbors throughout the world **juletrær** (Christmas trees) are rigged on the mastheads. And, on board ships, as in Norwegian homes, Christmas is celebrated Norwegian style, which means little differently than the way others celebrate this very special season.

Of course, the shops along Oslo's Karl Johan resemble main street and malls elsewhere throughout the world. Fanciful window displays beckon eager-eyed children pressing noses against the glass for a better view of Christmas "goodies." Streets throng with Norwegians on the customary Christmas shopping spree. Big, lighted Christmas trees brighten up the squares, and street lights and poles are festooned with garlands and lights. Adults, already weary of shopping excesses, dream about the good, "old-fashioned" Christmas the way **Mormor** (grandmother) used to celebrate it.

Christmas in Norway is an especially happy time for everyone since Norwegians celebrate the season for an entire month. Preparations begin in early December, and by preparations we don't mean simply gift buying. To a Norwegian housewife a clean house and boxes filled with seven kinds of Christmas cookies are of major importance.

Every corner of the house is cleaned. Curtains and windows are washed, carpets, pillows and bedclothes are brought out for a thorough airing then beaten until the last particle of dust has disappeared. Silver is polished and the crystal is washed until it shines.

In many farm kitchens throughout the country, preparations include the brewing of **Juleøl** (the special Christmas beer). In addition, for most families, there is a trip to the woods to select with great care the Christmas tree. Oslo residents Bjørn and Kari Johansen purchase their Christmas tree at Trysil, "not far from where we have our cabin. It is 190 cm. high, and with the base and the star in the top, it reaches the ceiling." (It was only during the late 19th century that

*A wide variety of **Julenissen** (Christmas elves or gnomes) can be seen at the **Tregaarden Julehus** in Drøbak, Norway. Many of these "kitchen witch" designs represent the creative artistry of Eva Johansen, who founded the Julehus in 1976, with her husband, Willy. Children from all over the world write to "Santa Claus" or **Julenissen** in Drøbak, the official Christmas post office in Norway.*

the custom of a Christmas tree was introduced into Norway from Germany.)

As Christmas draws closer, the baking is started. Many kinds of small cakes (biscuits and cookies) are baked, the minimum being seven different kinds, in addition to the **julekake**, the sweet Christmas bread filled with raisins, candied peel, and cardamom. Every cookiebox is filled with delicious cookies and then stored away for the holidays. The cookie recipes may vary from household to household, but seven kinds of cookies are traditional.

Julefeiring, the Christmas celebration begins when a Christmas tree is brought in and decorated on **Lille Juleaften** (Little Christmas Eve), and not a day before. It is decorated with all kinds of ornaments, handmade and store bought. Little Norwegian flags are also used and the children always make paper tree baskets from shiny colored paper to fill with cookies and nuts. Then they hang them on the **juletre**.

Some families still use real candles for their trees; however, this is a very dangerous, if beautiful, custom and is being given up more and more in favor of the little white electric lights.

The Christmas celebration starts at 4 o'clock on Christmas Eve. All the churches

Julekake

Christmas Bread

Preparation

⌘ Warm two cups of milk to about 120 degrees.

⌘ Set aside 1/4 cup of warm milk to cool to about 100° F, then add package of yeast and stir.

⌘ Put 1 3/4 cup of the very warm milk into blender jar, and add softened butter, then following ingredients, blending on low for a few seconds following each addition to ensure thorough mixing: Sugar. Cardamom. Egg.

⌘ To blender mixture, while on low speed, add 1-2 cups of flour. Mixture will soon become too thick to continue.

⌘ Add 4 cups of flour to large mixing bowl and attach dough hook.

⌘ Add to liquid mixture raisins and sukat in mixer bowl and while on slow speed, allow several minutes for dough hook to work into a soft, wet dough. Then, slowly add remaining flour to dough until it is well blended.

⌘ Let rise about 20 minutes in warm place, or until doubled in size.

⌘ Punch down and divide dough into two equal portions.

⌘ Shape into proper size for two 9" round pans or two loaf pans.

⌘ Let rise for about 25-30 minutes, or until again doubled.

⌘ Preheat oven to 400° F.

⌘ Brush with beaten egg.

⌘ Bake for about 35-40 minutes or until done.

Ingredients

2 cups milk
1 package dry yeast
1/3 cup sugar
1/2 cup butter, softened
1 egg
2 teaspoons cardamom
7 cups flour

3/4 cup raisins
1/2 cup "Sukat" (candied lemon peel) or chopped, candied fruit
1 egg, beaten

Marie's Original Recipe

Julekage

Til hvert 1 mark Mel, tages 4 lod Smør, og 6 lod Sukker. Kardemomme. Citronskal, rosiner efter smag 1 spiseske gjar til hvert mark.

Background

Julekake is really a delicious Christmas sweet yeast bread. There are many different recipes or variations, but the basic ingredients are simple: plain, white flour (not self-rising), yeast, sugar, milk, and margarine or butter. Many of the holiday versions of sweet yeast breads become much more elaborate, and may contain eggs, more butter, raisins, cardamon, cinnamon, candied fruit or orange peel, or sukat, candied lemon peel.

This recipe makes up into a moderately soft dough, slightly sticky, which may be kneaded on a floured surface.

Flour, butter, sugar, cardamom, candied lemon peel, raisins, and yeast. The basic ingredients for a delicious sweet yeast bread that fills your home with holiday aromas while its baking, and is a delight to eat by itself, or with coffee.

Berlinerkranser
Berlin Crowns

Ingredients

4 hard-boiled egg yolks
4 fresh eggs, separated
1 cup sugar
1 pound unsalted butter, softened
3 3/4 cups all-purpose flour
crushed loaf sugar

Quantity

Makes 96 wreath cookies.

Preparation

⌘ *Mix all the egg yolks together. Add sugar.*
⌘ *Blend in butter and flour.*
⌘ *Roll out into three thin sausage pieces and refriger-
 ate 30 minutes.*
⌘ *Preheat oven to 350º F.*
⌘ *Take a strip and cut off 1/2 inch. Roll this into a
 four-inch-long strip, forming a circle and overlap-
 ping the ends to form a wreath.*
⌘ *Dip into egg white and then coarsely crushed sugar.*
⌘ *Bake on an ungreased cookie sheet for about 10
 minutes or until golden brown.*

Marie's Original Recipe

Barlinerkrandse

2 haardkogte Aggeblommer gnides sammen med 8 lod finstodt Sukker og røres saa ud i 2 raae Aggeblommer, derpaa haves 1 mark Mel og 1/2 mark udvasket Smør deri. De rulles ud til smaa krandse; bestryges med pidskede hvidder og bestraes med gravstodt Sukker og Mandler.

Fattigmann
Fried Crullers—"Poor Man's Cake"

Ingredients

3 egg yolks
1 egg white
1/3 cup confectioner's sugar
1/4 cup whipping cream
1 tablespoon cognac (or brandy)
1 1/2 cups flour
1/4 teaspoon cardamom
1/4 teaspoon lemon peel
Vegetable oil for deep fat frying
Confectioner's sugar for tops
 (optional)

**Note: See safety tip on deep
 fat frying on p. 220.**

Preparation

⌘ *Beat eggs and sugar. Blend in cream and cognac,
 beating well.*
⌘ *In a separate bowl, mix flour, cardamom and lemon
 peel.*
⌘ *Gradually add to egg mixture.*
⌘ *Refrigerate one hour (overnight if possible).*
⌘ *Preheat oil to 375º F.*
⌘ *On a well floured board, roll dough very thin, about
 1/8-inch thick sheets.*
⌘ *Cut into diamond shapes, approximately 3-inches
 long by 2-inches wide. Make a 1-inch slit lengthwise
 in center of each. Pull one end through the slit and
 twist dough under.*
⌘ *Fry in hot oil until lightly browned. Turn to brown
 other side. (About 2 minutes on each side.) Drain on
 paper towels.*
⌘ *Cool. If desired, sprinkle lightly with confectioner's
 sugar (to which might be added some vanilla sugar).*
⌘ *Store in sealed container.*
⌘ *Makes 20-30 depending on size.*

join together in welcoming Christmas by ringing church bells. It is a beautiful and touching moment. At Christmas, the bells are rung differently than on other special occasions. This is no slow, steady "ding dong," but an intense and protracted ding-ding-ding lasting several minutes.

A very informal church service, called the Children's Service, is held and the congregation joins in singing the Christmas carols and the minister wishes everyone a very merry Christmas. Then it's home, where the family gathers, young and old, for the big dinner. Christmas peace settles over the land in farms and villages. Stragglers who have not yet reached their destinations hurry to join family and friends. In many areas, the snow creaks and crunches under foot. Light from the windows glows invitingly as the dark winter afternoon rapidly turns into evening.

Pork, potatoes, sweet and sour cabbage, pork sausage, cranberry sauce and pickles are favorites. For dessert, homemade ice cream or a Norwegian delicacy called **Tilslørte Bondepiker** (Brown Betty) may be served.

During a recent Christmas season, Bjørn and Kari baked **Sandnøtter**, **Tyske skiver**, **Krumkaker**, **Serinakaker**, **Berlinerkranser**, **Smultringer**, and **Sandkaker**. "I call them 'in and out cakes,' because you carry them in and out from the coffee table during the entire season," Bjørn notes, with tongue in cheek. As usual," he

Countless Yule logs have cast a special glow from this corner fireplace in Sunndalen. Many generations of the Fladvad family have celebrated Juletid around its blazing fire.

noted, "we are going to serve **ribbe**, **julepølse** and **medisterkaker** on Christmas Eve, when Trond and Nina, Kari's mother, two sisters, one husband and a daughter are coming for the traditional dinner in our home. It is all served with boiled potatoes, a gravy and a Norwegian type of sauerkraut and **Tyttebær-syltetøy**."

For many families on Christmas Eve it is still the custom to make a trip to the barn with a bowl of **graut** (porridge) for þe **nisse**, the gnome who—according to superstition—is the protector of the farm. Today, the ceremony is performed mainly for the children, but **Mormor** (grandmother) may still have the uneasy feeling that the little fellow might actually exist.

The **nisse** is not the only one remembered with a treat at Christmas. The **julenek**, a bundle or sheaf of oats for birds, is mounted on a pole atop the barn, and the farm animals are also given a special Christmas feed.

Yule Log Cake

Yule log cakes are named after the yule log which burned brightly on the hearth to keep King (Father) Frost at bay. In Norway, the fourth Sunday before Christmas marks the start of Advent. During this period, many Christmas preparations are made, and Norwegian kitchens are sweetly fragrant with holiday baking. Apple candelabras are created with candles, apples, and brightly colored bows to celebrate the Yuletide.

Dinner is served and enjoyed for a long, long time. (At least for the children it seems like a very long time.) A lot of **akevitt** (aquavit) with beer chasers is consumed by the adults and there is one **skål** after another as the Norwegians wish each other **God Jul, God Jul**. (Of course, the "designated driver" is selected in advance. Norwegians are very strict about drinking and not driving.)

Akevitt or **dram** is made from potatoes or barley. You always say "**skål**" before sipping *Akevitt*.

Julenissen Brings Gifts

Suddenly there is someone at the door. It is **Julenissen** with his big sack filled with gifts. He is an elf-like creature, short, round and good natured.

He has something for everyone.

If you're a troll, as any lover of Norwegian folklore knows, you live in an underground cavern, are kind to people in spite of the fact that you enjoy stealing their provisions, can foretell the future, endow humans with fortunes or superhuman strength, if you feel so inclined, and are probably quite ugly.

Trolls apparently enjoy being something less than beautiful and make the most of it at the **Syttende Mai** celebration in Stoughton, Wisconsin, each year when the ugliest troll contest is held. School children, under the guidance of their school art departments, design and make their own terrible looking troll heads in an effort to outdo each other in looking hideous. Perhaps, trolls

would not be so homely if they received a steady diet of Norwegian dishes and delicacies such as ones you can buy at the **syttende mai** celebration. The women prepare sumptuous **smørgåsbord**, and there are snacks and other foods and specialties. Brats or **varme pølser** (hotdogs), served in novel ways as they sometimes are in Norway, where **lefse** may substitute for hotdog rolls.

The Christmas celebration itself begins with the reading of the Christmas story from the Bible; often from a family Bible that is several hundred years old, with generations of births and baptisms, confirmations and marriages and deaths recorded inside the front cover.

After this, the family sits down to enjoy the traditional meal, which to the unaccustomed, may seem to contrast strangely with the festive occasion. Often the main dish is porridge. Sometimes fresh cod, or possibly **lutefisk**, cod treated in a lye solution and served boiled. This is traditional food, and likely survives from pre-Reformation times, when Christmas Eve was devoted to fasting and abstinence. The Christmas meal these days includes a variety of dishes that remove all thoughts of fasting– or abstinence–for that matter.

For the children however, food is important, but not all-important. Their eyes keep turning to the presents under the tree, sometimes kept behind the closed doors of the living room. As their elders linger over

Pepperkaker

Gingerbread Cookies

Preparation

⌘ *Preheat oven to 350° F.*
⌘ *Mix all ingredients.*
⌘ *Cover cookie dough and chill four hours (or overnight) in refrigerator.*
⌘ *Roll out (thinly) 1/4 of dough at a time (leaving remaining dough in refrigerator) on generously floured surface (counter top or canvas) with a covered rolling pin.*
⌘ *Bake on ungreased cookie sheet 10-12 minutes.*
⌘ *Makes 150 cookies.*

Ingredients

1 cup butter, softened
1 cup sugar
1 cup molasses
1 1/2 teaspoons cinnamon
1/2 teaspoon ground cloves
1 1/2 teaspoons ground ginger
1/2 teaspoon salt
1 1/2 teaspoons diced orange peel
1/2 teaspoon nutmeg
1 1/8 teaspoon baking soda
1/2 cup heavy cream
4 egg yolks
4 3/4 cups flour

Background

There are many versions of this cookie recipe. After trying several of them we found this version made the biggest hit with our families. The added orange peel gave the cookies extra flavor. Perfect to serve on crisp autumn days.

"Pepperkaker" is a reminder of the fact that in medieval times, ginger and pepper were always used together and their names became almost interchangeable. That is why so many ginger flavored cookies and cakes are called "pepper." Although they contain none of that spice today, they are still spicy or "peppery" in flavor. Enjoy!

Peppernøtter

Ball-Shaped Spice Cookies

Preparation

⌘ *Cream butter and sugar until light and fluffy.*
⌘ *Add egg yolks, cream, and almonds.*
⌘ *Mix together thoroughly.*
⌘ *Add flour mixed with spices*
⌘ *Roll into logs 4-6 inches long.*
⌘ *Wrap in plastic wrap and refrigerate 6-8 hours, or overnight.*
⌘ *Slice into rounds 1/4 inch thick*
⌘ *Bake in pre-heated 350° F. oven for about 15 minutes.*

Alternate Method

⌘ *Shape into 1-inch balls.*
⌘ *Bake in 350 degree oven for about 15 minutes or until slightly brown at the edges.*

Ingredients

2 sticks butter, softened
2 cups sugar
3 egg yolks
1/2 cup cream
1/2 cup chopped almonds
3 cups flour
1/4 teaspoon finely ground white pepper
1/2 teaspoon ginger
1/2 teaspoon cinnamon
1/2 teaspoon cloves

Peppernøtter
Ball-Shaped Spice Cookies

Ingredients

2/3 cup butter
4 pieces crystalized ginger
1/2 cup molasses
1/2 cup cane syrup
3 cups flour
1 teaspoon soda
2 teaspoons allspice

Preparation

⌘ *Melt butter in pan with crystalized ginger.*
⌘ *Add molasses and syrup.*
⌘ *Stir in flour with allspice and soda.*
⌘ *Roll into small balls.*
⌘ *Bake at 350º F. on greased cookie sheet for 15 minutes.*

Notes

Peppernøtter (pepper nuts), a pleasantly spicy holiday cookie, contains both ginger and pepper. In medieval times, cooks always used ginger and pepper together. These delicious cookies have an interesting flavor. They taste especially peppery right out of the oven. They mellow somewhat when stored in a tightly covered container for several weeks.

Since there are no chopped almonds in supermarkets, if almonds are required, use slivered almonds and chop them up a little. Or, just sprinkle slivered almonds on top of cookies before baking.

Using white pepper avoids having to explain to your guests the origin of those "little black specks" in your cookies. Also, it has a somewhat milder flavor than black pepper.

Hvite Peppernøtter
White Ginger Cookies

Ingredients

2 cups sugar
2 sticks butter
2 cups milk
1/4 cup rum
6-7 cups flour
1 teaspoon soda
1 teaspoon ginger
1 teaspoon cloves
1 teaspoon cinnamon
1/2 teaspoon hjortesalt or
  baking soda
5 teaspoons baking powder

Preparation

⌘ *Preheat oven to 375º F.*
⌘ *Cream sugar and softened butter.*
⌘ *Add milk slowly and allow to mix thoroughly. Then add rum.*
⌘ *To flour add cinnnamon, ginger, cloves, soda and baking powder.*
⌘ *Mix thoroughly, then add to liquid mixture and beat smooth.*
⌘ *Roll into small balls.*
⌘ *Bake on greased cookie sheet for 15 minutes.*

Marie's Original Manuscript Recipe

Hvide Pebernödder

1 pun löst hvidt sukker; 1 1/2 pun hvedemel; 2 lod smør; 9-10 sker god sur melk eller römme; 1 theske potaske; 1 do hjortesalt; 1 do kanel; 1 do ingefar; 1 do nellikker. Spekkelasier bruger man også heraf.

delicious morsels, the youngsters start to fret at the unbearably slow pace. It seems like an eternity will pass before the big moment arrives and the dazzling presents can be opened.

Finally, the adults are stuffed and the time honored ritual of "circling the Christmas tree can begin." Everyone joins hands to form a ring around the tree, and then all assembled walk around the tree as they join together in singing Christmas hymns.

The gifts are then distributed, and the children marvel at the surprises inside for them. The remainder of the evening is spent playing games. Cakes, cookies, and other *julemat* are served throughout the evening to keep any possible hunger pangs at bay.

GLEDELIG JUL
Merry Christmas

The next morning family and friends again gather together for more eating and celebrating. Often the family goes to church. In previous years there was an early morning service, followed by a big breakfast at home. These days however, the service is later in the morning, and is often held at a small wooden church that may have served the community since the Middle Ages. At Flatvad, it is the Romfo Church which is over 200 years old, one of only four octagonal churches in Norway.

Some of these churches have runic inscriptions on the darkened walls, highlighted by paintings and carvings done during the centuries since those distant times. Perhaps, if you listen closely, you can hear the faint echo of hundreds of earlier Christmas

---

Julekost

Breakfast: Whole grain bread with cheese, herring, smoked eel, liverwurst or jam. Soft boiled eggs. Milk or coffee.

Sunday: Fried eggs, potatoes and bacon

Lunch: Open faced sandwich, coffee, tea or milk and fresh fruit

Dinner: (eaten at 4:30 p.m. in most homes) Usually a plain meal consisting of fish or meat, boiled potatoes and a vegetable.

Coffee: (served after a little nap at 6:30) Served in the living room on the big coffee table. Coffee and several kinds of cookies.

Aftensmat: (evening meal served about 10 p.m.) Open faced sandwich and a glass of milk.

---

services, with hymns being sung by voices now stilled and resting in the nearby *gravlund*.

The church service is followed by the traditional *Julefrokost* (Christmas breakfast). It starts in the morning and lasts most of the day. All kinds of delicacies are served *smørgåsbord* style. It is all created beautifully because to Norwegians it isn't just what you serve, but how you serve it that is important.

After the coffee portion of a holiday meal, Norwegians often go for a stroll if it is summertime or settle down for a little knitting or embroidering if it is during the long winter evenings.

Many Norwegian families, including the Johansens, visit the cemetery during the Christmas Day afternoon. There they find the graves of their relatives and place a lighted *stearin lys* (paraffin wax candle) on the grave. "At that time of the year it is dark at about 4 p.m in Oslo," Bjørn Johansen points out. "You can imagine the sight when thousands of stearin candles are burning in the snow at an Oslo cemetery."

Christmas Eve and Christmas Day are certainly the high points in the Norwegian Christmas Season. However, they do not conclude the season's celebrations. For many, they are the beginning of a season lasting at least to Epiphany, and in some places until January 13th–the twentieth day of Christmas, and the feast day of St. Canute. Then, as the saying goes, "twentieth-day Canute drives away Christmas."

Christmas is the season for socializing. In some places, people still use horses and sleighs, and the jingle of sleigh-bells can be heard through the snow frosted trees. It is a season of welcomes and warm greetings, of light streaming out of open doors as guests are received, a season of good food, games, and merriment, when bedtimes are relaxed for the children.

"To go *julebukk*" (lit. "Christmas goat") is an old custom dating back to the Middle Ages still enjoyed by the children, who dress up in fancy clothes and visit nearby farms. There they are treated to cakes and other delicacies. This is the kind of Christmas that is still a rich part of the heritage, particularly in country districts, a Christmas that **Mormor** knew and loved. However, it is very likely that when St. Canute had finally put end to the festivities, **Mormor** felt like going into hibernation. The work involved was, and is, staggering.

Most of us don't stop to think about our Christmas traditions, we accept them without question, as do Norwegians. These traditions take on more meaning however, when we remember that they are a kind of museum, providing glimpses of our forefather's beliefs and way of life–from pagan customs to ancient Christian traditions.

Christmas, a great Christian tradition, has assimilated customs from many religions and peoples. Each country has added its own special contribution to the rich tapestry of Christmas tradition.

Consider our Christmas tree, usually an evergreen, conveying the idea of vitality and growth, despite the temporary darkness of winter. It incorporates both Christian and pagan symbols. The Celtic people gave us mistletoe, the Saxons, holly. The custom of giving gifts was adopted from a Roman New Year festival. Along with these customs, the people of Norway have included their own Christmas customs, some of which can be traced back to the pagan sacrificial offerings of their Viking ancestors.

Even the word Yule, or in Norwegian **Jul**, which is the name for the holiday itself, dates back to pre-Christian times. **Joulu** or **Lol** was a pagan feast celebrated all over Northern Europe. Historians cannot agree as to exactly what kind of feast the **joulu** was, or even the exact time of year when it was celebrated. However, there is general agreement that it must have fallen on a date

Marzipan Pig

Here's how you can make a marzipan pig or other shapes at Christmas time.

Ingredients

1 cup almond paste (8 ounce can)
1/4 cup light corn syrup
3/4 cup confectioner's sugar
2/3 cup marshmallow creme (or melted marshmallows)

Directions

Cut up almond paste into small pieces in a bowl, then mix until smooth. Add 1/4 cup light corn syrup, 3/4 cup confectioner's sugar, and 2/3 cup marshmallow creme or melted marshmallows. Divide batch, and add coloring as desired. Shape into marzipan candies and tint.

Christmas Fun With Children

Steps

⌘ Cover work surface with a plastic table cloth
⌘ Provide 1 sheet of waxed paper, a small bowl (custard cups are good size)
⌘ Give each child approximately two tablespoons of marzipan "dough" in each cup. Let child choose shade.
⌘ Adult put one drop of food color on depression in each cup of dough.
⌘ Child molds, kneads "edible clay" until pastel color is uniform throughout dough.
⌘ Begin making shapes: pig, watermelon slice, fruits, and vegetables.
⌘ Small details may be painted on candy with food color drop in candy wrapper, such as leaves on strawberry.
⌘ Decorate with sprinkles.
⌘ Set to dry on paper plate.

Bergen Peppernøtter

Bergen Pepper Gingersnaps

Preparation

⌘ *Preheat oven to 375º F.*
⌘ *Mix thoroughly molasses, sugar, and eggs.*
⌘ *Add pepper, cinnamon, orange peel, ginger, and baking soda.*
⌘ *Add flour slowly, mixing thoroughly as it is added. We used a blender during these first two steps. Then, poured out the syrup mixture into a mixing bowl, and slowly added the flour to create the dough.*
⌘ *Roll into 1 1/2 inch balls or*
⌘ *Roll out 1/2 - 3/4 inch thick onto floured surface, then cut into squares.*
⌘ *Place on greased baking sheet.*
⌘ *Bake for 20-25 minutes.*

Ingredients

2 whole eggs
1/2 cup molasses or dark syrup
1/2 cup sugar
2 1/2 cups flour
1/4 teaspoon white pepper
1 teaspoon cinnamon
1 teaspoon orange peel
1/2 teaspoon ginger
1 teaspoon baking soda OR
   1/2 teaspoon baking soda
   and 1/2 teaspoon hjortetsalt

Notes

This spicy ginger snap reminds us of old fashioned thick ginger snaps made without butter and therefore far lower in calories. The gentle but tangy pepper taste lingers for a few minutes after the cookie-biscuit is eaten. The combination of ginger, cinnamon, and orange peel is delightful. Of course, the degree of spiciness depends on the quantity used. Scale back the spices if you prefer a milder flavor. Another variation can be the syrup selected. Molasses can be replaced by another favorite syrup such as maple or cane syrup.

Marie's Original Manuscript Recipe

Bergenske Pebernödder

   1/2 mark Sirup; 1/2 mark Sukker; 1 mark Mel; 2 Ag; en tappet theske Peber; 2 do Canel; 2 do Pomerantskal; 1 do ingefar, og 1 do Natron eller 1/2 Natron og 1/2 Hjortetsalt.

Background

In the days of early Christianity, small heart-shaped cakes were baked on saints' days. They were called Life Cakes or Saints' Hearts. Later, these cakes were ornamented and bestowed as gifts on saints' days. The name became distorted from Saints' Hearts to Sand Tarts. The museum at Bath, England has a collection of old cutters used in making these cakes.

Ingredients

1 cup butter
3/4 cup sugar
1 egg, beaten
2 1/2 cups flour
1 teaspoon almond extract
1/2 cup ground or finely
    chopped almonds

Sandkaker
Norwegian Sand Tarts

Preparation

⌘ *Preheat oven to 325º F.*
⌘ *Cream butter and sugar until fluffy.*
⌘ *Add egg, almonds, and flour. Mix thoroughly.*
⌘ *Chill for an hour (or overnight).*
⌘ *Roll dough out very thin.*
⌘ *Press pieces of the thin dough into greased* Sandbakkelse *or other small fancy forms (or tiny muffin pans). A little flour on your fingers will keep the dough from sticking to them. Or, if you're not concerned about strict uniformity in thickness, simply press walnut-sized pieces of the dough evenly into the bottom and around the sides of* Sandbakkelse *forms.*
⌘ *Place the filled* Sandbakkelse *forms on a baking sheet.*
⌘ *Bake 12 to 15 minutes or until golden brown.*
⌘ *Remove cakes from forms while still warm by tapping edge of form gently against table top.*

Quantity

Makes about 3 dozen tarts, 3 1/2 inches by 1 1/4 inches.

Serving Suggestions

These can be served plain or filled with fruit and whipped cream. Norwegians enjoy these tart shells served plain, like cookies.

Smørpletter
Butter Dots

Preparation

⌘ *Mix all ingredients well.*
⌘ *Shape into a sausage about 2 inches thick.*
⌘ *Chill well.*
⌘ *Slice into 1/4 inch slices.*
⌘ *Arrange on cookie sheet.*
⌘ *Decorate with almond slices or walnuts.*
⌘ *Bake in 350º F. oven for about 15 minutes.*

Ingredients

1/2 cup confectioner's sugar
1 1/2 cups flour
1 1/2 sticks of butter, softened

Quantity

36 cookies.

during late autumn or early winter. Most historians do agree that its focus came to be associated with, a sacrificial feast for the dead.

Perhaps that seems strange today, however we must remember that this was an agricultural society, solidly linked to the yearly cycle of spring, summer, autumn, and winter, which corresponded to birth, reproduction, and death. It probably seemed natural to associate fertility and death--life's emergence from and return to the unknown.

The oldest of our Christmas customs seem to be the remnants of this feast. They concern sacrifices to the gods and to the dead, and they generally include food and drink.

Certainly of ancient origin is the special *juleøl*, the Yuletime beer that is brewed on the farms, and in modern times by the breweries. This custom can be traced back through the years to the time when horns filled with beer during the Joulu festivities were dedicated to the Norse gods **Odin**, **Frøy**, and **Njord.**

Today, when Norwegians lift their glasses each Christmas in the traditional Scandinavian "**Skål**," (pronounced "scawl"), they give little thought to their Viking ancestors who lifted the horns of sacrificial beer to drink for peace and a good year to come.

Juleøl as a tradition survived Norway's conversion to Christianity. People simply refused to give it up. Wisely, the country's leaders chose instead to give the old tradition a new symbolic meaning. Beer, they decided, was no longer considered to be a sacrificial drink. It was to be called holiday beer. The laws of the land directed that it should be "blessed on Christmas night, to Christ and the Virgin Mary."

Associating pigs with Christmas dates from another ancient tradition. It is believed that a pig was sacrificed to **Frøy** at some point during the Joulu celebration. In fact, the pig provided the main dish for the subsequent feast.

This is perhaps why, even today, pork is served in most Norwegian homes at Christmas. It may be a whole roast piglet, or it may be in the form of pressed pork, roast pork with sour cabbage, smoked ham, or pickled trotters.

Marsipangriser

Marzipan

Pigs A

Charming

Christmas

Tradition

A favorite gift at Christmas celebrations in Norway is a marzipan pig. The Christmas pigs

Woven Paper Hearts

Woven paper hearts are traditionally made of red and white paper at Christmas time in Norway. Tove sent us one that she had made to hang on the *juletre* (Christmas tree). Perhaps they were invented by Hans Christian Anderson. Because the little hearts are so much a part of Christmas in Norway, we wanted to include them here.

You'll need red and white paper, pencil, ruler and scissors to make a heart.

1. Cut two rectangles of paper (one red, one white) 3" x 9."

2. Fold each piece in half, lengthwise, making them 4 1/2" x 3".

3. Draw a line 3" from the folded edge on each piece, giving you a marked off square.

4. Draw lines one inch apart (or 1/2 inch apart, if you wish to have more loops).

5. Opposite the folded edge, cut around each rectangle to make a curved edge.

6. Cut carefully along the lines from the fold up to the marked off line.

7. Weave the red and white loops together, creating a heart basket that will open at the top. Make a paper handle the same size as one of your loops: 1/2" x 3", or 1" x 3" and attach with glue. Or, punch a hole at the top of the heart and tie a narrow satin bow.

are quite popular and sometimes they are rather large, too. Tante Jeanne Willumsen recalled a Christmas pig she had received and remembered fondly as "such a beautiful piggy." Norwegian children greatly enjoy the holiday custom of making marzipan confections, shaping the dough into tiny fruit replicas such as bananas, apples, cakes and even hard cooked eggs, sliced.

The Italians called the holiday **marchpane** which at first meant "a box for fine confections." The Germans called it **marzipan**. Since this confection, which is a paste of almonds, sugar, and egg whites shaped into a variety of forms, was imported from Germany, Norwegians and Americans call it marzipan.

In addition to seeing marzipan pigs at Christmas time, the pig may also appear as a holiday symbol on a Christmas postcard—the pig all dressed in a colorful knitted scarf and hat, perched on a sled racing down a snow-covered hill.

The belief in the **nisse** also recalls pagan times. His ancestry as protector of the **gård** (farm) can be traced back to the man who, in the distant past, had first cleared the land. Often this man was believed to be interred in one of the burial mounds near the farm buildings. At Yuletide (the feast for the dead), food and drink was brought out to the mound for him, and he was believed to come out to eat and drink. Over the centuries, the popular image of this much respected (and sometimes feared) ghost changed into the less dangerous, but still at times destructive and leprechaun-like **nisse** found in traditional Norwegian fairy tales.

A strange intermingling has taken place between the Nordic **nisse** and the St. Nicholas of central Europe. The result is the queer mixture of gnome and saint described to American children in "twas the night before Christmas." Interestingly, the author of those immortal words in "A Visit From St. Nicholas," Clement C. Moore, lived in Newport in the house next door to the Cottrell home at 23 Catherine Street. Today, in Norway too, the native **nisse** contain strong elements of the imported Santa Claus.

Nisse were not the only ghosts thought to be present at Yuletide. The dead were believed to travel about in great numbers during this season. Food was left on the tables for them on Christmas night, or in some places during the entire Holiday period. For some guests, it is an *eerie* thought, as they help themselves to the abundant food on the Christmas buffets in Norwegian restaurants, that the tradition of these meals probably goes back to the ghostly banquets of superstition. Others believe (with more justification), that the abundance and variety of dishes can be traced to another tradition. People believed that the quantity of food served at Christmas augured poverty–or plenty–in the year to come. Naturally, they outdid themselves to ensure a year of abundance.

Other Christmas traditions are traceable to the Middle Ages: the use of straw decorations and the sheaf of oats set out for the birds.

SOURCES & SUGGESTED READING

Forbes, Kathryn (1943). *Mama's Bank Account*. The story of a Norwegian immigrant family living in San Francisco and based on biographical sketches by Forbes.

Du Chaillu, Paul (1882). *The Land of the Midnight Sun*.

Henriksen, Vera (1992). *Christmas in Norway*. Oslo: NORINFORM for the Ministry of Foreign Affairs.

Undset, Sigrid (1923). *Kristin Lavrinsdatter*. New York: Alfred A. Knopf.

Norwegian Royal Crowns

Preparation

⌘ *Preheat oven to 375º F.*
⌘ *Cream butter and sugar; add egg yolks.*
⌘ *Add flour and almond extract; mix well.*
⌘ *Chill.*
⌘ *Force through cookie press onto cookie sheet.*
⌘ *Bake for 10 to 15 minutes.*

Quantity

Makes 90 Cookies

Ingredients

1/2 cup butter
1/4 cup sugar
yolks of 2 hard-boiled eggs,
  mashed
1 cup flour
1 teaspoon almond extract

Serinakaker

Serina Cookies

Background

This is a buttery, golden little cookie.

Preparation

⌘ *Preheat oven to 350º F.*
⌘ *Cream butter, sugar and vanilla until light and fluffy.*
⌘ *Add beaten egg.*
⌘ *Add baking powder and salt to flour.*
⌘ *Gradually stir into egg mixture, mixing well.*
⌘ *Chill in refrigerator for at least an hour.*
⌘ *Roll pieces of the cookie dough into small, 1-inch balls, then dip in beaten egg white and roll in chopped nuts.*
⌘ *Place on cookie sheets, separating somewhat as they tend to spread out during baking.*
⌘ *Flatten each ball of dough slighting using tines of a fork.*
⌘ *Lightly brush with beaten egg white.*
⌘ *Place in oven and bake about 10-12 minutes, watching closely. The cookies themselves do not brown, just the nuts and egg white.*
⌘ *Cool on wire rack.*

Ingredients

2/3 cup butter, softened
1 cup sugar
1 teaspoon vanilla
1 egg, beaten
1 teaspoon baking powder
1/2 teaspoon salt
2 1/2 cups flour
-----
1 egg white, beaten
1/2 cup chopped almonds

Sirupsnipper
Molasses Diamond Cookies

Background

Bjørn and Tove's mother, Nina Johansen, always baked these at Christmas. "It made my kitchen smell like Christmas," she said.

These cookies are mild but full of flavor. The ginger and molasses are not overpowering (like gingerbread). The combination is more subtle. It's a chewy cookie, especially when they first come out of the oven. It's akin to eating a cookie-candy hybrid.

"Snipper" refers to their diamond shape.

Ingredients

1/4 cup (or 4 tablespoons)
   molasses
1 cup sugar
2 1/4 cups flour
1/2 cup heavy cream
1 teaspoon baking soda
1 teaspoon ginger
10 1/2 tablespoons butter,
   softened (1 stick, plus 2 1/2
   extra tablespoons)

Preparation

⌘ *Preheat oven to 350º F.*
⌘ *Mix everything together except the butter, which is worked into (*elte*) the dough last.*
⌘ *Cover dough in plastic wrap and chill in refrigerator overnight.*
⌘ *Roll out thinly and cut with cookie cutter into diamond shapes.*
⌘ *Bake on cookie sheet for about 10 minutes.*

Quantity

Makes 80-90 cookies.

*Asbjørn and Nina Johansen
on their wedding day.*

Mølsgraut

Møls Porridge

Ingredients and Preparation (Norwegian)

8 liter melk kokes inn til ca halv mengde. Sprenges med 4 dl kulturmelk og kokes videre inn til passe tykk grøt. Tilsett ca. 2-3 spiseskjeer smør, 2 kopper sukker, 1 ts kardemomme. Lag en jevning av 3-4 spiseskjeer mel og 2 1/2 dl fløte og jevn grøten La den kokes godt opp. Fyll i skåler. Når den er litt avkjølt legges over et tynt lag smeltet smør (om ønskes kan strøs pa kanel og lage ruter).

Preparation

⌘ *8 liters of milk cooked down to about half its original amount.*
⌘ *Add 4 deciliters (2 cups) buttermilk and continue cooking until it becomes a thick porridge.*
⌘ *To that add about 2-3 spiseskjeer butter and two cups of sugar and one teaspoon of Cardemom.*
⌘ *Separately mix three tablespoons of flour with 2 1/2 deciliters of cold, heavy cream (fløtekrem). When thoroughly mixed, add to cooking mixture.*
⌘ *Let the mixture boil slowly for about 15 minutes, then remove from heat and pour into serving bowl.*
⌘ *Let stand until cool.*
⌘ *Spoon a little heated (liquid) butter over the top, which will form a very thin layer when cooled.*
⌘ *Sprinkle a little powdered cinnamon in criss cross patterns over the top.*

Background

Mølsgraut is a regional dish from the Sunndalen where it is a holiday recipe often served in the Flatvad home with waffles and coffee following weddings, Confirmations, Christenings, and at Syttendemai and Christmas. Recipe courtesy of Randi Flatvad.

Ingredients

8 1/2 quarts milk
2 cups cultured buttermilk
2-3 tablespoons butter
1 teaspoon Cardemom
3 teaspoons flour
2 1/3 cups cold, heavy cream

Traditional Norwegian Dinner

Får i Kål (lamb and cabbage)

Preparation

⌘ *Divide meat in serving pieces, wash and dry.*
⌘ *Place in layers with all other ingredients.*
⌘ *Boil water and pour over mixture until the level is about half way up.*
⌘ *Let simmer for several hours (2-3 hours).*
⌘ *Serve with boiled potatoes.*

Note

Tove explains, "This is a traditional dish eaten in the fall. I recommend it highly."

Ingredients

5 pounds stewing lamb, bones and all
6 pounds cabbage, sliced not too thin
1 tablespoon whole pepper
50 grams flour
1 tablespoon salt

The Fladvad and Bjørke Families

by

Bjørn Fladvad Johansen
and
Tracy Daniel Connors

With special appreciation for contributions provided by Lars Flatvad

Marie Theresa Fladvad emigrated from Christiania (Oslo), Norway to the United States in 1895. She left behind in Oslo, her father Tron Fladvad and mother, Oline Bjørke Fladvad, plus several sisters and brothers. Settling in Newport, Rhode Island, she soon married and began a new life. The Fladvad and Bjørke families from which she came have been established in Norway since before written records were kept. This is their story.

To better understand and appreciate the history of these two old Norwegian families—the Fladvads and the Bjørkes—we need to begin with a brief overview of the historical background and the circumstances in which they lived. Tron's family had lived on three neighboring farms in Western Norway near Sunndalsøra for several hundred years. Oline Bjørke's family was from Furnes, about six miles north of Hamar and about 30 miles south of Lillehammer, the site of the 1994 Winter Olympic games.

*The Norwegian **bumerke** for the Hoås, Fladvad, and Bjørnhjell families of Nordmore.*

In many important respects, these two families and the land which they farmed represented the majority of Norwegians who emigrated to the United States. By following their story in so far as possible, we get a much better understanding of these families and times in which they lived.

The following is a broad outline and summary of Norway's history and events—including some interesting information explaining different systems of taxation, weights, and money.

Throughout the chapter we mention historical events ranging from military actions to changing customs, in Norway, Scandinavia, America, and elsewhere. We have added these to provide perspective and comparison between events at the farms and in Norway with trends, developments, and changes taking place around the world.

In the second part of the 12th century the Norwegian Kingdom consisted of the Norway as we know it geographically today, plus it then included parts of Sweden. In addition, the King of Norway collected taxes from Isle of Man, The Hebrides, The Orkney Islands, The Faroe Islands, Iceland, and Greenland.

Starting in the 13th century, Norway developed its own traditions and folklore which continued throughout the Middle Ages. People sang and danced to folk songs, and passed stories from one generation to another. It was the beginning of Norwegian customs and culture as we know it today.

Church and Crown

Between 1000-1300, the population in Norway increased from 150,000 to about 400,000, as new land being brought under the plow provided new sources of food. During the Viking Age, most farmers had owned their own farms. Much of the land had changed ownership by 1300, with the majority of farmers being tenants under the King, the Church, or the "overlords." Together, they owned about 70 percent of Norway's arable land.

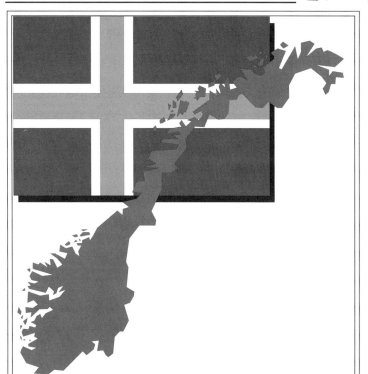

About Norway

Northernmost country in western Europe

Official name: *Kongeriket Norge* or *Kongeriket Noreg* (Kingdom of Norway)

Government: limited, hereditary, constitutional monarchy

Legislature: *Storting* (115-member Parliament), divided into *Odelsting* (75 percent of the members) and the *Lagting* (25 percent of the members). A *"ting"* was an assembly of free men at various assembly places or *"thingstad,"* to make legal or judicial decisions.

Local Administration: divided into 19 counties (*fylker*), which are, in turn, divided into 452 municipalities (*kommuner*)

Area: 125,181 square miles

Highest Elevation: Galdhøpiggen (8,121 feet)

Population: 4 million

Major Languages: Norwegian (*Bokmål, Nynorsk*), Samisk (Lapp)

National Anthem: *Ja, Vi elsker dette landet* (Yes, We Love This Land)

Major Holidays: May 17, commemorates the signing of the Norwegian Constitution in 1814. June 23rd, St. John's eve is celebrated with festive bonfires lit in the Viking tradition. July 29th commemorates the death of King Olav Haraldsson (Saint Olav) at the Battle of Stiklestad in 1030

Roads: over 15,622 miles of national roads.

In addition to collecting taxes, the most important source of income for the earlier kings was the practice of confiscating property belonging to enemies and as fines for breech of the law (by whomever determined). In this way over time, the king came to possess a great deal of land which provided him considerable income in the form of land rent.

The process of land acquisition was slow, but ultimately very effective. Any farmer who defied the king had his land acquired. The king demanded title to all untitled lands. Any industrious farmer who cleared new lands made himself a tenant of the king. During periods of bad harvest, farmers had to borrow from the king, church, or larger land holders. If they could not repay their debts, their land or rights were turned over. The farmer continued to work the land, but now as a tenant, a *"leilending."*

In the 1300s, most of Norway's land was farmed by tenant farmers. While they paid rent to the landowner, they were free. Rent, taxes, and tithes were paid in corn, butter, furs, fish, or hides. They were required to maintain their farm buildings. Most farms had several owners, with one or more of them actually working the land. A typical Norwegian farmer was both freeholder—and tenant.

The upper-class was supported by the unrelenting and physically exhausting labor of the farmers and their families. The farmers paid rents to the landowners, taxes to the King, and tithes to the Church. Those adjudged to have broken the law were fined and could be forced to pay fines to both King and Church. The average Norwegian farmer in the 13th century paid about one-fifth of his family's annual production to the land owner, the Church, and the King.

The introduction of Christianity and the establishment of the (Catholic) Church in Norway took place with the cooperation of the farmers, although some of them resisted conversion for quite a while. (Note: Until the Reformation in 1537, the Church in Norway was the Roman Catholic Church. After 1537 it was the Lutheran Protestant Church.) The clergy was under the leadership of the bishops, who were under the supervision of the King.

The King continued to add land to the bishop's churches. Throughout the middle ages the lands belonging to the church increased considerably through donations and gifts from private persons for the salvation of their souls, from The Crown, and from wealthy people. Donations of land came as well from ordinary farmers, and through mortgages for unpaid fines, loans and tithes. The church itself also bought land from people who for some reason had to sell. Over time and in these ways, the Church became the largest landowner in Norway, and in the early 1300s it owned approximately 40% of all land.

In 1103, an archbishop's Residence was established in Lund, Sweden, and placed under authority of the Archbishop of Hamburg-Bremen, Germany. Until 1152, the church of Norway was controlled by the archbishop in Lund, when the Residence of the Archbishop of Nidaros (now Trondheim) was established. The last archbishop in Norway fled the country in 1537.

The time up to 1300 was a time for expansion both in terms of population economics and political development. From then and up to the middle of the 1500s was, tragically, a time dominated by pestilence, depopulation and reduction in agricultural production.

The Black Death

In 1347, the Black Death (bubonic plague) began the first of several outbreaks which periodically devastated Europe, at times killing a third of the entire population. Between 1347 and 1351, for example, approximately 75 million people throughout

Akershus Festning (Castle), today one of Norway's best known landmarks was built by King Håkon Håkonson in the 13th century. He also moved the capital from Bergen to Oslo. At the time, Bergen had approximately 7,000 inhabitants, Oslo, about 2,000.

Norwegian farms from the Middle Ages at Maihaugen in Lillehammer. *Solid, practical buildings designed to provide protection and useful function for farmers trying to survive in Northern latitudes. Even today the Norwegian diet reflects in many important ways its origins in the foods able to be grown on relatively isolated upland farms. Looking at what they were able to grow, from grain to cattle, we can better understand why certain grains are used in traditional baked goods more than others. Because dairy cattle were always at hand, butter and cheese were staple foods, included in many traditional recipes. Today, butter is in some disrepute for its cholesterol content. For that reason, we have tried to reduce the amounts where possible in our recipes. However, we should keep in mind that these early farmers worked long hours, with plenty of demanding physical activity. They burned far more calories than we do today, and probably could tolerate the relatively high levels of fat in their diet. Certainly, their grain heavy diet was high in fiber content.*

Europe died of the Black Death. Norway was not exempted and the disease found its way to both Bjørke and Flatvad.

The plague came to Bergen in 1349 carried by an English ship. It soon spread up the coast to the Sunndalen. By that fall, one third of the population was dead. By 1400 the population was half that of the 12th century, Norway's "Golden Age." Ironically, even as Norway began to lose its identity as a nation-state, for those that were left life was somewhat better—they took over the best land. Whole communities had been wiped out, the aristocracy all but eliminated. These lands would not be reclaimed until the 1600s. Farmers paid less in taxes and tithes. In 1500 taxes were half of what they had been two hundred years earlier.

Consider the economic and emotional toll represented by the death of two out of every three people in a country. Entire families were wiped out.

Sweden-Denmark-Norway

Because both Sweden and Denmark had more arable land and therefore larger populations, they dominated Norway. In the 14th and 15th centuries, the Hanseatic League based in Bergen, took economic control of Norway's foreign trade.

The Union of Kalmar (1389-1521) brought Norway, Sweden, and Denmark together as a national union for the first time in 1397. Margrete was a Danish princess who became Queen of Norway following her marriage to Håkon VI Magnusson. Eventually, she survived her father, her husband, and her son to then arrange for her young relation, Eric of Pomerania, to be elected King of both Norway and Denmark. The visionary queen then attacked Sweden. The nobility there were convinced to send the German king packing. Eric was crowned King of Scandinavia in 1397. However, Margrete was the power behind the throne until her death in 1412.

In 1513, Christian II became King of Denmark and Norway. Since Sweden had pulled out of the Union of Kalmar, Christian attacked and conquered Sweden. However, following his coronation in 1520, he had 82 nobles and clergy murdered in his attempt to frighten others into submission. Both the Danish and Swedish nobility rebelled at this brutality, and he fled to The Netherlands in 1523. Norway stayed in the background during this struggle.

In 1536, Danish King Christian III signed the Royal Charter. It stated that Norway was now a part of Denmark and not a separate kingdom. Increasingly, Norway was administered from Copenhagen.

Between 1536 and 1814 Denmark-Norway had ten kings called Frederik or Christian. One, King Christian IV, is remembered today. He reigned for 60 years, a warrior king with bad luck.

After the Reformation, when the Norwegian Church became Lutheran, the Church lost most of its powerful domain, and the Ecclesiastical aristocracy disappeared. After the Reformation, the aristocracy consisted mainly of Danish nobility who came to Norway as administrators.

The Reformation

In 1537, King Christian III's forces defeated the Archbishop of Nidaros. The new

Norway's population increased after 1500. *For the next century, farms that had been abandoned in the late Middle Ages following the Black Death were reclaimed and again used to produce crops. Soon, there was not enough land for everyone who wanted to own a farm. After about 1660, a large, new class of cotters (**husmenn**) began to increase in many rural areas.*

king introduced Lutheranism to Norway. On Easter Sunday, April 1, 1537, Olav Engelbrektsson, the Archbishop of Nidaros, sailed down the Trondheim Fjord enroute to The Netherlands. On that morning, the Catholic Church owned 40 percent of Norway's land. As the last Catholic bishop was leaving Norway for the last time, the King was exappropriating this land for the Crown. In the future, the King would be the real power in Norway.

From the end of the 1600s, Norwegian farmers began reclaiming title to their lands. When King Frederick III introduced the absolute monarchy in 1660, only twenty percent of Norway's land was owned by the farmers. By 1800 however, nearly 60 percent of the land was owned by those who farmed it. To pay his huge war debts, the King had given land to the merchants carrying his debts. They soon resold it—to the farmers.

Farmers and Cotters

After 1500, Norway's population increased. Until about 1600, farms that had been abandoned in the late Middle Ages were reclaimed and put under the plow. Soon, this was not enough, and after about 1660, a large, new class of cotters increased in many rural areas. Cotters ("**husmenn**") were allowed to clear a small area on a larger farm. For this land, he had to pay a rent, usually by working for the farmer on the main farm. The entire family shared in the work.

During the Reformation, the State had confiscated large tracts of Ecclesiastical property. By this means, the State gained control of over half of all land in Norway.

In the 1660s, the State began to sell land. Many of the buyers were earlier tenant farmers. This change in status from being a tenant farmer to that of a freeholder provided another important benefit over and above actual control of the land. As a freeholder, the right of inheritance of the farm was guaranteed. While any inheritance rights (or lack of them) on a tenant farm was dependent on the land owners, for a freeholder inheritance followed standard rules—primogenitor. This meant that the oldest living son had the right to take over the farm undivided. It also meant that after a family had owned a farm for a certain number of years it had the right, if the farm was sold, to take it back from the new owner within a certain number of years.

By about 1700, arable land was no longer in surplus. By then people were looking for new ways to support themselves—to make a living. As a consequence, the landowners regained power and began increasing the land rent for tenant farmers or "**leilendinger**," who still represented about 70 percent of all farmers. As Norway moved into the 18th century, farmers were administratively, economically, and socially subordinated to the upper class and rich commoners.

For the next century, the social differences grew deeper. The rich citizens and

During the 1700s, Norwegian social differences grew deeper. *Rich citizens and civil servants strengthened their position towards farmers having little status. Increasingly, farming communities became divided into one group of real (land-owning) farmers, and another group consisting of cotters and servants. In 1825, there were 90,000 farmers and 96,000 cotters and tenants in Norway.* ***Husmenn*** *lived in extremely crowded houses little better than cabins such as this one at Maihaugen.*

the civil servants strengthened their position towards the lower social classes in the towns and with those farming populations having little status. Increasingly, farming communities became divided into one group of real (land-owning) farmers, and another group consisting of cotters and servants. In 1825, there were 90,000 farmers and 96,000 cotters and tenants in Norway.

Norway Under Sweden

As a reward to Sweden for its support to Russia in its war against Napoleon, the Russian Czar promised the Swedish King support for his wish to assume control of Norway from Denmark. After Napoleon was defeated in Leipzig in 1813, King Carl Johan of Sweden with an army of 60,000 men, declared war on Denmark. When the hostilities were over, the peace agreement required Denmark to give Norway to Sweden. Iceland, the Faroe Islands, and Greenland remained under Denmark's control.

The Conferees had not consulted the Norwegians about this arrangement. As it turned out, they were unwilling to be a part of Sweden. They gathered at Eidsvoll, prepared their own Constitution, and elected the Danish Prince Christian Fredrik as King of Norway. He pledged to follow the new Norwegian Constitution, but surrendered when he was threatened by the Swedish king. Norway and Sweden went to war over the matter. Eventually, the Swedish government accepted the new Norwegian Constitution, which among other things gave Norwegians the right to have their own Parliament (The *Storting*). In October, 1814, the Storting accepted the union with Sweden which lasted until 1905.

In just fifty years, from 1815 to 1865, the population in Norway doubled—from about 900,000 inhabitants to 1.7 million. This dramatic increase in population, coupled with the relatively fixed amount of land, most

Food storage room *for a* **gammle gård** *or old Norwegian farm. Hard money in Norway was scarce. Most land rents were stipulated in farm products, of which there were many types, from dairy products and grains, to fish or fish products for those farmers and land owners near a river or the sea. Each product had a different value. One pail of butter made in this churn for example, was the equivalent of four pails of grain.*

increase in numbers came after the U.S. Congress enacted a homestead law in 1862. This declared enormous tracts of land open for cultivation and eventual ownership— homesteading. More than 800,000 Norwegians emigrated to the United States during the forty years after the homestead law was enacted.

The Landowners

In the Middle Ages, both economic and political power in Norway were based on the size of the yield from the farms. Because the population was spread over vast distances and the country's mountainous geography, seldom did anything like large units of landed property come into being. Instead of creating large tracts of contiguous holdings, land owners often owned different parcels of land. They benefited from the yield of the tenant farmers (**leilendinger**) through the land rent (**landskyld** or simply **skyld**). There were very few free holders.

The Land Rent
Landskyld

Originally, the size of a farm in square meters or other measures was not the basis for determining its rent, taxes, or tithe. Instead, the yield of the farm was the basis for such assessments. Even freeholders were taxed on the basis of what was calculated as a "land rent."

Since hard money was scarce, the land rent was usually stipulated in farm products, of which there were many types. Some farms produced mostly dairy products, others grains, and others on or near the coastline, fish or fish products. Therefore, the type of products called for by the land rent depended on the farm's production.

Different products had different values. For example, one pail of butter was the equivalent of four pails of grain, which in turn, had its equivalent value in a certain number of loads of fish.

In 1647, for example, the skyld for all the Fladvad farms was 5 pails (**spann**), probably of butter. Adding to the complication was the fact that farm products often differed in value at various locations across the country.

of which would be passed along to the eldest son, led to a great number of cotters and tenants. As renters, they had a very uncertain future, dependent on the land owners.

This set the stage for the great emigration to America—from 1865 to 1915. Of course, the first emigrants left Norway for America in 1825. However, the real

Fladvad or *Flatvad*, *means a shallow fording place. This name was probably derived from its location beside the Driva River in the Sunndal valley of west central Norway. The Driva River carries the melt-off of snow and rain from the Dovrefjell. Its plunging "V"-shape tells geologists that the valley was formed primarily by glacier action. Throughout history, the river would rampage through the valley doing great damage to the farms. Farming there was both risky and remote. This view of the Driva is from a pedestrian suspension bridge on the Flatvad farm. Built in 1933, it was whimsically named the Brooklyn Bru (bridge), probably by Theodor Fladvad who had lived in the Brownsville section of Brooklyn, New York. He stayed at Flatvad for lengthy visits during the late 20s and early 30s.*

The Land Register *"Matrikkel"*

Originally, the **Matrikkel** or land register, was an official register of all real property outside the towns which stipulated the value of individual parcels. The first official Norwegian land register was set up between 1665-1669, and used for tax purposes. A new register was established in 1836, and revised in 1863.

The Fladvad farms got their new **Matrikkel** in 1838, and a revised one in 1886. It probably took some time for the process to move throughout the country. Significantly, this **Matrikkel** is expressed in money, even in different currencies. At the time of the 1863 revision, the value of all real estate in the country (except Finnmark in the far north), was stipulated at 936,000,000 **Kroner**. This was distributed over 500,000 **debt marks**, each Mark having a value of 100 **debt øre**. Each farm was assigned a pro rata share of the **debt øre**.

The Named Farms and the Land Registered Farms

Norway's original farms were given names, very often referring to some unique characteristic. For example, Fladvad or Flatvad, means a shallow fording place. This name might have been derived from its location beside the Driva River in the Sunndal valley. The farm nearby is called Hoås, literally meaning "high place."

As arable land became scarce, it became increasingly common to divide the original named farm into more units. The new farms carried the same name as the original farms. Since taxation was linked more to the farm than to the person owning or tilling the land, the tax authorities had to solve the problem. They devised a system in which the new farms usually kept the original name, but added an "east" or "west" or "lower" or "upper" to the original name, and given their own **Matrikkel**.

This was the case for the Fladvad family, who owned "Fladvad Number One," the eastern farm or **Østigård**.

*The **Romfo Church** (above) has been the Fladvad family church for several centuries. At one time, the church owned a part of Flatvad. The tithe was introduced in 1100, and was the first ordinary tax in Norway. At first, the tithe was a ten percent tax based on the annual production of grain. But, as is the habit with taxes of any kind, the number of taxable products and items was steadily increased. Later, the tithe was based on the value of all that was owned by the farmer. The tithe was abolished in 1918.*

Taxes

At first, officials and citizens did not pay taxes. During the 1700s, a small portion of the total taxes was paid by the privileged classes. The real taxpayers were the farmers. Taxation was based on the farm's yield—the greater the yield, the greater the tax. Land rent was based on the same principles, and when taxes were calculated, they were based on the land rent as well.

Measures and Currencies

When people during the Middle Ages paid land rent or taxes, or when they needed to purchase something, they did so most often with products of the soil. Because they were in such frequent use as a "currency," these products acquired their own more or less fixed value and rate of exchange vis-a-vis other products.

At one time, for example, 3 **laup** (or pails) of butter = 3 hides = 1/3 mark of burned (smelted) silver. One **laup** is the equivalent to 15.4 kilograms or 35.96 pounds. Roughly then, 107.88 pounds of butter equalled the value of three tanned hides, which equalled the value of 82.5 grams of refined silver. Over time, payment in currency was preferred, then required.

From 1544 to 1875, the **Daler** was the main currency throughout Norway. The coin's name was taken from a 25-30 gram silver coin from Joachimstal in Bohemia, Germany.

The coin became the **Joachimstaler**, then simply, **Taler**. In the United States, it became the "Dollar."

The weight of the Daler was 25 grams of silver. The silver content was stable throughout the period. This was not the case for smaller coins in which the silver content was considerably reduced. This increased the number of smaller coins equalling one Daler. To begin with, one Daler was 3 Mark, or 48 Skilling. In 1625, one Daler = 6 Mark = 96 Skilling.

In 1875, Norway introduced **Kroner** ("crowns") and **øre**.

Flatvad & Bjørke

The basis for Flavors of the Fjords was the manuscript cookbook of Marie Theresa Fladvad who emigrated from Christiania (Oslo) in 1894. Her father was Tron Fladvad and her mother was Oline Bjørke. Tron Fladvad's family had owned a farm in Western Norway near Sunndalsøra for several hundred years. Oline Bjørke's family was from Furnes, near Hamar.

The Fladvad farm is on the floor of a valley carved through the mountains by the glaciers and the Driva River. Its plunging "V"-shape as opposed to a "U"-shape signals

Anders Nilsen Bjørke
January 20, 1792 -

Oline Andersdatter Bjørke
April 9, 1837-November 12, 1908. Born near Furness, Norway. Died in Oslo, Norway.

Marie Larsdatter Bakken
April 4, 1804 -

Marie Theresa Fladvad
December 22, 1865 - 1947. Born in Kolvereid, Norway. Emigrated to Newport, Rhode Island in 1895. Married Charles Middleton Cottrell.

Tron Olesen Fladvad
May 17, 1831-1914. Born at Flatvad, Grøa, Norway. Died in Oslo, Norway.

Ole Endresen Fladvad
1794-1842

Anne Olsdatter
1798-1848

that the valley was largely formed by glacier action. Periodically, the river would rampage through the valley doing great damage to the farms. Farming there was both risky and remote. The nearest town of any size was Kristiansund many miles away by boat down the fjord. It was until recently called Kristiansund N(orth), to differentiate it from Kristiansand, which is located in the south of Norway.

The Bjørke farm was located on the North shore of Lake Mjøsa, Norway's largest inland lake. The countryside there was somewhat less challenging and more settled, with pastures and fields gently sloping down toward the water.

FLATVAD

Kristiansund, Norway is about one fourth the way up the long west coast of Norway, and situated on one of the many islands that protect the entrance to several fjords carved into the interior of central Norway.

Behind and southeast of Kristiansund are several fjords, cut deep into the country's interior, including the Tingvoll-fjord. Like a huge question mark tilted 45 degrees to the

The Driva begins *about one hundred rugged miles away from Flatvad in the Dovrefjell (above), a barren, high mountain plateau. Gaining strength as it collects melted snow and rain, the Driva has carved the Sunndalen (Sunndal valley) from Oppdal to Sunndalsøra. The Driva cuts through mountains rising from about 3,000 feet to over 6,000 feet.*

left of vertical, the Tingvoll-fjord becomes the Sunndalsfjorden at the point on the "?'s" lower third where the curve becomes a straight line.

At the bottom of Sunndalsfjord, where the point would be on the "?," is Sunndalsøra, the southernmost point on the Sunndalsfjord. The heart of Nordmøre. Here, the Driva River, a clear, fast flowing mountain river flows into the Sunndalsfjord, carving a steep valley between the Snøhetta and Trollheimen mountain ranges.

Today, Route 70 from Oppdal to Sunndalsøra follows the Sunndalen for about fifty miles from the Oppdal valley to the fjord. At times the road runs alongside the Driva, at times it climbs sharply up the side of the valley offering breathtaking views of the bottomland and its neat farm houses, many of them carved out of the side of mountains. Within a few miles the route can change from a mountain highway to a flat lands road hugging the side of the mountain on one side with the Driva roaring down the valley a few feet away on the other.

Flatvad was the name of the farm where Tron was born and where he spent his childhood. He was born in 1831, and was number six of a large family of nine children, in which the first child was born in 1819 and the last born in 1840. There were five girls and four boys. Two of the boys were older than Tron, which meant that his chance of becoming the successor on the farm was minimal. His oldest brother, Endre, eventually inherited the farm. Tron had to prepare himself in other ways to make a living.

Bjørnhjell

Flatvad

Hoås

Traditional Names

The family history however, begins a very, very long time before this—at a farm named Hoås.

There is one custom regarding names in those old days which we should explain. The first name was always given, and it had a tendency to be repeated through the generations. The second name was chosen to indicate the father's first name. Therefore, if you were the son of Ole, your second name would be Olesen (son of Ole); or, if a daughter of Ole, Olesdatter (daughter of Ole). The third name was the name of the farm on which you lived. By this custom, the third name of Tron Fladvad's ancestors in the early days was Hoås, since they were then living on that farm. Then, for a time, it was Bjørnhjell, and finally, Flatvad.

In the earlier days in Norway (as elsewhere in the world), it was quite common

that ordinary people never learned to read or write. So, instead of writing their names on legal documents, they used a mark. In Colonial America, the mark was customarily an "X." The English word "Mark" is written **bumerke**, in Norwegian, the "bu" meaning "live." It originally meant a stamp indicating the farmer's place of residence. As time passed, the mark was used on all property belonging to the farmer in question. Today we might call the bumerke a brand or even a logotype.

As far back as this history begins, the records are sketchy. With only the barest of detail, tithes and taxes mentioned together with the names of long-vanished farmers, the following brief history of the farm cannot hope to lift itself far from the inevitable arithmetic of land ownership. What's missing, but implied, is the constant struggle waged each year by the farmers against the land and climate to successfully raise and harvest the crops so essential for their very survival. However sketchy, we do get glimmers of the people and their lives. We note them here to provide whatever understanding we can about them, and to better appreciate the continuity and steadfastness of these hardy land owners whose descendants are still working the land today.

Hoås

The name Hoås literally means "high place," and the farm itself is situated on a plateau. The first time the farm is mentioned in written sources was in 1520. At that time the Archbishop of Nidaros (in Trondheim), owned a 1/2 pail interest or share in Hoås. After the Reformation, that share was assumed by the King, and in 1756, this share was bought by the farmer at Hoås farm no. 1. Between 1730 and 1747, the farmer also bought all other parts not belonging to the Church.

Halvor and Halfdan

As far as records reveal, Hoås was one farm until 1620, when it was divided into two farms.

In the taxpayers register from about 1520, two men are mentioned as living at Hoås. One of them, Halvor, was the farmer actually renting the land. Halfdan was subordinate to him. It may have been that they were brothers-in-law. During that period it was common that two men had one farm together. Their standard of living at that time was not such that they could pick and choose. Even a relatively subordinated position at a farm was better than having no farm at all.

Simon, Tore Simonsen and Bersvend Toresen Hoås

In 1548, the farmer at Hoås was named Simon. After him, between 1550 and 1590, the farmer on the land was called Tore Simonsen Hoås. From 1590 until 1621, the Hoås farmer was named Bersvend Toresen Hoås.

It cannot be confirmed that Simon is the father of Tore, or that Tore is the father of Bersvend. However, circumstantially we can make this assumption. In a letter from about 1630, it was witnessed that Lars Bersvendsen Hoås paid his fellow heirs a sum of money to ensure he was the sole owner of the farm. The document stated that the farm has now followed the same family "to the fifth man," meaning that the same family had lived on the farm for three generations before Bersvend Toresen Hoås.

Bersvend was the police officer in Sunndalen after 1600. He died in 1621, and his widow farmed the land until 1627.

Lars Bersvendsen Hoås

Lars and his wife farmed the Hoås farm no. 2 from 1627-1665. Following in his father's footsteps, he served as the police officer of Sunndalen from 1648 until his death in 1662. In addition, he served as the church warden of Løken Kirke from 1642 until his death.

Lars was married to Ildri Hågensdatter, a sister of Jon Hågensen Fladvad of farm no. 5. She was a strong woman, and after her husband's death she postponed the division of the inheritance for six years. Another example of her strength was the fact that her eldest son was given the name of her father instead of her husband's father as was the common practice.

They were relatively wealthy people, owning several shares in other farms in addition to their own. The four children living at the time of the division of the inheritance collectively got the equivalent of 339 1/2

The Hoås farm *sits on a plateau and the name literally means "high place." Written records mention Hoås for the first time in 1520, when the Archbishop of Nidaros owned a 1/2 pail interest or share.*

Daler. The widow kept for herself: five barrels of grain; two cows (which stayed on the farm) and one cow which she hired out; one silver can of 52 weights; four silver spoons engraved with her and her husband's initials; two linen sheets; one rug; four goats and two sheep (which stayed on the farm); one copper kettle (18 kilos); and, two barrels of seed grain.

Significantly, Ildri made an agreement with her children that if she in any way should not be satisfied with this arrangement, that she would be entitled to live free of charge with any of them for the rest of her life.

Hågen Larsen Hoås

The eldest son of Lars and Ildri, Hågen and his wife farmed Hoås from 1666 until 1703. He married twice, and his second wife's name was Marit. Between them he had six known children.

Hågen was church warden for Løken Kirke from 1682 until 1688. He must have been a peaceful man, at least we don't hear very much about him in the records.

Tore Hågensen Hoås

Hågen's first three children, probably with his first wife, were all boys. Son number three, Tore, was born about 1665, and grew up to become a farmer at Bjørnhjell.

Bjørnhjell

The first time Bjørnhjell is mentioned in written sources is about 1440. The land most probably belonged to Hoås. A tenant at Hoås had, according to tradition, made a girl pregnant and therefore had to marry her. The people of Hoås then gave the tenant Bjørnhjell which at that time was a wilderness, overgrown with trees.

Most probably Bjørnhjell had been a farm as early as the Middle Ages, because we know that the Archbishop of Nidaros owned some of it before the Black Death came in 1349. The dread disease killed everyone living on the farm and it was desolated for generations. Most probably Bjørnhjell became subordinated to Hoås during this period.

Avalanche

Compared to Hoås and Flatvad, Bjørnhjell was not as exposed to the dangers of flooding from the Driva River. However,

The first part of the name **Bjørnhjell** *either refers to a man's name* **Bjørn**, *or to an animal's name, which translated into English means "bear." The second part of the name indicates that the land is situated on a plateau. In the case of Bjørnhjell, the plateau is several hundred feet above the floor of the valley. The "ledge" is what is left of the "sea shore" when sea levels were much higher than they are now.*

it was exposed to another natural peril—avalanche.

The first known catastrophe came in January, 1684 when an avalanche destroyed the houses and outbuildings, killing six people, and all the livestock on the farm. Only one farmer and a small girl survived.

The girl, Magnhild, was dug out of the snow still lying at her dead mother's breast. The farmer, Ole Knutsen Bjørnhjell, moved the houses on the farm to another, undoubtedly safer location. Ole died in 1701 and his daughter, Magnhild, inherited the farm. Tore Hågensen moved from Hoås to Bjørnhjell and married Magnhild.

Avalanche! *Compared to Hoås and Flatvad, Bjørnhjell was less exposed to the dangers of flooding from the Driva River, but it was exposed to another natural peril—avalanche. The first known catastrophe in January, 1684 destroyed the houses and outbuildings, killing six people, and all the livestock on the farm. The surviving farmer moved the houses on the farm to another, undoubtedly safer location. The "stick figures" of people in the distance where the field meets the tree line give some idea of the sheer drop from the mountain to the fields of Bjørnhjell. In winter the mountainside is covered with massive layers of snow and ice from the **foss** (waterfall).*

Tore Hågensen Bjørnhjell

Tore and Magnhild farmed Bjørnhjell from 1702 until her death in 1733. He continued until 1740. They had nine children together. Their first son, Hågen, was born shortly after 1700 and their last child, Anna, was born in 1723.

In 1723, the farm had two horses, 18 cows, and 20 sheep and goats. They paid a tithe of 21 5/8 barrels of grain.

When Magnhild died, the joint property was appraised at 165 Daler. There were no debts.

Tore died in 1742, one year after he had given the farm to his eldest son, Hågen.

Hågen Toresen Bjørnhjell

Hågen farmed Bjørnhjell from 1741 until 1766. We do not know the name of his wife, although it was probably Ingrid. In 1789, a female named Ingrid Bjørnhjell, born about 1700, died.

We do know that Hågen and his wife had four children. The first born was a son, Tore, born in 1744, then came Randi in 1746, Ivar in 1748, and finally, Endre in 1750.

In 1766, Hågen sold the farm to his eldest son, Tore, for 48 Daler.

Tore Hågensen Bjørnhjell

Tore farmed Bjørnhjell from 1766 to 1789, and then moved to Flatvad, which he switched ownership with Anders Sivertsen. Some accounts say it was as a result of a card game wager. Another account says they both wanted each others farm—a "grass is greener" attitude. Most family members agree that whatever the real cause it was probably helped along by too many trips to the beer bowl. Family history remembers that neither of their wives were consulted about the switch in advance and were understandably very upset. Unfortunately, soon after Tore bought Flatvad, it was devastated by severe flooding along the Driva River that Spring.

Water pushed down the Driva valley in wild torrents. The Driva River, even at normal level, is a thrashing, rolling river fed by rains and runoff from the Dovrefjell highlands to the east. During flood periods it is unpredictable and turns the valley farmland into a "flood plain."

This flooding however, was particularly severe, part of a major natural disaster which hit all the valleys in western Norway running south and west from the mountain ranges of Jotunheimen, Dovre, and Rondane. The previous winter, enormous masses of snow had fallen in the mountains. The following spring, unusually warm weather combined with heavy rain caused a sudden, rapid melt-

The Flatvad farm is first mentioned about 1440, when it was partly owned by the Archbishop of Nidaros in Trondheim. Flatvad's value plummeted after the Black Death. "**Flatvad**" has always meant "the flat or shallow ford" across the Driva River, which cuts through the property from right to left at the base of the forest covered cliffs.

ing of the snow. Called the **Storofsin**, or **Ofsen**, the enormous quantity of water released by the rainy, warm weather in 1789 poured down the Gudbrandsdalen to the south, filling up the entire bottom of the valley with several meters of water, and sweeping away farmland, trees, houses, animals, and people. Mjøsa, the largest lake in Norway, rose several meters, and a somewhat smaller lake further south rose 17 meters.

Flatvad

The Flatvad farm is first mentioned about 1440, when it was partly owned by Aslak Bolt, the Archbishop of Nidaros in Trondheim. For the first time he created a list showing all land owned by the Archbishop. Collectively, the Archbishop owned land representing about 3,000 farms, having a total value of 155,000 kilos of butter. This was

the estimate before the Black Death. Afterwards, the value was much less.

Before the Black Death, the annual land rent on Flatvad was 15 pails. After the Black Death, the rent had plummeted to 5 pails. In 1550 the Archbishop brought suit against the owners to collect the unpaid 1 2/3 pail of "municipal" land rent. The suit was later cancelled with the remark: "Not Won," meaning the dispute had gone to court and that the municipality of Trondheim had lost the case.

The name **Flatvad** has been spelled many different ways over the years:

Flatawade or *Flatauade*	(1440)
Flettewodh	(1520)
Flatvad	(1530)
Fladuaae	(1643)
Fladvad	(1723)

Today, the farm is shown on the map

The Sunndalen was first settled during the Bronze Age.
*Flint discoveries revealed settlements over 4,000 years old.
Today, farm land and cultivated forest areas make up 140
square kilometers of the area, the remainder being mountain
wilderness. About eight miles east of Sunndalsøra is the village
of Grøa, a pleasant little community sitting astride the Driva.
Today, it offers boating and fishing accommodations, plus ski
recreation in the winter which arrives as early as October-
November. About two miles east of Grøa, Flatvaddalen cuts
down from the north, separating the Trolla (7,200 feet) from
the Satbakk-kollen (6,400 feet). There the Hoås, Bjørnhjellen,
and Flatvad families have lived for hundreds of years. The
Flatvad farm is located at the spot where the Flatvaddalen
joins the Sunndalen. The Hoås farm is about two miles to the
west. Bjørnhjell is about a mile to the east along the shallow
valley floor of the Driva.*

as "*Flatvad.*" It has always meant "the flat
or shallow ford" across the river, in this case,
the Driva River. The family has usually
spelled it "Fladvad." Most likely, spelling it
with "ad" instead of "at" is the result of a
Danish clergyman's preference for soft Danish consonants, instead of the harder Norwegian "t." In this work we use "Flatvad"
to refer to the family farm in Nordmøre,
and "Fladvad" to refer to the family at large.

Modern Flatvad

The "modern" history of the Flatvad
farm begins about 1520, with a taxation
list. This far back, of course, the records
are sketchy.

The farmers who owned Flatvad until
1789 are not directly related to the present
family. However, we have included the history of the farm from earliest records to give
the reader a better understanding of the farm
and of life in the Sunndal.

About 1520, in the first known taxation list, three men are mentioned as farmers at Flatvad: Gude, Ole, and Engebret.
That year Gude had to pay the tithe with
two weights of silver, plus one weight of silver for the land rent. Ole paid one weight
of silver; and, Engebreth 2 1/2 weights of
silver, plus one weight for the land rent. The
total value of the farm and its holdings that
year was set at 55 weights of silver, plus 40
weights of silver for the land itself.

About this time as well, chocolate was
brought from Mexico to Spain. Eventually,
it would find its way into Norwegian, as well
as into world cooking.

The Widow Called Synnøve

In 1548 the records mention at Flatvad,
a widow called Synnøve, apparently a
farmer's widow. She paid an annual land
rent of one cow, and one sheep. Her farm
had a land rent of 2 2/3 pail.

As previously noted, from time to time
we will add historical footnotes to help the
reader correlate events in Norway by pointing out events taking place elsewhere at
about the same time. For example, at this
time King Henry VIII had died in England
the year before, and was succeeded by his
and Jane Seymour's son, Edward VII. However, Edward, too would die in 1553 after a
very short reign. Lady Jane Grey would be
proclaimed Queen of England, only to be
deposed nine days later. Finally, Mary I,
daughter of Henry VIII and Catherine of
Aragon, became the Queen "Bloody" Mary.

From 1609 to 1626, Peder Helsing,
probably a newcomer to the area, farmed
Flatvad.

Elsewhere, in Constantinople, the Turks
were starting the Blue Mosque. Tea from
China was being shipped to Europe for the

The Sunndal Valley

Flatvad

Bjørnhjell

Sunndalsfjord

Leikvin

Sunndalsøra

Trolla

⌘

Vinnu-fjellet

Flatvaddalen

Såtbakk-kollen

Hoås-nebba

Tverrådalen

To Oppdal

⌘ Løykja

Litlsomrung-nebba

Kling-fjellet

⌘

Grøa

LitlKalkinn

Kaldfonna

Serkjedalen

Stoplan

Ø **Driva River**

⌘

Hornet

Gråhøa

Hoås

Romfo Church

first time by the Dutch East India Company. And, Henry Hudson sailed through Hudson's Straits to discover Hudson's Bay.

In 1611, the War of Kalmar was declared by Denmark on Sweden. And later that year, Charles IX of Sweden died. He was succeeded by Gustavus II (Gustavus Adolphus). In England this year, the first edition of the Authorized Version of the Holy Bible, the "King James Bible," was published.

Ivar, Dordi, and Ingrid

About Ivar Pedersen, born in 1620 near Flatvad, we know much more. He was married twice, first to Dordi Nilsdatter, with whom he had three children: Ivar, Morten, and Helga. After their mother died, they received 34 Daler.

Ivar married "the girl next door" after Dordi's death. Ingrid Sivertsdatter lived on the adjacent farm and was the sister of Erick Sivertsen, and Even Sivertsen. She had two children, Ivar and Dordi, before her husband, Ivar, died in 1678.

There was war this year between Sweden and Poland, with Gustavus Adolphus occupying Livonia. After leaving Plymouth, England, the Pilgrim Fathers landed in Massachusetts to found the Plymouth Colony. In England, there were more serious matters at hand. Oliver Cromwell was denounced because he participated in the "disreputable game of cricket."

Tithe Based On Grain Yields

Records show the tithe paid on the

The first church in Sunndalsøra was located at Løykja, about three miles east of the town. The site was near what today is the largest preserved Viking burial ground in Norway, consisting of about 200 graves, mostly burial mounds. The oldest of the graves were from the fourth century A.D. and were used to bury cremated remains. In 1685, an avalanche destroyed the church, leaving only a few scattered fragments, including these pieces of the altar rail and a carving of Christ. They have been incorporated into a special Chapel room at the nearby Leikvin Parish Museum. Services are held weekly.

Flatvad farm was based on representative yields from 1621-1622 of 84 barrels of grain a year. In that year as well, potatoes were planted for the first time in Germany.

For twenty years after 1626, Ingebrigt farmed at Flatvad, his tax record entry being the only time he appears in "history."

The tithe paid on the Flatvad farm is based on a representative yield from 1628-1635 of 74 1/2 barrels of grain a year. Far from the farming challenges at Flatvad, Sweden and Denmark signed a defense treaty, and King Gustavus Adolphus entered the Thirty Years' War. In America, the following year, the colony of Massachusetts was formed.

Ole, Gjertrud's Husband

From 1646 until his death in 1656, Ole, Gjertrud's husband, farmed Flatvad.

The Swedish army captured Prague, then invaded Bavaria with the French. In England, the Civil War between the Royalists and Parliamentarians ("Roundheads") ended with Cromwell victorious after the battle of Naseby the year before.

King Christian IV of Denmark died in 1648, and was succeeded by Frederick III.

In Flatvad, Ole chafed under the sometimes heavy-handed law enforcement meted out by his neighbor. From 1648 to 1662, Lars Bersvendsen Hoas owned and worked the adjacent farm. He was also the Sheriff for the area in and around Flatvad. Apparently, he liked the authority it gave him. As Christian Willumsen, noted much later, "rumor had it that he was something of a big shot."

Willumsen married Gunhild Charlotte

Over the centuries flooding *was a "clear and present danger" to the farmers who worked the land in the Driva River valley. In 1666 taxation at Flatvad was reduced by 12.5 percent, one of the ways flood damage is revealed in the records. Flooding by the Driva river has often left its mark on the Fladvad family and the Sunndalen.*

Fladvad in 1912. She was the younger sister of Marie Fladvad Cottrell, to whom she was quite close despite their age difference. He was a very successful businessman and entrepreneur. Another passion, fortunately for the reader, was research into family history. We are very much indebted to his memory for providing important information used throughout this work.

Horses, Cattle, Sheep and Goats

In 1657, the Flatvad farm included 4 horses, 33 cattle, 13 sheep, and 20 goats. The horses provided transportation, the goats gave milk for *Gjetoast*, the sheep provided mutton and wool, and the cattle furnished beef, hides, and meat, plus other products produced by the family from milk.

Denmark attacked Charles X of Sweden, while he was distracted by his on-going wars with Russia, Poland, and Austria.

In England, Cromwell rejected the title of "King." And, in London, chocolate drinking was first introduced.

In 1660, Charles X of Sweden died. He was succeeded by Charles XI. The Peace of Copenhagen ended the war between Sweden and Denmark.

Cotters Gain Status

There were few available cotters on Norway's west coast as the 17th century came to an end, therefore they had higher status and somewhat less work. In addition to work on the farms, they supplemented their earnings with fishing and handicrafts. The number of cotters increased from 17,000 in the 17th century, to 48,000 in 1800. At that time, cotters equalled farmers in Norway.

The world's first written absolutist constitution went into effect in 1665 giving the king total authority in all matters. Ironically, the officials selected to administer the country were often Norwegians and increasingly viewed Norwegian matters through the eyes of "native sons." Absolutism actually reduced the power of the aristocracy in favor of more centralized control exercised in the name of the people.

Flooding Ravages Flatvad

Historical records over the centuries make it clear that flooding was a "clear and present danger" to the farmers who worked the land in the Driva River valley. Interestingly, one of the ways flood damage can be detected from the records is to note when taxation was reduced.

In 1666, the same year that London's center city burned to the ground, taxation at Flatvad was reduced by 12.5 percent. Flooding by the Driva river had left its mark on the Fladvad family and the economic picture for the region. In that year as well, the first Cheddar cheese was made.

Taxation of Flatvad in 1667 was based on an annual yield of 71 barrels of oats. In England, the blind poet John Milton completed "Paradise Lost."

Ingrid, A Widow With Property

At Flatvad in 1678, with Ivar's death, Ingrid was a widow with property. Mons Toresden, son of Tore Andersen Ørsund, married the Flatvad widow. They would have two children. Russia and Sweden went to war. In England, there was great consternation over the "Popish Plot." Trials were conducted of many leading Roman Catholics.

Mons and Ingrid welcomed a daughter, Asbjorg, in 1680. She later became a farmer's wife at the Toske farm number 1 nearby.

Absolutism was imposed in Sweden under King Charles XI. In America, the French organized a colonial empire stretching from Quebec to the mouth of the Mississippi River. In Germany, an enterprising restaurateur opened the first coffeehouse.

At Flatvad in 1682, a second daughter was born to Mons and Ingrid. Marit remained unmarried and in her later years, became insane.

In America, La Salle claimed the Louisiana territory for France and took possession of the Mississippi Valley.

Ingrid buried her second husband, Mons Toresden, in 1687. He left an estate estimated to be worth 86 1/2 Daler. His widow was a stalwart lady. Ingrid took a third husband, this time Ole Ivarsen, born about 1650. In Athens, the Parthenon and Propylaea were badly damaged during a bombardment by Venetian forces.

Timber Trade

The timber trade became a principal industry in Norway during the 17th century. England was the largest market. Even with the real threat of deforestation, exports increased. Farmers and cotters helped their earnings by supplying and transporting timber. Typically, the merchants in the towns made the largest profits. In 1688, the King issued a decree shutting down many sawmills. Soon, profits were monopolized by a few, very powerful and wealthy individuals close to the Crown.

Ingrid Ivarsen died in 1692. Her widower, Ole Ivarsen (needing help to harvest the 200 horse loads of grain), remarried. Unfortunately, we don't know her name. However, in a dispute brought to court in

Kristiansund became a town on June 29, 1742 *by decree of the Danish-Norwegian King Christian VI. Until that time the merchants in Trondheim had all trading rights in the area. Its ideal geographical and strategic position, near the coastal traffic, and having a good sheltered harbor, plus its timber and fish exports, were all important factors helping the growth of the town. At one time, Kristiansund was Norway's leading area for processing exporting of fish, especially klipfish. Today Kristiansund has about 18,000 residents and the town is the center for oil drilling exploration in Central Norway. Kristiansund Folk Bibliotek.*

1729, one of the farmers at Flatvad mentioned was a widow named Kari Fladvad. This is probably Ole's widow.

In Scotland, the Clan Macdonald was massacred at Glencoe. In America the following year, Carolina was divided into North and South.

Sivert Olesen, Kari and Ole Ivarsen's first son, was born in 1696. As the eldest son, he was destined to inherit the farm.

In England, naturalist John Ray described for the first time the aromatic herb peppermint.

Ole, Ingrid and Ole's second son was born about 1698, and became a farmer nearby. A sister, Beret, followed. She became a farmer's wife at Toske farm number 1 nearby.

Flatvad: Good Earth

In Germany, Leopold of Anhalt-Dessau introduced goose-stepping into the Prussian army. In London, Mrs. White opened a Chocolate House. It would soon become the headquarters of the Tory Party.

The Fladvad family not only farmed and harvested the fields nearby, but they also used the nearby mountain pastures as sources for winter fodder. In 1723, from fields and pastures, they collected 123 horse loads of grass.

Taxation papers this year characterize Flatvad as having "good earth," and the certainty of a good crop of grain. The yield at the Flatvad farm is estimated at 20 barrels of mixed grains, and 90 barrels of oats.

It was "good cattle land." In addition, each of the three farmers living on and working the farm has a small mill used to grind the grain they grew.

The records show that cotter's farms are virtually unknown at Flatvad. Those who worked the land, owned the land.

Sivert and Ingrid

After Ole's death in 1725, his eldest son, Sivert Olsen, followed him on the farm. He married Ingrid Toresdatter, a sister of

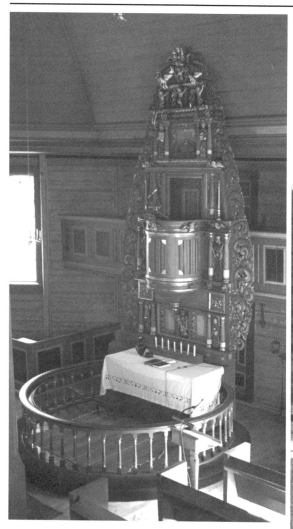

Confirmation into the Lutheran Church *was introduced in Norway in 1736. One important change it made was the requirement that children learn to read in order to learn religious tenets by reading the Lutheran catechism. The present Romfo Church was built in 1821. The altar was carved in about 1713 and incorporated into the present building.*

Hågen Toresen Bjørnhjell. In Russia, Peter the Great died and was succeeded by his wife, Catherine.

Anders, first son of Sivert and Ingrid was born about 1726, and followed his father on the farm. Next was Olaug, who became a farmer's wife at Tøfte farm number 2. In London, Jonathan Swift published "Gulliver's Travels."

Driva Flooding=Land Dispute

Sometimes damage caused by Driva River flooding created problems beyond crop and land damage for the families owning land on its banks. Over the years, the Fladvad and Hoas families inter-married and generally treated and respected each other as "kin." However, on June 29, 1736, the two families found themselves in court.

The dispute was over land boundaries and borders between adjoin-ing farms. Of course, these had long since been established. How-ever, someone forgot to tell the river which, dur-ing several periods of flooding, changed its course. In doing so, the Driva gave the Hoas family some land that had originally belonged to the Fladvads. The dis-pute was finally settled

Detail of altar carving at Romfo Church.

by making a new distribution of land.

A second daughter, Ingrid, was born to Sivert and Ingrid at Flatvad about 1739. She became a farmer's wife at Tronstua (lit. "Tron's room") in Husby.

At the time Sivert took over Flatvad, he bought 15 marklag land rent from some-one named Femmer at Kvalvåg. On Janu-ary 30, 1745, he bought another 1 øre 5 marklag lease and land rent at a price of 200 Daler, partly from his brother, partly from his brother-in-law. After these pur-chases, the only part of the farm he did not own was that part owned by the Romfo

Church, a part the church was not allowed to sell.

One In Four Newborns
Died Before A Year

In the second half of the 18th century, Norwegian farmers paid between 4 and 10 percent of their gross incomes in tithes and taxes. By comparison, a French farmer had to pay between 60 and 75 percent.

Even after the plagues were over, mor-tality was still higher among children. Even as late as the 18th century, nearly one quar-ter of all newborns died before they were a year old.

Anders and Dordi

Anders Sivertsen took over responsibility for Flatvad in 1758 and married Dordi Olsdatter Leangen, who was born about 1732. They had five children, including: Ingrid, born in 1758, and died in 1764.

As Anders was tak-ing over Flatvad, George Washington was taking Fort Duquesne, later re-named Pittsburgh.

In 1760, the home fields of the Flatvad farm alone provided 40 horse loads of grass for winter fodder. These were the flood plain fields on the valley floor.

Grass was greener too, for the future King George III. His grandfather, George II died and he succeeded him. For the Germans, it was scorched earth. The Russians occupied and burned Berlin.

The British opened new Botanical Gar-dens at Kew. Some attendees were wear-ing new silk hats imported from Florence.

In this year as well, Sivert legally trans-ferred Flatvad to his son, Anders, and took accommodation and support from him.

Ole, the first son for Anders and Dordi was born in 1761, and followed his father on the farm. In London, the Society of Arts opened the first exhibition of agricultural

Ole and Anne's second son, Ole (right), *moved to Melhus (south of Trondheim) with his family. Soon however, he moved his family to Brunsvika, Kristiansund. His descendents still live there, some of them in the original farmhouse.*

machines. Anders and Dordi could have used them, but undoubtedly never did. At the time, they were still mourning the death of their daughter, Ingrid who died suddenly at the age of six.

Ingrid, a second daughter was born in 1765. Anders and Dordi named her after her older sister who had died the year before. She would grow up to become a farmer's wife at Hoås farm number 2.

America Revolts, Driva Floods

While Anders and Dordi celebrated the birth of their new daughter, Americans were denouncing the passage by Parliament of the Stamp Act for taxing the colonies. The Virginia Assembly immediately challenged the right of Great Britain to the tax. At a Stamp Act Congress in New York, delegates from nine colonies drew up a declaration of rights and liberties.

Meanwhile, the potato had become the most popular European food. And, a clever man named Spallanzani, suggested that food could be preserved through hermetic sealing.

In 1766, taxation of the Flatvad farm was reduced by over 20 percent. Driva River flooding was to blame.

Bersvend, a second son for Anders and Dordi, was born in 1767. In America, taxes were being added by England on imports of tea, glass, paper, and dyestuffs.

Ole, born in 1774 at Fladvad, was Anders and Dordi's third son.

By the 1780s, the total dry fodder collected at Flatvad was about 200 horse loads. The several Fladvad families working the land at that time had a common dairy farm nearby in which they owned shares.

The circular saw was invented, and the first Sunday newspapers appeared in London.

In America, the British took Charleston, but French troops arrived in Newport. The Americans were defeated at Camden, but the British army was trounced at King's

In a few places, the old road through the Sunndal can still be seen, as here where it passes near Bjørnhjell. *After an avalanche in about 1715, the Leikvin farm was moved to where it stands today. In 1880 it was bought by Lady Barbara Arbuthnott, a Scot who was also known as Sunndallen's uncrowned queen.* **Leikvin** *means "playground," and comes from the Viking era. Today, fully restored, it continues its usefulness as the Leikvin Bygdemuseum.*

Mountain, North Carolina.

In 1786, Anders gave Flatvad over to his eldest son, Ole, for 150 Daler. Frederick the Great died and was succeeded by his nephew Frederick William. Poet Robert Burns published "Poems chiefly in the Scottish dialect." In Charleston, S.C. the American Golf Club was established.

Tore's Bad Luck

Ole moved his household from Flatvad to Bjørnhjell (bear + mountain ledge), and his parents followed him to this farm. Here, Anders wife, Dordi Olsdatter, died in 1820.

After Anders took over his several farms in Bjørnhjell, he decided to sell Flatvad. Tore Hågensen Bjørnhjell bought Flatvad in 1789 when he was about fifty years old. He had been a farmer at Bjørnhjell from 1766 to 1789. He was in for some bad luck. Soon after he bought Flatvad, the Driva rampaged through the Sunndalen in the summer of 1789.

In New York, the first U.S. Congress convened. The French Revolution began, the mob stormed the Bastille, and Lafayette became commander of the National Guard.

The Flatvad farm obtained tax exemption for seven years for one fourth of its taxes after the great flood in 1789.

Philadelphia became the federal capital of the new United States. Lavoisier published "Table of Thirty-One Chemical Elements." Washington, D.C. was founded.

Endre and Sogni

Endre Hågensen was born in 1750, the son of Hågen Toresen Bjørnhjell. In 1793 he married Søgni Ivarsdatter, daughter of a farmer named Einar Ivarsen, who owned Flatvad farm number 2. Their son, Ole, was born in 1794, and later inherited Flatvad.

In Paris, Louis XVI was executed, the Reign of Terror had begun. Later, Queen Marie Antoinette was executed. In the United States, a new law compelled escaped slaves to return to their owners.

Perhaps tiring of the struggle to farm this demanding land in the face of an untamed river, Tore transferred Flatvad to his brother, Endre in 1794 for 600 Daler.

In the United States, the Navy was established. From Paris to Lille, the first telegraph line was put into operation.

Tore died in 1797, but his wife lived until 1822.

In Paris, Napoleon, arrived to command forces for the invasion of England. John Adams became President of the United States.

In the autumn of 1800, Endre bought the allodial privilege from his brother's son, Haagen Toresen, for 90 Daler. The allodium was land held in absolute ownership, and without obligation or service to any feudal overlord. Endre was ensuring he had sole ownership of Flatvad.

Taxes on the Flatvad farm were reduced 12.5 percent for five years—1800-1804—due to severe flooding by the Driva River.

Napoleon established himself as First Consul in the Tuileries. In the U.S., Federal offices were moved from Philadelphia to Washington, D.C. Thomas Jefferson was elected President.

Potatoes Feed More People Than Grain

In 1800, Norway's population was still below a million people. By 1865 however, that figure was up to 1.7 million, and reached 2.2 million by 1900. Reduced infant mortality, and better nutrition were major factors. Herring and potatoes replaced barley porridge as the staple dish. By 1830, potatoes were provided a stable, nutritious yield double that of a grain product.

Grave marker at Romfo for Endre Fladvad, Tron's brother, who inherited Flatvad.

The population in Christiania increased from about 9,000 in 1800 to almost 40,000 in 1855. The sleepy little capital was waking up. The Storting invested money in the Royal Palace, the University, the National Hospital, and the Bank of Norway.

During the Napoleonic Wars, Norway tried to stay neutral, but failing that, finally sided with France. Soon, Britain's fleet prevented Norwegian ships from exporting or importing critically needed goods and supplies. In 1808, the volume of shipping from Norwegian harbors was only one percent of what it had been in 1805. Southeastern Norway, dependent on Danish corn, soon faced starvation and famine. Finally, the King worked out an arrangement with Britain to sell Norwegian products to them in return for free transport of Danish corn.

In the autumn of 1814, Endre transferred Flatvad to his son, Ole, for 100 Daler, plus accommodation and support.

Christian Frederick of Denmark was elected King of Norway. In America, the British burned Washington, D.C.

Norway Ceded To Sweden

When Sweden joined the Great Powers against France, they promised Crown Prince Karl Johan a special prize if they won—Norway. By 1814, Danish King Frederik VI admitted defeat, and signed a peace treaty at Kiel. He had ceded Norway to the King of Sweden.

Danish Prince Christian Frederick refused to accept the agreements made at Kiel. Calling on strong Danish loyalty by Norwegian decision-makers, he convened a constituent assembly at Eidsvoll. By late May, 1814, the assembly's 112 members had agreed on a new constitution for Norway, with sovereignty of the people as its guiding principle. Power was to be shared among the new national assembly—the Storting—the judiciary, and the king.

Unfortunately for Prince Frederick, Napoleon's defeat left Swedish Crown Prince Karl Johan free to put into place the provisions of the Treaty of Kiel. Following a short war, Christian Frederik's 30,000 poorly trained Norwegian farmer volunteers, lost to Karl Johan's 50,000 professional soldiers. However, Karl Johan accepted the most of the Eidsvoll Constitution. While Norway emerged the "junior partner" in the new union with Sweden, Norway retained significant autonomy, including her own flag and her own bank. On November 4, 1814, the new Storting elected Karl XIII as King of Norway.

Ole and Anne

The year before Endre died, Ole, then age 24, married Anne Olsdatter, aged 20, the daughter of Ole Tronsen, who owned Flatvad Farm no. 5. They would have nine children.

Endre died in 1819, and his wife, Søgni followed him in 1829.

Søgni, Ole and Anne's first child was born that year and named for her grandmother. She would marry the farmer who owned Tøfte farm number 1.

In America, the U.S. purchased Florida from Spain, and Alabama joined the Union. In England, a maximum 12-hour working day for juveniles was established.

Anne, named after her mother, was born in 1820. She would marry a cotter's son, Halvor Paulsen Snøvasmyren. Sadly, he died of tuberculosis in 1861. The next year, she moved to Kristiansund.

In England, George III died. In the United States, the Land Law fixes land prices at a minimum of $1.25 per acre.

Endre, the third child for Ole and Anne, was their first son. He would inherit Flatvad.

Ole, Ole and Anne's second son was born at Flatvad in 1827. In 1850, he would move to Melhus (south of Trondheim) with his wife, Marit Retsel. Soon however, he moved his family to Brunsvika, Kristiansund. There he and his industrious wife Marit farmed and operated many successful businesses. Their descendents still live there, some of them in the original farmhouse.

Olaug, born in 1830 at Flatvad to Ole and Anne, died as an infant.

Gudrun Holm Opdøl, *wearing a **bunad** or national costume which had belonged to Ingrid Flatvad, the wife of Endre Flatvad, Tron's brother. The silver jewelry she is wearing was made by Ingrid's father, Per Gjøra, who was working as a silversmith. These precious heirlooms are still in the family.*

In Christiania, Henrik Wergeland published his epic poem *Skabelsen, Mennesket, og Messiah* (Creation, Humanity, and Messiah). He went on to fire his own and succeeding generations with his poetry, prose, articles, and political activity. He died in 1845 at the age of 37.

Tron Fladvad, was born in 1831 to Ole and Anne at Flatvad. He would marry Oline Bjerke of Furnes, near Hamar. One of their daughters was Marie Theresa Fladvad.

Belgium separated from the Netherlands. Cholera continued spreading from Russia into Central Europe, reaching Scotland in 1832. The first horse-drawn buses appeared in New York.

Norwegian farmers finally succeeded in

electing a majority of representatives from their own ranks to the Storting. This would lead, in 1869, to the formation of Norway's first political party, the Liberal Party or "Venstre."

Potatoes Arrive At Flatvad

By 1835, in addition to raising horses, cattle, sheep, and goats, the Fladvad family also raised pigs.

The tithe paid on the Flatvad farm was based on yields in 1835 of 16 barrels of barley, 1 barrel of mixed grain, 19 1/2 barrels of oats, 1 barrel of rye, and 7 1/2 barrels of potatoes. This was the first mention of potatoes being grown at Flatvad.

That year Texas declared its right to secede from Mexico. The first negative photograph, "*Lacock Abbey, Wiltshire,*" was taken by William Henry Fox Talbot.

Olaug, born to Ole and Anne in 1836, became a farmer's wife at Svisdal farm number 2.

Davey Crockett was killed at the Alamo. Texas won independence from Mexico and became a republic.

Marit, Ole and Anne's last child was born in 1840 when Anne was 42, became a cotter's wife at Romfobrekkan. In England, Queen Victoria married Prince Albert of Saxe-Coburg-Gotha.

In the 1840s and 1850s the Storting passed laws making it easier for entrepreneurs to go into business in such fields as timber and sawmills.

Endre, Anne, and Ingrid

Ole died in the Spring of 1842. In the division of the inheritance after him Flatvad was given to Endre for 450 Daler. He was twenty years old. Anne lived until 1848, she was 52 when she died.

The polka, a Czech folk dance, came into fashion. In England, Queen Victoria made her first railroad trip—from Windsor to Paddington.

In 1849, Endre Olsen, married Anne Jonsdatter, aged 25, the daughter of Jon Larsen of Bjørbekk. Tragically, the next year, Anne died the day after bearing a child, and the child died less than four months later.

In the Spring of 1852, Endre married Ingrid Pedersdatter, aged 28, daughter of Peder Evensen, owner of Gjøra farm number 1.

Ole, Endre and Ingrid's first child was born. Ole would live on at Flatvad until 1900. He never married.

Commodore Perry negotiated first treaty between America and Japan. The first form of the light bulb was invented.

In 1854, the first railway was opened from Christiania to Eidsvoll. Mainly it carried timber to Oslo to help with housing construction.

Anne, Endre and Ingrid's first daughter was born in 1855. She became a farmer's wife at Opdøl in Ålvundeid.

In Christiania, Camilla Collett, Henrik Wergeland's sister, published Norway's first realistic novel, "*The Governor's Daughters.*" It attacked marriage for its subjugation of women. It would help inspire Norway's women's liberation movement.

Czar Nicholas I of Russia died and was succeeded by Alexander II. The first iron Cunard steamer crossed the Atlantic in just over nine days. Florence Nightingale introduced hygiene into military hospitals during the Crimean War.

On March 10, 1908, Ingrid sold the farm to her daughter's son, Endre Eysteinsen Opdøl for 8000 Kroner. Ingrid lived until early in 1918.

Endre Eysteinsen Opdøl was born in 1888, the son of the farmer, Eystein Olsen Opdøl, and the "daughters son" of the previous farmer at Flatvad.

At Flatvad in 1913, Endre Eysteinsen Opdøl married Gudrun Holm, a teacher, who was born in 1888. They had five children.

In London, Suffragettes demonstrated for the right to vote. in London. A Federal income tax was introduced in the United States, zippers became popular, and the foxtrot became fashionable.

Hamar. *This Norwegian stamp commemorates Hamar's* **Domkirkeodden** *(cathedral ruins), a medieval cathedral and Bishop's castle, the only visible traces of the old market town of Hamar. These four Romanesque arches date from about 1150 and remain the symbol of the city.*

BJØRKE

Norway's largest inland town, Hamar, is located about forty miles northwest of Oslo. The city was founded in 1049, and its first "tourists" were pilgrims coming from throughout Europe, resting in Hamar during their long, arduous journey to St. Olav's tomb in Nidaros Cathedral in Trondheim. Hamar's first cathedral was built shortly after Christianity was introduced in Norway. The remains of the cathedral and bishop's palace (from about 1150) are still to be found in Hamar.

The oldest written sources refer to Bjørke ("birch tree") in 1322, eighteen years before Geoffrey Chaucer was born (1340). The farm exists to this day near Furnes, a small farming community approximately five miles northeast of Hamar on Lake Mjøsa.

At about the same time as the first mention of Bjørke in the records, at the Battle of Bannockburn in 1314, Robert the Bruce's Scots routed the English under Edward II.

In Germany, Grey Friar Berthold Scharz invented gunpowder. The sawmill was invented in 1328, and would eventually find use at both Bjørke and Flatvad. In the late 19th century, the Bjørke family would be heavily involved in the timber trade made possible by the sawmill.

From the time Bjørke was first mentioned in the records, until the next mention, nearly 200 years would pass.

Norwegians Retain Their Identity

Farmers, fearful of dying and wanting to ensure their souls a better after life donated their land to the Church. Soon, the Archbishop of Nidaros became the most powerful man in Norway, the uncontested leader of the Council of the Realm. Most of the church tithes were paid in dried fish. The Archbishop then sold these to the German Hanseatic merchants in Bergen.

While Danish became the written language, Norwegian customs and dialects continued. Norwegians understood they were a separate nation. While control for a period was exerted from Copenhagen, each King referred to himself as the King of Denmark and Norway. Even coins minted in Norway bore the Norwegian coat of arms.

In 1483, Henry Tudor, Earl of Richmond, defeated and killed Richard III at Bosworth. When Henry succeeded as Henry VII, he established the Tudor dynasty. Further north, King John II of Denmark defeated the Swedish army (1497) at Brunkeberg. He occupied Stockholm, and revived the Scandinavian Union. In 1500, records tell us that part of the Bjørke farm belonged to the Church, under the "St. Michaels altar in Hamar."

From August 17-19, 1624, the citizens of Oslo fought a raging fire. They lost. King Christian IV decided to move the town closer to Akershus Castle. He came to the provincial capital to personally direct construction and named the new town, "Christiania."

Coaching Inn

In 1649, Bjørke was totally owned by Vice Regent Hannibal Sehested, but later it

The Bjørke farm sits atop a knoll, flanked on the southside by an apple orchard. The house overlooks Lake Mjøsa to the West, and slopes down into a small valley to the East. Route 222, the "old road" between Hamar and Brumunddal, winds down the valley where the predominate industry to this day is farming. Occasionally, scenic views of Lake Mjøsa and Helgøya—the holy island—can be seen across the rolling pasture land, dotted with neat homes and cottages. Helgøya was a regional center of pagan worship before Christianity was introduced.

became a part of Storhamar farm.

In 1769, the local inn was moved from Stor-Ile to Bjørke, and the farm became a coaching inn, serving food, hospitality, and lodging for travelers north to Fangberget, and south to Hjellum.

The first complete census revealed that Norway had a population of 723,618. In London, the Privy Council decided to retain a duty on tea destined for the American colonies.

Nils and Kari

In 1773, Bjørke was sold as a "freehold." Nils Jensen Tomter was born at Rafstad in Vang in 1737. He married Kari Larsdatter, born about 1750. Tomter bought Bjørke from Jens Grønbeck Wessel for 1650 Riksdaler. In addition to being a farmer, records indicate he was an inn keeper and an Army Guard.

In Boston, a "tea party" was held. In Vienna, the waltz became fashionable. British engineers built the first cast-iron bridge at Coalbrookdale, Shropshire. It stands to this day.

At Bjørke, Nils and Kari had the first of eight children that we know of: Ole, born in 1774. Later, he would live at Koos in Ringsaker, and marry Grete Eliasdatter, the daughter of the county police officer, at Jerdrum in Stange.

In Philadelphia, the Continental Congress decided on the nonimportation of British goods to American colonies.

Eli, the first daughter for Nils and Kari, was born. She would marry Erik Knutsen Jevanol. While Nils was riding for the doctor, Paul Revere was riding from Charleston to Lexington, Massachusetts. George Washington was riding as Commander-in-Chief of American forces. England hired 29,000 German mercenaries for the war in North America.

In 1777, Nils and Kari had a second daughter, Alis. She married Ole Eriksen Kvernengen in 1800.

Fire at Bjørke. *Today there is no trace of the fire at Bjørke in 1783. It spread so fast that three houses, two good horses, and 10-12 barrels of grain were destroyed. It left the owner, Nils Bjørke, a poor man.*

Meanwhile, Americans adopted the Stars & Stripes as the flag of the Continental Congress. Washington defeated the British at Princeton, New Jersey, then himself was defeated at Brandywine, Pennsylvania.

Bjørke had one cotter in 1778, two in 1801, and one in 1875.

In 1778, Nils added to the land at Bjørke by purchasing the adjacent farm, Furunaever for 460 Riksdaler from Erik Brynildsen Narud.

Washington defeated the British at Monmouth, New Jersey.

Lars, a second son for Nils and Kari was born in 1779. However, it would be, Lars not Ole who would inherit the farm.

The British surrendered to the Americans at Vincennes. Spain declared war on Britain.

Jens, Nils and Kari's third son, was born at Bjørke in 1781. He lived for some time at Murstad, and later at Bjørke where his business ventures included selling.

The Americans defeated the British at Cowpens, N.C., then cornered the British at Yorktown.

Fire At Bjørke

In 1783, Bjørke was hit by a fire which spread so fast that three houses, two good horses, and 10-12 barrels of grain were destroyed. Despite all his work, the fire at Bjørke left Nils a poor man.

Britain recognized America's independence. And, in Germany, Beethoven's first works were printed.

Kari was born to Nils and Kari Bjørke. She would marry Ole Larsen Maelumeie.

At this time, Denmark abolished serfdom. And, Scottish millwright Andrew Meikle invented the threshing machine.

In 1789, at Bjørke, Lisbet was born to Nils and Kari Bjørke.

In France, the mob invaded Tuileries, and the revolutionary Commune was established. The royal family was imprisoned. Gustavus III was assassinated in the Stockholm Open House. In America, Kentucky became a state. Two political parties were formed: the Republicans under

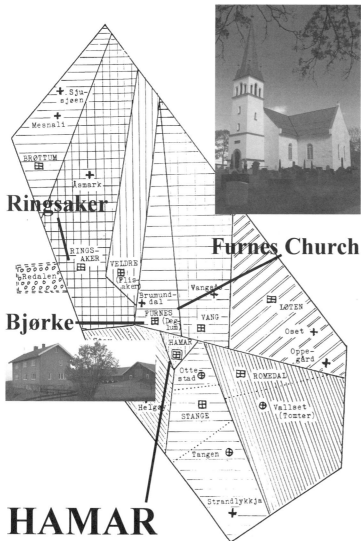

HAMAR

Parish map of the Hamar region showing the areas served by the various churches. The Furnes Church parish included the town of Brumunddal. In 1963 the parishes were consolidated. (Parish map furnished by Hamar Statarkiv)

rest together in the well tended church yard. The Bjørkes plot is next to the cemetery wall and their grave stones are among the largest in the "**gravlund**."

The Bjørke land also included a parade ground and drill field for two companies of Dragoons.

Anders and Marie

Anders, Nils and Kari's fourth son was born at Bjørke in 1792. Anders left Bjørke in 1814 at the age of 22. In May of that year he married Marie Larsdatter Bakken.

Early in their marriage they lived at a small farm in Furnes called **Nederkverneie** ("lower mill"). In the beginning of 1826 they decided to move to a nearby municipality named Ringsaker, a few miles north of Hamar. They already had three children by then, two girls and a boy. Marie went first in the middle of June, and took with her their eldest daughter, Karen, born in 1823, and an infant, Agnete, born in 1826. Nils arrived in Ringsaker on June 27, 1826, with their year old son, Niels.

Their next son, Lars, was born February 2, 1829. Then came another son, Even, born on February 17, 1831.

During this period they lived on two different farms in Ringsaker, and after Even was born they moved to a third farm called Kommerstadbakken, and then to another called Flisagereie. Here Oline Bjørke was born on April 9, 1836. After Oline, their seventh child, Andreas, was born in 1839.

Nils Jensen Tomter died at Bjørke in 1823. That year, Mexico became a Republic. In America, the Monroe Doctrine closed the American continent to colonial settlements by European powers.

Norwegian emigration to America began in 1825 with 52 Quakers leaving Stavanger to go to Illinois. However, the mass exodus did not start until the 1860s.

Thomas Jefferson, and the Federalists under John Adams and Alexander Hamilton.

In 1811, inn privileges were divided between Bjørke, the Deglum farms and Hov. The decision reached was for these three farms to provide inn services in turn, each for two years.

Tomter added the Pinnerudvollen lands to Bjørke. The new Furnes Church was built on land belonging to Bjørke, and the farmers paid an annual land rent to the owner of Bjørke. The church was constructed to the South of the farm, less than a quarter of a mile away.

Today, the Furnes Kirke is solidly constructed of white stucco and topped with a grey slate roof. The Bjørkes and Bakkens

Battle of Market Square. Norwegians clashed violently with Swedish officials on May 17, 1829. The Swedes were disturbed over celebrations during Constitution Day, which they regarded as a day of rebellion. When the Swedish governor sent soldiers to disperse the crowd in the square, the Battle of Market Square took place. Eventually, it became Norway's national day of celebration. (Historic Norwegian stamps from the Bjørn Fladvad Johansen Collection)

During the period 1860 to 1930, 800,000 Norwegians emigrated to America.

In 1828, the King of Norway received an application from Bjørke asking for the right to become the sole coaching inn. The following year, Bjørke's petition was answered with "good news and bad news." The good news: it would again have inn privileges. The bad news: the rights for coaching were not granted. (Some political realities never change.)

In America, Andrew Jackson became President of the United States. And, the first U.S. patent on a typewriter is granted.

Norway's National Day

On May 17, 1829, there was a violent clash with Swedish authorities who were disturbed about Norwegian celebrations during Constitution Day. The Swedes regarded May 17th as a day of rebellion and November 4th, the date the union with Sweden was inaugurated, as the more suitable day for celebration. The Swedish governor sent soldiers to disperse the crowd in the square. The Battle of the Market Square, as the episode was soon to be called, eventually resulted in no further appointments of non-Norwegian governors, and the establishment of May 17th as Norway's national day of celebration.

Kari Larsdatter Tomter died in 1834.

In 1875, Christiania and the area around the capital contained 10.6 percent of the country's population. By 1930 it would reach 17.4 percent.

Henrik Ibsen published "*A Doll's House*," in 1879, a psychological, realistic drama expressing the struggle of the individual caught in an institutional trap.

In 1880, Alexander Graham Bell himself traveled to Norway to inaugurate the country's first telephone line. By 1900, there were 24,000 telephones in Norway.

Oline Andersdatter Bjørke

A great deal can be learned from study of the church records of that time. You can learn who married whom, the names of children christened, whether or not they were legitimate, who was confirmed, who died, who moved out, and who moved into the parish. And so we find that on April 9, 1836, the churchbook for Ringsaker notes that Oline Andersdatter Bjørke at the age of 14 moved from Flisagereie in Ringsaker to Nybakkenn at Furnes to serve at that farm as a tenant.

Moving to other places to find work was not unusual. It indicated the difficulty

Church record books in Furnes and Ringsaker *reveal that Oline Andersdatter Bjørke, age 14 and again at age 16, accepted work on farms in both communities. It indicated the difficulty of finding work in one's home community. Many young people at that time had to leave their families to seek work on other farms. For their efforts they received room and board, some clothes—and very little money. In 1853, when Oline returned to Ringsaker seeking employment on another farm she presented a testimonial from her previous employer.*

of finding work in the place where one presently lived. To leave your family and seek work as a tenant was often the case, at least for some period of time in a young person's life.

When the day for seeking new employment arrived in the spring or autumn, young people met their future employers at church or at markets, making agreements with them regarding work. For their work they received room and board, some clothes—

and very little money. Often this was the first step before moving to entirely new places. However, it could also just be an episode in their life, after which they returned to the place they came from, and either entered into a new arrangement there, or married and settled down.

In 1853, Oline returned to Ringsaker seeking employment on another farm. In the churchbook, the clergyman noted her age—"16 winters old"—and further, that she presented a testimonial from her previous employer.

Niels and Lars Bjørke

We now leave Anders Nilsen Bjørke and the rest of the family, and concentrate on Oline's two brothers, Niels and Lars, who would play an important role in her future.

Her eldest brother, Niels, who was born in 1825, decided to move to Namsos, a small community about 150 miles north of Trondheim. Lars followed Niels.

In 1845, Namsos was undergoing a timber-boom. This small town is located at the outlet of the Namsen River, which runs through the vast forests of Namdalen—then virgin land almost untouched by man. A sharp increase in timber prices, combined with an increase in the export volume of timber and boards to England, France, and The Netherlands, offering an opportunity to make a fortune in timber trading. Both Norwegian and foreign investors took advantage of this and established themselves in Namsos as merchants, saw-mill workers, craftsmen, shipowners, or sailors.

In 1845, Namsos had just two houses and a few warehouses. By 1858, there were 70 houses. The increase continued until 1872 when eighty percent of the town was destroyed by fire.

In 1860, foreigners had invested some 200,000 Spesidaler in Namsos timber trade. One English company bought an enormous tract of land, as big as the entire county of Akershus—4,500 square kilometers, including ownership of 140 farms. From 1865, when the boom reached its peak, and for twenty years thereafter, over six million logs were exported from a district where before hardly an axe had been used in the forest.

By the middle of the 1880s it was all

over. Prices were dropping, and it was increasingly difficult to get the timber out of the forests. Niels, however, had established himself as a merchant in Namsos in the later 1850s.

Oline Travels To Namsos

In the spring of 1859, Oline, now age 23, again appeared before the clergyman of Ringsaker, this time to report that she planned to leave Ringsaker. She was following her two brothers to Namsos.

We don't know exactly how Oline traveled, but she might have taken a steamboat part of the way from Hamar to Lillehammer. Travel in Norway at that time was not easy. The first railway had been built in 1854, but it only went from Oslo to Eidsvoll on the southern bank of Lake Mjøsa—a trip taking about three hours. From there you could go by boat to Hamar and further north to Lillehammer which is situated at the northern end of Mjøsa.

In July, 1875, an American traveler, E. L. Anderson, began a journal which ultimately he turned into a book, "*Six Weeks in Norway*." The book chronicles his journey throughout Norway, from Christiania (Oslo) to Throndhjem (Trondheim), Aak, Bergen, and concludes in Oslo.

The American Consul to Norway from 1869 until 1894 was Gerhard Gade. "During the morning of our arrival," Anderson wrote, "I called upon Mr. Gerhard Gade, consul for the United States, and found him ready to give us every assistance in preparing for our journey. I can not express our obligations to the gentleman for his attentions and kindness, and it was at his delightful country-house, 'Frogner,' that we first learned that northern hospitality does not partake of the coldness of the climate."

Anderson learned from Mr. Gade that the roads had been "greatly improved of late years," so much so that "a light carriage might be substituted for the inconvenient and wearying two-wheeled carriole mentioned in the guide-book." As you might expect, this was "a very agreeable piece of information, for I had looked with dread upon the long rides, day after day, in a seat that gives no support to the back."

During his travels in England, Anderson found the carriole still in use by the English, who "do not believe in innovations, and who pride themselves upon following the customers of a country, even at the expense of comfort," he sniffed. For the "natives," who can afford to travel in a more luxurious manner, "it is a thing of the past."

So helpful to Anderson was Gade, that Anderson dedicated "*Six Weeks in Norway*," to "Consul Gerhard Gade, of Christiania." Twenty years later, Gade was no longer in Christiania. He was in Boston at the residence of Mr. and Mrs. Thomas S. Nowell, who lived at 337 Commonwealth Avenue. He was there as an honored guest at the wedding held in the Nowell's home of Charles Middleton Cottrell of Newport, Rhode Island to Marie Theresa Fladvad, formerly of Christiania. Harriet Nowell was Mr. Cottrell's domineering sister. Harriet was present at the start of the Cottrell-Fladvad marriage, and she was there when it ended some twenty years later. In fact, when he later became ill, she would make "Charlie" choose between her and his wife, Marie.

Anderson's "*Six Weeks in Norway*," provides an interesting portrait of the country as it was during the period Marie Fladvad's mother, Oline was traveling through the same country Anderson describes. The comparisons to the Norway of today are striking. Yet, in many important respects the country's scenery and its fine people remain the same.

It is not likely that the Cottrells knew Consul Gade. They had some infrequent ties with Midleton, Ireland, the family's original home there, but none in Norway. It is most probable that Consul Gade was invited to the wedding as a friend of the Fladvad family who met him during his service in Norway, sometime after they moved to Christiania in 1884.

The fact that Consul Gade accepted the invitation to attend the wedding suggests that he both knew and liked the family. By today's standards, travel in those days was highly inconvenience and uncomfortable. Arranging to attend the wedding was a major commitment.

To Andersen the "Christiania fiord" had

none of the characteristics that made the western bays of Norway "celebrated for their grandeur of scenery…" However, he thought it was beautiful and would remind Americans of the "upper Hudson." In July, the sun shines for about 18 hours a day. So, when Anderson arrived in Christiania at midnight, there was "still light enough to see the vessels in the harbor, and to admire the old fortress of Akershus, that pretends to guard the town." His mooring site was probably in Pipervika, near the present Aker Brygge and the Oslo City Hall, the Rådhus. He hurried through customs, and took the short walk "through the deserted streets that brought us to the Victoria Hotel, one of the best inns in Northern Europe."

He found Christiania to be a "well-built city, beautifully situated about the head of the fiord, seventy miles from the sea." It had, he reported, a population of 80,000.

Christiania was then, and is now, the "first commercial port of Norway, and supplies nearly the whole of the southern part of the country with foreign imports. The harbor is without a rival, and the flags of all nations may be seen upon the shipping."

"Many of the public edifices are of imposing appearance, and the residences in the suburbs exhibit taste and wealth."

The hills in the vicinity "furnish many pleasing prospects, and the roads are excellent."

"Three miles from the city rises Frognersæter[en], from whence an extended and varied view may be had. The city, the silver fiord dotted with islands, the pine-clad hills, and the distant peaks, with their snowy caps, are presented to the eye.

Overlooking the fiord, and in a setting of emerald trees, is Oscar's Hall, a summer palace of the king. Here may be seen some

Oslo's Old Town. *Following his arrival in Oslo, traveler E. L. Anderson hurried through customs, and took the short walk through deserted streets to the Victoria Hotel. He might have walked past these very houses, now relocated to the grounds of the Norsk Folk Museum and restored to their former charm.*

The "white swan of Mjøsa"—Skibladner—is the world's oldest paddle-steamer still in active service. Today, as it did when Oline Bjørke went aboard in 1859, Skibladner plies the Mjøsa during the summer months. This beautiful little ship takes its name from Norse mythology, where "Skibladner" was a vessel which could sail with equal ease on land or sea. Lake Mjøsa is still the "beautiful sheet of water," Anderson found. Seventy miles long, its greatest width is ten miles.

of the master-pieces of Norwegian painters, landscapes by Gude, and pictures of peasant life by Tidemand."

Anderson found few railroad lines operating in Norway at that time. However, the system of "posting has been brought almost to perfection. At point seven miles apart, or as near that distance from each other as is practicable, posting-houses (**skys-stasjoner**) have been established, where the traveler may obtain fresh horses and lodging, if he require it, at prices fixed by the local government. These stations are, for the most part, the homes of the farmers, and the accommodations, as might be expected, are of a primitive character, but they are the best that the country can afford, and the guest is always assured of civility and attention."

"The Norwegian peasant—and except on the coast there are few towns—is proud of his ancestry and of his hard-won freedom, but, unless his dignity is touched, he is the most polite and hospitable of mortals."

Anderson recommended have "a courier who understands the language." His experience led him to conclude that "all Norwegians are thoroughly honest, even to the couriers," and he recommended Matthias Johanssen of Christiania, as a "most capable, energetic, and trustworthy man."

Norwegian Horses Would Not Kick

Anderson and his wife, spent a week "pleasantly in Christiania." The evening before they left for their journey "through Gudbraandsdalen, over the Dovre-field to Throndhjem (Trondheim)," Johanssen called them into the court yard of the hotel to examine the carriage in which they were to ride, and the provisions he had obtained for the journey. "We found a light caleche carriage, closely packed with preserved meats, crackers, etc., while an ingenious contrivance, pendant from the dash-board, held a dozen small bottles of Bordeaux wine. My fears in regards to the safety of these latter fragile goods were set at rest when Johanssen assured me that Norwegian horses would not kick." A board fastened to the rear axle carried a single trunk.

After the inspection, the "richly laden" carriage was left in the hotel court yard, "where it remained undisturbed throughout the night." Not an article was missing in the morning. Anderson made a point of noting that "it was our custom to leave our property in the carriage, as it stood by the roadside, night after night, at the inn door, and our faith in the honesty of the people was never shaken."

Johanssen had the carriage loaded on the train from Christiania to Eidsvoll, the end of the rail line. However, nearby by was the "pretty little steamer King Oscar,"

in the Vormen river, "ready to take us to Lillehamar, at the head of Lake Miosen (Mjøsa)." There the carriage was placed on the foredeck, while the three travelers rested under an awning on the quarter-deck."

The King Oscar is long gone. However, one of its contemporaries is still sailing.

On August 2, 1856 the steamboat "Skibladner," had taken its maiden voyage down Lake Mjøsa, Norway's largest lake. Its name was taken from Norse mythology, where **Skibladner** was a ship which could sail with equal ease on land or sea. With the railway open between Oslo and Eidsvoll since 1854, the Skibladner would help bring the capital and many inland towns and villages much closer together.

Remarkably, the **Skibladner**, the single remaining paddle wheel steamer of that period, is not only still afloat, but also still in commercial use. Homeported in Eidsvoll, it makes regularly scheduled stops at various ports around lake Mjøsa, much as it did nearly 150 years ago. Now the world's oldest paddle steamer remaining in operation, the **Skibladner** still sails the length of Norway's largest lake. On board, you can eat a tasty meal of salmon and strawberries as you glide slowly past the beautiful landscape along the Mjøsa.

About midway up Lake Mjøsa is the island of Helgo (Helgøya), a "splendid farm" in Anderson's time, and "formerly the estate of one of the wealthy nobles."

Hamar is about 65 miles north of Oslo, in the heart of rich farmland. It is Norway's largest inland town. One of its more notable features is what remains of a medieval cathedral, built around 1150. "Four arches of the ancient cathedral, built in the year 1152 by the bishop, who was afterward Pope Hadrian IV, have a commanding position on a point of land running into the lake from the site of ancient Hamar," Anderson noted, "and show that a splendid edifice once occupied the site." These symbolic reminders of the ancient cathedral have survived centuries of neglect and weathering. However, they fared less well in standing up to acid rain. They are protected by conservationists and are being restored.

Above Helgøya, lake Mjøsa narrows to "a uniform width of about two miles, until it meets the river Lågen at Lillehamar." It was during this part of the journey that the captain of the Oscar struck up a conversation with Anderson. The "master of the vessel approached me, and in very good English asked me if I knew General So and So, or Colonel Blank, or Major Ditto, and seemed very much disappointed that I did not have the honor of an acquaintance with any of these heroes, who, he assured me, were fellow-countrymen of mine. It turned out that the skipper's hobby was the collection of visiting cards; and, as every American who travels abroad takes a title, if he may by chance lay any claim to one, he had a very pretty collection of the names of the American nobility." With straight-faced sarcasm, Anderson reports that the captain "threw my card, which had simply the prefix of 'Mr.,' into the lake."

Anderson was somewhat premature in his predictions for Lillehamer, which in 1875, had only 1,700 inhabitants. Reaching the town in the early evening, Anderson dryly observed that Lillehamer is "built on the hillside, and will not cause much loss should it fall into the lake, as is reasonably to be expected." Since *Six Weeks In Norway* is long since out of print, we suspect the Olympic Committee was not unduly alarmed by his predictions. He was not impressed with the town or its meager accommodations.

The food was so bad in Lillehamer that he said he preferred "taking the chances for such food as the farmers could offer, or that the courier might prepare on the road." Perhaps he preferred canned meat washed down with Bordeaux.

As quickly as possible, Anderson had Mr. Johanssen pushing the carriage up the road running through "Gudbrandsdalen, one

The Gudbrandsdal. *Once leaving the shores of Lake Mjøsa at Lillehamer, today's E-6 highway follows the Lågen river to Dombås. The two lane road is rarely straight, but winds back and forth up the Gudbrandsdal. At times the scenery is restricted to rows of evergreens on either side. Then, without warning the highway breaks out of the forest and reveals a broad valley 5-7 miles across dotted with neat farms and a patch work quilt of fields and pastures. Some cattle, but far more sheep, graze in the pastures which seem at times to be more vertical than horizontal.*

The Royal Road Across the Dovrefjell. *After leaving the town of Dombås, Norway's main highway artery—E-6—begins to climb sharply through a series of switchbacks. The land changes quickly from pasture and farms, then highland plateau—the Dovrefjell. Evergreens give way to barren rocks, covered in grey-green lichens.*

of the grand valleys that make Norway habitable, which, with its continuation, the Romsdal, extends from the upper end of Lake Miosen to the sea at Veblungsnoes (Veblungnes), and is the great artery of trade."

"The Laagen (Lågen) river, that takes its rise in the Lesjeverksvan, flows down the length of this valley, while the Rauma, that flows from the same sources, runs northwardly down the Romsdal. These rivers, swift and strong, add much to the beauty of the valley, and they keep the traveler company through the journey from lake to sea."

At Dombas E-6 continues more sharply north towards Trondheim. Highway 9 continues west down the Romsdalen to Andalsnes. Leaving Dombås, E-6 begins to climb sharply through a series of switchbacks. In minutes the gentle Gudbrandsdal is left behind. The ecology changes quickly from pasture and farms, to highland plateau—the Dovrefjell. The tall evergreens give way to shorter trees, then just barren rocks, covered in grey-green lichens. Small lakes dot the barren terrace.

For about fifty miles, the road points north-north-east as it moves across the ridge. At Hjerkinn, 36 miles from Dombas, the Driva river begins as a mountain stream, then grows slowly into a river as the highway parallels its flight down the rugged valley. At Oppdal, the Driva curves to the West and continues carving away at the Sunndalen valley, a process that has continued for many thousands of years.

The Royal Road

Before the carriage track was built at the bottom of the valley in 1820, the old road to Nidaros (Trondheim) crossed the mountains from the settlement of Dovre,

Sunndalen. *Tron Fladvad took this road in 1860 when he left Sunndalen and set out for Kolvereid, about thirty miles north of Namsos. He had known all his life that he would eventually have to leave the Sunndal. He could not inherit Flatvad since he had an older brother. There was no more arable land in his valley. He would have to develop other skills and move away.*

Gautstigen, since the Middle Ages. From Dovre to Hjerkinn, the Royal Road passed the farms at Tofte, then cross the Hardbakken and descended to Fokstugu. Norwegian kings since Harald Håfagre used the road, first on horseback, then after 1704, in carriages.

It was a dangerous journey. Travelers erected a stone altar to kneel and pray for a safe journey or for a safe arrival. A rock heap at the highest point on the road near Hardbakken, still exists from the time when travelers would throw a stone on the pile to bring them good luck.

Probably Oline took the **Skibladner** for the first 60 kilometers along Mjøsa to Lillehammer, then went by road up the narrow Gudbrandsdalen for another 110 km. to Otta, when the climb up into the mountain plateaus of the Dovre begins. Then down from the mountains another 250 km to Trondheim. The land route was still maintained by farmers who helped travelers enroute to Trondheim. From there she probably went by ship to Namsos, a distance of about 200 kilometers. She would have spent at least several days on the journey.

Tron Olesen Fladvad
Oline Andersdatter Bjørke

In 1860, Tron Fladvad left Sunndalen and set out for Kolvereid, about thirty miles north of Namsos. Since his eldest brother would take over Flatvad, Tron knew he would have to leave his childhood home. He would need to develop other talents and skills to make a living other than inheriting the family farm.

Perhaps in his travels through Namsos enroute to Kolvereid, he met Oline Bjørke, and they fell in love. She had arrived some months before. On May 6, 1861, two years to the day since she left Ringsaker, Oline

Born in 1861, Anna Fladvad was the first child for Oline and Tron Fladvad who had married and settled in Kolvereid. They leased a farm--Sjølstad West--and Tron became a ship owner. They had two more children while they lived at Sjølstad, a son, Ole Andreas, and a second daughter, Marie Theresa. Anna married Martin Johansen.

Bjørke married Tron Fladvad in the Kolvereid Church.

In the fall of 1861, Oline and Tron settled in Kolvereid and leased a farm called Sjølstad West. At the end of that year, their first child, a girl, Anna, was born.

In 1861, Oline and Tron were joined by her two brothers, Niels and Lars. Niels moved from Namsos in September, 1861, and leased the farm, Rokka. Lars married the eldest daughter of the farmer owning Sjølstad east.

In 1863, Tron bought Sjølstad West for 870 Daler.

Oline and Tron had two more children while they lived at Sjølstad. Their first son, Ole Andreas was born on October 11, 1863, the same year the first paper mill went into operation at an Oslo suburb. By 1890, Norway had sixty pulp mills.

A second daughter, Marie Theresa was born on December 22, 1865.

Tron seemed to be more interested in trade and seamanship than in farming. At first he bought a **jekt**, a single masted Norwegian boat very common along coastal waters. Lars Bjørke was the skipper for the vessel. In addition, Tron became a partner in a sloop called the **Amalie**.

By 1867 however, over extension and an economic downturn forced Tron to liquidate his holdings. In 1867, he and Oline moved to Kristiansund that autumn.

A second son, Frederick was born in 1868. When he lived in Christiania, he worked as an office clerk. Later, he moved

Kristiansund harbor in 1880. *The city is spread over three islands, Kirkelandet, Innlandet, and Nordlandet. Its ideal geographic and strategic position near coastal traffic, a good sheltered harbor, and its timber and fish exports, were important factors contributing to the town's growth. Unfortunately, they were also factors in the decision by the German occupation forces, to bomb the town for three days in 1940.*

Tron Fladvad and Oline Bjørke Fladvad *and eight of their nine children in a photograph taken during the time they lived in Kristiansund. In the back row, Ole Fladvad, born in 1863, stands next to his sister, Anna Fladvad Johansen, born in 1861, who rests her hands on her parents shoulders. Second row, left to right, Fredrik Fladvad, born in 1868, died later in Brooklyn, NY. Tron Fladvad, Oline Fladvad, Marie Theresa Fladvad, born in 1865, and her youngest brother, Theodor ("Toddy") Fladvad, born in 1870 and died in 1944. Front row, Gina, Olise, and Otilie ("Otta"). Lower left,* **Marie Theresa's Confirmation photograph** *taken when she was about 15 years old.*

The Kristiansund skyline (below) as it looked at the time Tron and Oline settled there in about 1867. (Historic photograph from the Collection of the Kristiansund Folk Bibliotek)

Kristiansund's main street, *Parkveien, in 1866 (left) and in 1880 (below). Tron and his brother, Ole both lived nearby and would have used this main thoroughfare daily. (Historic photographs from the Collection of the Kristiansund Folk Bibliotek)*

Shoppers and strollers *(left) move about on Kristiansund's Longveien (formerly Parkveien), at the turn of the century.*

A Parade in the Rain. *At right, a small parade of musicians passes the torvet (market) and Kirken (church) in 1905. (Historic photographs from the Collection of the Kristiansund Folk Bibliotek)*

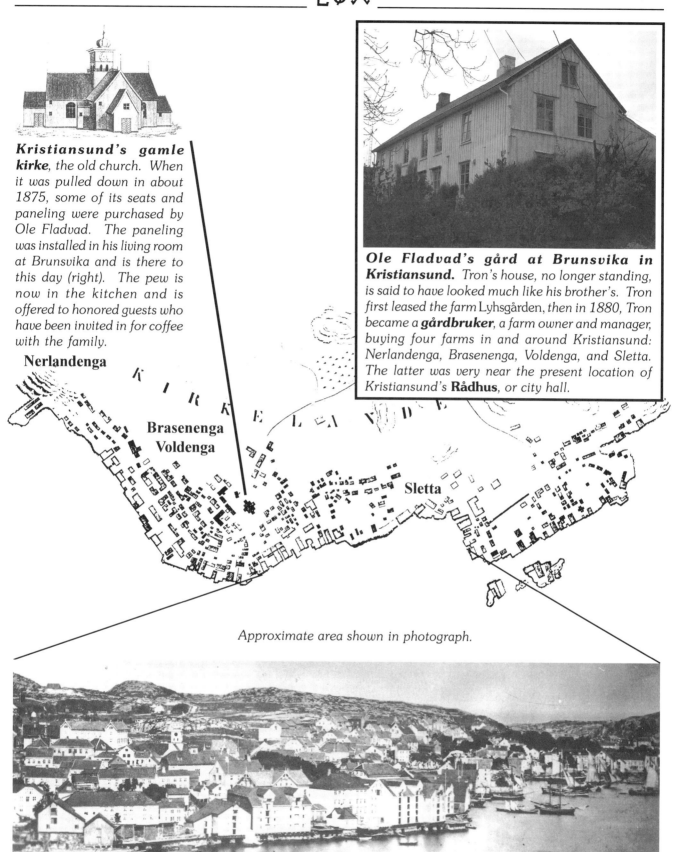

Kristiansund's gamle kirke, the old church. When it was pulled down in about 1875, some of its seats and paneling were purchased by Ole Fladvad. The paneling was installed in his living room at Brunsvika and is there to this day (right). The pew is now in the kitchen and is offered to honored guests who have been invited in for coffee with the family.

Nerlandenga

Brasenenga
Voldenga

Sletta

Ole Fladvad's gård at Brunsvika in Kristiansund. Tron's house, no longer standing, is said to have looked much like his brother's. Tron first leased the farm Lyhsgården, then in 1880, Tron became a **gårdbruker**, a farm owner and manager, buying four farms in and around Kristiansund: Nerlandenga, Brasenenga, Voldenga, and Sletta. The latter was very near the present location of Kristiansund's **Rådhus**, or city hall.

Approximate area shown in photograph.

This harborside view of Kristiansund was taken in 1867. While the Kart (map) was drawn in 1854, it is the only available map of that period in the collection of the Kristiansund Folk Bibliotek. Viewed together however, they provide us with a better understanding of how the town looked at time Tron and Oline lived there with their children. (From the Collection of the Kristiansund Folk Bibliotek)

*Tron's farm, **Sletta**, was very near the present location of Kristiansund's Rådhus, or city hall.*

In 1884 Tron and Oline left Kristiansund *(below) and moved to Olso. According to family history, Tron used his knowledge of boats and sailing to carry out the move. Marius Fladvad of Kristiansund, related that Tron loaded his family, his belongings, and his cattle aboard a **jagt** similar to the **Embla**, and sailed around the Southern coast of Norway and up the Oslo fjord to reach their new home. At the time, he was 53 years old and Oline was 45. Anna was 22, and Marie was 18. Oslo would be the home for Tron and Oline for the rest of their lives. (Historic photograph from the Collection of the Kristiansund Folk Bibliotek)*

to Brooklyn, New York, where he died. He had no children.

Lars was also having difficulties. After trying with no success to save the Sjølstad, he sold it.

Niels came to an even sadder end. In the autumn of 1871, while floating timber down the River Kvista, he fell in and drowned. Later, when his body was found, it had no head.

Tron and Oline Move to Kristiandsund

In Kristiansund, Tron and Oline leased the farm **Lyhsgården**. Tron hired a man to help him with the farm work, and one woman assisted Oline in the kitchen and with the household chores. While living in Kristiansund, Tron and Oline had six more children.

The 1870 census sheet for section number 586 in Kristiansund provides a great deal of important information about the family. For example, it notes that Tron Fladvad was the **Jordbruger**, or farmer, and that he was born in 1827 in Sunndalen. Oline is listed as his wife, born in 1837 in Hedemarken (Furnes, near Hamar). Daughters Anna and Marie were born in Kolvereid in 1861 and 1865 respectively. Son Ole was born in Kolvereid in 1863. Sons Frederick and Theodor were born in Kristiansund in 1868 and 1870 respectively.

In addition to family members, the census notes others living on the "**gård.**" Elen Gjekling, for example, was a servant from Sunndal. Others were listed as helping Tron farm the land, including: John Hansen, Ingebrikt Aas, and Thor Rasmusssen.

Theodor Fladvad, Tron and Oline's third son, was born in 1870. His son took the name Leif Norgreen.

In 1870, only 20 percent of Norway's population lived in towns. By 1900, over 30 percent, lived in towns. From 1870 to 1900, the population of Christiania increased from 75,000 to 230,000.

In 1872, another daughter, Gina, was born to Tron and Oline. Cryptic records note she "died young."

In 1874, Olise Fladvad was born to Tron and Oline. On a visit to Newport, Rhode Island in 1918, to see her sister, Marie, following the end of World War I, she would

Lars Ole Fladvad, Tron's brother had his farm at Brunsvik, a small inlet about half a mile from the center of Kristiansund at that time. Today, the city has grown up around it, but Ole's grandson and his family still live there and maintain the house as both a city historical residence and their ancestral home. During **World War II German Wehrmacht occupation troops** *forced the family to leave the house and then used it as a headquarters for troops prepared to defend the city from an Allied invasion which never materialized. They built bunkers on the property ("pill boxes") which remain to this day (below). In addition, their hobnailed boots seriously damaged the floors, in many places grinding doorway oak thresholds down to thin strips. Stair treads were ruined. They nearly collapsed the house when they overloaded the second floor with ammunition until the rafters became swaybacked from the weight. Extensive repairs were required after the war, but at least the family got the house back. Thousands of other families in Krisitiansund were not so fortunate. During three days of bombing in 1940, the Germans destroyed over two thirds of the city. To this day family members cannot understand why this outrage was visited on the city which had no weapons, and put up no resistance to the overwhelming forces.*

die suddenly of typhoid fever.

In 1876, Otilie ("Otta") Fladvad was born. She later married an American, Thomas Hinds of New York. They had no children and she died about 1920.

Gunhild Charlotte (Jeanne), Tron and Oline's last child, was born November 23, 1881 in Kristiansund. She would later marry Christian Willumsen of Christiania.

Although he leased farm land at first, in 1880, Tron became a **gårdbruker**, a farm owner and manager. On August 25th of that year, he bought four farms in and around Kristiansund. Their names were Nerlandenga, Brasenenga, Voldenga, and Sletta.

After farming them for two years, he sold them on September 9, 1882. All were bought and sold on the same dates.

In 1882 alone, almost 29,000 people

*Tron's daughter, **Marie Theresa**, was fifteen in 1880, old enough to learn important business skills from her father and from the example set by Marit Flatvad with the **kaffestue**. Nearly 40 years later, she would need these skills when she would be forced to support herself and her four daughters in Newport, Rhode Island. Drawing upon her experience and additional training at a home economics school in Oslo, Marie would establish a boarding house business in Newport. She was active in its all-male Chamber of Commerce, which commended her for her service as hospitality chairperson during efforts in the 1920s to raise money to build the Viking Hotel.*

left Norway for the United States, more than the combined populations of Trondheim and Tromsø.

As far as family records and history reveal, Tron and Oline always lived near relatives. In Kolvereid, Oline's brothers lived and farmed nearby. In Kristiansund, it was Tron's brother and sister who lived close by and provided social and business support. There were no social "safety nets" in those days and it was important to have family members to whom you could turn for help in a crisis.

Norway's First Kaffestue

The primary occupation for Tron and Ole was farming, but there was another "Flatvad" in town who became a local celebrity in a different line of work: Marit Flatvad established and managed for many years Norway's first real "coffee house." She was described as both "pleasant" and "temperamental" in newspaper accounts written about her and her role as Krisitiansund's **kaffevertinne** or coffee hostess.

She operated the **kaffestue** (coffee house) in Loennechengården from about 1880 until after 1900. She established high standards for her patrons. Those wanting a steaming cup of coffee and one of her famous rolls or **boller**, had to descend a long staircase from the **Fisketorvet** (fish market) . She had rented several rooms in the building, one for her kaffestue and the others she sublet to a printer and another to a building materials store ("**Bygningsartikkel forretning**").

Marit Kårbø Fladvad was born in 1833 in Lesja, in the Romsdal valley to the east of Kristiansund. She met and married Lars Olsen Flatvad, who was a farmer and businessman in the town. Records are not clear, but he had probably taken his name "Flatvad" from the farm, although he was not directly related to the ancestral family, who spelled it Fladvad.

Family historians believe he might have been a cotter at Flatvad. It is highly probable in such a small town and having ties with the farm, that the Fladvads knew Lars and his enterprising wife, Marit. The newspaper later concluded that it was Marit who was probably "the real leader" of their business enterprises. She was called a "business genius" and an extremely clever human being.

At first she sold vegetables and flowers (**blomster**) from a basement store in

Holbergsgate 27. *Tron and Oline, plus their daughters Otilie, Olise, and Jeanne lived together at Holbergsgate 27 in Oslo. Today, their former home is across the street from the main entrance of Oslo's SAS Scandinavia Hotel. When Marie visited them in 1907, their apartment was too small for her and her three daughters. She spent much of her time that summer at a waterside **hytte** she called Guthus (the good house)*

Stangvik, a section of downtown Kristiansund. Later, she added leather goods and supplies. Her flowers and vegetables were "very popular" one account reported, and she "probably made a good living on this little business."

It was her **kaffestue** however, that put Marit Flatvad into the history books. She was soon known for her good coffee and her cleanliness. Her **kaffestue** became very popular.

Weary, hungry Kristiansund fishermen at four and five o'clock in the morning would be welcomed at Marit's **kaffestue** which was open and doing a brisk business. They looked forward to the delicious aroma of her coffee and her famous specialty, **skillingskaker**, a large bun with raisons and coarse sugar on top. She would top them with butter and lots of **gamelost**, a type of aged, pungent cheese.

On one occasion Marit had a celebrity visit her **kaffestue**. Alexander Kielland, Norwegian novelist, short-story writer, and dramatist. He ranks among the "big four" of Norwegian classic writers, along with Björnson, Ibsen, and Lie. Even though he came from a wealthy merchant family, Kielland wrote about the glaring discrepancies between wealth and poverty, and obviously felt a deep aversion to the dehumanizing effects of industrial capitalism. He sympathized with its victims and had parted company with his own class. He saved his worse literary punishment for the representaives of conservative, institutionalized life, ranged from the clergy and bureaucrats, to schoolmen. Although the newspaper article does not state the specific date for Kielland's visit to Marit Flatvad's **kaffestue**, it was probably during the period when he was district governor for

Marie Fladvad Cottrell (right) spent almost a year and half in Norway in 1906-07, visiting her parents and relatives. Her return to America in 1907, aboard the SS Oscar II, marked her last trip home to Norway. Her mother, Oline (left) died in 1908. On the return trip, she and her sisters met Captain Roald Amundsen who had recently discovered the magnetic North Pole and transited the Northwest Passage.

Romsdal (1902-1906).

How many cakes do you want, Marit asked. "Oh well, I guess I have to have quite a few," he said, somewhat absent-mindedly, probably thinking about other things than **skillingskaker**.

Marit brought out a whole stack of **skillingskaker** for him, as well as coffee which she served in mugs. He enjoyed this "original" service and took his time eating his food.

Not much of a "news hook" for American journalists, however that one visit prompted a Krisitiansund writer to create a brief story on February 18, 1949 and to include her name in the headline. Forty five years later in the Kristiansund Bibliotek while leafing through a 4-inch high pile of clippings in a folder, that headline caught

the author's attention. While it did not provide much information about Kielland, the article gave us a colorful portrait of Marit Flatvad and Norway's first *kaffestue*.

Marit was very strict about behavior in her establishment. She kept order among its patrons. If a customer did something of which she disapproved, they "wouldn't get away with it," the newspaper reported.

In addition to their **gård** at Brunsvik, Marit and Ole bought an apartment house in downtown Kristiansund near the Grand Hotel—the old Rennie building (**den gamle Renniegården**) built in about 1780 by Lars Lund, then Superintendent of Customs for Kristiansund. The property is now owned by the Grand Hotel. [Note: **gård** can mean both farm or a house in town. In this context, we have translated **gård** as "building" or "house."]

She kept an apartment there for herself, and she expanded her business operations into the sale of old clothes and provided rooms for lodgers.

She was a "popular and orginal character in town," the newspaper reported. She dressed in a short, gray skirt with a checkered apron. She wore a knitted scarf around her waist and around her head. Her hands, the report noted, were usually placed at the hips and she looked very strict. She was active politically and was a "liberal."

When Marit Flatvad died on February 14, 1912, Kristiansund lost one of its "most popular and exceptional figures." However, in Newport, Rhode Island, Marie Fladvad Cottrell remembered well her example and business skills. She would put them to use herself soon enough.

Life in Christiania

In his travelogue, *Six Weeks in Norway,* Anderson reported that Christiania "is a well-built city, beautifully situated about the head of the fiord, seventy miles from the sea, and, it is asserted, has a population of 80,000 souls. It is the first commercial port of Norway, and supplies nearly the whole of the southern part of the country with foreign imports. The harbor is without rival, and the flags of all nations may be seen upon the shipping." Many of the public "edifices are of imposing appearance, and the

residences in the suburbs exhibit taste and wealth."

In Christiania, Tron started a new career—trading livestock. Later, he expanded his business to build a slaughterhouse. This lasted for about four years, when he sold his holdings and started over as a carpenter. He soon became a master joiner and continued in this trade for the rest of his active life.

Tron and Oline, plus their daughters Otilie, Olise, and Jeanne lived together at Holbergsgate 27 in Oslo. Today, their former home is across the street from the main entrance of Oslo's SAS Scandinavia Hotel.

It seems likely that two of their sons also lived in Christiania at that time. Theodor was employed by the Norwegian State Railway System. Ole served as a waiter for some time at the Loge Restaurant (for the Freemasoners of Christiania).

Martin Johansen who had married Anna Fladvad, also worked at the same restaurant at that time. Later, Martin and Anne would own and operate the Victoria Park Hotel in Hamar.

During this period Tron and Oline came to know the United States Consul in Christiania, Gerhard Gade, who served there from 1869 until 1893. Perhaps the relationship was established through Tron's Masonic (Free Mason) affiliation. The relationship was cordial and close enough for Gade

After sailing his family from Kristiansund to Christiania, Tron started a new career—trading livestock—expanding his business to build a slaughterhouse. Later, he sold his holdings and started over as a carpenter. He soon became a master joiner and continued in this trade for the rest of his active life.

to be an honored guest at the wedding of Marie Theresa Fladvad in Boston, Massachusetts in 1895. Marie had left Christiania in 1895 for the United States. She married Charles Middleton Cottrell of Newport, R.I. the next year.

Margaret Cottrell, a first daughter, was born to Marie Fladvad and Charles Cottrell in 1900. Despite several previous pregnancies, Margaret was the first to survive. She never married.

By 1900, manufacturing accounted for over 28 percent of Norway's gross national product, and employed over a quarter of the country's work force.

Endre died at Flatvad in the spring of 1902. His widow, Ingrid, ran the farm until 1908, with the help of Lars Jørgensen Toske.

In that year the Boer War ended, China and Korea were recognized as independent nations, and the U.S. acquired the Panama Canal.

In 1903, Marie and Charlie Cottrell celebrated the birth of a second daughter, Eleanor Oline Cottrell, named for Marie's mother, Oline Bjørke. She would marry Kenneth Stevens Kaull of Newport, Rhode Island.

A third daughter, Marie Theresa Cottrell was born to Marie and Charlie Cottrell in 1905. She would marry William Mead Raymond, Jr. of Stamford, Connecticut.

In the spring of 1905, the Storting voted unanimously on a resolution that the union with Sweden under one King has ceased to exist..." After some blustery protestations, Sweden acceded, and Norway's throne was offered to Prince Carl of Denmark. The people voted overwhelmingly in favor of the monarchy, and the new king took the name Haakon VII and gave his young son the name Olav. Norway was once again a free and sovereign nation.

In 1907, aboard the SS Oscar II, Marie Fladvad Cottrell returned from her last trip home to Norway. Her mother's health was failing. It was the last time she would see her parents.

On the return trip, she and two of her sisters traveling with her, met Captain Roald Amundsen who had recently discovered the magnetic North Pole and transited the Northwest Passage. He was photographed with them and signed the photo.

In 1908, a fourth daughter was born to Marie Fladvad and Charlie Cottrell in 1908. Cecile Middleton Cottrell was the last child born to them. She would marry James Edward Irving of Darien, Connecticut.

Oline died in Oslo in 1908.

Elsewhere, the General Motors Corporation was founded, and Ford Motor Company produced the first Model "T" (15 million would be sold). Wilbur Wright flew thirty miles in 40 minutes.

Tron Fladvad died in Oslo in 1914.

Sources & Suggested Reading

Anderson, E. L. (1875). *Six Weeks in Norway*. Boston, Massachusetts: Author.

Castberg, Frede (1961). *The Nowegian Way of Life*. London: William Heinemann, Ltd.

Flom, George T. (1909, 1993). *A History of Norwegian Immigration to The United States*. Bowie, Maryland: Heritage Books.

Friis, Erik J. (Ed.)(1976). *The Scandinavian Presence in North America*. New York: Harper's Magazine Press.

Grun, Bernard (1963). *The Timetables of History*. New York: Simon and Schuster.

Libek, Ivar and Øivind Stenersen (1992). *History of Norway*. Oslo, Norway: Grøndahlog Dreyers Forlag AS.

Thorne-Thomsen (1963). *In Norway*. New York: The Viking Press.

Urdang, Laurence (Ed.) (1981. *The Timetables of American History*. New York: Simon and Schuster.

Wright, Esmond (Gen. Ed.)(1984). *History of the World: The Last Five Hundred Years*. London: The Hamlyn Publishing Group Limited.

THE LEAST MERRY CHRISTMAS IN NEWPORT

by
Tracy Daniel Connors
&
Faith Cottrell Raymond Connors

On a bleak December day in 1916, 65-year old Charles Middleton Cottrell sat on the second step of the staircase leading to the upper levels of the family's big Victorian home at 23 Catherine Street at the corner of Catherine and Fir Streets in Newport, Rhode Island. The three story house was built in 1825 by John Easton and had been the "cottage" of James Gordon Bennett.

Never a big man physically, Charlie Cottrell now looked smaller than ever as he sat hunched over, pained in body and soul, sobbing. He was an empty shell, a mirror image of his business, formerly a thriving partnership with his brother, Robert Clarke Cottrell. "The Cottrell Block," one of Newport's largest mercantile and undertaking establishments at 320-360 Thames Street, had been drastically reduced this year and moved to a bay-windowed store front at 20 Bellevue Avenue.

Charlie's daughter, Theresa, then about 11, later remembered this was the last time she ever saw her father—sitting on the staircase of his house—crying. His home now, not theirs.

Some years before, their next door neighbor, Clement C. Moore had penned the now immortal words of "*A Visit From St. Nicholas.*" Christmas was just days away, but this was to be the least "Merry Christmas," in the family's history.

Charlie's Norwegian-born wife of twenty two years, Marie, and his other three daughters, Margaret (16), Eleanor (13), and Cecile (8), were there too, standing in the foyer, their stricken faces framed in the large, floor-to-ceiling mirror which hangs to this day in the entrance hall. Marie still loved Charlie and felt pity for him. After all, he was in constant pain with rheumatoid arthritis.

The John Easton house at 23 Catherine Street in Newport, Rhode Island was the Charles Middleton Cottrell home from 1910 until 1916. The Cottrell family enjoyed its best times there--until his health failed. (Below right) The stairs where Charlie said goodbye to his family.

Charles Middleton Cottrell

MARIE'S DILEMMA

But at that moment, Marie's mind was reeling with the implications of the ultimatum Charlie and his older sister, Harriet Cottrell Simes-Nowell had just delivered to her. Charlie sobbed wretchedly into his elbow, never looking Marie in the eye, keeping his head on his crossed arms.

Hattie stood to one side, stiffly laced into her high-necked brocade dress over the whalebone corset, her ever present lorgnette hanging on a black ribbon nearly to her knees.

Harriet was Charlie's sister, the oldest living child, only daughter, and most domineering of Michael and Catherine Cottrell's five children. She had married George Symes of Plymouth, Massachusetts in 1875, with whom she had a daughter, Ethel. By 1881, she had divorced Symes and married Thomas S. Nowell, fifteen years her senior, a leather merchant from Portsmouth, New Hampshire.

During their courtship, Nowell at one point brought her five engagement rings from which to choose. She couldn't decide which of the beautiful rings to keep. Totally in character, she kept them all.

After they were married, she changed the spelling from "Symes" to "Simes" and hyphenated the names to become Mrs. Harriet

Harriet Cottrell Simes-Nowell. *Harriet was Charlie Cottrell's domineering sister, known to her nieces as the infamous "Aunt Hattie" and "her royal highness." (Barker Family Collection)*

Cottrell Simes-Nowell. Her daughter, Ethel, adopted the hyphenated name as well. When Thomas Nowell died in 1914, Harriet dropped the "Simes" from her name, while Ethel decided to retain her father's name in hers, but changed the spelling back to "Symes-Nowell."

From 1881 until 1914, Harriet had lived at 337 Commonwealth Avenue in Boston, Massachusetts. Charlie and Marie had been married in her living room in 1895 with the former Consul to Christiania, Gerhard Gade, an honored guest. However, Newport was not that far away by train or boat. She spent lengthy periods "in residence" in Newport.

[Mr. Gade's title was "Consul" instead of Ambassador because technically Norway still belonged to Sweden. In fact, from 1869

Marie Theresa Fladvad Cottrell. *When her husband's health failed leaving her on her own, Marie Cottrell's sister-in-law offered her and her four daughters a "home" in the basement and Marie a job--as the cook. Instead, Marie chose independence and self-sufficiency.*

until 1894, he was the de facto U.S. Ambassador to Norway, which would dissolve the "union" and regain her independent nation status in 1905. Norway's capital city, "Christiania," would be renamed "Oslo" in 1925 by The Storting.]

Thomas Nowell decided to put the better part of a continent between himself and his wife, leaving the leather business and moving into the mining business--in Alaska. There is no record of Harriet going to Alaska. At the time of Charlie's marriage to Marie, Nowell was serving as a Congressman from Alaska to the 53rd Congress, and had been a Commissioner to the World's Fair in Chicago in 1893. Although he died in 1914, he had made his home in Alaska long before his death. He died at the home of his son, in Seattle.

Meanwhile, Harriet, living in Boston, "was prominent in social and club circles," according to the *Newport Mercury*. [The *Newport Mercury* was founded in June 12, 1758 by James Franklin, Jr., nephew of Dr. Benjamin Franklin. It remains the oldest continuously published newspaper in the United States, still published as a weekly companion to the *Newport Daily News*. A subscription cost $2 per year.] After Nowell's death, she returned to Newport in about 1914 and moved into the family's Greek Revival home at 105 Pelham Street house with her daughter, Ethel. As the snapshot at lower right shows, she was still there in 1928.

Harriet was a member of Trinity Church, of St. Martha's Guild, and "managed the first rummage sale in this city, in the interest of the Galahad Club Camp. She was also a member of the Art Association, the Sunshine Society, Newport Historical Society, and the Newport County Woman's Republican Club." Hattie had moved into Newport society since her return five years before. It was all too apparent that she had taken control over Charlie's life as well.

Charlie was too sick, Hattie announced. He could not take care of Marie and the children anymore. He was ending his business career, but he was moving into rooms at the rear of 20 Bellevue Avenue, where he and Robert had relocated the business. (In 1919, Charlie would be moved to a sanitarium on Jamestown, just across Narragansett Bay from Newport on Conanicut Island.)

Ethel Simes-Nowell *(above left) and her mother, Harriet Cottrell Simes-Nowell. Hattie was present at the start of the Cottrell-Fladvad marriage, and she was there when it effectively ended some twenty-two years later. When he became ill, she would make Charlie choose between her and his wife, Marie. (Barker Family Collection)*

(Below) ***"At my dressing table,"*** *Hattie wrote on the back of this 1928 snapshot taken in her bedroom at 105 Pelham Street. (Barker Family Collection)*

"When I was at home with papa...he called me his doll-child, and he played with me just as I used to play with my dolls."
Nora Helmer, *"A Doll's House"*

Henrik Ibsen, *the internationally honored Norwegian playwrite and author, in 1898. The Fladvads were proud of him and were very familiar with his work. Marie had several photographs of him, including this one which she probably acquired during her 1897 visit to see her parents in Christiania. "Ibsen, like Wagner and Manet, has lived down his commentators," H. L. Mencken wrote, "and is now ready to be examined and enjoyed for what he actually was, namely, a first-rate journeyman dramatist, perhaps the best that ever lived." One of the "Ideas" Ibsen had, Mencken pointed out, was that it is "unpleasant and degrading for a wife to be treated as a mere mistress and empty-head."*

MARIE REJECTS "THE DOLL'S HOUSE"

Being a loving, not to mention resourceful woman, Marie tried to assure her husband of over twenty-two years that she would find a way to take care of him. After all, she had watched and assisted her father, Tron Fladvad, for many years. Through him and her mother, Oline, she had gained experience in timber sales, fishing, farming, and cattle. Her Norwegian family was old, land-owning, hardworking, and entrepreneurial. She could take his place in the business and turn things around.

Hunched over on the staircase, Charlie adamantly refused to listen, shaking his head on his sleeve. They had had this one-sided conversation before. Women, at least Cottrell women, could be educators or lead philanthropic organizations, but they simply didn't go into business. It wasn't right. People might think he was a failure...that he couldn't provide for his family. No, it was all settled, he mumbled into the stair carpet. He said no more.

Hattie's next announcement left Marie even more stunned, if that were possible, unable to breathe for many endless seconds. They were putting the house up for rent. Dr. Samuel Parker Cottrell, Marie's brother-in-law, who had moved to Catherine Street to help Charlie cope with arthritis, now planned to move his office and residence to 59 Bellevue Avenue. Marie and "her" daughters, she said icily, could move into the house at 105 Pelham Street--the same house Marie and Charlie had lived in when they were first married 22 years before. This time however, their rooms would be in the basement.

In addition, Hattie explained, Marie, who was known for her delicious Norwegian cookies and cakes, and for her skills as a hostess, could become the cook for the Simes-Nowells and "earn her keep" at the kitchen stove. "After all," Hattie explained in what she thought was a compliment, "you are an excellent cook, even if you speak the English language very poorly."

Involuntarily, Marie started to reach for the balustrade to steady herself, but then, totally in character, drew herself up to her full

The Grand Hotel *in Oslo, Norway, 1993. Ibsen was often seen in the Grand Cafe after his return to Christiania in 1891. Occasionally, Marie and her friends would see him there when they went in for* **frokost.** *Of course, they saw his plays when they were presented at the nearby National Theater. The Grand Cafe is still serving delicious meals to the crowds thronging Karl Johan. The entrance to the* **Storting***, Norway's parliament, is seen at right.*

height, head back, chin up and said--absolutely nothing. Inwardly however, furious, icy winds in her head were roaring in circles, tumbling the words "basement," and "cook" around and around. They began to sound more like a sentence, than a compliment. She was shivering not from the cold, drafty hall, but from the sudden absence of warmth from her husband's heart.

Nora's tortured revelation to her chauvinistic husband in Henrik Ibsen's *"A Doll's House,"* provides an eery parallel and important comparison between a Norwegian dramatic heroine, and a real Norwegian woman of the early Twentieth century facing a similar crossroads in her life.

Marie had seen the world renowned drama many times at the National Theater when she lived in Christiania, Norway. She

went there often with her younger sister, Olise. Ibsen appeared nearly every day at the Cafe of the Grand Hotel in downtown Oslo, just four blocks from their house on Holbergsgate. They had often seen him there.

Ibsen revealed the emptiness and tragedy in the lives of a comfortable, if ordinary family--Torvald Helmer, his wife Nora, and their three little children. Torvald sees himself as ethical, and the upholder of family position and pride. Nora has assumed the role of a dutiful, flighty, even irresponsible wife in order to flatter and please him. To help Torvald regain his health and to save his life, Nora acquires a loan by forging a signature. She makes the payments by copying documents at home. However, when the forgery--fraud--is exposed, Torvald is outraged and berates

The **Cottrell's Catherine Street** home as it looked when Marie left it in 1917 for the last time. They enjoyed six happy years in its spacious Victorian rooms. However, Charlie Cottrell's health was deteriorating and over the years their differences had not been resolved, only temporarily repressed.

her out of concern for his own social reputation.

Utterly devastated and seeing the "real" Torvald, a shallow, empty hypocrite, Nora declares her independence of him and their children. She leaves to start her own life and to find own own way in the world.

Christiania audiences were outraged and scandalized by Ibsen's refusal to cobble together a "happy ending." Marie, when she thought about it, was probably glad he had resisted. After all, A Doll's House was all about knowing oneself and being true to that self.

"I was simply transferred from papa's hands into yours," Nora cries with tragic understanding. "You and papa have committed a great sin against me. It is your fault that I have made nothing of my life."

"Our home has been nothing but a play room," Nora continued. "I have been your doll-wife, just as at home I was papa's doll-child; and here the children have been my dolls."

"It was then it dawned upon me that for eight years I had been living here with a strange man, and had borne him three children—. Oh, I can't bear to think of it! I could tear myself into little bits!"

Her head spinning, Marie looked at her

"The Cottrell Girls" as they looked when they moved to Catherine Street. Left rear, Eleanor and Margaret, front, Cecile and Theresa.

Ø

precious daughters. Their tear-filled eyes were riveted on hers. These were not "dolls." These were her flesh and blood. She had suffered a great deal and lost many other children to bring these beautiful girls into the world.

Marie was even worse off than Ibsen's Nora. She had been Charlie's wife for twenty-two years. They had had four children together that had lived. Others had not survived, including twin boys. Now, horrified, she realized with icy immediacy that she did not know this side of Charles Cottrell at all--an exhausted, beaten shell of the man she married.

She had admired his intellect and his gentleness. He spent hours reading and thinking. His friends and family called him "a dreamer," but it was to Charles that they turned when Robert's son, Edwin Cottrell needed help with his studies. He was not a particularly good student, but with "Uncle Charlie's" tutoring,

Edwin's scholarship improved dramatically. [He went on to become a Professor at Stanford University and the Mayor of Palo Alto, California.]

But now, a sick, broken man, Charlie was not his former self. With the pressures in his life suffocating him, he was close to panic and total exhaustion. He was no longer the man Marie had married.

Ibsen made a harsh, and even selfish decision for Nora—she left her husband and her children. "There is another task I must undertake first, I must try and educate myself—you are not the man to help me in that. I must do that for myself. And that is why I am going to leave you now."

Marie was no Nora. She had never been Tron's "doll child." There was not a selfish bone in her body. She knew what she had to do. Marie was a doer, not a talker.

When at last she could speak, she told Charlie

59 Bellevue Avenue. *When Marie set out from 23 Catherine Street, she was heading for this house (left) at 59 Bellevue Avenue on the corner of Mill Street. In this 1905 view, we see a woman (at right) walking her dog past the home of Mary H. Tompkins. When Mrs. Tompkins died in the mid-1930s, she bequeathed the property to the Redwood Library. Her house was torn down, the property landscaped, and Abraham Redwood's "summer House" was moved to the rear of the lot. The Redwood's fence was extended around the Tompkins property at that time. Marie Cottrell later bought her home from Mary Tompkins, who was then living in New York. In the background, near the intersection of Bellevue Avenue and Redwood Street, a man on horseback stops to talk to a neighbor in a carriage drawn by a white horse. (From the Collection of the Newport Historical Society)*

Newport, Rhode Island. In this 1890's postcard view we are looking North towards Washington Square. The Cottrell store is seen at right, a Sailor passing in front of the raised awnings. Newport was enjoying an economic boom. Jobs were plentiful. The population was soaring. Yet, even now, "an occasional cow wandered into the downtown city streets." The building of the "mansions" was well underway. Newport's population was 20,000 and the shops on Thames Street had begun installing newer, wider, plate glass windows. (Barker Family Collection)

Newport's Thames Street
as it looked when Marie Fladvad arrived in Newport.

This photograph of the same general period was taken from almost the exact location as the postcard view above. The Cottrell store with its large awnings raised in good weather is seen at right next to the Western Union telegraph office and just steps away from the U.S. Customs House with its flags painting the breeze. Carriages line the streets, their horses waiting patiently for shoppers. A boy in knickers races by the store, while a man in a dark frock coat follows behind. Chairs and furniture spill out of the store onto the sidewalk. The advertising on the Cottrell storefront has changed however. In the postcard view above, "Carpets and Rugs" are featured. In the photograph below, "Mattresses and Feathers" share the billing. (From the Collection of the Newport Historical Society)

firmly, with her lilting Scandinavian accent, that she did not know what she would do or where she would go, but it was certainly NOT into the Pelham Street basement. Yes, she would continue to make those delicious meals and Norwegian baked goods, but from now on it was for her daughters—and no one else, unless they were her guests or paid for the privilege.

Taking the by now nearly hysterical girls in hand, Marie buttoned her coat, opened the door, and told them, "We are leaving now." In Norwegian, she reminded the girls, to watch their step on the icy street. The three oldest

Marie Theresa Fladvad was passing by the Cottrell dry goods store on Thames Street when Charles Middleton Cottrell looked out and saw her. Turning to his brother, he announced, "Robert, I am going to get married."

The Cottrell Block. *In 1894, when Marie first met Charlie, the Cottrell store occupied an entire block on Newport's well-known Thames Street (above). It was a large brick building at Numbers 320 to 330, known to local residents as "The Cottrell Block." (Today the site is occupied by the Newport Post Office.) In this late 1890s photograph we see Charlie (left) and Robert Cottrell (right) in suits and ties in front of their flourishing business. The store offered customers a wide variety of products and services, from furniture and wallpaper to undertaking and embalming. High windows and three sets of glass doors were framed by large, scalloped awnings which could be let down on hot summer days to provide cooling shade. The center door served as the main entrance. Nine or ten wicker chairs and sofas were lined up outside on the sidewalk to display some of the furniture for sale inside. Several of the chairs had animal pelts thrown over the back, including bear, leopard, and sheep skins. In those days, coffins were usually made of fine hard woods by local craftsmen. When the "box" was completed it was lined with expensive cloth. Therefore, it was not unusual for a furniture store to also provide mortuary services--building the coffin to order and providing horses and carriages for the funeral party.*

Newport Harbor *as it looked when Marie Fladvad arrived from Norway. At far left is the spire and clock tower of Trinity Church. Located in Newport's Queen Anne Square, Trinity Church is the most prominent landmark on Newport's skyline. (From the Collection of the Newport Historical Society)*

girls had known Norwegian before they could speak English. Holding hands together, they set off down Catherine Street towards Newport and Bellevue Avenue, the girls' stiff hair ribbons bending forward in the icy breeze.

Marie was now on her own. It was frightening, but exhilarating to be able to make her own decisions. No longer would she have to defer to her husband. From now on she would be known in Newport as Mrs. Marie T. Cottrell. She had gotten back far more than her name.

CHARLIE MEETS MARIE

Charles Middleton Cottrell was 43-years old in 1894, the eldest living son of Michael and Catherine Cottrell. He owned the store at 320-330 Thames Street in partnership with his brother, Robert Clarke Cottrell. They had inherited it from their father, Michael. As an 1880 graduate of the Cincinnati School of Embalming, Robert handled the embalming and undertaking duties. Charles, with prior

experience at Boston's Jordan, Marsh & Company and other "dry-goods" stores, handled the department store side of the business.

"Charlie," as he was called by friends and family, was better known as a "dreamer," than as an aggressive businessman. However, he must have thought he really was dreaming one day in 1894 when a beautiful young woman walked by. She was on her way to Minnesota for a visit, but had stopped in Newport to visit a teacher friend. She never made it to Minnesota.

"I was a bachelor nearly fifty years old [he was actually 43[, and planning to stay single," Charlie would later explain to friends. "One day I looked out of my store and saw the most beautiful young woman walking by. I turned to my brother at that moment and said, 'Robert, I am going to get married!'"

Charlie Cottrell had just spotted Marie Theresa Fladvad, a visitor from Christiania (Oslo), Norway. She was 32, unmarried, and about to meet her future husband.

[Another, less "romantic" version of how they met is through Eleanor Mack, from Boston's Beacon Hill, who Marie had met on the boat enroute to the United States. Perhaps Mack also knew Harriet Cottrell who also lived in Boston at that time.]

In light of future events, it is significant

Charlie (above) was in partnership with his brother, Robert (below) and doing business as C.M. & R.C. Cottrell. In 1894, Charlie was an aging, bachelor uncle watching Robert's children grow up. "A couple of handsome Irishmen," chuckled Samuel Barker, Robert's grandson years later.

"Purgatory," a cleft rock formation in Middletown, RI near the present Norman Bird Sanctuary, was a favorite haunt of picnicing Newporters. When he was a boy during the Civil War period, Charles Middleton Cottrell used to climb down into Purgatory to collect birds' eggs. In 1949, this story was related to ten-year old Faith Cottrell Raymond by her cousin, Louise Cottrell. Louise also related a Narragansett Indian tale about an Indian "Princess" who had two suitors. The one that truly loved her would leap across Purgatory. Both attempted the leap. Unfortunately, the one she truly loved fell to his death. The other young man, although he completed the leap successfully, decided that he did not want to marry her after all. Young Faith, was fascinated by these tales. So much so, that Sarah Cottrell Ackerman's husband, Alexander ("Lex"), thoughtfully took this picture for her album.

James Cottrell arrived in Boston in 1823 from Middleton, Ireland (near Cork). He was a college graduate and linguist, speaking several different languages, conversing fluently in English, Latin and Greek. James and his wife, Honora Mountain of Kilmartin, Ireland lived in this house on Newport's John Street. James helped supervise construction of the Fort Adams fortifications.

that after being a bachelor for 43 years, Charlie decided to get married the year after his mother, Catherine died, and just two years after his father, Michael had died. Charlie had lived with his parents for much of his life in their home at 79 Thames Street.

NEWPORT MERCHANT

Charlie Cottrell had been born and educated in Newport. The year following the end of the Civil War, in 1866, at the age of fifteen he moved to Boston for five years where he worked at Jordan, Marsh & Company. Later, he joined Jacob Fullarton & Company of Boston and "engaged in the tea, coffee and spice business." In 1874, when he was 23-years old, Charlie returned to Newport to work for his father in the "furniture store." In 1875, he was off to New York City where he worked in the "wholesale department of A.T. Stewart & Company's Store."

In the 1880's, Charlie returned to Newport and rejoined his father in the business on Thames Street. Charlie's father, Michael, died in 1893, and his mother, Catherine, followed him down "Farewell Street" to Newport's Island Cemetery the following year.

Charlie was now in partnership with his brother, Robert and doing business as C.M. &

R.C. Cottrell. They were appointed trustees of their father's estate. Charlie also served as treasurer of the City Steam Laundry Company, which he had helped found and incorporate. Charlie was a member of the Coronet Council, Number 63, Royal Arcanum, a member of the Trinity Episcopal Church, and "in political faith, he adhered to the principles of the Republican Party."

In 1894, Charlie was an aging, bachelor uncle watching Robert's children Edwin (14), Harriet (10), Sarah (9), Catherine (5), Samuel (1) grow up. Robert's wife, Annie Johnson Southwick would give birth to Annie Louise, the following year.

After 71 years in America, the Cottrell family was settled in a comfortable, if not boring niche in Newport business and society. They had worked hard to leave their immigrant status behind. They were proud of their efforts over half a century to build Newport and to become accepted into its mainstream. However, Charlie the Dreamer was about to shake up the family hierarchy. Charlie was about to marry, not a young lady from an established Newport or New England family, but a Norwegian immigrant just "off the boat" from Christiania.

THE COTTRELLS ARRIVE IN NEWPORT

James Cottrell, Charlie's grandfather, had arrived in Boston in 1823 from Midleton, Ireland (near Cork). He was 21, "the son of well-to-do parents, and a descendant of one of England's substantial and influential families." Genealogical Records and Historical Sketches of Prominent and Representative Citizens of the Old Families of Rhode Island reported that James "was given an excellent educational training, being a college graduate. He was a linguist, speaking several different languages, conversing fluently in English, Latin and Greek."

James Cottrell married Honora Mountain of Kilmartin, Ireland "whose father and grandfather were large land owners of their native land." Traveling with his valet, he arrived in Boston, then moved to Newport where he "accepted a position at Fort Adams, working on the construction of the fortifications." Honora followed with six-months old

Michael soon after.

For years he was a prominent and active member of St. Mary's Roman Catholic Church, where he served as the church's clerk. [Later, St. Mary's would be the church in which Jacqueline Bouvier and John F. Kennedy were married.] James taught the parishioners Gaelic. He would be remembered for "instructing those less fortunate than he, and he was the first in Newport to teach night school." He could be "somewhat arrogant in his make-up," but he was also "courteous and kindly, and as a result had hosts of friends." When he died in 1860, his funeral was one of the "largest of his day."

After a "short and painful illness," the Newport Mercury reported on June 16, 1860, "Mr.

James Cottrell, [died] in the 68th year of his age. Mr. Cottrell was a native of County Cork, Ireland; he emigrated to this country in 1827 [family records say 1823], and was one of our oldest sons of adoption--making Newport his home, where he has left a large family circle and numerous friends to mourn his loss."

James and Honora Mountain Cottrell are buried in Newport's Irish-Catholic Cemetery on Warner Street.

SHIPPING OUT
ON THE AUDLEY CLARKE

After a public school education, Michael Cottrell apprenticed himself to a cabinet maker. In 1849, together with many other Newport men, Michael "got the gold fever."

During the "excitement incidental to the discovery of gold in California," he became interested in the voyage of the ship "Audley Clarke." On February 15, 1849, together with many other young men from the town, Michael shipped out from Newport to California aboard the bark.

The officers of the ship were a well-known group of Newporters, including: William A. Coggeshall, president; Aaron F. Dyer, treasurer; George W. Langley, secretary; and, William A. Coggeshall, George Vaughan, Isaiah Crooker, Charles Cozzens, Levi Johnson, Ayrault W. Dennis, James H. Demarest, directors. Ayrault Dennis served as captain. He was

backed up by Charles Cozzens, first mate, and George B. Slocum, second mate.

The group was given a big send off. George Taylor, organist of Trinity Church collaborated with Edward Moore to write an appropriate song for the occasion to which they gave a lumbering title: "*Sail On, Thou Gallant Bark, or the Departure of the Californians.*"

The lyrics were written by "Edward Moore, M.A., Esq. of the Classical School for Boys, Newport." Great lyrics they were not; however, despite their unachieved aspirations for lofty verbal heights, they do offer a glimpse of the dreams shared by the men of the Audley Clarke.

"Sail on, sail on, thou gallant bark, God speed thee o'er the wave. When tempest rage and nights are dark, May he be nigh save. For 'tis no poor or worthless freight, That thou art call'd to bear. No gorgeous silks or robes of state. No glit'ring toys are there.

"But oh! more valued far than these, than gems of price untold. Thou bearest o'er the stormy seas, Stout hearts, and spirits bold. High hopes are there and visions bright, Of wealth in distant climes. Of glad return and friends' delight, and happy future times.

"More precious still, there hover near, And all their perils share, The mother's sigh, the fond wife's tear, The loving maiden's prayer. May God then guide thee o'er the main, Wherever thou may'st roam.

Michael Cottrell. *The son of James Cottrell, Michael was brought to Newport as an infant by his mother Honora Mountain Cottrell. Tiring of his trade as a cabinet maker, in 1849 he got "gold fever" and shipped out on the Audley Clarke, around the Horn to 'Frisco Bay. He returned in 1850 to open a store on Newport's Thames Street. Michael was a better businessman than gold miner and the business "met with marked success, due to his energy and untiring industry."*

Until thou bring thy freight again, To happiness and home."

Mr. Taylor wrote the music. He had been trained in Liverpool, and it was pointed out, had "been last to play the Berkeley organ."

RETURN TO NEWPORT: BUSINESS ON THAMES STREET

By 1850, Michael had returned to Newport, "not satisfied with the conditions that surrounded him in that far Western region."

Together with Stafford Bryer, Michael apprenticed under David M. Coggeshall, then a cabinet maker. In 1850, he and Bryer became partners and opened an establishment on the corner of Division and Church

Streets. "Cottrell and Bryer...engaged in the furniture and undertaking business."

"Cottrell & Bryer, dealers in furniture, feathers, mattresses, looking-glasses, etc.," noted their advertisement in the Newport City Directory. "Ready-made coffins of all sizes in rosewood, walnut, and mahogany, constantly on hand. 37 Church Street." The city directory noted that Michael Cottrell lived at 13 John Street.

The Cottrell-Bryer partnership lasted until 1869, when it was dissolved and Michael opened his own business on Thames Street. He stayed in the Free Library building until

Catherine E. Wallace Cottrell *(below). The Notman Photographic Company of Newport, Rhode Island created this formal pose. Wife of Michael Cottrell, she was born and raised in Augusta, Maine and Fall River, Massachusetts, and was descended from a noble family. Her great grandparents were Thomas Wallace and Lady Catherine Butler, who was the sister of the Duke of Ormond.*

1872, when he bought a large brick building at Numbers 320 to 330 Thames Street. It would be the home of the Cottrell family business for the next 45 years.

Michael also provided undertaking services to merchant seamen. "A Washington dispatch," the Newport Mercury reported on July 7, 1883, "says that the Surgeon General has made arrangements for the care of sick and disabled seamen at the various marine hospitals in New England. In Newport, the Newport Hospital medical attendance is to be furnished by an acting assistant surgeon, the Newport Hospital to furnish quarters, subsistence, nursing and medicines at 95 cents per day. Michael Cottrell to provide for the burial of deceased patients at $11.50 each."

Michael was a good businessman. His business career "met with marked success, due to his energy and untiring industry, coupled with natural business ability and foresight. He was a genial, courteous gentleman, possess-

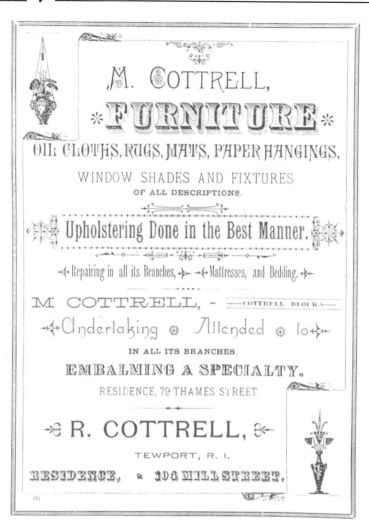

An advertisement from a Newport City Directory (above) *of the late 1880s notes that "M. Cottrell" sold furniture, oil cloths, rugs, mats, paper hangings, window shades and fixtures of all descriptions. EMBALMING A SPECIALTY" the bold faced ad emphasized. Note the typographical error in "Tewport."*

ing an unassuming manner, all of which made him many staunch friends."

MICHAEL AND CATHERINE

About 1760, Thomas Wallace married Catherine Butler, sister of the Duke of Ormond. The Butler family, according to Burke's peerage, moved to Ireland with Henry II, husband of Eleanor of Aquataine. The head of the family was made chief butler to the king, hence the name "butler." He built Kilkenny Castle, owned by the Butler family ever since.

Richard Wallace, a son of Thomas and Catherine Butler Wallace, married Ellen

From the late 1880s, the Robert Clarke Cottrell family lived at 104 Mill Street, one of the very few brick colonial houses in Newport. It was built about 1758 by Benjamin Reynolds, a Jamestown ferryman. Other owners included Samuel Mumford, 1784, Robert Brattle, 1797, William Ellery, 1800. It was restored by George Mason between 1858-1860, and then purchased by Charles Hammett in 1867.

Michael Cottrell. *Newport residents read the sad report by the Newport Mercury on August 23, 1893, that "Mr. Michael Cottrell died at his residence, on Thames Street [79 Thames] at 12:30 p.m. yesterday, after an illness of much longer standing than his friends and even his family thought, for he bore his suffering, of fully a year, with remarkable fortitude and without complaining, lest he give pain to those about him."*

Gorman. Their son, Patrick Wallace, married Margaret Cahill. Following the birth of their daughter, Eleanor, they emigrated from Ireland to America about 1830. From 1830 to 1860, they made their home in Augusta, Maine, where daughters Catherine and Margaret were born. Then they moved to Fall River, Massachusetts, where they remained until his death.

Eleanor Wallace married Patrick Collins, "about whom no record is at hand," family records state with cold efficiency. As for Eleanor, they record she was "a faithful Catholic, lovable and efficient. She supported herself and her children by conducting a high class employment agency on Charles Street in Boston. Eleanor Collins had only one daughter, also named Eleanor (but always called "Millie"). She "was attractive and popular with her Newport cousins, whom she frequently visited." The Newport and Fall River Street Railway trolley made the trip from Fall River to Newport in about 90 minutes.

Millie married Will Cashman, "a bright Irish gentleman, much interested in Boston politics." She died "in middle life leaving three children"--Mildred Collins, Eleanor Collins, and William Collins.

Catherine, Patrick and Margaret's other daughter, was born March 20, 1825 and died February 8, 1894. She was a "woman of strong character and decided ideals, who sway those about her for good."

Catherine Wallace Cottrell was a "woman of strong character and decided ideals, who sway those about her for good," reported her contemporaries. "Aunt Kate," as she was called by relatives, "never hesitated to administer correction to her own and her sister's children when they needed it."

Catherine married Michael Cottrell, "who conducted a furniture and undertaking business in Newport on the site of the present Post Office. She left the Catholic Church and influenced her husband to do so as well," according to the records.

Catherine and Michael would have six children, including: James Wallace Cottrell, who lived from May 13, 1846 through September 21, 1847; Harriet Cottrell, born September 15, 1848; Charles Middleton Cottrell, born September 19, 1851; Robert Clarke Cottrell, born September 24, 1853; Samuel Parker Cottrell, born July 25, 1860; and, William Wallace Cottrell; born July 26, 1862 and died February 18, 1889, of tuberculosis in Newport at the age of 24.

Undoubtedly, William's disease was not helped by the fact that he smoked. His silver

(Above) ***Antique postcard view*** *of Newport's* ***Trinity Church.*** *The Cottrell family joined Trinity at Catherine's urging. Years later, after attending Sunday School the Cottrell girls would go over to Robert Cottrell's home on Frances Street to "read the funny papers." Robert, a business partner with their father, Charles, was Mayor of Newport in 1906.*

helped by the fact that he smoked. His silver cigarette case engraved with "WWC," was later given by his niece, Marie Theresa Cottrell Raymond, to her son, Lieutenant William M. Raymond III.

As Michael, assisted by Charlie, continued to expand his business, elsewhere in early 1890s, Henrik Ibsen had just published "*Hedda Gabler*." Idaho and Wyoming had joined the Union. In Baltimore, rubber gloves had been used for the first time during surgery at Johns Hopkins Hospital. Global influenza epidemics ravaged countries around the world. And, the first entirely steel-framed building was erected in Chicago. The pace of change was picking up throughout the world, changes that were

Harriet Cottrell with her father, Michael. The initials NAVA indicate that he is wearing his uniform as a member of the Newport Artillery. The Newport Artillery Company was chartered in 1741 by George II. It is the oldest military unit in America operating under its original charter.

Patrick Wallace. According to information provided by the family, Patrick Wallace (above) remained "a gentleman of the old school, wearing little curls in front of his ears, and arriving at the station an hour before train time. Many of his descendants," the family notes point out, "also have a dread of being late." Patrick Wallace was not "a penniless immigrant, but received remittances from his grandmother, Lady Catherine Butler, as long as she lived. In addition, he owned land in Augusta, Maine as shown by a deed in his daughter Catherine's possession."

echoed in Newport.

In 1893, living in Christiania with her father, Tron and mother, Oline, Marie Fladvad read that Hawaii had proclaimed itself a Republic, Dvorak performed the Symphony from the New World, and Fridtjof Nansen had begun his unsuccessful expedition to the North Pole. Until recently, she had heard or read little about Newport, Rhode Island. Now she was corresponding with a friend who lived there and had invited Marie to visit Newport before going on to Minnesota.

Although in ill health for over year before his death, Michael "was confined to his home though only a fortnight, gradually growing worse till he sank into a condition of unconsciousness during which death came." He left his widow, Catherine Wallace Cottrell,

This Oslo street of the late 19th century has been completely restored and reconstructed by the Norsk Folkemuseum. The houses and shops are used by artisans and craftsmen in the **Gamlebyen**, or Old Town. Marie Fladvad would find this "gate" a familiar scene, looking much the same as when she left Oslo in 1894.

and four children, including: ex-Alderman Robert C. Cottrell, Charles M. Cottrell, Dr. Samuel Parker Cottrell, and Mrs. Thomas Nowell ["Hattie"] of Boston. His brother John, and a half brother, Representative James B. Cottrell, also survived him.

Michael was often asked to run for public office, but never did so. However, he did serve as "asylum commissioner, for which a beneficent and sympathetic nature peculiarly fitted him."

He was a member of the Newport Artillery, "when it gallantly went to the defence of the state's honor in the time of the Dorr revolution." He was a member of numerous business and civic organizations, and a director of the Union National Bank.

The Mercury concluded Michael Cottrell's obituary by noting that his "life was marked by sterling integrity and his death is a loss to the business community. The first tendencies of his nature were toward kindness and frankness, the chief qualities of a man."

MARIE FLADVAD ARRIVES IN NEWPORT

In Christiania, Marie Fladvad was preparing to leave Norway. She had broken off her engagement to a doctor. Later, she would explain to her daughters that he had told her an "untruth." Family records suggest she had planned to visit California and perhaps open a stitchery school.

The newspapers in Christiania were reporting the arrest of French army Captain Alfred Dreyfus on charges of treason. He

Charles Middleton Cottrell *and **Marie Theresa Fladvad** at the time they were married in 1895. Their wedding took place in his sister's Boston home. The former U.S. Consul to Christiania, Gerhard Gade, was an honored guest.*

would be convicted, and deported to Devil's Island. In New York, Thomas Edison opened a Kinetoscope Parlor. Marie was probably more interested in the news that composer Jean Sibelius had performed "*Finlandia*." She loved music and knew many major operatic works by heart.

In Newport, the Mercury reported that "golf has put in an appearance at Jamestown. A very interesting game was played at the Dumplings on Tuesday by Newport and Jamestown players."

"Steamers Conanicut and Anawan came into collision while off Rose Island Saturday morning (August 4, 1894) The damage was slight," the Mercury reported.

As usual, Newport was a very busy little city. The New York Yacht Club began its fiftieth annual cruise in August. "Reports of saluting guns echoed throughout downtown

*"**Cliff Walk, near Bailey's Beach**, Most Beautiful Walk in the World, Newport, R.I." proclaims this 1909 postcard. Marie Fladvad Cottrell would fix a picnic basket on Sunday afternoon and the family would make the scenic walk between the rocky shore and the mansions of Newport millionaires.*

This antique post card explains that these are the residences of E.D. Morgan and boat landing of Commodore James. Scenes from Newport's **Gilded Age**.

Newport announcing that the yachts were arriving in the harbor."

The Newport Yacht Club held its first "Ladies Night" at its headquarters "and a very enjoyable affair it proved," the Mercury reported. "Tasteful decorations, fireworks, music and refreshments were features of the evening's entertainment."

Just north of Newport on Aquidneck Island, in Middletown, the soil was rich and in good weather years, could produce bumper crops of vegetables. In 1894, for example, the Mercury pointed out, "Mr. Benjamin T. Brown of Middletown planted three acres of potatoes this year on which the yield has averaged from 60-80 barrels to the acre. Some of the potatoes have weighed 19 ounces each."

In 1894, the first class Newport-to-New York fare via the Fall River Line had been reduced from $3 to $2. The overnight trip with luxurious accommodations on a magnificent steamboat such as the Priscilla or the Commonwealth, completed Marie's journey in time from the provincial capital of Christiania, into Newport's **Gilded Age**.

The term was taken from the title of a novel written by Mark Twain and Charles Warner in 1873 which satirized the excesses of the time. At this time Newport was the hot weather destination of the wealthy. When the Astors, the Vanderbilts, the Belmonts, and other wealthy families of the period began spending their summers in Newport, they brought with them money, friends, and battles for social standing.

Newport fairly crackled with sights, sounds, and smells when Marie stepped off the steamboat. Newport's smells included the fragrances of hawthorne and honeysuckle, whose delicious fragrances were countered by horse droppings and cesspools. The sounds included the whistle of the Fall River steamers, the Jamestown ferryboat, and the bells of warning buoys at the harbor entrance. The sights included Colonial homes, the hustle of a lively port and wharf, and the bustle of merchants and servants to meet the needs of those living in the mansions along Bellevue Avenue.

Ida Lewis, the legendary lighthouse keeper who saved at least 18 people from watery deaths at the entrance to Newport Harbor, was still living at the Lime Rock lighthouse. By act of Congress in 1872, Ida Lewis was not only the sole officially appointed female Keeper in the Lighthouse Service, but she was the highest paid Keeper

Marie was delighted to move to the **"Top of the Hill"** and into 105 Pelham Street in 1900. Touro Park, one of the highest points in Newport, was just across the street. Next door at 115 Pelham was the Swinburne House, an 18th century Greek Revival with rusticated corners and ionic columns supporting the portico. Best of all the neighborhood was much quieter than busy Thames Street.

Touro Park is the home of the mysterious Stone Tower (below), which many believed was built by Viking explorers in the 11th century. Current theory attributes the tower, whose arches face the basic points of the compass, to Rhode Island Colonial Governor Benedict Arnold, who owned most of this land at the time. On a vacation to Newport in 1949, Margaret Cottrell sent this postcard to her sister, Marie Theresa ("Petie"). "Having a wonderful time. They're digging around the old mill, trying to find out who built it." The stone tower stands across the street from both 105 Pelham Street and 108 Mill Street, houses in which the Cottrells lived for many years, most of Margaret's childhood.

The Old Stone Mill, Newport, R. I. Ancient Viking Tower

Margaret Cottrell was born May 1, 1900 to Charlie and Marie. *Margaret was born after her mother had suffered numerous miscarriages, a condition then known as "uterine exhaustion."*

Marie might have considered taking a medication which the Mercury was touting as a cure to "remove tumor and cure other female weakness...another case of womb, kidney and bladder trouble cured by Lydia E. Pinkham's Vegetable Compound."

Perhaps her miscarriages made the emotional climate more volitile, but it was already clear that their vastly different backgrounds would not be easily overcome.

Of course, there was the obvious fact that she was Norwegian and he was Irish-American. The language differences were to be a sore point throughout their marriage. Later, when her sisters would visit, Charlie would complain if they talked for too long in Norwegian. "Stop talking about me," he would say, sharply. Most of the time he was right, they were talking about him.

Perhaps of even more importance in the long run was Marie's much greater background in business. Despite the fact that he seemed to be the businessman in the family, the truth was he preferred to read and think,

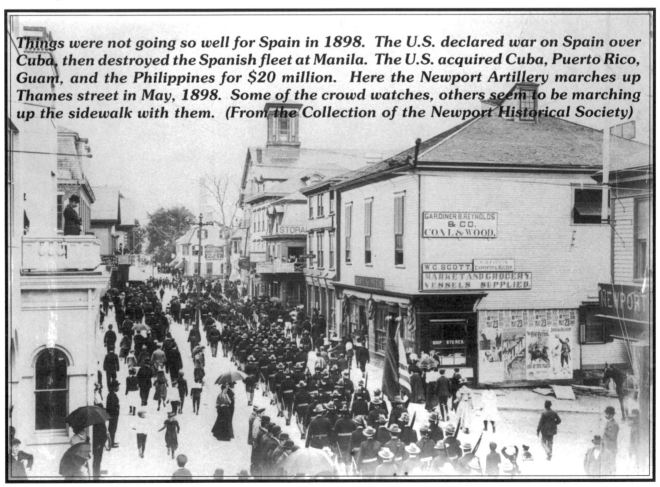

Things were not going so well for Spain in 1898. The U.S. declared war on Spain over Cuba, then destroyed the Spanish fleet at Manila. The U.S. acquired Cuba, Puerto Rico, Guam, and the Philippines for $20 million. Here the Newport Artillery marches up Thames street in May, 1898. Some of the crowd watches, others seem to be marching up the sidewalk with them. (From the Collection of the Newport Historical Society)

Marie was delighted to move to the **"Top of the Hill"** and into 105 Pelham Street in 1900. Touro Park, one of the highest points in Newport, was just across the street. Next door at 115 Pelham was the Swinburne House, an 18th century Greek Revival with rusticated corners and ionic columns supporting the portico. Best of all the neighborhood was much quieter than busy Thames Street.

Touro Park is the home of the mysterious Stone Tower (below), which many believed was built by Viking explorers in the 11th century. Current theory attributes the tower, whose arches face the basic points of the compass, to Rhode Island Colonial Governor Benedict Arnold, who owned most of this land at the time. On a vacation to Newport in 1949, Margaret Cottrell sent this postcard to her sister, Marie Theresa ("Petie"). "Having a wonderful time. They're digging around the old mill, trying to find out who built it." The stone tower stands across the street from both 105 Pelham Street and 108 Mill Street, houses in which the Cottrells lived for many years, most of Margaret's childhood.

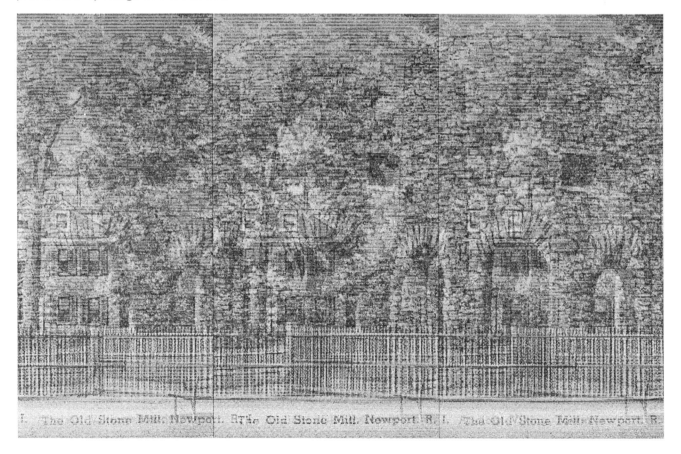

Margaret Cottrell was born May 1, 1900 to Charlie and Marie. *Margaret was born after her mother had suffered numerous miscarriages, a condition then known as "uterine exhaustion."*

Marie might have considered taking a medication which the Mercury was touting as a cure to "remove tumor and cure other female weakness...another case of womb, kidney and bladder trouble cured by Lydia E. Pinkham's Vegetable Compound."

Perhaps her miscarriages made the emotional climate more volitile, but it was already clear that their vastly different backgrounds would not be easily overcome.

Of course, there was the obvious fact that she was Norwegian and he was Irish-American. The language differences were to be a sore point throughout their marriage. Later, when her sisters would visit, Charlie would complain if they talked for too long in Norwegian. "Stop talking about me," he would say, sharply. Most of the time he was right, they were talking about him.

Perhaps of even more importance in the long run was Marie's much greater background in business. Despite the fact that he seemed to be the businessman in the family, the truth was he preferred to read and think,

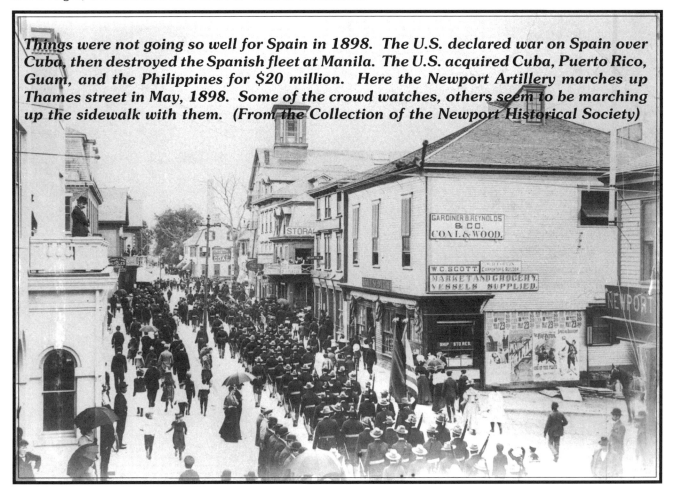

Things were not going so well for Spain in 1898. The U.S. declared war on Spain over Cuba, then destroyed the Spanish fleet at Manila. The U.S. acquired Cuba, Puerto Rico, Guam, and the Philippines for $20 million. Here the Newport Artillery marches up Thames street in May, 1898. Some of the crowd watches, others seem to be marching up the sidewalk with them. (From the Collection of the Newport Historical Society)

rather than to stay involved in the details of business. The family referred to Charlie as the "dreamer."

Marie had been born in Kolvereid, Norway, a seaport and timber town about 200 kilometers north of Trondheim on Norway's west coast. There, and later in Kristiansund and in Christiania, she had helped her father, Tron Fladvad, in his many entrepreneurial activities.

At various times, Tron was engaged in timber, fishing, farming, cattle, and cabinet making. His fortunes followed those of the country as a whole. Often he would do quite well. At other times, when the economy was bad, he would have to sell his holdings

Margaret Cottrell. *Marie was dismayed when the Cottrell relations pampered Margaret to extreme, carrying her up and downstairs until she was five years old. As an adult, Margaret was unlike her sisters, Eleanor (1903), Marie (1905), and Cecile (1908), never marrying and becoming more of a recluse with passing years. According to the custom at the time, she was taught to curtsey to adults when being introduced. When girls reached their teens, they no longer curtsied, but shook hands. Margaret was over 20 before she could break her habit of curtseying to adults.*

greatest benefits on mankind in the fields of physics, physiology and medicine, chemistry, literature, and peace. In London, Gilbert and Sullivan produced their last comic operetta, "The Grand Duke." In Athens, the first of the modern Olympics games was held. In Alaska, another gold rush was on--to the Klondike. No Cottrell was interested this time.

In 1898, things were looking up for Charlie and Marie. He had gained a position as Treasurer of the City Steam Laundry Company at 220 Thames Street, just a block or so towards Washington Square from the Cottrell's Thames Street Store. He would have additional income for the next fourteen years.

and start over. However, no matter how bad things got, he never gave up. He was always able to come back, even if it meant doing so in an entirely new business area.

As the 19th century came to a close, Charlie helped Marie follow events and to learn English by continuing to read to her. They followed such headlined stories as the campaigns of British General Kitchener against the Mahdi in the Sudan; and, the establishment of five annual Nobel Prizes for those who during the preceding year had conferred the

come for the next fourteen years.

More important to Marie in 1900 was a move. Charlie announced they were moving to 105 Pelham Street, right across the park from his brother, Robert's home at 104 Mill Street.

The move to much more spacious quarters pleased Marie no end. Also, the neighborhood was much quieter away from the bustle of Thames Street. She needed more rest these days, she was again expecting and had to be especially careful since they had lost

> *A friend once made a derogatory remark about a mutual friend who was pregnant with an "unplanned" baby. Marie gently reminded her that "every baby brings its own love with it."*

Marie Cottrell *stands several inches taller than her husband, Charles in this snapshot taken at 105 Pelham Street on June 4, 1905, after Marie Theresa's Christening at Trinity Church. The house in the background was the home of Elizabeth H. Swinburne, who bequeathed it on her death in 1924 to the Civic League of Newport. It is now the Swinburne School. Interestingly, this photograph was cut into three pieces when the family separated in about 1916. Louise Cottrell later obtained the pieces and glued them back together, reuniting the family once more, at least on paper. (From left) Six-month old Theresa is held by her cousin Harriett Cottrell Barker, Marie looking somewhat melancholy, Charlie, Catherine Wallace Cottrell, and Jeanne Fladvad, Marie's beautiful younger sister. In the foreground, Eleanor and Margaret. Eighteen months later, Marie was back in Norway and Charlie was writing plaintive letters of fatherly affection to Margaret.*

several other children.

Marie was beginning to read English more easily now. As she waited for the next birth, she followed the demands of the Philippines for independence from the United States. She made a note to get a copy of Henrik Ibsen's "*When We Dead Awaken*," which he published that year. She admired his work and had several photographs of Ibsen. She had seen him many times on the streets and the restaurants of Christiania.

Local advertisements in the Newport Mercury kept her up to date on "specials." Today they provide telling glimpses of life in Newport at the beginning of the 20th century.

"Get Your Ice Cream at Koschny's at 230-232 Thames Street."

"Hams shoulders and bacon" were to be had at Coggeshall's Market on Washington Square and Thames Street.

Both stoves and ice were available at the Arctic Ice Company, at 163 Thames Street, W.K. Covell, proprietor.

Coke could be delivered to your door by the Newport Gas Light Company, 36 bushels for $3.50.

Schreier's on Thames Street was advertising a "Special Sale in our Trimmed Hat Department to reduce our large stock."

Royal Baking Powder was reminding readers in a large ad that it was "absolutely pure" and made from "grape Cream of Tartar, the most healthful and efficient of all leavening agents." It warned Newport housewives that "many mixtures, made in imitation of baking powders, are upon the market. They are sold cheap, but are dear at any price, because they contain alum, a corrosive poison."

Barney's Music Store at 164 Thames Street was running a special on their Edison "Gem" Phonograph. The "Graphophone Outfit" was complete for only $13.75, and included a graphophone, nickel horn, 6 records, the graphophone carrying case, the graphophone reproducers, and blank records."

For those Newporters feeling "a bit shaky," the Mercury's ad for Dr. Pierce's Golden Medical Discovery gave "strength to the nervous system." The Discovery "does not brace up, but builds up. It is entirely free from alcohol and from opium, cocaine, and other narcotics usually found in so-called nerve medicines."

*"**Greetings from Pelham Street**," reads the note which accompanied this photograph of a somewhat formal evening card party at Pelham Street. Charlie (center, holding a Christmas card), and Robert Cottrell (looking on at far right), play host to friends and relatives. Charlie appears not to notice Harriet Cottrell Barker's elbow on his left shoulder. Louise Cottrell, in "middie" blouse at left, is about 13 years of age. Therefore, the photograph was probably taken during the period Marie was living in Norway with her daughters. Ethel Simes-Nowell (center left) studies her cards, while her mother, Harriett Cottrell Simes-Nowell says something to the man at far right (unidentified).*

A NEW CENTURY, A NEW BABY

In 1900, a girl, Margaret, was born to Charlie and Marie, the first of their children who would reach adulthood. However, she was "different," than the sisters who would follow her.

Robert Cottrell and his family were living at 104 Mill Street. However, now his brother, Dr. Samuel Parker Cottrell was living there as well and serving as Secretary to the Board of Health, with offices in City Hall.

"Uncle Parker," as he was known to his family, was a graduate of Jefferson Medical College. After practicing in St. Paul, Minnesota and Boston, Massachusetts, he had returned to practice in Newport. During the Spanish-American War he had served as a 1st Lieutenant in the U.S. Army Medical Corps and had seen active service in Cuba and the Philippine Islands. He also served as executive surgeon at Simpson Hospital, Fortress Monroe.

The following year, Marie tried to improve her English by reading aloud to Margaret a new book by Beatrix Potter entitled "*Peter Rabbit*."

As she waited for the birth of another child in 1903, a daughter, Eleanor Oline, Marie was delighted to read the news that Norwegian author Björnstjerne Björnson was awarded the Nobel Prize for Literature. She was amazed at the news that brothers, Orville and Wilbur Wright, successfully flew a powered airplane. And, it was almost too much to believe that a car had actually crossed the American continent in 65 days.

When Edwin Cottrell asked to board with his father, Robert, Dr. Samuel Parker Cottrell moved over to 105 Pelham Street. [Edwin later studied Economics and Political Science at Swarthmore College.] Marie had mixed feelings about the move. On the one hand, Parker, a physican would be in the house if the children or she ever needed him. On the other, some of their privacy would be gone (and would never come back). She felt her privacy was being invaded. People were now

Marie spent long periods in Norway visiting relatives including her sisters, Otilie (Otta) and Jeanne (left), and her mother, Oline Bjerke Fladvad (above right). They lived in Christiania (Oslo) at that time. However, her sisters also wrote frequently and visited her in Newport, where this photo postcard was taken at the Rugen Studio. It was addressed to their sister, Olise Fladvad. "Otta and I were out. We got a kick from having a couple of photographs taken. Here's how we looked."

Although badly water damaged, this picture at *Guthus* (good house) was taken in "summer 1907" in Norway. Marie looks stressed and pensive as she poses with her sister, Olise, and with Margaret, Theresa (in Marie's lap), and Eleanor. Marie spent long periods in Norway with her first three daughters who spoke Norwegian as their first language. *"Jeg er gamle"* (I am grownup), Theresa used to tell adults, always provoking a good laugh.

showing up at the house for treatment.

1904 began tragically for the Cottrells. On January 20th, Annie Southwick Cottrell, Robert's wife, died. The funeral took place on a rainy Saturday. Large crowds braved heavy rain and muddy streets to pack Trinity Church where Robert was a Vestryman. Robert had long been involved in local government and would later serve as Mayor of Newport. The overflowing crowds included many leaders of government as well as civic organizations. Robert would miss her greatly, but he would continue to be a loving father and uncle to his family. His children would go on to achieve major successes in their careers.

In 1904, Marie was busy with two very small children, Margaret, 4, and Eleanor, 1. In addition, she was expecting another child. Her disposition wasn't improved when Charlie let Parker list Pelham Street as his office as well as residence. Parker had given up his position with the Health Department.

The fact that Theodore Roosevelt had won the U.S. Presidential election did please her. He seemed like an industrious, energetic

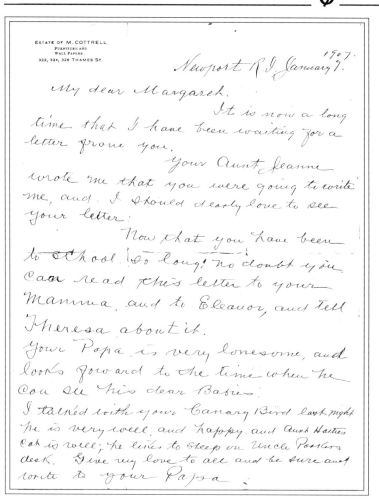

ESTATE OF M. COTTRELL
FURNITURE AND
WALL PAPERS.
322, 324, 326 THAMES ST.

Newport R.I. January 7. 1907.

My dear Margaret,

It is now a long time that I have been waiting for a letter from you.

Your Aunt Jeanne wrote me that you were going to write me, and I should dearly love to see your letter.

Now that you have been to school so long! no doubt you can read this letter to your Mamma and to Eleanor, and tell Theresa about it.

Your Papa is very lonesome, and looks forward to the time when he can see his dear Babies.

I talked with your Canary Bird last night he is very well and happy and Aunt Hatties cat is well; he likes to sleep on Uncle Posskins desk. Give my love to all and be sure and write to your Papa.

Charles M. Cottrell *wearing an unusual cap, and smoking a cigar.*

man. And, she read where France had established the 10-hour work day. In New York, through which she had passed just several years before, the Broadway subway was opened. And, a New York policeman had arrested a woman for smoking a cigarette in public.

In 1905, on January 16th, Marie had another baby girl, Marie Theresa Cottrell. She would be a mischievious sprite, a tom boy some family members nicknamed, "Indian Pete." Later, that would be shortened to simply, "Peter." However, throughout her life her Newport friends and relatives would call her "Theresa." Her Stamford, Connecticut friends at her church would call her "Marie." And, her family, including her sisters, called her "Peter" or "Petie."

Marie Cottrell was overjoyed in 1905 by news from home. The Norwegian Parliament (Storting) had decided to separate from Sweden. Norway was again taking its place in the world as an independent nation. Prince Charles

Marie Theresa Cottrell *would be a mischievious sprite, a tom boy some family members nicknamed, "Indian Pete." Later, that would be shortened to simply, "Peter." However, throughout her life she had three names. Her Newport friends and relatives called her "Theresa." Later, after she was married, her Stamford, Connecticut friends at church would call her "Marie." However, to her immediate family, including her sisters, she was always, "Peter" or "Petie."*

Annie Southwick Cottrell, *Robert's wife, died January 20, 1904. The funeral took place on a rainy Saturday. Large crowds braved the heavy rain and muddy streets to pack Trinity Church where Robert was a Vestryman. The overflowing crowds included many leaders of government as well as civic organizations. (From the Collection of the Newport Historical Society)*

of Denmark was elected King Haakon VII of Norway.

MARIE RETURNS TO NORWAY

Even as she was tending baby Theresa, Marie was making plans--to go back to Norway. Family records and oral history are sketchy. What is known is that throughout their marriage, Marie and Charlie had to work

constantly to overcome cultural and age differences. Not only did some members of his family look down on her as an immigrant, she was frequently confronted by gender restrictions. At that time, women had very few "career" options available to them. While Marie had gained valuable business experience in Norway, Charlie was adamant in refusing to give her any role in his business. Throughout their marriage he rebuffed her attempts to help him, even as his part of the business went steadily downhill.

Theresa had been born in January, 1905. Some months later, Marie lost twin boys. Sadly, they died at birth, probably in early 1906. In May, 1906, Marie took her three daughters with her and moved to Norway. She would not return to Newport until October, 1907, an absence of nearly a year and a half.

While no family evidence exists to indicate a rift before her departure, the length of her absence clearly indicates where her heart lay at that time. She also suffered from asthma and thought a trip home might help the condition. Meanwhile, Charlie moved out of 105 Pelham Street and lived at 71 Washington Street.

While she was enroute, on May 23, 1906 Henrik Ibsen died. She remembered him fondly. She felt a great sympathy and kinship with his characters who are stripped of their disguises and forced to acknowledge their true selves. She had strong misgivings about her own life. Would she ever be able to stand on her own two feet withouut the domineering interference of the men in her life, she wondered.

Meanwhile, Norwegian explorer Roald Amundsen was transiting the Northwest Passage to determine the position of the magnetic North Pole. She had no idea that they would meet the following year.

Marie spent the remainder of 1906 and the following year at home--in Norway. She visited with her parents, Tron and Oline, in their rather cramped housing in Christiania. Her sisters, Jeanne, Otilie ("Otta"), and Olise Fladvad were living there as well. During the warm, light-filled summers, she took a house near the water. On the photographs taken there in 1907 during those carefree months

Thames Street looking East *at the corner of Franklin Street sometime before 1915. A man bends down to give his dog some water from a fire hydrant in front of the U.S. Customs House. At right foreground, the Western Union Telegraph Office. At far right, the Cottrell store with signs advertising furniture, carpets, and undertaking. The Cottrell horse drawn hearse with driver in black mourning clothes and top hat is pulling away from the curb in front of the undertaking establishment. (From the Collection of the Newport Historical Society)*

she referred to it as **Guthus**, the good house. However, neither in these or in any of the other photographs she had taken of her over the years did Marie ever smile.

On May 17, 1907, Marie joined her family in celebrating Norway's second National Day. In national custume and carrying small Norwegian flags, they walked down the hill to **Slottet** (the Norwegian palace for its Royal Family) and joined thousands of their countrymen in parading past the new King and Queen during the Independence Day Parade ("**syttendemai tog**").

The visit was especially poignant for Marie, since Oline's vision was failing. It was hard to see her mother so obviously near the end of her life. Jeanne later remembered her mother crying over the fact that blindness kept

her from reading her Bible.

They spent a great deal of time in the country at Guthus. Surviving photographs taken during that visit show Marie, her daughters, and her sister outdoors. The children, dressed in short sleeved dresses, are playing on the rocks near the water, Marie and Olise sitting watchfully nearby.

For Christmas 1906, Marie bought Charlie a copy of Björnstjerne Björnson's *bonde-novellen*, a peasant romance novel entitled "*Synnöué Solbakken*"--Synnöué of sunny hill.

Björnson was also a song writer whose songs were often described as having a delicious freshness. They possessed "a natural music which defies the translator," wrote Edmund Gosse in the foreward to the edition

As the Gjøa looks today at the Fram Museum in Oslo. A replica of a Viking ship is seen in the foreground.

Marie sent Charlie.

"Of his political lyrics, at least one, ***Ja, vi elsker dette landet*** ("Yes! we love this our country!"), achieved popular success, and in the musical setting made for it by Nordraak, has become the national hymn of Norway, Gosse pointed out.

A week later, even before receiving the book Marie had bought for him in one of the shops along Karl Johan, Charlie sat down to write to his daughter.

"My dear Margaret," Charlie wrote on M. Cottrell Estate letterhead. "It is now a long time that I have been waiting for a letter from you." Margaret was then seven and attending school in Norway.

"Your Aunt Jeanne wrote me that you were going to write me, and I should dearly love to see your letter. Now that you have been to school so long, no doubt you can read this letter to your Mamma and to Eleanor, and tell Theresa about it."

"Your Papa is very lonesome, and looks forward to the time when he can see his dear Babies.

"I talked with your Canary Bird last night. He is very well and happy and Aunt Hatties (sic) cat is well; he likes to sleep on Uncle Parker's desk. Give my love to all and be sure and write to your Papa."

We don't know if Margaret wrote. Charlie would not "see his dear Babies" for another ten months.

Meanwhile, Samuel Parker Cottrell was maintaining his medical office and residence at 105 Pelham Street. In addition, Aunt Hattie and her daughter, Ethel K. Simes-Nowell were boarding there as well. By January, 1907, Charlie was living at Pelham Street once more. When she returned, Marie would find a very crowded household.

Marie's departure from Christiania was painful. Her father, Tron, and mother, Oline saw her and the children off from the docks at Aker Bryge. Marie's sisters, Otilie ("Otta") and Olise went with her. Somehow Marie knew it would be the last time she would see her parents. Her mother died the following year. Tron stayed busy at his final business enterprise, master joinery, until his own death in 1914.

Famed Norwegian explorer Roald Amundsen *traveled with the Fladvad family on several occasions. In this picture taken in 1907, he stands with Marie's sisters, Otta (left) and Olise. Later, he autographed and dated the photograph.*

On the back of the battered autographed photograph, Otta has noted: "Memories from my first trip to USA aboard the SS Oscar II. The photo is of Captain Hemple during a very interesting game called shuffle board with Captain Roald Amundsen!" The photograph however, shows Captain Amundsen posing with Otta and Olise. The photograph to which she referred has not been located.

Historic Norwegian stamps from the Bjørn Fladvad Johnansen Collection

Marie Fladvad Cottrell and her sisters *frequently sailed back and forth to Norway. In 1906 she remained there for over a year. Marie took her children with her for these extended stays in her homeland. In this photo taken during the return voyage home in October, 1907, she is flanked by her sisters, Olise and Otta. Standing in front are her young daughters Eleanor, Margaret and Theresa. This photograph is virtually identical to the photograph on the preceeding page in which Captain Roald Amundsen posed with Marie's sisters. Marie warned her daughters not to go out on the "weather decks" during the stormy crossing. Theresa disobeyed. A wave swept down the deck and carried her to the very edge. Fortunately, a heavy deck chair landed on her, pinning her down until help arrived. But for the chair she would have been lost at sea.*

Between polar expeditions Roald Amundsen explored a new challenge-- Shuffleboard.

Roald Amundsen was only a young man of seventeen when he witnessed the triumphal homecoming of Fridtjof Nansen, Norway's famed Arctic explorer in 1889. At some point during this time he fixed on the idea of mastering the Northwest Passage. His practical mother would have none of that, she wanted him to be a doctor, to pursue a career in medicine, and he did become a medical student. However, upon her death, he gave up the idea of hanging out a "shingle," and took the mate's examination instead.

His first chance at Arctic exploration was in 1897-1899 aboard the Belgian ship "Belgica," under the command of Adrian de Gerlache. He was first mate on this expedition that was the first to winter in the Antarctic. However, he wanted to set his own course with destiny.

In 1901, he conducted oceanographic research along the northeast coast of Greenland. Finally, he was able to buy the Hardanger sloop Gøja, ("Sea"), and set out in 1903 for Arctic seas. His aim was to locate the magnetic North Pole. He spent two winters in Gjøahavn, learning Arctic survival skills from local Eskimos, for whom he had enormous respect.

In 1905, he finally breached the Northwest Passage making the first voyage around the northern Canadian coast. During the incredible journey, he also located and charted the magnetic North Pole. Even after coming through the passage, the Gjøa had to spend yet another winter in the Arctic. Amundsen left the boat for a harrowing 3-month sled ride to Eagle City to let the world know they had breached the Passage. Finally, on August 31, 1906, the Gjøa reached Nome, Alaska.

Amundsen's name doesn't show up again in the logs of history, until 1909. However, we do know where he was on October 15, 1907. He was not enduring the hazards of a

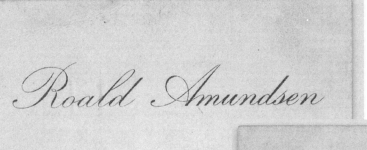

The Fladvad sisters stayed in touch with Amundsen. *They corresponded over the following years and met at least once more. Just eight months after reaching the South Pole, Amundsen sent Otta his personal card. He noted on the back, in English, that he would "be glad to see you again."*

harsh arctic climate. He was engaged in activities potentially much more dangerous-- socializing aboard a passenger ship enroute to the United States.

Otilie and Olise were enroute to the U.S. for her first visit to this country. They were traveling with their older sister, Marie, and her three children who were returning from an extended visit to her beloved Norway. Jeanne stayed with Oline and Tron at their Holbergsgate apartment until her mother died.

On the back of an autographed photograph, Olise noted that she was traveling on the SS Oscar II. The photo is "of Captain Hemple during a very interesting game called shuffle board with Captain Roald Amundsen."

It is interesting that she mentions Captain Hemple first, then Captain Amundsen. After all, at that point Amundsen had simply spent three winters stuck in the ice. If he had any dreams about reaching the Pole, it was probably the North Pole, not the South, he

had in mind. In any event, she thought enough of his friendship and accomplishments to have him pose with her and to autograph the photograph. It would take him several more years to achieve his highest goal: to be the first to reach one of the Poles.

Even as he was considering an attempt to reach the North Pole by drifting across the Arctic Ocean, as Nansen had done, word was received that Robert E. Peary had reached the Pole on April 6, 1909. Amundsen was still determined to reach a pole. He simply changed his direction. In August, 1910 he left Kristiansand on a new voyage of discovery. Aboard that ship only he knew that his real goal was through dangerous Southern waters. When the Fram reached the island of Madeira, Amundsen informed the crew members who were jubilant. They were not alone. British Captain Robert Falcon Scott had established an Antarctic base and was planning to move toward the pole. The race was on.

105 Mill Street as it looks today.

Amundsen started for the South Pole on October 20, 1911. With him were four companions, 52 dogs, and four sledges. He took enough food for four months. On December 14, 1911, celestial observations confirmed they had reached the Pole. Amundsen's detailed planning, done in secret, had paid off. They were all safely back at their base by January 25, 1912. In fact, his planning and foresight saved their lives. Captain Scott reached the Pole on January 17, 1912 to find Amundsen's flag. Scott and his eleven man team all died from hunger and cold on their return trip. In terms of danger, daring, and difficulty, few feats of human exploration can equal Amundsen's success in reaching the South Pole in 1911--and with the safe return of all hands.

In another unusual footnote, Amundsen became embroiled in the controversy over who "really" discovered the North Pole. In 1907, a New York native and surgeon, Dr. Frederick Cook,

told the press he was going on a hunting trip. He sailed to Annoatok in northern Greenland, crossed over the ice to Ellesmere Island, and set out northward onto the polar ice with two Eskimos and 103 huskies. He returned 14 months later in 1909 to claim he had reached the North Pole. Two days later, Navy Captain Robert Peary cabled from Greenland that he had discovered the North Pole. Peary was outraged at Cook's claim, since Peary had many numerous exploratory expeditions, and an unsuccessful attempt in 1906 when he was stopped by bad weather.

After studying Cook's journal, Amundsen was convinced that Cook had indeed discovered the pole nearly a year before Peary. Other evidence was contradictory. In fact, the claims to discovering the North Pole of both Cook and Peary were challenged. The first uncontested surface attainment of the North Pole was achieved by a four-person snowmobile expedition led by American Ralph Plaisted on April 18, 1968.

With funds gained from his Antarctic successes, Amundsen established a successful shipping business. In 1925 he was still reaching out to open new horizons in arctic exploration--this time with the airplane. He flew within 170 miles of the North Pole. The next year, he did fly over the North Pole in a dirigible, crossing from Svalbard, north of Norway, to Alaska. The Captain of the Italian-built dirigible Norge was Umberto Nobile. In June, 1928 when Nobile was reported lost after flying over the Pole again, Amundsen set out by airplane from Tromso to search for him. Amundsen's plane was never seen again.

In this winter snapshot taken behind 105 Pelham Street, we see from left, Margaret, Theresa, an unidentified girl, Eleanor and an unidentified boy holding a dog.

MOVE TO MILL STREET

Upon Marie's return to Newport in October, 1907, if they had any major differencies, they resolved them—at least temporarily. A fourth and final daughter, Cecile, was born to Charles and Marie in 1908.

Marie was frustrated by Harriet Cottrell Simes-Nowell's attempts to run the house. Her histrionics were almost a daily event, especially over her rings.

Hattie still had the five "engagement" rings her second husband had bought for her when she could not select just one. He had presented her with five from which to choose the "right one." She couldn't make up her mind--and kept all five rings.

Every night, to protect them from thieves, she would hide them in a different location in and around the Pelham Street mansion. However, on many mornings, she would temporarily forget the location of one or two of them. On those occasions, she would become highly emotional and begin accusing members of the family of stealing her rings. Eventually, the rings would be located and the house return to peace and quiet—until the next time she forgot where she put them. The ritual became a family joke.

Marie could take no more. Finally, Charlie worked out an arrangement with his brother, Robert. Just prior to Cecile's birth, he moved Marie and the girls to 104 Mill Street. Robert, who had served as Mayor of Newport in 1906, moved his family to 21 Greenough Place.

They were now comfortably settled in the big, three-story gabled roof house that had been the Robert Cottrell home since 1886. Built in 1758 by Benjamin Reynolds, a Jamestown ferryman, it was one of the very few brick colonial houses built in Newport. Sitting near the large, south-facing windows, Margaret and Eleanor tried their newly acquired reading skills to decipher Kenneth Grahame's "The Wind in the Willows."

(Below right) **Standing beside 104 Mill Street**, *from left, Theresa, Eleanor, Margaret holding Cecile. The three older sisters would sit near the large, south-facing windows of their new home reading Kenneth Grahame's "The Wind in the Willows." (Below center)* **In 1911 Charlie and Marie took the second and last of their vacations together**, *they rented a house in Jamestown, just across Narragansett Bay. The Cottrells called the nearly identical houses "The Three Sisters." Their names were (from left) "The Anchorage," "Betty Cottage," "Nina Cottage," and "Myra Cottage." As advertised, "Myra and Nina Cottages each have Reception Hall, Parlor, Dining Room, Kitchen, eight Chambers and Bath Room. The Betty Cottage and The Anchorage each have Reception Hall, two Parlors, Dining Room, Kitchen, nine Chambers, and two Bath Rooms. All have modern improvements and are completely equipped for House-keeping." (From the Collection of the Jamestown Historical Society)*

*The **Easton-Cottrell home** at 23 Catherine Street as it looks today.*

Busy with her growing brood, Marie took little notice, at first, that "Fountain" pens were becoming popular. About this time she did begin to see--and hear—a new automobile chugging along Newport's streets and avenues. The Ford Motor Company had recently produced the first "Model T"—15 million would eventually be sold.

In 1910, Marie noted, sadly that Björnstjerne Björnson had died. She remembered the Christmas of 1906 when she found the small, tan volume of *Synnöve Solbakken*

In 1911 a film company arrived in Newport *to produce an early movie which included a "fairy scene." Two of the six children appearing in the scene were Eleanor Cottrell and Marie Theresa Cottrell. In the Fifties, Eleanor ("Ellie") Cottrell Kaull who was then living in New York City, saw it on television and called Theresa to tell her, excitedly, "Peter! We're on television." Newport youngsters in the movie included (l. to r.) Natalie Muenchinger, Elizabeth Sayer, Eleanor Cottrell, Kathryn Lee, Marie Theresa Cottrell, and Irma Richardson.*

in the shop along Karl Johan. She wished she could be a little more like Synnöve, safe and secure with her family at their ancestral farm, growing up to marry Thorbjorn, the boy next door. Then she remembered how passive Synnöve was, how accepting of whatever fate had in store for her, and finally, how manipulated by both sets of parents into accepting a marriage proposal from Thorbjorn. No, she could never be Synnöve Solbakken, she was too strong-willed.

When her household and mothering duties allowed, Marie was very active in local Suffragete meetings and marches. Therefore she felt a strong personal loss, when Julia Ward Howe died at the age of 92 in Newport on October 17, 1910. She had caught pneumonia shortly after returning from Smith College where she had received another honorary degree.

Marie had heard Mrs. Howe speak on numerous occasions and felt strong kinship with her views on woman's suffrage. She supported as well, Mrs. Howe's international thinking, including the benefits of having a general congress of women to promote alliances between different nationalities to settle international questions amicably.

Elsewhere in Newport that year, over 1,000 Newporters out of a population of 27,500 had been employed as servants. Later, while the population in 1920 had swollen to over 30,000, fewer than 700 were listed as servants. This trend would first give Aunt Hattie frustration, then "ideas."

1910 was a big year for Marie. After living for three years at 104 Mill Street, they were moving again. This time it was to a big Victorian home at 23 Catherine Street, right next to the Clement Clarke Moore home.

Built about 1825 by John Easton, the house was later acquired by James Gordon Bennett. There would be plenty of room for everyone. It was just a short walk down Catherine Street towards Easton's Beach to the Tolethorpe School for Girls. Uncle Bob and his family, were now living at 11 Francis Street.

There was more good news in 1911. Roald Amundsen had reached the South Pole. Marie wrote excited notes to her sisters.

Margaret, Eleanor, Therese, and Cecile attended the Tolethorpe School for Girls at the former Chanler estate, Bath Road [now Memorial Boulevard] and the cliffs. Their cousin, Ethel K. Simes-Nowell (left), daughter of Harriet Cottrell Simes-Nowell, was principal. Above right, in the distance, is Middletown, Rhode Island. The former school is now a restaurant with a stunning view of Middletown, R.I. and Easton's Beach.

LIFE AT 23 CATHERINE STREET

After attending Trinity church, Theresa remembered later, she and her sisters would walk back home, stopping off at Uncle Bobs to read the Sunday papers. For many days they could talk of nothing else but the tragedy they read about in the Sunday papers in 1912. The liner Titanic sank on its maiden voyage after hitting an iceberg. 1,513 people had been lost, including many who were well known to Newporters.

After serving as Treasurer of Newport's City Steam Laundry for over 14 years, Charlie lost that important source of income. Their financial problems grew rapidly, even as Marie began to worry about how they would educate their children. She was even more worried by Charlie's physical deterioration. His health was very obviously being undermined by arthritis. He was increasingly less able to help Robert with the business on Thames Street. Slowly, inexorably, Marie began to feel that some important tide was turning against them.

The strains on their marriage were growing. In many important respects, about the only things they had in common were their children. Charlie moved to 119 Gibbs Avenue. Marie and the girls remained at 23 Catherine Street.

The Cottrell girls were quite popular and good dancers. In the years after its introduction in 1913, the Foxtrot became one of their favorites.

Theresa read that a new railroad station, the Grand Central Terminal opened in New York. She gave it only passing note at the time. Later, when she was a professional secretary commuting into New York City from Darien, Connecticut, she would pass through the huge building every day.

In 1914, Charlie quietly moved back into 23 Catherine Street. Not so quietly, World War I began following the assassination of Archduke Francis Ferdinand, heir to the Austrian throne.

Margaret, Eleanor, and Theresa enjoyed reading Edgar Rice Burroughs' new book

During World War I *Newport echoed with the boom of cannon firing during "sham battles" at the nearby Naval Training Station.*

"*Tarzan of the Apes*." They liked "*Penrod*" by Booth Tarkington even better.

One Sunday in 1915, they learned that the Germans had widened the war in Europe. The Germans began unrestricted submarine warfare by sinking the liner "*Lusitania*," and launching Zeppelin attacks on London.

Like more than 5 million people in America every day at that time, the girls enjoyed attending a movie. They were amazed when they first saw a new film by D.W. Griffith titled "*Birth of a Nation*."

During this period, Margaret, Eleanor, Theresa, and Cecile were educated at the Tolethorpe School for Girls at the former Chanler estate, Bath Road [now Memorial Boulevard] and the cliffs. The principal there was their cousin, Ethel K. Simes-Nowell, daughter of Harriet Cottrell Simes-Nowell.

As reported in her obituary, Ethel Simes-Nowell was "prominent in amateur theatricals, a pioneer in the wo-man's suffrage move-ment, and an educator. She was a leader

In 1917, *Charlie and Robert moved the Cottrell business to 20 Bellevue Avenue. It signalled the end of an era for the Cottrell family.*

of the Unity Club as both an actress and director of its productions. The Club held its plays in the Parish Hall of the Unitarian Church. "She was among those in the van here when the fight for women's suffrage was being conducted, and national women leaders came to this city for that cause," the Newport Mercury reported in February 9, 1940.

During World War I, she produced a number of plays for the War Camp Community Service for the "many enlisted men here in the Naval Reserves and others."

Dressed for the occasion, *the Cottrells prepare for a drive on Bellevue Avenue. Harriet Simes-Nowell (third from left) and Catherine Wallace Cottrell (center foreground) are recognizable.*

BEGINNING OF THE END FOR CHARLIE AND MARIE

In 1916, the average annual wage was $633.00 a year. It is doubtful that Charlie was earning much more than this. They were still living at 23 Catherine Street, but they were struggling. The Cottrell business was floundering. There was talk of closing the store and moving to another location. What little of Michael Cottrell's estate that was left was now being rapidly used up.

Marie wanted her daughters to know about the family's finances. Charlie seemed dead set against having them know anything at all.

To make matters even worse, Charlie's health continued to fail. Parker moved into 23 Catherine Street. He wanted to help his brother.

Marie knew that their future looked about as gloomy as events in Europe. There the allies had suffered through the Battle of Verdun, and the Somme defensive. Food was rationed in Germany. There was very little to be happy about.

As they followed events in the newspaper, the Cottrell girls were gripped by the wide diversity of happenings around the world in 1917. Bread was rationed in Great Britain. In Russia, the Czar abdicated. [In 1918, the Czar and his family would be gunned down on Lenin's orders. Their remains were discovered and identified in 1992.] In Britain, the Royal Family renounced its German name and titles. They cheered at the news that the first United States Army division had landed in France. With money particularly short for them, the Cottrells could hardly believe their eyes when they read that Charlie Chaplin's yearly

Eleanor and Theresa whimsically dressed for a Newport parade.

Two ladies in long winter coats and warm hats, pass three children on the sidewalk in this view of 59 Bellevue Avenue from Touro Park, Newport's "Top of the Hill." Park benches (foreground) face the Old Stone Tower in Touro Park. (From the Collection of the Newport Historical Society)

A 1910-era view of Jamestown, Rhode Island (above) on Conanicut Island. *Charlie Cottrell spent the last year of his life at Maplewood, a sanitarium near the Jamestown Ferry landing seen here. (Below)* **Maplewood Sanitarium**, *where Dr. W. Lincoln Bates and his family operated a combined sanitarium, hospital, and hotel for many years in the late 19th and early 20th centuries. Maplewood burned in 1944. (Left) Close examination of the Maplewood photograph revealed the ghostly image of a woman sitting in the second from left window on the second floor. (From the Collection of the Jamestown Historical Society)*

salary had reached one million dollars.

Sometimes, when they passed a "watering hole" on Thames Street they could hear men inside singing a new song by George M. Cohan, called "Over There." They begged Marie to let them bob their hair, the latest fashion sweeping the U.S. and Britain. She wouldn't hear of it.

However, when the U.S. Senate rejected President Wilson's suffrage bill, they heard a lot. Marie was quite upset that women had lost another round in the struggle to gain the right to vote.

Charlie and Robert moved the Cottrell business to 20 Bellevue Avenue in 1917. The move signalled the end of the Cottrell business on Thames Street, a landmark since Michael first opened his own store on Thames Street in 1870. An era was coming to a close.

Charlie's arthritis, always a troublesome ailment, was worsening. He was increasingly less able to work. His income began to fall off.

Charlie and Marie had numerous arguments over the plight of the business. She wanted to get involved in the business, to use her own initiative and past experience in Norway to help save Charlie's part of the business.

He was adamant. Her place was in the home, with their daughters age 17, 14, 12, and 9. Meanwhile, the Michael Cottrell Estate was depleted. The little store with the bay window on Bellevue Avenue was only big enough for Robert to use for his mortuary business.

Years later, Mr. William Sherman, a life-long Newport resident and former President of the Newport Historical Society, remembered Robert Cottrell doing business at the 20 Bellevue Avenue address. Reminding the authors of Robert's many years of service to Newport, including a term as Mayor in 1906, Sherman recalled Robert "sitting in the window," of 20 Bellevue Avenue, watching the passers by, and "waiting for business," he said, joking and with a twinkle in his eye, meaning that "business" would come when someone died.

In mid-1916, Charlie gave Marie his tearful goodbye and turned his welfare over to his family, especially Aunt Hattie. When Marie left 23 Catherine Street, she sought out

her brother-in-law, Robert. Together with Parker, they arranged for her to stay with Parker at 59 Bellevue Avenue (below).

Soon after, Charlie moved to 20 Bellevue Avenue. The Catherine Street house was rented out.

A brief story in the Newport Mercury during this period announced that a local renter, Frederick H. Paine had rented for Charles Cottrell, "his house on Catherine and Fir streets, formerly the James Gordon Bennett

Catherine Wallace Cottrell *stepped in to pay her uncle's medical bills--in exchange for all his household goods.*

cottage, to Baron Renaud Ungern-Sternberg, second secretary of the Russian embassy and gentleman in waitin to the Czar of Russia. Baron Ungern-Sternberg, who occupied this cottage last summer, will have with him Commander I. V. Mishtowt, naval attached of the embassy."

Charlie needed the income.

Parker treated Charlie at his Bellevue offices for a while. However, on December 1, 1917, Uncle Parker died. The Cottrell girls had lost both their well liked uncle and their doctor. Now who would minister to Charlie's worsening arthritis?

In 1918, an Armistice was finally signed between the Allies and Germany. Sadly, it came too late for Cousin Samuel Cottrell. He had been killed in France on September 30th. He was only 25 years old.

*"**Mr. Charles M. Cottrell**, a well known Newport business man, died at Dr. Bates' Sanitarium in Jamestown on Monday after a long illness."*

Always an avid reader, Charlie read the good news in his cramped quarters at 20 Bellevue Avenue. His body was ravaged by the disease, but he tried to stay up on things in the world. He still loved his daughters, but it is believed that he never saw them again. Theresa remembered that the tragic scene on the stairs at 23 Catherine Street was the last time she ever saw her father.

In 1919, Germany signed a peace treaty at Versailles. In the United States, the Volstead Act was passed making prohibition the law of the land. The bars on Thames Street would be hard hit.

More important to Marie was the ratification of the 19th Amendment to the Constitution giving women the vote for the first time. In Newport, shortly after passage of the act, 3,826 women registered to vote in the 1920 election, including Marie T. Cottrell. The Newport County Woman Suffrage Association, led to victory by Mrs. Elliott, the Sturtevants, and their friends, became what it remains today, the League of Women Voters.

CHARLIE AND THE ELECTRIC SPARK

In 1919, Charlie's arthritis was very advanced. He required constant care and drastic measures. The family decided that Charlie would be helped by a period of treatment at Dr. Bates Sanatarium in Jamestown.

Dr. W. Lincoln Bates (1855-1932), together with his wife, Dr. Martha Boyce Bates, M.D., and a son, William, operated the combination sanitarium, hospital, and hotel for many years. Locally, it was known as Maplewood. Dr. Bates died in 1931 and Maplewood burned in January 1944.

Dr. Bates published the *Electric Spark* from 1910 to 1935. A January, 1913, article noted that "if the reader of this paper is afflicted with any of the following diseases

pack up and come to Dr. Bates Electropathic Sanatarium at Jamestown, R.I.: Acne, Angina pectoris, Aphonia, Cancer, Catarrh, Constipation, Dyspepsia, Epilepsy, Infantile paralysis, Lumbago, Mental diseases, Neuralgia, Rheumatism, Sciatica, Spinal diseases,. Electricity is a mechanical, physical and therapeutic agent covering a field of possible activities greater than that of any other natural force. The electric current is utilized as a motive power for healing purposes."

Charlie Cottrell's three remaining years would be spent in the care of Dr. Bates and "the electric spark."

CHARLIE PAYS HIS BILLS-WITH HIS HOUSEHOLD

By now Charlie was an invalid confined in a sanitarium on Jamestown. He had not been able to function as a businessman in years. The bills for his treatment continued to mount. He contributed no income. Funds from the Michael Cottrell estate had been used up long before. A cryptic legal document explained what happened next—Catherine Wallace Cottrell, his niece, agreed to pay his

When the Unknown Soldier was buried in Arlington National Cemetery in 1921, the family knew that it wasn't their Sam, seen here at Camp Upton shortly before he was shipped over to France.

bills. Her price was all Charlie's worldly goods.

Marie learned from the family that Charlie had sold all of their household furnishings to his niece, Catherine Wallace Cottrell—for the sum of $1. In return, she paid for his stay with Dr. Bates and the electric spark. In a shaky hand on that cold December 2nd, Charlie signed over all his personal property at 23 Catherine Street to Catherine Cottrell.

"Know all men by these presents," the Bill of Sale of Personal Property executed on December 2, 1919 begins with standard legal jargon, that "I, Charles M. Cottrell of the City and County of Newport in the State of Rhode Island in consideration of one dollar and other good and valuable considerations paid by Catherine W. Cottrell, of said Newport, the daughter of my brother, Robert C. Cottrell, the receipt whereof is hereby acknowledged, do hereby grant, sell, transfer, and deliver unto the said Catherine W. Cottrell the following goods and chattels, namely, 1 hall mirror, 1 hall chair, 1 hall clock, 1 black rocking chair, 1 leather chair, 1 library table, 1 secretary, 7 dining room chairs, 1 china closet, 1 sideboard, 1 broken set china, 1 small set steps, some framed pictures, and each and every other singular thing, chattel and article of personal property belonging to me now in the house known as and numbered 23 Catherine Street in said Newport."

The hall mirror was not taken from the house. It refused to budge, so firmly attached was the mirror to the left side of the front hall. It remains in the hallway to this day.

Charlie signed the bill of sale in a shaky hand that started on the line, then dropped below the line by the time he reached the "a" in Charles. Prophetically his last known signature went down hill.

Catherine Wallace Cottrell had returned to Newport in early 1918 after graduating from the School for Social Service of the Cathedral of St. John the Divine in New York City. She then completed another brief course of study at the first Red Cross Institute in Boston. She would serve as the Executive Secretary of the Newport Chapter of the American Red Cross for the next 27 years.

The United States was entering World War I and there was much to be done in

When Charlie died, *Marie and her daughters were living at 59 Bellevue. Marie had already begun to take boarders into her rooming house. The house as it appears today from the grounds of Newport's Redwood Library.*

Newport. "It was in the war days that many features were added to the Red Cross services," the Providence Journal noted in a July 8, 1945 article praising her career contributions. "The nutrition, first aid, and home nursing courses, the motor corps, and bandaging classes were initiated. In this war other new additions were the Nurses' Aides, the Camp and Hospital Committee, the Arts and Skills Committee which works with patients in the realm of physical therapy, and the motor corps ambulance service."

Catherine noted in the article that "helping people to help themselves" had been her goal in the 5,000 cases she handled, and they proved to be the most challenging and satisfying aspect of her career.

She received praise for her efforts in such disasters as the Mackinac Steamboat Explosion, the Bath Road fire, the Washington Square fire, and the hurricanes of 1938 and 1944, when "the Red Cross was called upon to provide doctors and nurses, food, quarters, and clothing."

"Out of these experiences she remembers particularly," the journalist concluded, "a wild ride in a Coast Guard cutter to Block Island during the 1938 hurricane when the tidal wave had just passed through. That was her most exciting experience."

But in 1919 she needed household furnishings. She had returned to live in her father's large, three story home at 11 Francis

When Marie needed help *"getting into real estate," she turned to her brother-in-law, Robert Clarke Cottrell. (Barker Family Collection)*

Street. Charlie needed money for medical bills. Catherine had the money and wanted the Cottrell family furniture, including the 300-year old clock made in Cork, Ireland brought to Newport by James Cottrell. She got the furnishings, and paid for Charlie's electric spark treatments at Dr. Bate's Sanitarium.

"MR. COTTRELL IS SURVIVED BY FOUR DAUGHTERS..."

Theresa's education changed course as a result of Charlie's health and money problems. In 1917 she and her sisters had attended the Tolethorpe School for Girls. From now on there would be no private school for Marie's daughters. In September, 1919,

Theresa enrolled at Rogers High School. She graduated in the Class of 1923 with a "Commercial" diploma.

Marie began to frequent local auctions to refurnish her home and the rooms in it she planned to rent out.

Life in Newport during the 1920s was lived almost entirely in the local "back yards." Going off the island was a frustrating affair. Long waits for ferry rides, and unpredictable coach connections made excursions a risky undertaking for those living life at other than a leisurely pace. Life really went on in the neighborhood, and through membership in Newport's religious and civic associations.

One did not need to venture far anyway. Small grocery stores, barbers, and dry goods shops were mixed in among the houses in each neighborhood. Street vendors brought in fresh vegetables and "ices." The five or six city grocers large enough to sell meat, like Tisdalls on Broadway, sent their delivery trucks out all over town. Coal was delivered to the chute behind the house.

On March 19, 1921, the Newport Mercury ran the following brief obituary: "Mr. Charles M. Cottrell, a well known Newport business man, died at Dr. Bate's Sanitarium in Jamestown on Monday after a long illness. He had been a sufferer from rheumatic trouble for a long time, and for the past three years had been an invalid.

"Mr. Cottrell was the oldest son of the late Michael Cottrell and was born in Newport on September 15, 1851. While still a boy he went to Boston and was employed for a number of years in some of the large dry goods houses of that city, and afterward was employed in the A.T. Stewart store in New York. Returning to Newport, he entered his father's store and after the death of the latter, carried on the business with his brother, Mr. Robert C. Cottrell, until a few years ago. He was also engaged for a time in the laundry business in partnership with Mr. Charles T. Sterne. Mr. Cottrell is survived by four daughters, also a brother, Mr. Robert C. Cottrell, and a sister, Mrs. Thomas S. Nowell."

Significantly, the notice mentions only that he had four daughters. They are not named. His wife of 26 years, Marie Fladvad Cottrell is not mentioned at all.

Marie did not attend the funeral. Instead, she and a friend wept their way through their own private memorial service for the husband who had in so many ways, died years before. Her family remembers that despite the pain and hardship he had caused his family, Marie never said anything negative about him. She possessed a dignified and stoic quality that reflected her basic courage and **rettskaffenhet** (honesty, rightness and integrity). Through all the many challenges she would face as a result of his illness and death, she never, ever thought of herself as a "victim."

Her daughter Theresa once asked her mother what the future would bring. "If you knew," Marie answered with wisdom so tragically acquired, "you wouldn't have the strength to live."

In other events that year, Hitler's storm troopers begin to terrorize the opposition. Irving Berlin opened the first of his "Music Box Revues" in New York. (Later, Theresa would see some of them herself.) She would also listen to Graham McNamee broadcast baseball games from the Polo Grounds in New York. He did so the first time in 1921. And, in Pittsburgh, station KDKA transmitted the first regular radio programs in the U.S. Some years later, Marie's favorite radio program was the "Arthur Godfree Show."

The Unknown Soldier was interred at Arlington National Cemetery in 1921. It wasn't Sam, he was buried in France.

ON HER OWN

On August 18, 1920 Marie celebrated the news that Tennessee had become the 36th State to ratify the Woman's Suffrage Amendment to the U.S. Constitution. The law went into effect on August 26, 1920. As a naturalized U.S. citizen, Marie took great pride in voting in every election thereafter.

The year after Charlie died was somewhat strange for Marie. She expected to miss him after his death. After all, they had been married for 26 years. However, his lengthy illness had pulled them apart years ago. Once he had been taken to Jamestown, he was all but dead to her.

Marie and as noted in the city directory, "three dependents" (her unmarried daughters over 21, including Margaret, Eleanor, and Theresa), were living at 59 Bellevue Avenue. Marie's tenants included John F. Madden,

(Below) **Marie Theresa Cottrell** *(left) with her sister, Cecile at about the time she graduated from Rogers High School in 1923.*

Marie Theresa Cottrell vacationing in Miami, Florida in the late 1920's. Before marrying William Raymond, Jr. of Stamford, Connecticut on January 17, 1933, she had started a business career in New York City. She served as secretary to Harry Payne Whitney and to Paul Whiteman, the band leader. On her employment application for a new job she noted that she left the Whiteman organization because of "insufficient salary. No advancement." She had earned $18 per week. In January, 1925 she went to work for the Guaranty Trust Company in New York. On her new salary of $25 per week, she was able to afford a radio, a fur coat, and best of all, a car.

they had to be close by to facilitate her being able to oversee the activities of her tenants. The house next door, 65 Bellevue Avenue was perfect. All she needed was the money--$10,000--to buy it from its owner, Mary H. Tompkins who was living in New York City.

In September, 1922, Marie signed an agreement to purchase 65 Bellevue Avenue, and to pay the owner $10,000 by the following May 1st. Soon after she concluded the

Norman T. McLean, and Norman R. VanderVeer. The Newport Mercury was keeping its readers up to date on the Teapot Dome oil scandal hearings which had begun in Washington. P.G. Wodehouse published "The Inimitable Jeeves," which they enjoyed reading. At the theatre on Washington Square they enjoyed watching Douglas Fairbanks swash and buckle his way through "Robin Hood."

Prophetically, elsewhere, Lee de Forest first demonstrated the process to incorporate sound in motion pictures. And, German aircraft designer Willy Messerschmitt established his airplane factory.

Marie had little in the way of cash assets. Of course, she did have 59 Bellevue Avenue, a large, two story home, with double chimneys and a sun porch. Two multi-flued chimneys carried away the smoke from the fireplaces which warmed almost every major room. The large kitchen was in the rear of the building, on the right. The high ceilings rooms were airy, and well lit.

While strapped for cash, she had her good name and key support from Robert. She needed more rooms to rent out; and,

agreement, she paid a visit to Newport Savings and Loan Association. They knew Mrs. Cottrell and welcomed her request. Despite the lack of collateral, they loaned her the money. Marie had "gone into real estate," which provided the major source of her income for the next 18 years.

"Going into real-estate," as it was termed, was a big step for Marie. In this she had support from some family members, including her brother-in-law, Robert Cottrell. Because they were all "strapped" at that point, mostly it was moral support, no money. From the time Charlie died in 1921, Marie would be totally on her own until her daughters were old enough to work and send some money home to "Mother." Theresa later explained to her daughter, Faith, that "I was my mother's right arm."

In a letter to Theresa, some years later, Marie echoed the challenges of all land lords everywhere. Since she did not write very well in English, her daughter Margaret wrote it for her.

"I am trying to raise the rents here [at 59 and 65 Bellevue Avenue], and I've some tough ones to deal with. They haven't, yet, answered whether they're staying or leaving. I've had a great many people looking at apartments, but they all want to pay small rents. Of course, I've a great deal of painting and cleaning up to do, and very little to do with. So, you see, I have some figuring to do."

TEENS IN THE TEENS

The Cottrell girls were very popular. And, they were good dancers, improvising to such tunes as: "*Yes, We Have No Bananas,*" "*Barney Google,*" "*Tea for Two,*" and "*I Want to be Happy.*"

Friday evening, May 11, 1923 was a big evening for Marie and for Theresa. They had busied about for weeks getting Theresa ready to celebrate her graduation from Rogers High School with the Class of '23. The school's athletic association was the sponsor for the Third Annual Red and Black Ball.

Marie enjoyed watching her daughters get dressed up to go out on a date (always heavily chaperoned). With teenage annoyance, Theresa would scold her. "Mother, please don't watch me." Marie would smile

Marie Theresa Cottrell *chose a "Fotomat" machine to produce these candid photographs of her in her stylish "cloche" hat in the early 1920s.*

and remind her that "a cat can look at a Queen." Marie had a quote for every occasion. However, she did not swear. Regardless of the provocation, her strongest "oath," was "Oh, Applesauce." When used under trying circumstances however, this term for bland apple mush acquired a miraculous ability to motivate those around her.

Perhaps looking to her mother as an example, Theresa did not swear either, but she came close. Depending on the circumstances, she might use one of her two trusty oaths: "Holy jumped up Judas priest," or "Jesus Christ in the foothills." Later, her daughter, Faith, recalled that "when I reached the 'foothills,' I knew I was in big trouble."

Theresa had plenty of strength to live that Friday night. The restored R.H.S. Gymnasium was gaily decorated that evening, with music provided by the "Premier Augmented Orchestra." The high school had been restored during 1920-1922 following a fire which had completely gutted the school, causing $250,000 in damage. An entire new building, including a new gymnasium and auditorium, had been added behind the old building.

On Wednesday, June 22, 1923, Marie Theresa Cottrell graduated from Rogers High School along with 133 others in her class. On either side of the platform in the school's new assembly hall, were the national and state

Marie Theresa Cottrell sat *for this silhouette by Julia Brown September 12, 1916.*

flags, and in the center the seal of the class of 1923, which reminded all those attending of its motto: "Fit Via Vi." It was the largest class to graduate from Rogers in the city's history up to that point.

Dr. William Herbert Perry Faunce, President of Brown University, led off his remarks by noting that the "finest thing in Newport are its boys and girls." The audience nodded approvingly.

Dr. Faunce then posed the question as to which studies are most useful. "Some think we exist for what can be done through us," he pointed out, "others for what can be done in us. The first are the advocates of vocational training; the second the advocates of cultured training. Nothing, however, can be done through us until something is done in us, and this is the point of reconciliation between vocationalists and culturalists. One never knows what is useful if he defines the word too narrowly. The man of liberal training falls upon his feet in *every* emergency of life, and becomes a valuable citizen of the republic," he said.

A liberal education, Dr. Faunce emphasized, gives a man the power to think straight and to come to a focus. Education gives us "breadth and horizon," he continued, "which is not so common in a large country as in a small one. We are not so broad as our ancestors were in Colonial times, and we have grown narrower and more self-centered since our great wars," he concluded. "Eventually we shall have physical nearness, but perhaps mental alienation," he said, prophetically.

However, through "study and travel we come into sympathy with men of other nations and become ambassadors of good will. A liberal education frees us and a real teacher's knowledge flows over into the vacant mind of the student."

In conclusion, Dr. Faunce urged the graduates, by now undoubtedly getting restless in spite of their vacant minds, to "go forth to help, as soldiers of the republic, with energy and enthusiasm. He closed with a motto from Rupert Brook, the brilliant young British poet who had been killed in France during World War I. "Now God, be thanked who hath matched us with His hour," Dr. Faunce said, stepping aside for the Glee Club, followed by the presentation of medals to various outstanding graduates.

The Samuel Middleton Cottrell Memorial Medal, created to honor Theresa's cousin, Robert Cottrell's son, was presented to Harry Lee Burgess by the president of the RHS Alumni Association, John H. Nolan. Like Brook, Sam had been killed in France. The better part of an entire generation of young men from many countries had gone "Over There"--to stay.

Thinking of her handsome, dead cousin, Theresa had to swallow the lump in her throat. She remembered a photograph of Sam and his sister, Louise. Sam was pulling baby Louise on a sled. Their innocent faces smile out at the world to this day. On the back young Sam in a childish script had endorsed the picture proudly, "To Uncle Charlie and Aunt Marie."

The exercises were concluded when the audience rose and sang together, "Fair Rogers." Sitting in the audience with Margaret and Eleanor, Marie was so very proud. Cessie could not be with them. She was living in Brownsville (Brooklyn) with Marie's Norwegian relatives (probably her brother).

During the exercises, Theresa flipped through the class yearbook. A class picture sufficed for photographs in those days, but the yearbook included the class history, the oration, and the class poem. She was particularly interested in the poem. Her friend Sydney Greason had written it.

"Of our true purpose on this earth we know but little, save that Conscience bids us live according to the social and the moral codes we have," he wrote, echoing the best thinking of young minds growing up in the Twenties. These were not the empty, hedonistic thoughts of "Flappers," but of serious, responsible young people.

"And it is very well we do," the poem continued, "for time and acts have shown that Right is true and good, and should be prevalent and strong, no matter what the charge shall be to men, because we live not for ourselves alone but for the ones who follow in our path."

Echoing the concerns of the first post-World War generation, Young Greason warned that "in these times when governments and laws are undermined by wrangling, vicious knaves who curse the standing orders, and declare that things are wrong, and that our middle class, should bow before the dictates of a mass, rapacious, superficial, and untaught, we needs must use our Reason and our staunch Integrity to route the menace, and to hold our own, and keep our peace and ways. Good friends, that is the problem of the day. Unless we check this radical unrest, and strive to break its wretched, grasping hold, posterity is cursed; then all is lost."

The class history chapter of the yearbook singled out Greason's poem. "We wish special notice be given to our gallant troubador, Sydney Greason, whose poem, we predict, shall be, in a thousand years, the great American epic." There may have been a coorelation between the special notice, and the fact that Theresa was also on the yearbook committee.

The class history noted that "this has been a year of club movement at Rogers." The first foreign language club was organized with Thomas Sweeney as President. Theresa Cottrell was elected vice president. The

Her new business career *in New York enabled Theresa to take a vacation in Florida in about 1925.*

history noted that the club "has provided many entertainments during the year for the student body, in the form of musicales and

DR. HORACE P. BECK
VICE PRESIDENT
JOHN J. CONRON
VICE PRESIDENT

BOARD OF DIRECTORS
—
GEORGE W. BACHELLER, JR.
DR. HORACE P. BECK
DAVID C. CAESAR
THOMAS B. CONGDON
JOHN J. CONRON
MARION EPPLEY

CHARLES TISDALL
PRESIDENT
W. C. CAMPBELL
MANAGING SECRETARY

Newport Chamber of Commerce

NEWPORT, RHODE ISLAND

SHERMAN BUILDING, THAMES STREET

TELEPHONE 558

GEORGE H. PROUD
TREASURER
HARRY A. TITUS
VICE PRESIDENT

BOARD OF DIRECTORS
—
WILLIAM A. LEYS
DANIEL J. McGOWAN
JAMES T O'CONNELL
EDWARD A. SHERMAN
CHARLES TISDALL
HARRY A. TITUS

My dear Mrs Cottrell

Please accept my sincere appreciation of the splendid entertainment furnished to members of the Chamber of Commerce and myself on the occasion of the recent conference on hotel proposition with Mr. Kenny.

Very sincerely yours,

W. Campbell

Newport R.I. Mch 24"

Mrs Cottrell
59 Bellevue Ave.

plays. It is a great success and a credit to the school, for a foreign language club gives a student deeper insight of a language that mere classroom study."

That night, the Alumni Association hosted a reception and dance for the Graduating Class of 1923. The Honoree was Head Master Frank E. Thompson, who was celebrating his Fiftieth year with Rogers High School. During the program, many speakers rose to recognize and praise Thompson's leadership. "Those who, within these fifty years, have come under Mr. Thompson's care and guidance, and have passed out of that care into the work-a-day world, come back this evening and lay before him in this leaflet their gratitude, their appreciation and their love."

A few days later, on Friday, June 25th, from 8 p.m. until midnight, Theresa attended the Banquet Dance of the RHS Senior Class, in fact, she served on the dance committe with classmates, George Halpin, Sydney Greason, Vernon Stoneman, and Laura Chase. She danced six of the 18 dances that night with Syd Greason, the Class Poet and "troubador." The dance highlighted the changing tastes of the new generation. Of the 18 numbers played by the Rialto Orchestra, only two were waltzes, and other 16 were Fox Trots.

THE 'BIG APPLE' FOR THERESA

Louise Lawson wrote the Prophecy chapter of the yearbook. She looked into Theresa's "future" and saw that she "went to Paris for a few years. She came back to Newport and opened a shop on the Avenue where she sells all sorts of odd and beautiful things." Lawson wasn't even close.

59 Bellevue Avenue as it appears today, one of two Newport houses Marie T. Cottrell bought and rented to provide for herself and her four daughters.

New York, not Paris was in Theresa's future. Her main concern in the weeks and months after graduation was getting a job. They were scarce in Newport.

During the summer of 1923, she served as "social secretary" to Mrs. Howard Spencer Graham, who lived on Eastons Point. Her pay was $20 a week.

By March, 1924, Theresa was working for Mrs. John F. Hubbard, who operated a real estate business at 136 Bellevue Avenue. She was paid $15 per week as a stenographer. The extra income helped a great deal. She stayed with the Hubbard business until December, 1924, when she boarded the Fall River Line for the overnight trip to New York.

Marie would allow Theresa to go to New York only if both she and her sister, Eleanor went together. They found lodging in a convent and employment in Manhattan.

By December 8, 1924 she had found a job in New York. In fact, she was, almost, in "show biz." She joined the business operation of Paul Whiteman, the world famous band leader, whose offices were at 160 West 45th Street. Her "show business" career lasted for six weeks, until January 17, 1925, when she left the Whiteman operation due to "insufficient salary" and "no advancement."

MARIE BECOMES A NEWPORT BUSINESS WOMAN ON HER OWN

The newly created Newport Chamber of Commerce was quite busy in 1924. It had set a goal of developing a large new hotel in Newport--without the assistance or interference of outside developers. Newport citizens were solidly behind the project which needed $500,000 to capitalize the project. Marie strongly favored the new hotel. She shared their vision for the new tourist facility.

On March 24th, W.C. Campbell, the managing secretary for the Chamber of Commerce wrote to ask Marie to "Please accept my sincere appreciation for the splendid entertainment furnished to members of the Chamber of Commerce and myself on the occasion of the recent conference on hotel propositions with Mr. Henry." Her skills as a hostess and caterer were highly valued by Newport's business community.

Once again, Marie's talents and abilities as a hostess were in evidence. She couldn't help but remember that had she accepted Hattie's offer, she would now be in the basement at 105 Pelham Street, baking for Hattie's social set. Instead, although she had suffered

Marie Theresa Flatvad Cottrell *(right foreground) in a mid-1930's photograph with her daughters and granddaughter, Joan Kaull. From left, Eleanor Cottrell Kaull, Marie Cottrell Raymond, Margaret Cottrell, Joan Kaull, and Cecile Cottrell (Irving). "Petie," was working in New York as Secretary to Harry Payne Whitney and had paid for the cottage in which Marie and her unmarried daughters were then living. The rented house was in Cedar Gate, near Darien, Connecticut, a rustic area with lots of trees and lodge-like houses.*

through some very thin years, now she was a Newport business person in her own right. She was very proud of her support for the Chamber.

"My dear Mrs. Cottrell, we certainly appreciate your most enthusiastic letter of October 15th," W.C. Campbell, the managing secretary for the Newport Chamber of Commerce wrote on October 17, 1924. He went on to "assure you that we are all tremendously pleased with the outcome of our hotel drive."

It took several years for the public to dig deep enough to buy half a million in common and preferred stock. However, the project was a success. The Hotel Viking was opened in 1926. Its "Skoal Room" was designed by Harriet Cottrell's husband, Ralph Barker.

[In 1961, the Viking's "Skoal Room"

was the scene of the first meeting between Marie's granddaughter, Faith Raymond, and Naval Officer Candidate, Tracy Connors of Jacksonville, Florda. Neither knew at the time that her grandmother had been heavily involved in supporting its development.]

In 1925, Marie was delighted with the news that the Storting had renamed Christiania, Norway--"Oslo." She followed closely the news that Roald Amundsen and Lincoln Ellsworth had conducted a successful arctic amphibious exploration. (The following year Roald Amundsen, Ellsworth, and the Italian explorer, Nobile flew over the North Pole to Alaska in the airship "Norge.")

She was not so enthusiastic about the popularity of a dance called the Charleston. Her daughters helped her stay current with the changing fashions of the period which

Marie dreamed of building a handsome new apartment building _on property at the corner of Bellevue Avenue and Mill Street. New York architect Hobart Upjohn prepared these sketches based on her directions._

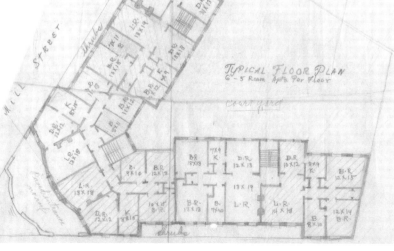

Upjohn proposed _a handsome, four-story, arrow- shaped Palladian building. The "point" faced the corner of Bellevue and Mill Streets. Each floor had six, 5-room apartments, each with its own fireplace._

featured straight dresses without waistlines, skirts above the knees, and "cloche" hats. She had helped Theresa pack her bags in late 1924, and move to New York. Theresa had the right clothing, but how would she fare in the big city.

ESTABLISHING THERESA

IN NEW YORK

In January, 1925, Theresa began working through the Brown Employment Exchange which saw itself as the "Agency for High Class Business Positions." They charged her $2.50 "remitted weekly until the balance is paid!" The balance was $17.50 for a job.

Theresa applied for a job at the Guaranty Trust Company of New York on January 12th. She listed her address at the time as 225 West 14th Street. Mr. Henry Miller, the employment manager screening her application, wrote in parentheses "(convent)." At the time it was one of the few places in New York City considered to be safe and secure lodging for young, single women.

As "special qualifications," she listed bookkeeping, typewriting, adding machine." She listed as references: Mrs. Elizabeth Hodson, Mrs. William Andrews, and Mrs. J.C. Easton. The personnel department noted "OK," after their names.

Emma Hubbard verified Theresa's employment period, and said she found her "very efficient, and of excellant (sic) character as far as I know." However, she pointed out that "she left with the declared intention of returning after a two week visit but evidently changed her mind."

Guaranty Trust Company was very thorough in their screening process. They verified all references in writing. "Dear Madam," Mr. Miller wrote to Mrs. Howard Graham at Eastons Point, "Miss Marie T. Cottrell...in applying for a position with this Company, claims employment with you from June 1923 to August 1923, stating that she resigned of her own accord. Any information you can give us concerning the correctness of these statements, together with your candid opinion of the applicant's character, ability and personal habits, will be appreciated and held strictly confidential." Someone noted at the

bottom of the office copy: "Mrs. Graham abroad, so reply will be delayed."

Mrs. Andrews and Mrs. Easton did reply to Mr. Miller's letter.

"I have known Miss M. T. Cottrell since she was a child," wrote Mrs. Andrews, who lived at 21 Catherine Street, Theresa's next door neighbor for years. "I believe her to be a very bright, clever girl. I know she got through high school at an early age. I believe her to be in every way desireable for the position she seeks."

Mrs. Gardner C. Easton ("Florence") "wish to state I have known Miss Cottrell all her life, and feel confident in saying that she is a girl of excellent character and habits, and charming manner. In the positions she has held since leaving school she has given complete satisfaction. I am sure you will find her dependable."

Theresa got the job. Only six months after graduating from high school she had moved to New York to find employment. She did not go to Paris, nor did she return to Newport to open a shop. After a nine-year business career in New York, during which she helped her mother a great deal financially, she attended a party in Darien, Connecticut. There she met a handsome young man who had just graduated from Lafayette College in Easton, Pennsylvania, William Mead Raymond, Jr. from Stamford, Connecticut. They married in 1933.

MARIE'S APARTMENT

BUILDING

Marie had a larger vision for her property on Bellevue Avenue and Mill Street. Her participation in Newport's efforts to build the new Viking Hotel had rekindled her desire to build her own building. Newport had no apartments at the time, but she owned adjoining lots at a prime location. In addition, she knew about apartment living from her years living with her parents in their Oslo apartment on Holbergsgate.

Joining Petie in New York in early 1925 Marie sought out a noted architect, Hobart Upjohn. She took with her the plot plans for her two properties across from the Redwood Library. After she explained her dream of a

Marie Fladvad Cottrell in her early 80's, *shortly before her death in 1947. Nap time for Monnie (pron. "Money") and Faith. Faith Raymond relaxing with her grandmother at the Kenneth Kaull home at Five Mile River Road in Darien, Connecticut. Monnie lived with her daughters during her last years. She spent a great deal of time with little Faith, teaching her to play Fish while Theresa prepared a meal or baked her mother's Norwegian cakes or cookies. Marie would sit on Faith's bed and hold her hand while she fell asleep. She died at the Dance family house on Five Mile River Road in Darien, Connecticut where she was receiving medical care in a small, first-floor bedroom. With her when she died was her son-in-law, Kenneth Kaull, who listened to her last words. Unfortunately, he could not understand them. She was speaking in her native language, Norwegian. (Photo by William Raymond, Jr.)*

beautiful new apartment building, she commissioned him for $554 to prepare architectural drawings.

On February 20, 1925, he completed his preliminary sketches. He proposed a handsome, four-story, arrow point shaped Palladian building. The "point" faced the corner of Bellevue and Mill Streets. The

Robert Cottrell's family as young adults. *Left to right, Edwin Angell Cottrell, Sarah Cottrell Ackerman, Harriet Cottrell Barker, Annie Louise Cottrell, Samuel Cottrell, and Catherine Wallace Cottrell. (Barker Family Collection)*

wings were separated by a triangular courtyard. Each floor had six, 5-room apartments, each having its own fireplace. She returned to Newport determined to see it completed.

ALONE ON BELLEVUE AVENUE

Marie spent several years trying to raise money to build the new apartment building. As time passed and her efforts were not successful, the Upjohn's sketches were folded carefully and put away. She never saw her dream realized, but she kept the tissue paper sketches until she died.

For the first time ever, in 1927 Marie lived alone at 59 Bellevue Avenue. While she had her tenants and boarders to serve, she was quite lonely. She did get to see Al Jolson in *"The Jazz Singer."* And, she followed Sonja Henie's victories with great interest.

Like many Newporters, she read with keen interest that Lizzie Borden, the accused murderess of her parents in near by Fall River, Massachusetts, had died. However, this year was especially empty. Three of her beloved daughters had moved to New York City. [Margaret rarely left her mother's side, never married, and only lived by herself following her mother's death.]

Not long after, Marie wept when she read that Roald Amundsen had been killed while attempting to rescue the Italian explorer Nobile whose airship had crashed north of Tromso, Norway. She remembered the shuffleboard games aboard the SS Oscar II. Now it was so long ago.

The Newport Directory notes in 1927 that Marie T. Cottrell "has removed to Brownsville, New York."

EPILOGUE

In her final years, Marie Cottrell sold her homes in Newport and lived alternately with her daughters, Marie Theresa Cottrell Raymond ("Petie") and Eleanor Cottrell Kaull. They spent most summers vacationing in Jamestown.

When her granddaughter, Faith, was born in 1939, Marie spent a great deal of time with her, providing her with affectionate loving care. She called her "Sweetest." To Faith, she was "Monnie." When toddler Faith took a nap she would nod off to sleep with Monnie holding her hand. Faith never drank cold milk, Monnie heated it carefully to the proper temperature. The entire household enjoyed her Norwegian cookies and cakes. Truly, cardamom was the Queen of Spices in Monnie's kitchen.

Her grandchildren remember Monnie's "terrific sense of humor. She always had a smile and a twinkle in her eye when teasing." Marie loved to listen to Soap Operas on the radio, including "Stella Dallas."

Drivers in both Newport and Stamford learned to keep a sharp eye out for "Mrs. Cottrell." Like Norwegians to this day, Marie loved to walk and did so at any opportunity for hours at a time. However, when she wanted to cross the street she gave many hapless drivers a rude shock.

Without pausing to look much less to wait until the coast was clear, she would plunge off the sidewalk and head towards the far side holding up her hand or her cane if it was handy. Standing on their brakes, the apoplectic drivers would screech to a halt. Marie would continue on her way, oblivious to their jitters.

There was something about automobiles and what made them tick that intrigued her, however. She often accompanied family members back and forth from their homes in Connecticut to Rhode Island, or even to Florida. When the driver would stop at a service station for gas, Marie would also get out of the car. When the driver or service station attendant would open the hood to look inside, Marie would join the team as they peered at the engine and watch as the attendant pulled the dip stick to check the oil level.

"Remember to check the water in the battery," she would remind them, nodding her head seriously. Of course, she was right--and they always did when she rode with them.

Marie never did learn to drive, but she reminded the family that if she ever did, she would have to "know what was going on under the hood."

In addition to her character, Marie Fladvad Cottrell is remembered for her "bright curiosity, and her eagerness to learn."

In her early Eighties, Marie had become ill and the family made arrangements in 1947 for her to be given live-in care by a family nearby in Darien, Connecticut which provided those services. She was only there for several weeks when her condition suddenly worsened.

One of her sons-in-law, Kenneth Stevens Kaull, was on duty at her side for the family as her condition worsened. Suddenly, she sat up in her bed.

"Mama, Papa, I see you, I am coming soon," she said softly, all the while passing her hands across the top of the sheets. Then, she lay back down. As she slipped quickly into semi-consciousness she was talking, trying to say something.

However, in her last moments she forsook English and returned to her native Norwegian. Kaull was not fluent in Norwegian and did not have time to get Petie or her sister, Ellie who had learned the language as children. Petie was at home and Ellie was recuperating from surgery.

Annie Louise Cottrell, librarian of the People's Library died in June, 1965. Born in Newport in 1895, she was the daughter of former Mayor Robert C. and Annie Johnson Southwick Cottrell.

Catherine W. Cottrell, former executive secretary of the Newport Chapter of the Red Cross died February 25, 1971.

Harriet Cottrell Barker, wife of Ralph Randolph Barker, died in 1962.

Sarah Cottrell Ackerman, wife of Alexander ("Lex") Seymour Ackerman, died in 1983.

Edwin Angell Cottrell, born in 1881, died in 1953, after a distinguished academic career.

Marie Theresa Cottrell ("Petie"), after marrying William Mead Raymond, Jr. in 1933, gave up her New York career to live in Stamford, Connecticut where they raised their son, William M. Raymond, III, and daughter, Faith Cottrell Raymond. Petie died in 1969.

Sources & Suggested Reading

Allen, Everett S. 1976. *A Wind to Shake the World: The Story of the 1938 Hurricane.* Boston: Little, Brown and Co.

Bayles, Richard M. 1888. *History of Newport County.* New York: L.E. Preston & Company.

Downing, Antoinette Forrester. 1952. *The Architectural Heritage of Newport, Rhode Island, 1640-1915.* Cambridge: Harvard University Press.

Elliott, Maud Howe. 1944. *This Was My Newport.* Cambridge: The Mythology Company, A. Marshall Jones.

Gannon, Tom. 1952. *Newport, Rhode Island: the City by the Sea.* Woodstock, VT: Countryman Press.

Hammett, Jr., Charles E. 1887. *Newport Household Directory,* containing a complete street directory. Providence: Sanford Publishing Co.

Hartley, Alley. 1967. *A Gentleman from Indiana Looks At Newport & the Narragansett Bay Area.* Freeport, Me: Bond Wheelwright Co.

History of Newport in Pictures. 1939. Art Association of Newport, Newport Tercentenary.

Hopf, John T. *Photographs of Newport and Middletown, Rhode Island.* 210 postcards, loose-leaf binder. Photograph collection Redwood Library.

Mason, George Champlin. 1894. *Annals of Trinity Church, 1821-1892.* Newport, RI: Trinity Church.

Mason, George Champlin. 1884. *Reminiscences of Newport.* Newport. Charles E. Hammett, Jr.

Newport Chamber of Commerce. 1933. *Historic Newport.*

Newport Historical Society Staff. *The Business of Leisure: the Gilded Age in Newport.* In Newport History, Vol. 62, pt. 3, Summar 1989, p. 97-126.

Newport Mercury and Weekly News. 1870-1930. Newport: T.T. Pitman Corporation/Edward Sherman Publishing Company.

Newport Pathfinder: A Complete Handbook of Newport, R.I. Newport, 1910.

Panaggio, Leonard J. 1969. *Portrait of Newport.* 150th anniversary publication, The Savings Bank of Newport. Providence: Mowbray Company.

Parmenter, J.G. 1926. *Newport: Capital of Vacationland,* Newport, R.I. Chamber of Commerce.

Perkins, Wilma Lord. 1951. *Fannie Merritt Farmer: The Boston Cooking-School Cook Book.* Boston: Little, Brown and Company.

Powel, M.E. *The Long Wharf:* (In Reminiscences of Newport 50 Years Ago. 1926, p. 5-7.

Randall, Anne L. 1970. *Newport; A Tour Guide.* Newport, R.I.: Catboat Press.

Robson, Lloyd. *Newport Begins.* Reprint of issues of Newport Historical Bulletin from 1964-1967. Newport: Newport Historical Society.

Schumacher, Alan T. *19th Century Newport Guide Books,* Newport History, Fall 1978, no. 172, v.51, no. 4, p. 7393.

Simister, Florence Parker. 1969. *Streets of the City: an Anecdotal History of Newport.* Providence: Mowbray Company, 1969.

Swett, Lucia Gray. 1891. *New England Breakfast Breads, Luncheon and Tea Biscuits.* Boston: Lee & Sheperd.

The Newport Directory. Boston: Sampson, Murdock & Company, 1995-1930.

Trinity Church. 1955. Trinity Church in Newport. Newport, R.I.

Warburton, Eileen. 1988. *In Living Memory.* Newport, RI: Newport Savings and Loan Association/Island Trust Company.

Ward, John Stedman. *The Trolley Car Days of Newport, R.I.* Newport History, Spring 1974, no. 154, v. 47, part 2, p. 129-152.

Warren, Wilfred E. 1977. *Newport Harbor in the 1930s.* Unpublished manuscript in the Redwood Library.

Recipes for Cakes, Cookies and Breads

Marie and Anna Fladvad, were sisters born in the last half of the 19th century who grew up on a farm in Kristiansund, Norway, and later moved to Christiania (Oslo). Their father grew up on a farm near Grøa in Sunndalen, approximately 75 miles east of Kristiansund in West Central Norway which has been the Fladvad Family home for over 500 years. Members of the family reside in the area to this day.

Cooking for a large, farm family must have been a laborious process for the Fladvad family--mother Oline, father Tron, and nine children. The Christmas Season however, was special. Many hours were spent throughout the month of December creating numerous types of cookies and cakes to be eaten during the extended holiday period. Even today, the Christmas season is special in Norway combining as it does, wonderful tastes and aromas from a busy kitchen with the warmth of family visiting and catching up on the year's events.

Disappointed by her fiance, a doctor in whom she had discovered an untruth, Marie Theresa Fladvad left Norway in 1894 to visit Newport, Rhode Island. Although America became her homeland, the tastes and customs of Norway never left her and her family. Even as she married a Newport merchant, and began raising four daughters, Marie recreated the sweets and treats of Norway for her family and friends.

In addition to the recipes in Marie's manuscript cookbook, we have included contributions from family sources all over Norway. Marie's recipes alone reflected both her father's Sunndalen heritage and her mother's Hamar cooking traditions.

Substitutes are suggested for certain ingredients which are widely used in Norway, but are not readily available in some parts of the United States.

With special appreciation for the contributions made by Karen Connors Henson

*A doll **husfrue** prepares a meal--including Munker--at a miniature 19th century Norwegian wood stove in an Oslo Folk Museum exhibit.*

Amerikansk kake

American Cake or Lemon Currant Cake

Preparation

⌘ *Preheat oven to 350° F.*

⌘ *In electric mixer bowl, blend eggs, sugar, butter, vanilla, and lemon peel.*

⌘ *Dust currants lightly with 1/4 cup of the flour mixture, stirring to coat currants so they won't clump together in the batter.*

⌘ *Mix flour, baking soda, and baking powder.*

⌘ *Add dry ingredients to the egg mixture, beating well until blended.*

⌘ *Add currants to batter, mixing well.*

⌘ *Bake in greased bundt pan (or in loaf pan) about 35-40 minutes.*

Ingredients

3 eggs
1 cup sugar
1/2 cup butter, softened
1 teaspoon vanilla
1 teaspoon grated lemon peel
1 1/2 cups currants
2 1/2 cups flour
1 teaspoon baking soda
1 teaspoon baking powder

Marie's Original Manuscript Recipe

Amerikansk kage

1 pund hvedemel; 1/2 pund korinter; 1/2 pund lys havanna; 3 Æggeplommer; 1 pal melk; 3 lod klart smør; 1 theskje natron. Citrondraaber og krydderi efter behag. De 3 hvide piskes til skum, og haves i kagen. Steges i form med langsom varme.

Arendalskaker

Arendal Cakes

Preparation

⌘ *Preheat oven to 325° F.*

⌘ *Beat 2 egg yolks and 1 whole egg with sugar.*

⌘ *Add flour and baking powder.*

⌘ *Drop dough from teaspoon onto greased cookie sheet.*

⌘ *Decorate dough with almond slivers.*

⌘ *Bake for 12 minutes or until golden brown.*

⌘ *Makes about 40 cookies.*

Note

This recipe makes light, quick, delicious cookies. They are crispy outside with spongy chewy centers, much like meringues in texture. They spread somewhat on the cookie sheet, so make sure to leave plenty of room between them. They puff slightly and become a lovely golden brown.

Ingredients

2 egg yolks
1 egg
3/4 cup sugar
3/4 cup flour
1/4 teaspoon baking powder
3 tablespoons slivered almonds

Variations

Add 1/2 teaspoon of vanilla extract or 1/4 teaspoon rum extract to create subtle taste combinations.

Berlinerkranser I

Berlin Wreaths

Ingredients

2 hard-cooked egg yolks, sieved
2 raw egg yolks
1 teaspoon vanilla extract
1/2 teaspoon almond extract
1 cup butter, softened
1 cup sifted powdered sugar or
   1/2 cup granulated sugar
2 1/2 cups flour
-----
1 slightly beaten egg white,
   beaten until frothy
1/3 cup sugar cubes, crushed
   (12-14 cubes)

Serving Suggestions

These cookies are a family favorite. The dough will be smooth, but may be somewhat difficult to work with when warm. The hard cooked egg yolk is easily sieved through the tiny holes on a standard grater. Colored sugar can be used in place of the crushed sugar cubes during the holidays if desired.

There are many variations on this recipe. Some call for almond extract rather than vanilla. We've even seen one that had a small amount of orange peel included in the recipe.

Note: Use leftover egg whites to make meringues.

Background

Berlinerkranser are Christmas wreaths with a delicate buttery flavor. While Berlinerkranser may sound like German cookies, the recipe for these delightful wreath-shaped cookies is traditional Norwegian. These little cookie wreaths are made by hand-rolling the dough into pencil-thin strips. Wreaths are formed by looping the ends. The Norwegians decorate Berlinerkranser with **grovstødt Sukker** (coarse granulated sugar) which makes them sparkle.

Preparation

⌘ *Preheat oven to 325° F.*
⌘ *Sieve the cooled, hard boiled egg yolks.*
⌘ *Lightly beat raw egg yolks, mixing with vanilla and almond extract.*
⌘ *Add the raw egg yolk mixture, teaspoon by teaspoon, working each into the crushed egg yolks.*
⌘ *Rub sugar into egg mixture, working with the flat side of a spoon into the eggs until dissolved.*
⌘ *Add butter and flour little by little, mixing well between each addition.*
⌘ *Chill dough in refrigerator for about 30 minutes (or overnight).*
⌘ *Take small pieces of dough, roll into pencil thin strips approximately 6" long.*
⌘ *Curl dough strips into a circle and loop one end over the other, extending about one-inch—into wreaths.*
⌘ *Beat the egg white until frothy, brush on top of wreaths, then sprinkle with crushed sugar.*
⌘ *Bake in medium oven for 15-17 minutes. Cookies should be light golden in color.*
⌘ *Let stand for a few minutes before removing from cookie sheet to cooling rack. Remove carefully, or cookies may break.*
⌘ *Makes about three dozen cookies. More if you roll the dough out very thinly.*

Note

This process does require some effort. "Hard work, as Bjørn points out, "but as I see it, the only way to success."

Original Manuscript Recipe

Berlinerkrandse

2 haardkogte Æggeplommer gnides sammen med 8 lod finstödt Sukker og röres saa ud i 2 raa Æggeplommer, derpaa haves 1 mark Mel og 1/2 mark udvasket Smør deri. De rulles ud til smaa krandse; bestryges med pidskede hvidder og bestrøes med grovstödt Sukker og Mandler.

Berlinerkranser II

Berlin Wreaths

Preparation

⌘ *Sieve the hard-cooked egg yolk.*
⌘ *Cream together sugar and butter.*
⌘ *Add sieved egg yolk, raw egg yolk, and vanilla.*
⌘ *Add flour and mix thoroughly.*
⌘ *Chill dough in refrigerator for at least thirty minutes.*
⌘ *Preheat oven to 350º F.*
⌘ *Take small pieces of the dough (walnut sized) and roll into pencil thin (1/2 inch) strips.*
⌘ *Shape into wreaths overlapping about 1-inch from ends.*
⌘ *Place on ungreased cookie sheet.*
⌘ *Brush with slightly beaten egg white.*
⌘ *Bake in moderate oven for about 12-15 minutes.*
⌘ *Makes about 3 dozen cookies.*

Ingredients

1 egg yolk, hard cooked
1/2 cup confectioner's sugar
1 cup butter, softened
1 egg yolk, raw
1 teaspoon vanilla
2 1/2 cups flour
1 egg white, slightly beaten

Biskopskake

Bishop's Cake

Preparation

⌘ *Preheat oven to 350º F.*
⌘ *Using an electric mixer, beat the egg whites until stiff. Set aside.*
⌘ *Beat the egg yolks in medium size bowl. Beat in the sugar.*
⌘ *Coat raisins with 1 tablespoon of flour to keep them from sinking to the bottom.*
⌘ *Add floured raisins and almonds. Mix flour and salt together.*
⌘ *Alternately add flour and milk to batter and mix well.*
⌘ *Gently fold egg whites into batter. Save as many egg white bubbles as possible since this causes the cake to rise during baking.*
⌘ *Grease a round 9-inch cake pan or tube pan. Sprinkle bottom of pan with zwieback crumbs and pour in the batter.*
⌘ *Bake for 25 minutes or until the cake is done.*
⌘ *Remove cake when cool.*

Ingredients

5 eggs, separated
1 1/4 cups confectioner's sugar
3/4 cup seedless raisins
1 tablespoon cake flour
3/4 cup chopped almonds
1 1/8 cups cake flour
1/4 teaspoon salt
1/3 cup milk
1 zwieback (crumbled for crust)

Bløtkake I

Soaked Cake

Ingredients

4 eggs, separated
1/8 teaspoon salt
1 cup sugar
1 cup cake flour or potato flour
2 teaspoons baking powder

Preparation

⌘ *Preheat oven to 325º F.*
⌘ *Beat egg whites with salt until stiff.*
⌘ *Fold in half the sugar, fold in remaining sugar.*
⌘ *Beat egg yolks and blend into the mixture.*
⌘ *Mix flour with baking powder, then fold flour into egg mixture.*
⌘ *Bake in a greased, 9-inch round cake pan in a moderate oven for 20-25 minutes.*
⌘ *Test for doneness: insert wooden toothpick, which should come out clean of batter.*
⌘ *Remove from the oven and invert the pan on a wire cake rack.*

⌘ *Cool completely before removing from pan. Run a spatula or knife around the cake between the cake and the pan to loosen it if necessary.*
⌘ *Cut in three horizontal layers.*
⌘ *Spread each layer with Smør Krem, and rejoin.*

Bløtekake prepared by Bjørn Fladvad Johansen. For the berry topping, he used hand picked wild strawberries individually frozen. The tart berries made a delicious complement to the sweet whipped cream topping.

Bløtkake II

Soaked Cake

Ingredients

4 eggs
1 cup sugar
1 1/2 cups flour
2 teaspoons baking powder
1/3 cup water

Filling

1 8-ounce jar of apricot jam or preserves
2 ripe bananas
1 pint whipping cream
1/4 cup madeira or sherry

Preparation

⌘ *Preheat oven to 350º F.*
⌘ *Beat eggs and sugar until light and creamy.*
⌘ *Add flour, baking powder, and water, then mix thoroughly.*
⌘ *Pour batter into greased 9-inch round cake pan.*
⌘ *Bake in moderate oven for 20-25 minutes, or until done. Cool on wire rack.*
⌘ *Cut cake into three horizontal layers, sprinkling each layer with a little madeira or sherry.*
⌘ *Spread jam, sliced bananas, and whipped cream between each layer, then rejoin layers.*
⌘ *Cover the entire cake with whipped cream and decorate with sliced bananas.*

Bordstabel-bakkels

Boardpile Cookies

Preparation

⌘ *Beat eggs. Mix well with sugar.*
⌘ *Add cream, beating thoroughly.*
⌘ *Beat in flour and butter to egg mixture.*
⌘ *Chill dough for 30 minutes.*
⌘ *Preheat oven to 375º F.*
⌘ *Roll out thinly on a lightly floured board.*
⌘ *Cut into lengths 5-7 inches by 1-2 inches wide.*
⌘ *Place doughstrips on a greased cookie sheet.*
⌘ *Bake for 7-9 minutes or until lightly browned.*
⌘ *Leave cookies on cookie sheet, and spread a ribbon of almond paste the length of each cookie.*
⌘ *Return cookie sheet to oven for 3-4 minutes to allow almond paste to cook slightly.*
⌘ *Makes about 50 cookies.*

Almond Paste or Mandelrøre

Beat 3 egg whites until stiff peaks form. Gently fold in sugar and almonds until well mixed.

Background

The reason for this name, Bjørn points out, is the way the cookies are served. They are placed "as a pile of boards" (criss-crossed side by side in fours).

Ingredients

2 eggs
1 1/4 cups sugar
2 tablespoons heavy cream
3 3/4 cups flour
1 1/4 cups butter, softened
-----
3 egg whites
1/4 cup sugar
1 1/4 cups finely chopped blanched almonds (about 5 ounces).
Note: the food processor works well for chopping.
Almond paste

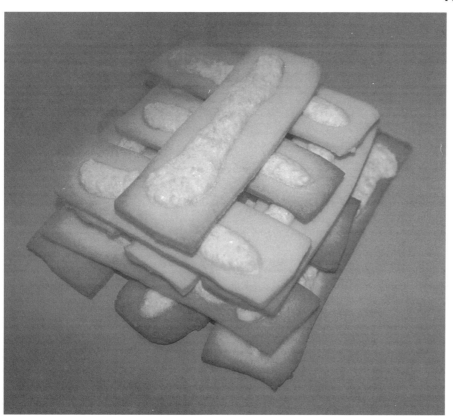

Clabbered Cream

Soured cream has traditionally been used both in cooking and in sauces by Norwegian cooks. It has a very pleasant taste, and a smooth texture. If you add some confectioner's sugar, you can spoon it over fruit or puddings. It can also be whipped.

Ingredients

2 cups heavy cream
2 tablespoons buttermilk

Preparation

⌘ *Heat cream in small saucepan to lukewarm (100º-105º F).*

⌘ *Remove from heat and pour cream into glass or plastic container. [We used a 3 cup plastic measuring cup, covered with plastic wrap and set aside on the kitchen counter top.]*

Add buttermilk and stir.

⌘ *Cover with plastic wrap and keep at room temperature (65º-75º F.) for about 24 hours or until it reaches the consistency of yogurt. It will be thick and creamy.*

⌘ *Keep covered and refrigerated. For a smaller amount, make half of the recipe.*

Olise Fladvad's travel diary, her hand painted china, and her solje pin resting atop her diary. Tyske skiver and lace cookies, an oval photo of Olise's sister, Marie Fladvad Cottrell with baby Theresa, two-year old Eleanor, and five-year old Margaret in 1905.

Diagonaler
Norwegian Diagonals

Preparation

⌘ *Preheat oven to 375º F.*
⌘ *Cream butter and sugar until light.*
⌘ *Add beaten egg, salt and flour.*
⌘ *Mix to a smooth dough.*
⌘ *Roll out about two-thirds of dough on a well floured board into a large oblong shape. Trim edges with knife or pastry wheel.*
⌘ *Cut oblong into 2" or 2 1/2" wide strips and place on greased cookie sheet.*
⌘ *With hands, roll remaining dough into pencil-thin strips.*
⌘ *Place lengthwise in center and at each side of each strip of dough.*
⌘ *Place a strip at top and bottom of length of dough (to keep jelly from draining out).*
⌘ *Between rows of dough place a thin row of jelly.*
⌘ *Bake in moderate oven 12-15 minutes.*
⌘ *While still warm cut in 1" diagonal slices.*
⌘ *Makes about 36 cookies.*

Ingredients

1/2 cup butter, softened
1/4 cup sugar
1 egg, beaten
1/4 teaspoon salt
1 1/2 cups flour
Currant jelly

Eggedosis
Egg Nog

Background

Eggedosis is similar to egg nog. It usually served on **Syttendemai**, the 17th of May, Norway's National Holiday—Independence Day. "In the old days," Tove explains with a twinkle, "it was always beaten stiff with a silver spoon. The maid did it."

Here is a recipe that will be a hit at holiday time. Note that a pasteurized egg substitute is used to avoid any potential health problems from raw eggs.

Preparation

⌘ *Mix first five ingredients.*
⌘ *Gently fold in the whipped cream.*
⌘ *Serve in small cups or glasses with a sprinkle of nutmeg on top.*

Ingredients

1 can sweetened condensed milk
1 teaspoon vanilla
1/8 teaspoon salt
1 quart milk
1/2 cup pasteurized egg substitute
1 pint carton whippping cream, whipped
Nutmeg to taste

Eplekake I
Apple Custard

Ingredients

5 apples (Granny Smith)
1/4 cup water
1/2 cup sugar
2 tablespoons butter
Grated rind of 1 lemon (or 2 teaspoons commercially prepared shredded lemon peel)
1/2 teaspoon vanilla
5 eggs, beaten
Topping: zwieback crumbs and whipped cream

Preparation

⌘ *Preheat oven to 350º F.*
⌘ *Slice thinly five cooking apples.*
⌘ *Cook on stove top or microwave in a little water (about 1/4 cup) until very tender. [In microwave use large (3 quart) covered (microwave safe) casserole dish and cook on high for 9-12 minutes.]*
⌘ *Stir carefully after about five minutes.*
⌘ *Add sugar, butter, lemon rind, and vanilla. Stir.*
⌘ *Beat eggs thoroughly using electric mixer or blender.*
⌘ *Pour well beaten eggs into casserole mixture. Mix thoroughly.*
⌘ *Bake for 35-45 minutes.*

Serving Tips

Sprinkle evenly with Zwieback or rusk crumbs. Top with whipped cream or a non-dairy whipped topping.

Marie's Original Manuscript Recipe

Frugtkage

10 Finstödte Kavringer; 1/2 pot Fløde; 1/4 mark Sukker; 1/2 mark Mandler; lidt Kanel; Æggene og Fløden slaaes tilsammen, derefter Sukkeret og Mandlene og Kavringerne, tilsist de pidskede hvidder Æble eller Pære kommer først i bunden paa fadet. Steges i 1 1/2 Time.

Note

In this recipe Marie placed the apple or pear slices on the bottom of the pan, then poured the batter over them before baking—an apple up-side-down cake.

Eplekake II
Apple Cake

Ingredients

4 tart apples
3 eggs
1 1/2 cups sugar
1/3 cup butter
2/3 cup milk
1 3/4 cup flour
2 1/2 teaspoons baking powder
1/3 cup brown sugar
1 1/2 teaspoons cinnamon

Preparation

⌘ *Preheat oven to 400º F .*
⌘ *Peel apples and slice thinly.*
⌘ *Blend eggs and sugar until foamy.*
⌘ *Melt butter, then add milk and heat to luke warm.*
⌘ *Blend warm mixture (blender on low).*
⌘ *Combine flour with baking powder. Fold into egg mixture.*
⌘ *Grease and flour a 9-inch round cake pan. Or, coat it with unseasoned bread crumbs as it is often done in Norway to give the cake a crusty surface.*
⌘ *Pour batter into pan.*
⌘ *Arrange apple slices on top in pleasing geometric pattern and sprinkle with brown sugar and cinnamon.*
⌘ *Bake for 30 minutes or until done.*

Marie Theresa Cottrell Raymond's
Dutch Apple Cake

Preparation

⌘ *Mix together flour, baking powder, salt and sugar.*
⌘ *Cut 1/4 cup butter into flour mixture.*
⌘ *Add egg and milk to flour mixture, beating well.*
⌘ *Place dough in greased 9-inch round pan.*
⌘ *Press three apples (cored and sliced) into dough in geometric or "pin wheel" design.*

Topping

⌘ *Cut butter into small pieces and distribute on top of dough.*
⌘ *Sprinkle sugar and cinnamon evenly on top of dough.*
⌘ *Bake at 350º F. for about 30 minutes.*

Ingredients

1 cup flour
1 1/4 teaspoons baking powder
1/2 teaspoon salt
2 tablespoons sugar
1/4 cup butter
1 egg
2 tablespoons milk
3 apples

Topping

1 tablespoon butter
2 tablespoons sugar
1/2 teaspoon cinnamon

Hard Sauce

1/4 cup butter creamed with 1 cup confectioner's sugar. Use small amount of cream or milk to soften. 1 teaspoon vanilla or 1/2 teaspoon rum extract for flavor. Refrigerate before serving on apple cake.

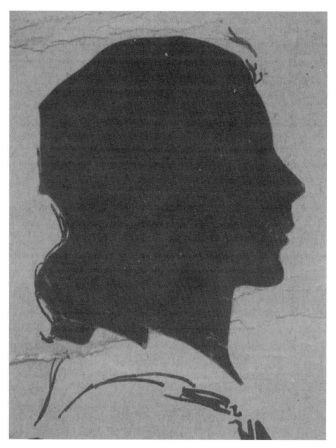

Eleven year old Marie Theresa Cottrell posed for this silhouette by Julia Brown in Newport, Rhode Island on September 12, 1916.

Flatbrød

Flat Bread

Ingredients

1 1/2 tablespoons sugar
1/4 cup butter, softened
1/4 teaspoon baking soda
1/4 teaspoon baking powder
1/2 teaspoon salt
1/2 cup buttermilk
1 1/2 cups flour

Preparation

⌘ *Preheat oven to 375º F.*
⌘ *Cream sugar and butter until smooth.*
⌘ *Mix in baking soda, baking powder, salt, and buttermilk.*
⌘ *Adding a small amount of flour at a time, mix to a stiff dough.*
⌘ *Divide dough into four equal pieces.*
⌘ *Roll out to about 1/8-inch thick on floured surface.*
⌘ *Bake on ungreased cookie sheet for 5-10 minutes or until lightly browned. The irregular rolled out pieces fit nicely on one cookie sheet.*
⌘ *Serve with cheese or softened butter.*
⌘ *Store in tightly covered container in a cool place.*

Fruktkake

Norwegian Pear Pudding

Ingredients

5 large pears (or apples), stewed
1/4 cup dry cooking sherry (or water)
6 eggs, separated
1/2 teaspoon sugar
3/4 cup cream (or half & half)
1/2 cup sugar
1/2 to 1 teaspoon cinnamon
10 Zwieback or rusk, crumbled
1/4 cup sliced almonds

Topping

1 cup whipping cream, whipped
Sweeten to taste

Preparation

⌘ *Preheat oven to 350º F.*
⌘ *Peel and core pears and slice thinly. [Can be prepared with apples as well as pears.]*
⌘ *Arrange in 3 quart (microwave safe) casserole. Add 1/3 cup water. Cover and microwave pears and sherry at 80 percent power for 9-12 minutes (or until tender in covered saucepan on stove top).*
⌘ *Separate eggs.*
⌘ *Beat eggs whites until stiff with 1/2 teaspoon sugar.*
⌘ *In blender, beat together egg yolks, cinnamon, cream. Add in sequence on slow speed: zwieback, and for last 15 seconds add the sliced almonds.*
⌘ *Fold liquid mixture gently into egg whites.*
⌘ *Arrange stewed pears on bottom of large (12" x 6") baking dish.*
⌘ *Pour egg mixture on top and even out with spatula.*
⌘ *Bake for 45 minutes.*
⌘ *Cut into squares and serve warm, topped with whipped cream.*

Fyrstekake

Prince's Cake

Background

"Fyrstekake is my favorite," explains Tove. "I make it both with the almond filling and with an apple filling—cooked apples with sugar, sort of a lumpy applesauce. Made with apples, it is delicious served with ice cream or whipped cream. My mouth waters at just the thought."

Preparation

⌘ *Sift together flour, sugar, and baking powder.*
⌘ *Cut in butter with pastry blender or with two knives until mixture looks like coarse crumbs.*
⌘ *With a fork, blend in 1 beaten egg until a dough forms.*
⌘ *Chill dough in refrigerator while making filling (about 20-30 minutes).*

Prepare Filling
⌘ *Prepare almond filling by mixing almonds, confectioner's sugar and 1 egg.*
⌘ *Apple filling is prepared by simmering apple pieces with water and sugar until tender, about 8 minutes. Drain water and mash apples until a lumpy applesauce is formed.*

⌘ *Preheat oven to 350º F.*
⌘ *Remove chilled dough from refrigerator and divide it into two balls. Refrigerate one ball until ready to use.*
⌘ *Place ball in an 8-inch round cake pan. Using hands, work dough in pan to cover bottom and sides of pan.*
⌘ *Spread almonds or apple filling onto dough.*
⌘ *Roll out other ball of dough on a well-floured board and cut into 1/2" - 3/4" strips long enough to form a lattice crust on top of filling. Trim lattice to fit edges. Seal.*
⌘ *Bake for 20-30 minutes, or until golden brown.*
⌘ *Cool completely before removing from pan.*

Ingredients

1 1/3 cups flour
1/2 cup sugar
1 teaspoon baking powder
1/2 cup butter
1 egg, beaten

Filling I - Almond

2/3 cup grated almonds
1 cup sifted confectioner's sugar
1 egg, beaten

Filling II - Apple

1 large apple, pared, cored, and cubed
1 cup water
1/4 cup sugar

Notes

Can be served in wedges like a pie. Great with vanilla ice cream. Very rich and moist, a crumbly but tender shell encasing a slightly chewy, nutty filling. The cardamom and cinnamon go very well together.

The lattice crust on top puffs up and turns a pretty speckled golden brown. Pipe whipped cream on top and sprinkle lightly with cinnamon.

Gjærbakst
Sweet Yeast Bread

Ingredients

2 (1/4 ounce) envelopes of
  yeast
1/2 cup warm water
1 1/2 cups milk
1/2 cup butter
1/3 cup sugar
1 egg
2 teaspoons ground cardamom
5 1/2 - 6 cups flour
-----
1 egg, beaten (use with water
  to brush on top of dough
  before baking)
1 tablespoon water

Sugar
Chopped almonds

Preparation

⌘ *Dissolve yeast in warm water (105º - 115º F).*
⌘ *In a pan, combine milk, butter, and sugar. Heat to lukewarm temperature. Butter does not need to melt completely.*
⌘ *Transfer to large bowl. Gradually add 2 cups flour and beat well. Blend in yeast mixture, egg and cardamom.*
⌘ *Gradually beat in additional 3-4 cups of flour to make a soft dough.*
⌘ *On a lightly floured board, knead dough for five minutes. Keep dough slightly sticky for a moist bread.*
⌘ *Place in greased bowl and turn once to ensure top is greased. Cover and let rise in a warm place until double (about 1 1/2 hours). Punch down dough.*
⌘ *Shape into buns or loaves and place in greased pans. Let rise again until double in size.*
⌘ *Preheat oven to 375º F.*
⌘ *Lightly brush tops with beaten egg mixed with tablespoon of water. Sprinkle with desired amount of sugar and almonds.*
⌘ *Bake loaves for 20 minutes or until lightly browned. Buns will take about 15 minutes.*
⌘ *Makes about 36 buns or 4 small loaves.*

Gjærbakst med Eple
Yeast Bread with Apples

Ingredients

1/2 batch yeast dough (see
  Gjærbakst recipe above)
1 egg, beaten
1 tablespoon water
2-3 medium-sized tart apples
1 tablespoon lemon juice
1 tablespoon cinnamon
3 tablespoons sugar
1/4 cup chopped or sliced
  almonds

Preparation

⌘ *Prepare sweetened yeast dough (Gjaerbakst recipe above).*
⌘ *After the first rising, punch down dough.*
⌘ *On very lightly floured board, roll out dough to fit a greased shallow baking dish, 8 x 11 inches or larger.*
⌘ *Shape the dough to fit the edges like a tart shell. Flute edges if desired.*
⌘ *Lightly brush dough with beaten egg diluted with 1 tablespoon of water.*
⌘ *Cut apples into quarters, core and pare. Thinly and evenly slice apples. Arrange in a thin layer on top of dough.*
⌘ *Sprinkle with lemon juice, cinnamon, sugar and top with almonds.*
⌘ *Cover and let rise in a warm place for 20 minutes.*
⌘ *Preheat oven to 375º F.*
⌘ *Bake for 25 minutes or until nicely browned.*

Gudbrandsdaler

Gudbrands Valley Cookies

The Gudbrandsdal ("Gudbrand's valley") runs from Lesjaskogsvatn southeastwards to Lake Mjøsa. This is *Peer Gynt* country, the setting for Henrik Ibsen's 1867 masterpiece later set to music by Edvard Grieg. Always a lure to summer travelers, the Gudbrandsdal scenery is among the most picturesque in Norway with mountains, farmsteads, fish-filled lakes, wild game, and alpine flowers. Oline Bjørke, Marie and Anna's mother, grew up in Furnes, on Lake Mjøsa, not far from the Gudbrandsdal.

Preparation

⌘ *Preheat oven to 350º F.*
⌘ *Stir together cream and potato flour.*
⌘ *Add butter, sugar, flour, and almonds.*
⌘ *Stir well. Using the dough hook on your heavy duty mixer helps a great deal when working this stiff cookie dough. Once you mix the cream with the potato flour, it "sets up" into a very stiff dough. Voila! The dough hook makes preparation much easier.*
⌘ *Roll the dough into 3/4-inch balls and press lightly with a fork to flatten.*
⌘ *Or, use a rolling pin to roll out dough on lightly floured surface to a thickness of approximately 1/4 inch. Use cookie cutters to create desired shapes.*
⌘ *Place on an ungreased cookie sheet.*
⌘ *Bake for about 15-20 minutes until pale golden brown.*
⌘ *Makes 50-60 cookies.*

Ingredients

1 cup cream
1 cup potato flour
1 cup butter, softened
1 cup sugar
2 cups flour
3/4 cup chopped almonds

Notes

Similar to **Sandnøtter**, these cookies are rich. However, we eat them only once in a while. And frankly, potato flour is sometimes hard to find. Many of the "health-food" or "gourmet" grocery stores do carry it. We keep our potato flour in the freezer since we find we use it infrequently. Buying it when we find it allows us to bake this tasty, rich variety of shortbread, with a buttery flavor whenever we feel the urge. We think it's just the right cookie to go with a hot cup of tea or coffee on a frosty afternoon.

In this recipe, the potato flour is used in combination with all-purpose white flour. Potato flour also makes a great thickener for soups and gravies.

The Gudbrands Valley

Guldkake

Gold Cake or Yellow Cake

Ingredients

8 egg yolks
2/3 cup butter
1 1/2 cups sugar
3 cups cake flour
3 teaspoons baking powder
1/2 teaspoon salt
1 1/8 cups milk
1/2 teaspoon lemon or vanilla extract
1/4 cup finely chopped almonds (in food processor)

Note

This recipe was prepared with cake flour for a fine and light texture.

Preparation

⌘ *Preheat oven to 375º F.*
⌘ *Beat egg yolks throughly.*
⌘ *Cream butter and sugar together until the mixture is light and fluffy. Gradually add egg yolks to creamed mixture, and beat until very smooth.*
⌘ *Sift flour with baking powder and salt. Add flour alternately with milk, beating well after each addition. When all flour is added, beat thoroughly again, then add extract and almonds.*
⌘ *Pour into three greased 8-inch layer pans and bake for 20-25 minutes.*
⌘ *Cool and remove from pans. Sprinkle with confectioner's sugar or spread with frosting to taste.*

Suggestion

Line pans with waxed paper cut to fit the bottom of your pans.

Hjortetakk

Norwegian Antlers or Dough Wreaths

Ingredients

2 eggs
2/3 cup sugar
1/4 cup whipping cream
2 teaspoons cognac or brandy
2 tablespoons butter
2 cups flour
1 1/2 teaspoons baking powder
1/2 teaspoon cardamom
vegetable oil for deep fat frying

Note

Read deep fat frying tips in Smultringer recipe.

Preparation

⌘ *Beat eggs with sugar.*
⌘ *In a separate bowl, whip the cream and add cognac; blend into egg mixture.*
⌘ *Melt butter and add to egg mixture.*
⌘ *Mix flour, baking powder and cardamom together.*
⌘ *Gradually add to egg mixture.*
⌘ *Place dough in a clean bowl and refrigerate 12 hours or overnight.*
⌘ *Heat oil to 375º.*
⌘ *On a floured board, roll small pieces of dough into pencil thin strips about 5-inches in length.*
⌘ *Curl strips into circles and overlap ends; press together to hold.*
⌘ *Make 4 diagonal cuts on outside edge to give antler appearance.*
⌘ *Fry only 3-4 at a time. This will keep the oil temperature constant and prevent overabsorption of fat in the dough.*
⌘ *Fry for about 2 minutes on each side or until brown.*
⌘ *Drain on paper towels.*
⌘ *Makes about 30.*

Honningkake

Honey Cake

Background

A delicious spiced honey "sponge type" cake which can be topped with whipped cream, vanilla cream, or butter cream.

In Medieval times, pepper and ginger were used almost interchangeably. In this recipe we see both are still used. Also note the use of "knife points" as a measure of baking powder in Marie's manuscript recipe.

Preparation

⌘ *Preheat oven to 350º F.*

⌘ *Separate eggs. In a small bowl, beat egg whites until stiff. Set aside.*

⌘ *In another bowl, beat together egg yolks, lemon peel, lemon extract, and sugar.*

⌘ *Gradually add honey and hot milk. Beat well.*

⌘ *Sift the remaining dry ingredients together.*

⌘ *Add to egg yolk mixture.*

⌘ *Gently fold egg whites into cake batter.*

⌘ *Pour into a greased bread pan (Marie's original recipe), or for a higher volume cake, pour into an ungreased tube pan.*

⌘ *Bake for about 20 minutes or until done.*

⌘ *Cool cake in pan upside down to preserve volume. When cool, remove from pan.*

Ingredients

4 eggs
1 tablespoon grated or finely chopped lemon peel
1/2 teaspoon lemon extract
1/2 cup sugar
1/3 cup honey
1/4 cup hot milk
1 cup cake flour
1 1/2 teaspoons baking powder
1/2 teaspoon salt
1/8 teaspoon ground black pepper
1/2 teaspoon ground ginger

Marie's Original Manuscript Recipe

Honning kage

9 Æg; 1/2 mark Sukker; 1 mark Mel; 1/2 mark Honning; 2 Theskeer Hjortesalt; Ingefær og en liden smule Peber. Steges som grovt brød.

Translation

9 eggs; 1/2 mark sugar; 1 mark flour; 1/2 mark honey; 2 knifepoints baking powder; ginger and a little bit of pepper. Bake as for whole wheat bread.

Hveteboller

Wheat Rolls

Background

These are delicious sweet rolls when cut in half and served with butter and/or strawberries. They are often served at children's parties in Norway.

Ingredients

1 package dry yeast
1 teaspoon sugar
1/4 cup lukewarm water
1 1/2 tablespoons flour

1/2 cup + 2 tablespoons butter
1 1/2 cups milk
2/3 cup sugar
1/2 teaspoon ground cardamom
1/2 teaspoon salt
5-5 1/2 cups flour
1 cup raisins
1 egg
1 tablespoon water

Preparation

⌘ *Dissolve yeast and 1 teaspoon sugar in luke warm water, not hotter than 110º F.*
⌘ *Add the 1½ tablespoons of flour.*
⌘ *Stir well. Put in warm place until double—about 10-20 minutes. It will become thick and foamy like pancake batter.*
⌘ *Heat the butter, milk, and sugar to a lukewarm temperature.*
⌘ *In a large mixing bowl, combine yeast mixture, butter, mixture, cardamom, salt, and 3 cups of flour.*
⌘ *Beat well.*
⌘ *Gradually add remaining flour. Dough should be slightly sticky.*
⌘ *On a lightly floured board, knead dough for a few minutes.*
⌘ *Place in a greased bowl. Turn dough once so top is greased.*
⌘ *Cover and set bowl in a warm place until dough doubles in size (about 1 - 1½ hours).*
⌘ *Punch dough down. Divide dough into about 28 pieces.*
⌘ *Roll each piece into a ball into which you place a few raisins (1-5).*
⌘ *Place on greased cookie sheets. Allow room for dough to double in size.*
⌘ *Let rise in a warm area for about 30 minutes to one hour.*
⌘ *Preheat oven to 375º F.*
⌘ *Beat egg and water together. Lightly brush "bolle" with egg mixture.*
⌘ *Bake for 15-20 minutes depending on "bolle" size.*
⌘ *Makes about 28 rolls.*

Jødekaker

Jewish Cakes

Preparation

⌘ *Preheat oven to 375º F.*

⌘ *Beat together eggs, sugar, butter, and cognac until creamy.*

⌘ *In a separate bowl, mix flour, baking powder and cinnamon.*

⌘ *Add dry ingredients to egg mixture and beat well.*

⌘ *Chill dough for 30 minutes or until it can be rolled out.*

⌘ *On a well floured board, roll out dough about 1/4 - 1/2 inch thick.*

⌘ *Using a round cookie cutter or biscuit cutter, cut out circular cookies.*

⌘ *Place on a greased baking sheet.*

⌘ *Brush the top with beaten egg white, then sprinkle with a few chopped almonds and sugar.*

⌘ *Bake for 12-15 minutes or until golden brown.*

Ingredients

2 eggs
2/3 cup sugar
1 cup butter
1 tablespoon cognac
2 1/4 cups flour
2 teaspoons baking powder
2 teaspoons cinnamon

Topping

1 egg white
1/4 cup chopped almonds
1/4 cup sugar

Model of a Norwegian cupboard from the the late 19th century seen in the Norsk Folke-museum in Olso, Norway's largest museum and the world's oldest open-air museum.

Marie's Original Manuscript Recipe

Jødekager

2 mark Puddersukker opløst i 3 pagler lunket Melk vaar det er opløst kommer deri 6 pidskede Æg, 1 glas Cognac, lidt Canel, Cardemomme og 2 Potaske og saa meget Mel saa deigen godt slipper bordet, derpaa tages 1 mark Smør, som udrulles som til butterdeig. Deigen settes om aften, dev udrulles tynd og udskjæres med en kniv og glass og steges ganske lys.

Julekake
Christmas Cake

Ingredients

1 envelope (1/4 ounce) dry
  yeast
1/4 cup warm water
1 1/4 cups milk
3/4 cup butter
3/4 cup sugar
1 teaspoon salt
1 egg
1 teaspoon cardamom
5-5 1/4 cups flour

1/2 cup raisins
1/2 cup chopped, candied fruit
2 teaspoons flour
1 egg, beaten
1 tablespoon water

Preparation

⌘ *Dissolve yeast in warm water (105º-115º F).*
⌘ *In a small pan, combine milk, butter, sugar, and salt. Heat to warm temperature. Butter does not need to be completely melted.*
⌘ *Transfer to a large bowl. Gradually add 2 cups flour and beat well with electric mixer.*
⌘ *Blend in yeast mixture, egg, and cardamom.*
⌘ *Gradually beat in additional 3-3 1/4 cups of flour to make a soft dough.*
⌘ *On a lightly floured board, knead dough for five minutes. Keep dough slightly sticky.*
⌘ *Place in greased bowl and turn once so that top is greased.*
⌘ *Cover and let rise in a warm place until double (about 1 1/2 hours).*
⌘ *Combine raisins and candied fruit. Stir in 2 teaspoons of flour to keep pieces from sticking together.*
⌘ *Punch down dough.*
⌘ *Knead fruit into dough and divide dough into two equal portions.*
⌘ *Shape portions into round loaves and place each in a greased 8" or 9" cake pan.*
⌘ *Brush tops with egg mixture.*
⌘ *Cover lightly and let rise until double, about 30-60 minutes.*
⌘ *Preheat oven to 375º F.*
⌘ *Bake for 35-40 minutes or until done.*

Norwegian Christmas Tree as a centerpiece at the Julehus in **Drøbak,** *a pleasant little town of some 3,000 people near Oslo. Hardly a household word—unless you're a child and want to send a Christmas card to Santa Claus. In which case, you address the letter to: Mr. Santa Claus, Julenissen N' 1440, Drøbak, Norway.* **"Julenissen"** *are Christmas elves or gnomes. In Drøbak however, Christmas does come 365 days a year at the* **Tregården Julehus** *("Christmas House built of Wood"). The quaint wooden house is chock full of Christmas presents and ornaments. Many children believe that Santa's workshop is nearby in some secret location. Another surprise. Drøbak is not at the North Pole. While it does sit beside the picturesque Oslofjord, most people get there by driving South for about 35 kilometers from Oslo. Over a quarter of a million people visit the Drøbak Christmas House every year.*

Kaffebrød

Coffee Bread

Preparation

⌘ *In a medium pan, heat butter, milk and sugar to a lukewarm temperature, not higher than 110º F.*

⌘ *Using a large mixing bowl, pour the warm milk mixture over the yeast. Stir to dissolve the yeast.*

⌘ *Add salt, cardamom, egg and 3 cups of flour. Beat well.*

⌘ *Beat in remaining flour. Dough should be soft and slightly stickly.*

⌘ *On a lightly floured board, knead dough for 6-8 minutes. A small amount of additional flour may be needed to keep dough from sticking to the board.*

⌘ *Place in a greased bowl. Turn dough once so top is greased.*

⌘ *Cover and let stand in a warm place until dough doubles in size (about 1-1 1/2 hours).*

⌘ *Punch down dough. Shape into two round loaves or make a braid by dividing dough into three portions, rolling into strands, and braiding.*

⌘ *Place on greased baking sheet. Cover and let rise again until double.*

⌘ *Preheat oven to 375º F.*

⌘ *Just before baking, brush dough lightly with a mixture of 1 egg and 1 tablespoon of water.*

⌘ *Sprinkle tops with sugar and almonds.*

⌘ *Bake for 20-25 minutes.*

Ingredients

1/2 cup butter
2 cups milk
1/2 cup sugar
2 packages dry yeast
1/2 teaspoon salt
2 teaspoons ground cardamom
1 egg
6 cups flour
-----
1 egg
1 tablespoon water
Sugar to taste, approximately 2 tablespoons
1/4 cup chopped almonds

Kaffebrød and King Haakon's Coffee Cake.

- -

Marie's Original Manuscript Recipe

Kaffebrød

1 mark Smør, 1/2 mark Sukker, 1 pund mel, 8 skeer vand, kanel og kardemomme efter behag udtrilles og udskjæres i spidser.

- -

Karamellpudding
Caramel Custard

Ingredients

1 cup sugar
1/2 cup boiling water
2 cups milk
1 cup heavy cream
2 tablespoons sugar
1 teaspoon vanilla
4 eggs

Slivered almonds
Whipped cream

Note

Often served with whipped cream. "A great favorite with all Norwegians," Tove notes.

Caramel Preparation

⌘ *Preheat oven to 300º F.*
⌘ *Over medium heat, melt 1 cup sugar in deep saucepan, stirring constantly.*
⌘ *Add boiling water (very slowly) and stir until syrup is thickened and smooth, about five minutes.*
⌘ *Immediately pour into baking dish, coating the side and bottom (or syrup will harden).*

Custard Preparation

⌘ *In same saucepan used for caramel, mix milk and heavy cream.*
⌘ *Stir while bringing to a boil over moderate heat.*
⌘ *Remove from heat.*
⌘ *Let cool for about five minutes.*
⌘ *Add vanilla.*
⌘ *Beat eggs and two teaspoons of sugar, then add slowly and carefully to the hot cream mixture, stirring slowly.*
⌘ *Pour caramel pudding mixture into caramel coated baking dish.*
⌘ *Set baking dish in larger pan of hot water, approximately 1-inch deep.*

One of the most beautiful views to enjoy in Norway as you savor a Karamellpudding is here at Golå Hotel, the late morning mist wafting gently over the smooth surface of Golåvannet. In the distance, the snow-capped shoulders of Storronden, Rondeslottet, Digerronden, Vesles-meden, and Smiubæljen rise from the Jotun-heimen masstif.

Kardemommemuffins

Cardamom Muffins

Background

Golden brown muffins. So easy to make and so delicious served warm with wisps of fragrant steam curling up alongside the steam from your coffee or tea.

Preparation

⌘ *Preheat to 350º.*
⌘ *Cream butter with sugar.*
⌘ *Add egg and mix well.*
⌘ *Combine baking powder, cardamom, flour and salt, mixing well.*
⌘ *Add flour mixture to egg mixture alternately with milk.*
⌘ *Grease and flour muffin tins or use paper baking cups. Fill muffin tins 3/4 full.*
⌘ *Bake for 15-20 minutes or until golden brown.*

Ingredients

1/4 cup butter, softened
2/3 cup granulated sugar
1 egg
2 teaspoons baking powder
1-2 teaspoons ground cardamom
1 1/2 cups flour
1/2 teaspoon salt
2/3 cup milk

Serving Suggestions

Serve with butter, preserves, fresh berries or other fruit.

Cardamom, Queen of Spices

Native to India, this richly perfumed dried fruit is a member of the ginger family of spices, and the world's second-most-precious spice. Today, it is mountain grown in Central America, Ceylon, or India, where it yields not more than 250 pound of pods per acre—each snipped individually from the plant with scissors. The pea-sized pods each contain 17-20 tiny aromatic black seeds.

Cardamom originated in India where it is still a favorite spice for curries and a wide variety of other dishes. In ancient times, physicians believed it warded off evil spirits and was a curative for many diseases, as well as an aphrodisiac. Some Indian physicians to this day believe strongly in its medicinal properties, claiming it is a remedy for indigestion, dysentery, nauseas, and even dental decay.

Throughout the Middle East, cardamom is used extensively—in coffee. Almost sixty percent of the entire world's production of cardamom is used for this single purpose.

When cardamom is used in coffee, it becomes a beverage called gahwa. Not only do Arabs find the flavor pleasing, but the service of gahwa has become ritualized. When used in this way, cardamom is purchased exclusively as green pods. A high premium is placed on the appearance of the cardamom pods, the greener the color, the most prized they are for gahwa.

Cardamom enjoys much broader use throughout Scandinavian, as the primary spice in a wide variety of baked goods.

Spice historians attribute Cardamom's popularity in Scandinavia, thousands of miles from India, to the Vikings. While it has not been proven conclusively, they conclude that Viking warriors who served for many years and in large numbers in the famed Varangian guards of Byzantine palaces, acquired a taste for cardamom and brought it back home with them.

Today, cardamom is used in many traditional Norwegian recipes.

Cardamom seed can be obtained in either the pod or decorticated (outer pods removed) states. Both pods and decorticated Cardamom can be obtained either whole or ground.

A buff colored pod means it has been bleached. Green pods are unbleached. However, the seeds of both are the same.

Kassandrakaker
Norwegian Cassandra Cookies

Background

The dough is remarkably easy to work. Even at room temperature it rolls right out without sticking if a little flour is spread beneath it. This recipe makes a delicious shortbread cookie.

Ingredients

1 egg
2/3 cup sugar
3 cups flour
1 cup butter, softened
1 egg white
Coarse sugar

Preparation

⌘ *Preheat oven to 375º F.*
⌘ *Beat egg and add sugar, mixing well.*
⌘ *Cream butter with flour until smooth.*
⌘ *Combine egg-sugar mixture with flour mixture.*
⌘ *Cover with plastic wrap and chill.*
⌘ *Roll out dough and cut into desired shapes with cookie cutter.*
⌘ *Place on cookie sheet, brush with egg white and sprinkle center with coarse sugar.*
⌘ *Bake for 10-12 minutes, or until golden brown at edges. Let cool.*

King Haakon's Coffee Cake
Lemon Cardamom Tea Bread

Background

A variation of Tebrød, but with a cardamom flavor instead of almond. A crunchy, dunking cookie similar to Italian Biscotte which is very popular in coffee shops.

Ingredients

5/8 cup butter, melted
3/4 cup sugar
4 eggs
1/8 teaspoon lemon extract
1 teaspoon ground cardamom
3 1/2 cups flour
4 teaspoons baking powder

Notes

Stores well in an air-tight container. Can also be frozen.

Preparation

⌘ *Preheat oven to 375º F.*
⌘ *Mix melted butter and sugar together.*
⌘ *Add eggs (one at a time), lemon extract, and cardamom to butter-sugar mixture.*
⌘ *Mix baking powder with flour.*
⌘ *Add flour mixture to the butter combination. Mix well.*
⌘ *Turn dough onto a lightly floured board.*
⌘ *Cut into four equal portions.*
⌘ *Shape each into a long, thin roll about 1-1 1/2 inches in diameter.*
⌘ *Place on a greased baking sheet.*
⌘ *Bake for 20 minutes or until golden brown.*
⌘ *Remove from the oven. Cut in slices while still warm, and separate pieces. Return to the hot oven for about five minutes to dry and brown lightly. It is similar to rusk, crunchy and tasty.*
⌘ *Makes approximately 40-45 slices.*

Kongevifter
The King's Fans

Preparation

⌘ *Preheat oven to 350º F.*
⌘ *Cream butter and sugar until light.*
⌘ *Add 3 unbeaten eggs, one at a time, beating well after each addition.*
⌘ *Add coarsely chopped nuts and almond extract (and vanilla extract if you prefer).*
⌘ *Mix baking powder with flour and add to mixture.*
⌘ *Chill for one hour or more.*
⌘ *Roll out on floured board to a rectangle, 1/8" thick.*
⌘ *Cut in 3 1/2" triangles or use cookie cutters in desired shapes.*
⌘ *Place on cookie sheet. Beat remaining egg. Brush cookies with beaten egg. Sprinkle cookies with almonds, pressing them gently into dough.*
⌘ *Sprinkle with sugar.*
⌘ *Bake for about 10-15 minutes.*
⌘ *Makes about 4 dozen.*

Ingredients

1 cup butter, softened
1 cup sugar
3 eggs
1/2 cup coarsely chopped blanched almonds
1 teaspoon almond extract (and 1 teaspoon vanilla extract if you want to enrich the flavor with a hint of vanilla)
1 teaspoon baking powder
3 1/2 cups flour
1/4 teaspoon salt

Topping

1 egg
Finely chopped almonds
Sugar

Suggestions

This dough rolls out very easily if the board is liberally sprinkled with flour. Work with 1/4 of dough at a time, as it becomes more difficult to roll when it's warm. Keep remaining dough in refrigerator until you are ready to use it.

Asbjørn Johansen took this picture of Gudrun Johansen (middle) and Reidar Johansen (standing behind Gudrun) during an outing in Rondane about 1920. They were three of Anna Fladvad and Martin Johansen's six children. His wife, Nina (right center), holds his coat and a six pence as she listens to the farmer who owns the wagon.

Korintkake
Currant Cake

Ingredients

1 cup dried currants
1 cup butter
2 1/3 cups sugar
6 eggs, separated
4 cups cake flour
1/4 teaspoon salt
3 teaspoons baking powder
3/4 cup milk
1 teaspoon vanilla extract
1/2 teaspoon almond or lemon extract
2 pieces zwieback, crumbled for crust (optional)

Preparation

⌘ *Cover the currants with cold water and let soak one hour or more.*
⌘ *Preheat oven to 350º F.*
⌘ *Cream butter and sugar together until well mixed.*
⌘ *Beat the egg yolks and add to the butter mixture.*
⌘ *Drain currants and combine with butter mixture.*
⌘ *Mix the flour, salt, and baking powder together and add alternately with the milk.*
⌘ *Add vanilla and almond (or lemon) extracts*
⌘ *With an electric beater, beat egg whites until stiff.*
⌘ *Fold egg whites into batter.*
⌘ *Grease three 9x5-inch loaf pans; sprinkle zwieback crumbs along bottoms and sides if desired.*
⌘ *Pour batter into pans.*
⌘ *Bake 40-45 minutes.*
⌘ *Remove from pans and cool on racks.*

Serving Suggestion

Marie includes 1 spoonful of citron (lemon extract) in her Korintkake. It is not as sweet as many American cake recipes. In its original form it is more like a coffee cake.

Marie's Original Manuscript Recipe

Korintkage

3 mark smelted Smør, skummes og alt tages bort, det røres i til det Bliver koldt, da kommes 3/4 mark Sukker i og røres stadig til det bliver en tyk salve, der efter 8 Æggeblommer, 1 mark Mel kun 1 spiseske ad gangen 1/4 mark Korinter skyllet godt, 1 Citron lidt Potaske tilsist de pidskede hvidder maa ikke steges for hurtig Formen smøres og strøes.

Kransekake I

Ring Tree Cake

Background

Serving Ring Tree Cake, a tier of cookies, is a special tradition in Norway. It is served at Christmas because of its attractive tree shape, at weddings because of its impressive height, and at anniversary parties because of its many layers as many rings as years to be celebrated).

Note: special equipment is needed in order to prepare this recipes as directed—Kransekake pans to produce the graduated rings.

Preparation

⌘ *Preheat oven to 350º F.*

⌘ *Beat together 2 cups butter, almond paste, 2 cups confectioner's sugar, and almond extract until smooth.*

⌘ *Beat in 4 egg yolks.*

⌘ *Gradually add flour, mixing until very smooth.*

⌘ *With a cookie press or your hands, roll 1/2-inch diameter strands of dough and fit against inside edges of greased kransekake pans.*

⌘ *Piece coils as needed (or force dough through a pastry bag or cooky press with a 1/2-inch plain tip).*

⌘ *Bake for 15 minutes or until delicately browned.*

⌘ *Cool on baking sheet.*

⌘ *Remove rings from pans with a long, thin spatula or knife.*

⌘ *To assemble cake, place largest ring on a flat plate.*

⌘ *Top with next largest ring.*

⌘ *Continue stacking rings in order of the next smaller until you've used all layers.*

⌘ *Decorate with garlands of icing and/or marzipan fruits.*

⌘ *Reinforce the layers with small wooden picks, sliding them between layers to hold in place.*

⌘ *To serve, lift off rings and break into bite-sized pieces.*

⌘ *Serves 30 to 35.*

Ingredients

2 cups butter, softened
1 cup canned or packaged almond paste
2 cups sifted confectioner's sugar
2 teaspoons of almond extract
4 egg yolks
5 1/2 cups flour

Kransekake Icing

Sift 3/4 cup confectioner's sugar into small bowl. Add approximately 1 tablespoon milk. Mix well. Use to drizzle on Kransekake rings. Make additional icing as needed.

Kransekake II

Almond Ring Cake or Wreath Cake

Ingredients

5 cups finely ground blanched
   almonds
5 confectioner's sugar
1/3 cup flour
3 egg whites

Preparation

⌘ *Preheat oven to 350º F.*

⌘ *Using food processor (or heavy duty blender), process almonds until a granular paste is formed.*

⌘ *In a mixing bowl, beat together almonds, sugar, flour, and egg whites.*

⌘ *Grease the kransekake pans for a 16-18 ring cake.*

⌘ *Spoon the dough into a pastry tube with a 1/2-inch wide tip. Press the dough into the rings, molding the ends together.*

⌘ *Bake 15-18 minutes, until lightly browned.*

⌘ *Cool and remove from the pans.*

⌘ *Decorate with garlands of white icing, one ring at a time, starting with the largest. Stack and move on to the next ring.*

⌘ *Add flags, candy, or other festive decorations.*

Kringle I

Pretzel Yeast Bread

Preparation

⌘ *Preheat oven to 375º F.*
⌘ *Mix flour, half of butter, half of sugar and cardamom in a bowl.*
⌘ *Dissolve yeast in a little warm water.*
⌘ *Heat milk until luke warm, add yeast, milk and eggs. Let rest for about 20 minutes.*
⌘ *Work in remaining sugar and butter. Let rest for another 15 minutes.*
⌘ *Work in raisins and citron.*
⌘ *Roll the dough into one long strip.*
⌘ *Arrange on a greased cookie sheet like a huge pretzel. Let rise until light.*
⌘ *Brush with beaten egg.*
⌘ *Decorate with almond slivers and bake for 30 to 40 minutes.*

Background

In Norway, the baker's logotype or sign is the shape of a pretzel. The shape we know as the pretzel came originally from the pagan calendar: a circle represented the path followed by the sun. The earth was shown as a small ball in the middle of the circle. When this shape was fashioned from dough, it evolved into the pretzel form as we know it today.

Ingredients

4 1/2 cups flour
3/4 cup butter
1/2 cup sugar
1 teaspoon ground cardamom
1 package dry yeast
2 cups milk
2 eggs
1 cup raisins
1/2 cup candied citron

1 egg, beaten
Almonds, slivered

Kringle II

Pretzel Cinnamon Cookies

These are slightly crunchy on the outside and moist on the inside. If the chocolate is omitted, the cinnamon flavor stands out, making very delicate tasting cookies.

The dough in this recipe is perfect for "thumbprints." Make indentations and fill them with 1/2 - 1 teaspoon of raspberry jam just before baking. The chocolate and raspberry combination is wonderful. This is the perfect cookie to serve with a cup of coffee.

Preparation

⌘ *Preheat oven to 350º F.*
⌘ *Combine sugar and sour cream.*
⌘ *Mix flour, salt, cinnamon and baking soda together.*
⌘ *Combine with the sugar mixture. If chocolate is used, melt and add last. The dough will be very thick and easily molded. Be sure to blend in the chocolate thoroughly or the cookies will be somewhat "marbled."*
⌘ *Roll into 1" balls and place on a greased cookie sheet.*
⌘ *Bake for 20 minutes.*
⌘ *Makes 72 (1-1 1/2 inch cookies).*

Ingredients

1 cup granulated sugar
1 cup sour cream
3 cups flour
1 teaspoon salt
1 teaspoon cinnamon
3/4 teaspoon baking soda
1 ounce chocolate (optional). Consider using semisweet chocolate and a tablespoon of malt.

Kringle III

Ingredients

2 cups flour
1/8 cup sugar
1/2 teaspoon salt
1/2 cup milk
2 beaten egg yolks
2 egg whites, stiff-beaten
1/4 cup luke warm water
1 package active dry yeast

Filling

1/2 cup butter
1 cup brown sugar
1 cup chopped nuts
1 cup finely chopped apples
(optional).

Preparation

⌘ *Soften dry yeast in warm water.*
⌘ *Sift flour, sugar, and salt together.*
⌘ *Combine egg yolks with milk, then add to flour mixture, blending well.*
⌘ *Place in greased bowl.*
⌘ *Cover and chill overnight in refrigerator.*
⌘ *Divid dough in half.*
⌘ *Roll each to 8 x 14 inches.*
⌘ *Place on greased cookie sheet.*
⌘ *Spread 3-inch strip down center length with egg whites.*
⌘ *Filling: combine butter, brown sugar, chopped nuts, and apples (optional).*
⌘ *Fold one side of dough over filling, and then the other.*
⌘ *Seal tight by pressing dough together along seam.*
⌘ *Cover and let rise until double.*
⌘ *Bake until golden brown in 400º F. oven.*

Asbjørn Johansen, Nina Johansen, and Tante Guri hiking in the Rondane region in the 1920's.

Krumkake Background

These crisp, curled cookies are an everpresent treat at special occasions in Norwegian homes. Making wafers is a cozy, traditional Norwegian custom. In the past, wafers or Krumkaker were called "broom cakes" because after baking they were coiled around broomsticks to give them their cone shape.

Wafers are crisp and delicious, by themselves or with a filling such as whipped cream, ice cream, or preserves. You can also dip them in melted chocolate, or drizzle them with icing sugar. The possibilities are limitless.

Krumkake Iron

A cookie iron consisting of 2 patterned disks, 5 or 6 inches in diameter, hinged and fitted into a cradle that supports the iron over the heat source. A krumkake iron can be used equally well over gas or electric heat. However, the gas stove has a slight advantage in offering pinpoint heat control.

Other cookie irons of similar design, for example the French *gaufrette* iron and Italian *cialde or pizzelle* irons, can also be used to make Krumkake. Conversely, these other cookies can also be made in the Krumkake iron. Today, many of these irons are electrically heated like most waffle irons.

We recently purchased our electric dessert-maker at a kitchen shop in a nearby mall. It's great and we highly recommend it. There are several multi-purpose dessert-maker electric irons on the market in which four Krumkake can be baked at a time. These electric irons may be used for pizzelles, waffles, and gaufrette, as well as for Krumkake. It's so much easier to use the electric iron—and easy to understand why many Norwegians have taken their traditional, non-electric irons to their hyttes.

Preparing Krumkake

Making Krumkake is the most fun and easiest to do when two people are working together. Prepare the batter according to the recipe you've chosen. Set your Krumkake iron over medium high heat, and turn it so both sides are evenly heated.

When you think the iron is ready to use, test with a drop of water. It should sizzle across the surface.

Our Krumkake iron is a small, round one, and requires only one tablespoon of batter spooned on its center. If your is larger, it may require as many as 3 tablespoons of batter.

Set a wooden cutting board on the counter near the stove top where you will be making your Krumkake. When you have spooned some batter onto your heated iron, close the iron and squeeze it shut with the handles. Then, remove the iron from the burner and hold it over the cutting board while you use a small spatula to scrape away any excess batter from around the sides of the Krumkake iron.

Return the iron to the heat and bake about 15-20 seconds on each side. When the Krumkake is golden brown, set the iron on the wooden board and remove the cookie with a fork. Use the fork and spatula to tuck or wrap the warm, pliable cookie around a "baking stick" or wooden clothespin and shape it into a cone.

The cookie is very hot to the touch, so use a spatula and fork to assist you in shaping it. Of course, **while working with hot tools and materials, you must be especially careful for yourself and for others who may be working with you or in the area**.

Krumkake
Norwegian Cones

Vanilla Krumkake

Ingredients
3 eggs
1/2 cup sugar
6 tablespoons butter, melted
2 teaspoons vanilla
1/2 teaspoon cardamom
2/3 to 1 cup flour

Sour Cream Krumkake

Ingredients
1 1/4 cups dairy sour cream
1/2 cup sugar
1 egg, beaten
Juice of 1/2 lemon
1 1/4 cups flour

Cardamom Krumkake

Ingredients
1 cup sugar
2 eggs
1/2 cup butter, melted
2/3 cup milk
1 1/2 cups flour
1/2 teaspoon cardamom

Almond Krumkake

Ingredients
4 eggs
2/3 cup sugar
1/2 cup chopped almonds
2/3 to 1/2 cup flour

Preparation
(non-electric Krumkake iron)

⌘ *Pre-heat krumkake iron over medium high heat. Be sure that your iron is well heated on both sides.*
⌘ *Mix all ingredients, then beat until smooth.*
⌘ *Test iron with few drops of water. If they skitter around, iron is at the proper temperature.*
⌘ *Apply the batter with a spoon or pour it on carefully. Drop 1/2 tablespoon batter on iron. Close gently.*
⌘ *Close the iron and turn it a couple of times during baking.*
⌘ *Cook until light golden brown, about 15-20 seconds on each side.*
⌘ *The wafers will be crisp and delicious when you bake them to a golden brown on both sides.*
⌘ *Keep iron over heat at all times.*
⌘ *Remove cookie with knife.*
⌘ *As soon as cookie is removed from the iron, wrap it around a wooden baking stick, or wooden clothespin.*
⌘ *Cool on wire rack.*
⌘ *Repeat the process with the remaining batter.*

Note
If you are using an electric Krumkake iron, follow manufacturer's directions for making these recipes.

Marie's Originial Manuscript Recipe

Krumkager
12 Æg vispes med 1 pund sukker, 1 pund smeltet smør og 1 pund mel.

Krydderkake I
Marie's Gingerbread

Preparation

⌘ *Preheat oven to 350º F.*
⌘ *Cream butter and sugar.*
⌘ *Add eggs and molasses. Beat until smooth.*
⌘ *Sift all dry ingredients together, then add alternately with buttermilk.*
⌘ *Bake for about 45 minutes in a 9"x12" greased loaf pan.*
⌘ *Cool slightly before loosening gently and removing from pan.*

Ingredients

1/2 cup butter
1 cup sugar
2 eggs, unbeaten
1/2 cup molasses
1 cup white flour
1 cup whole wheat flour
1 teaspoon baking soda
1 1/4 teaspoons ginger
1/2 teaspoon cinnamon
1/2 teaspoon allspice
1/4 teaspoon salt
1/2 cup buttermilk

Charles and Marie Cottrell in Newport with family members in late Spring, 1905. (Front row, left to right) Sarah Cottrell and Louise Cottrell, two of Robert Cottrell's daughters. Louise later served as Librarian of Newport's Peoples Library for over fifty years. Marie Fladvad Cottrell sits in the center with her daughter, Margaret to her left. (Back row, left to right) Jeanne Fladvad holds her niece, Marie Theresa Cottrell, with Samuel Middleton Cottrell peering over her shoulder. Sam was later killed in action in France during WW I. Harriet Cottrell Barker holds Marie's daughter, Eleanor. Charlie appears at far right. Just months later, Marie would depart for an 18-month stay in Norway with her parents and sisters.

Krydderkake II

Spice Cake

Ingredients

2 eggs
2/3 cup sugar
1 teaspoon cinnamon
1 teaspoon ginger
1/2 teaspoon cloves
1 1/4 cups flour
2 teaspoons baking powder
6 tablespoons butter, softened
2/3 cup sour cream

Preparation

⌘ *Preheat oven to 350º F.*
⌘ *Combine eggs and sugar until smooth.*
⌘ *Stir in cinnamon, ginger, and cloves.*
⌘ *Stir together flour and baking powder, then blend with egg mixture.*
⌘ *Mix in butter and sour cream.*
⌘ *Pour batter into greased 9-inch baking pan.*
⌘ *Bake for 45 minutes or until done.*

Note

This cake has a wonderful texture and flavor. It is a rich cake layered with spongy meringue, crunchy almonds and whipped cream. Serve with raspberries for a spectacular finish to a meal.

"I just love this cake," Tove noted in one of her letters. She served Kvæfjordkake to us when we visited her in 1993. Delightful!

Ingredients

1/2 cup butter, softened
1/2 cup sugar
4 egg yolks
3 tablespoons milk
2/3 cup flour
2 teaspoons baking powder
1 teaspoon vanilla

Meringue

4 egg whites
7/8 cup sugar

Filling

1 cup cream
1 cup prepared vanilla pudding
(or any basic vanilla custard)

Kvæfjordkake

World's Best Cake

Meringue Preparation

⌘ *Beat egg whites until thick.*
⌘ *Add sugar and beat until dissolved.*

Filling Preparation
⌘ *Beat cream until thick.*
⌘ *Mix with equal amount of prepared vanilla pudding.*
⌘ *Refrigerate until cake is baked and cooled.*

Preparation

⌘ *Preheat oven to 350º F.*
⌘ *Cream butter and sugar until fluffy.*
⌘ *Add egg yolks, milk, flour, baking powder and vanilla sugar. Beat well.*
⌘ *Bake in two greased 5"x9" loaf pans. Fill with batter (it will be a rather thin layer).*
⌘ *Cover batter in pan with with meringue. Sprinkle with finely chopped almonds.*
⌘ *Bake for 25-30 minutes.*
⌘ *Cool cakes and remove from pans.*
⌘ *Spread 1/2 cup pudding mixture down center of cake, spreading almost to sides.*
⌘ *Place other cake slice on top. Frost top and sides with remaining pudding mixture.*
⌘ *Chill overnight.*

Note

Cake may also be baked in one 9"x13" pan and when cooled, cut in half and prepare in the same way as the cakes baked in the loaf pans.

Linser

Custard Cups

Note

A small, round cake of sweet pastry with a custard filling—a custard tart.

Custard Preparation

⌘ *Heat the table cream to lukewarm.*
⌘ *Beat sugar, egg yolks, and flour. While beating continuously, pour the warmed cream over the mixture.*
⌘ *Pour into a double boiler and heat or carefully warm in a small pan over low heat. Slowly beat with a wire whip until mixture thickens. Continue cooking and stirring for another minute. Stir in vanilla or replacement amount of rum extract.*
⌘ *Whip the cream and fold gently into the custard sauce.*
⌘ *Chill while preparing pastry.*

Pastry Preparation

⌘ *Mix flour and sugar, then cut in butter until coarse crumbs form.*
⌘ *Add egg yolk and water; gently mix with a fork until a dough forms.*
⌘ *Wrap in plastic wrap and chill dough for 1 hour.*
⌘ *Preheat oven to 375° F.*
⌘ *On a well floured board, roll out thinly two-thirds of the dough.*
⌘ *In a muffin pan, line cups with dough.*
⌘ *Fill each cup with 1 heaping tablespoon of custard.*
⌘ *Roll out remaining dough and make small tops to go on each cup.*
⌘ *Pinch the edges to seal; use water to dampen edges if necessary.*
⌘ *Bake for 20 minutes or until golden brown.*
⌘ *When cool, unmold carefully.*
⌘ *Serve sprinkled lightly with confectioner's sugar.*

Filling Ingredients

1 cup table cream
2 tablespoons sugar
3 egg yolks
1/4 cup flour
2 teaspoons vanilla extract
1/2 cup whipping cream
Makes approximately 2 cups vanilla custard.

Pastry Ingredients

2 cups flour
3 tablespoons sugar
3/4 cup butter
1 egg yolk
4-5 tablespoons water

Mandelflarn
Almond Snaps

Note
These attractive, lace-like cookies taste like toffee candy.

Ingredients
1/2 cup butter
1/2 cup sugar
2 tablespoons whipping cream
2/3 cup skinless almonds, chopped fine (in food processor or blender).
1 tablespoon flour

Preparation
⌘ *Preheat oven to 325º F.*
⌘ *Melt butter, add sugar and heat to boiling point*
⌘ *Cool to room temperature.*
⌘ *Add cream, almonds, and flour. Mix well.*
⌘ *Drop by heaping teaspoons on a greased cookie sheet, 4-5 at a time. The dough spreads out to a 4-5 inch diameter, so allow plenty of space between cookies.*
⌘ *Bake 12-15 minutes until a light caramel color.*
⌘ *Cool 2 minutes.*
⌘ *Use a sharp knife to loosen cookies from pan. With a spatula, transfer to paper towels to cool.*
⌘ *Makes 24-30.*

Mandelkake
Almond Cake

Ingredients
1/2 cup butter, softened
1 cup sugar
3 eggs
3/4 cup ground or finely chopped almonds
1 cup flour
1 teaspoon baking powder

Preparation
⌘ *Preheat oven to 350º F.*
⌘ *Beat butter and sugar together in medium bowl until well combined.*
⌘ *Add eggs, beating thoroughly.*
⌘ *Add ground or finely chopped almonds.*
⌘ *In small bowl, combine flour and baking powder, then stir into batter.*
⌘ *Pour into greased, 9"x 9"x 2" baking pan.*
⌘ *Bake for 35 minutes.*
⌘ *Cool cake for 15 minutes.*
⌘ *Invert cake in pan on wire rack.*
⌘ *Gently loosen cake from pan with spatula.*

Almond Sugar Cake has a slightly coarse texture and nutty flavor.

Mandelkake med Krem
Almond Cake with Cream

Preparation
⌘ *Preheat oven to 325º F.*
⌘ *Beat eggs and sugar well together.*
⌘ *Add chopped almonds and baking powder.*
⌘ *Bake for 30-40 minutes in a greased 9-inch pan lined with waxed paper. Test for doneness with toothpick or straw. Should come out clean.*
⌘ *Cool on wire rack.*

Topping
⌘ *Spread cream on top of cake.*
⌘ *Arrange fruit on top.*
⌘ *Makes a very nice dessert cake. We like to top ours with blueberries. Any berry or fruit topping would be delicious.*

Ingredients
3 eggs
1 cup sugar, minus 2 table-spoons
1 1/2 cups finely chopped almonds
1 teaspoon baking powder

Topping
1 cup cream, whipped
1 small can fruit cocktail or peaches, drained.

Mandelkake med Krem

Mandelstenger
Almond Sticks

Ingredients

3 eggs
1 egg white
3/4 cup sugar
3/4 cup butter, melted
3 1/2 cups flour, sifted
1/2 teaspoon baking powder
1/4 cup blanched almonds,
    chopped

Preparation

⌘ *Preheat oven to 350º F.*
⌘ *Combine the 3 eggs with the sugar, mixing well.*
⌘ *Add butter and the flour sifted with the baking powder, mixing thoroughly.*
⌘ *Place dough on a floured surface.*
⌘ *Roll out thinly.*
⌘ *Cut into lengths about 4-inches long and 1-inch wide.*
⌘ *Place dough strips on a greased and floured cookie sheet.*
⌘ *Brush with egg white.*
⌘ *Sprinkle with chopped almonds.*
⌘ *Bake for 8-10 minutes, or until lightly browned.*
⌘ *Makes five dozen cookies.*

Marabukaker
Coconut Cookies

Background

These are wonderful. A dense cookie loaded with coconut flavor. Not at all crumbly, more of a cake-like cookie. Almost a tea cake with coconut—very buttery. If you have any difficulty slicing the dough, roll it into 1/2 inch balls, then flatten them slightly with a fork and sprinkle decorative sugar on them.

Ingredients

3 1/2 cups flour
2 cups sugar
2 cups butter, softened
1 teaspoon baking powder
1 teaspoon baking soda
1 teaspoon vanilla
1 cup flaked coconut

Preparation

⌘ *In large mixer bowl, combine flour, sugar, butter, baking powder, baking soda and vanilla*
⌘ *Beat at low speed, scraping bowl often, until well mixed—3 or 4 minutes.*
⌘ *Stir in coconut.*
⌘ *Divide dough into halves.*
⌘ *Shape each half into a 12" x 2" roll.*
⌘ *Wrap in waxed paper.*
⌘ *Refrigerate until firm, at least two hours.*
⌘ *Preheat oven to 350º F.*
⌘ *Cut rolls into 1/4 inch slices.*
⌘ *Place 2 inches apart on ungreased cookie sheets.*
⌘ *Bake for 9-14 minutes, or until edges are lightly browned.*
⌘ *Cool slightly, before removing cookies from baking sheets.*
⌘ *Makes about 8 dozen.*

Mor Monsen's Kake I

Mother Monsen's Cake

Preparation

⌘ *Preheat oven to 350º F.*
⌘ *Cream butter with sugar and vanilla.*
⌘ *Add eggs, beating well.*
⌘ *Stir together flour and baking powder.*
⌘ *Add to butter mixture, beating thoroughly.*
⌘ *Stir in the currants and the almonds.*
⌘ *Spread batter evenly on greased cookie sheet. Batter should be about 1/4 inch thick. It will not cover the entire cookie sheet.*
⌘ *Bake 20-25 minutes, or until light brown.*
⌘ *With a sharp knife (or pizza cutter), cut into small diamond-shaped pieces, approximately 2"x2".*

Ingredients

1/2 cup butter, softened
1/2 cup sugar
1 teaspoon vanilla
2 eggs, beaten
1 cup flour
1/2 teaspoon baking powder
1/2 cup currants
1/2 cup almonds, slivered or chopped.

Notes

At last! A sugar cookie without all the trouble of chilling, rolling, and cutting. You can omit the final slow baking or toasting step, and enjoy these as sugar cookie triangles. With different colored sprinkles, they can fit whatever holiday you are celebrating. Of course, this is not a traditional Norwegian topping. However, it is sometimes used in the United States. Makes 30-40 cookies.

If you enjoy your cookies extra crisp, re-set oven at 300 degrees F. and return the cookies to the oven for an additional 10 minutes or until crispy.

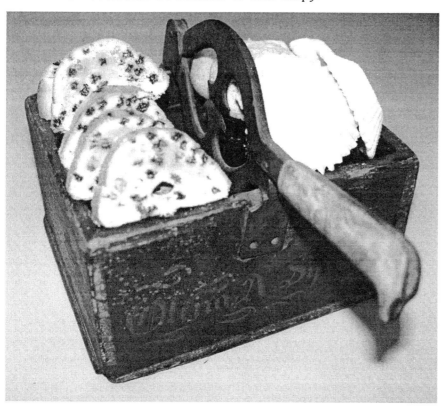

In the fall of 1861, Oline and Tron Fladvad settled in Kolvereid and leased a farm called Sjølstad West. At the end of that year, their first child, a girl, Anna, was born. Soon they were joined by Oline's two brothers, Niels and Lars. Niels moved from Namsos in September, 1861, and leased the farm, Rokka. Lars married the eldest daughter of the farmer owning Sjølstad east. In 1863, Tron bought Sjølstad West for 870 Daler. Oline and Tron had two more children while they lived at Sjølstad. Their first son, Ole Andreas was born on October 11, 1863, a second daughter, Marie Theresa was born on December 22, 1865. Left, full of currant cake and sandkaker, Olina's sugar box. In 1867, Lars built this sugar box for "Olina A. Sylstad." (Close up at right) The bone handle has "Aar 1867" engraved on one side and "Olina Bjerke" on the other.

Mor Monsen's Kaker II
Mother Monsen's Cake Cookie Bars

Background

In Norway, Mor Monsen's Kaker is often served at Christmas time. These little cookies can be made two weeks before you plan to serve them. Just store them in tightly covered tins or wrap them in aluminum foil and keep them in a cool place until you serve them to guests at your holiday table. Very pleasant tasting.

Ingredients

1 cup butter, softened
1 cup sugar
4 eggs
2 cups flour
1 teaspoon vanilla
1 cup currants
1/2 cup finely chopped or
    slivered almonds

Preparation

⌘ *Preheat oven to 350º F.*
⌘ *Cream butter and sugar in electric mixer.*
⌘ *Add eggs one at a time, beating thoroughly.*
⌘ *Beat in flour gradually.*
⌘ *Add vanilla and currants.*
⌘ *Spread batter smoothly into greased pan, approximately jellyroll size.*
⌘ *Sprinkle batter with currants and chopped almonds.*
⌘ *Bake in moderate oven for 20-25 minutes, until golden brown.*
⌘ *After cake has cooled in pan, cut into small diamonds, squares, or triangles.*
⌘ *Makes approximately 30 cookies.*

Marie's Original Manuscript Recipe

Fru Monsens kage

Man smelter 1 1/2 mark Smør; 1 mark fint Sukker; 14 Æggeplommer; 1 mark Mel; 14 hvidder. Bestrøes oven paa med Mandler efter behag.

Munker I

Apple Balls

Batter Preparation

⌘ *Combine dry ingredients: flour, baking soda, and baking powder.*

⌘ *Beat egg yolks and add to buttermilk (or measure buttermilk into blender, add eggs, and blend on low speed for a few moments).*

⌘ *Combine egg-milk mixture with dry ingredients.*

⌘ *Add butter.*

⌘ *Beat egg whites, then fold gently into egg yolks, milk, butter mixture.*

⌘ *Fry in Munkerpanne.*

Cooking Directions

⌘ *Heat Munker pan.*

⌘ *Place 1/2 teaspoon of butter into each well.*

⌘ *Pour batter into the wells, not quite up to the top, allowing room for batter to rise.*

⌘ *When the batter has turned a golden brown on the bottom, use a fork to turn the batter 1/3 of the way around (the munkkake looks like half a ball).*

⌘ *When that side is cooked, rotate the remaining batter into a round ball. Keep rotating the ball until the batter has been thoroughly cooked.*

⌘ *Cooking time is approximately 6-8 minutes per batch.*

Quantity

Approximately two dozen apple balls.

Munkerpanne

Shaped much like an inverted frying pan; on the surface are half sphere depressions—often seven or more. These are used over direct heat to make ball-shaped pancakes.

Serving Suggestions

Serve with confectioner's sugar and jam. Munker are easy to make, and you can keep your pan hanging in your kitchen as a charming decoration. Some of the most elegant hotels in Oslo have lovely copper **Munkerpanner** pans hanging in their main guest areas.

Ingredients

2 1/2 cups flour
1/2 teaspoon baking soda
3/4 teaspoon baking powder
2 eggs, separated
2 cups buttermilk
3 tablespoons melted butter

Munker II
Apple Balls

Ingredients

2 cups flour
1 teaspoon baking powder
1/2 teaspoon salt
1 teaspoon baking soda
3 eggs, separated
2 tablespoons sugar
2 cups buttermilk
2 tablespoons butter, melted (or spray pan with non-stick spray)
Jams, jelly, applesauce or finely chopped apple

Optional

1 teaspoon cardamom
1/2 teaspoon cinnamon

Preparation

⌘ *Combine dry ingredients (flour, baking powder, salt, and baking soda).*
⌘ *Beat egg yolks, add sugar and buttermilk.*
⌘ *Add dry ingredients and mix.*
⌘ *Fold in stiffly beaten egg whites.*
⌘ *Heat pan on medium heat.*
⌘ *Use non-stick spray or small amount of melted butter in each hollow of the pan. Place one tablespoon or more of batter in each hollow of the Munkepanner until 2/3 full.*
⌘ *Place 1 teaspoon of applesauce or jam on batter in each hollow.*
⌘ *When brown, turn over with fork and cook until golden brown on each side.*

Quantity

Approximately two dozen apple balls.

Serving Suggestions

These are very spongy on the inside. Roll balls in confectioner's sugar. Serve with jams and jellies.

The traditional Norwegian kitchen came equipped with a wide variety of pots, pans, kettles, and other cooking equipment. This arrangement was seen in an Oslo antiques store.

Norsk kake

Norwegian Sponge Cake
"Plain Cake"

Background

This recipe was given to Marie Fladvad Cottrell by a Norwegian friend on May 31, 1905 in Newport, R.I. She always referred to this recipe as "plain cake."

Preparation

⌘ *Preheat oven to 375º F.*
⌘ *Beat eggs with sugar and cream of tartar until fluffy*
⌘ *Fold in flour sifted with baking soda*
⌘ *Heat milk and butter*
⌘ *Add to flour mixture with vanilla*
⌘ *Bake in greased, floured pan about 25-30 minutes or until top of cake springs back when touched.*

Ingredients

4 eggs
2 cups sugar
2 teaspoons cream of tartar
2 cups flour
1 teaspoon baking soda
1 cup scalded milk
2 tablespoons butter
2 teaspoons vanilla

Comments

Sometimes a pound cake can be too heavy. This delicious, but simple cake (similar to **Formkake**) is very light as well as low in fat. It is the perfect backdrop for any number of toppings—lemon curd, ice cream, fresh fruit—or it is equally good by itself, perhaps with some strong coffee or espresso. In fact, we prefer it by itself since we love the robust vanilla flavor. **Formkake**, Bjørn explains, is baked in a loaf pan.

Sunndalfjord and Sunndalsøra.
(Photo by Hansen courtesy of Sunndal Reiselivslag)

Norwegian Spice Loaf
Marie Theresa Cottrell Raymond's Recipe

This recipe, another type of **Formkake**, bakes a lovely brown loaf. Shiny and not at all crumbly. It is a delicately flavored spice loaf, not strong like gingerbread. A mashed banana or two added to the batter makes a delicious banana spice loaf.

Ingredients

1 1/2 cups brown sugar, firmly packed
2 cups, plus 2 tablespoons flour (sifted)
1 teaspoon cinnamon
1 teaspoon ground or powdered cloves
1 teaspoon baking soda
1/2 teaspoon salt
2 eggs
1 cup light cream (Half & Half)
1/2 cup melted butter (or margarine)

Preparation

⌘ *Preheat oven to 350º F.*
⌘ *Sift together first six ingredients.*
⌘ *Beat eggs with cream to blend.*
⌘ *Slowly add flour mixture, mixing well.*
⌘ *Stir in melted butter and lemon rind.*
⌘ *Pour into medium loaf pan (9x5x3 inch), greased and floured. Or, use cupcake pans.*
⌘ *Bake in moderate oven for about an hour and five minutes, or until done. (About 25 minutes for cupcakes.)*
⌘ *Cool on wire cake rack for about 10 15 minutes before removing from pan.*
⌘ *Makes one 9-inch spice loaf or 20 cupcakes.*

Serving Suggestions

One cup floured, seedless raisins may be added to batter according to taste. May be baked in cupcake pans. In which case reduce oven time to about 25 minutes.

For loaf: bake in loaf pan, greased and floured. For cupcakes: replacing the light cream with an equal measure of yogurt will reduce the already low fat content of this delicious loaf.

One of Marie Theresa's handpainted calling cards. Her Newport relatives called her "Theresa." Her church friends called her "Marie." But her own family called her "Petie," short for Indian Pete, the Newport Tomgirl.

Marie Theresa Cottrell Raymond vacationing in Miami, Florida in the late 1920's. Before marrying William Raymond, Jr. of Stamford, Connecticut on January 17, 1931, she had started a business career in New York, City. She served as secretary to Harry Payne Whitney and to Paul Whiteman, the band leader. On her employment application for a new job she noted that she left the Whiteman organization because of "insufficient salary. No advancement." She had earned $18 per week. In January, 1925 she went to work for the Guaranty Trust Company in New York. On her new salary of $25 per week, she was able to afford a radio, a fur coat, and best of all, a car.

Norwegian Pancakes

Preparation

⌘ *In a blender mix eggs and sugar until smooth.*
⌘ *Add milk, cardamom and vanilla.*
⌘ *Blend well.*
⌘ *Add flour 1/2 cup at a time. Let rest for at least 30 minutes to allow the flour grains time to absorb some of the liquid.*
⌘ *Heat a small nonstick frying pan or omelette pan.*
⌘ *Place 1/2 teaspoon of butter in pan and pour in 1/8 - 1/4 cup batter.*
⌘ *Swirl pan until batter coats entire cooking surface.*
⌘ *Cook over medium heat until edges are light brown and center is no longer wet*
⌘ *Flip carefully and quickly cook for 30 seconds longer.*
⌘ *Transfer to plate.*
⌘ *Spread lightly with butter and raspberry jam.*
⌘ *Foll up gently and sprinkle lightly with powdered sugar.*
⌘ *Makes about 10 pancakes.*

Ingredients

3 large eggs
1/2 cup sugar
2 cups milk
1/2 teaspoon cardamom
1 teaspoon vanilla extract
1 1/2 cups flour
1/8 teaspoon salt

Butter
Raspberry jam
Powdered sugar

Serving Suggestions

These are very light and spongy—the cardamom taste goes beautifully with the raspberry jam. You can trim the ends of the rolled pancakes just a bit so that the pretty swirl of jam inside shows.

Pepperkake

Gingerbread

Preparation

⌘ *Preheat oven to 350° F.*
⌘ *Cream butter and sugar until light and fluffy*
⌘ *Add eggs and molasses, beating well*
⌘ *Sift the dry ingredients together and add alternately with milk to the egg mixture, beating thoroughly.*
⌘ *Bake for about 45 minutes in a large greased pan (about 9-inches square or 9-inch loaf pan).*

Ingredients

1/2 cup butter
1 cup granulated sugar
3 eggs
1/2 cup molasses
1 cup white flour
1 cup whole wheat flour
1 teaspoon baking soda
1 1/4 teaspoons ginger
1/2 teaspoon cinnamon
1/2 teaspoon allspice
1/4 teaspoon salt
1/2 cup sour milk (or buttermilk)

Pepperkake
Gingerbread Cookies

Ingredients

1 cup butter, softened
3/4 cup sugar
2/3 cup syrup or molasses
4 cups flour
2 teaspoons cinnamon
1 teaspoon ground cloves
1 teaspoon ground cardamom
1 tablespoon ground ginger
1 teaspoon baking soda
1/2 teaspoon salt
Sliced almonds for tops
Sugar for tops

Background

Very crunchy, hearty cookie with plenty of "zip" from the spices. It has a peppery tang that is balanced just right with its sweetness.

"We usually make diamond-shaped cookies," Bjørn points out, "and in the middle of each we put half an almond."

Preparation

⌘ *Cream butter, sugar, and molasses.*
⌘ *In a separate bowl, mix flour with remaining ingredients, except the almonds and sugar toppings.*
⌘ *Gradually add the butter mixture and mix well.*
⌘ *Roll dough into a "log" about 2-inches in diameter or a large ball. Wrap in plastic wrap and refrigerate overnight or for 2 hours.*
⌘ *Preheat oven to 350º F.*

There are three methods to form cookies:
⌘ *Slice log into thin cookies; or,*
⌘ *Roll dough into 1-inch balls; or,*
⌘ *Roll out large ball on lightly floured board, cut 2-inch strips and cut across into diamond shapes.*
⌘ *Place slices or diamonds on greased cookie sheets and decorate with almond slices.*
⌘ *Small balls of dough may be flattened with a cookie stamp or the bottom of a glass while on the baking sheet.*
⌘ *Sprinkle sugar on tops.*
⌘ *Bake for 10-14 minutes depending on thickness.*
⌘ *Cool on wire rack.*
⌘ *Makes about four dozen cookies.*

Peppernøtter
Ginger Cookies

Preparation

⌘ *Preheat oven to 350º F.*
⌘ *Cream butter*
⌘ *Add molasses or syrup*
⌘ *Stir in flour with soda, salt, ginger, and all spice*
⌘ *Roll into small balls*
⌘ *Bake on greased cookie sheet for 15 minutes.*
⌘ *Makes four dozen.*

You can refrigerate the dough before rolling into balls, but it really isn't necessary since the dough is not at all sticky. You can roll them in sugar before baking if you like a shiny, crackly type cookie outside.

Ingredients

2/3 cup butter, softened
1 cup molasses (as an alternative, use 1/2 cup molasses and 1/2 cup cane or maple syrup)
3 cups flour
1 teaspoon baking soda
1/2 teaspoon salt
1 teaspoon ginger
2 teaspoons allspice

*Marie Fladvad's hand carved **deig trau** or dough bowl is filled with Norwegian Christmas tree ornaments and tasty peppernøtter and ginger cookies.*

Peppernøtter
Peppernut Cookies

Ingredients

1 cup butter, softened
2 cups granulated sugar
3 egg yolks from large eggs
(alternative: one egg and one
egg yolk)
1/2 cup cream
1/2 cup chopped almonds
3 cups unbleached, sifted white
flour
1/4 teaspoon finely ground
white pepper
1/2 teaspoon ginger
1/2 teaspoon cinnamon
1/2 teaspoon ground cloves

Serving Suggestions

These taste especially peppery right out of the oven. They mellow a bit when stored in a tightly covered container for a couple of weeks. We thought they might taste even better by adding a little more pepper, but then, we like very spicy food. Cookies will be crispy on the bottom and just barely chewy in the middle—just right. The chopped almonds give them a nice nutty texture and flavor.

Background

Delicious! A refrigerator spice cookie to slice and bake. You'll love the fragrant aroma while they're baking. Peppernøtter, a pleasantly spicy holiday cookie, contains both ginger and pepper—perhaps a holdover from medieval times, when cooks used ginger and pepper together. These buttery little cookies have an interesting flavor. However, it is important to use white pepper (milder in flavor than black pepper), and to help avoid the questions we received about an early batch. "These taste great! But...what are these little black specks?"

Preparation
⌘ *Preheat oven to 350° F.*
⌘ *Cream butter and sugar until light and fluffy.*
⌘ *Add egg yolks, cream and almonds. Mix in thoroughly.*
⌘ *Add flour, sifted with spices*
⌘ *Roll into "logs" 4-6 inches long and wrap in plastic wrap. Refrigerate 6-8 hours or overnight*
⌘ *Slice chilled dough into rounds about 1/4 inch thick*
⌘ *Bake for about 15 minutes.*

Pleskener

Background

Plesken are small, thin cookies containing no fat. These spread a little so leave plenty of room. Once again, we are amazed at the many variations of delicious sweets the Norwegian cooks were able to come up with, considering the same basic ingredients. A lovely golden brown edged cookie.

Ingredients

3 eggs, separated
1 cup sugar
1/4 teaspoon salt
1 cup flour

Preparation
⌘ *Preheat oven to 325° F.*
⌘ *Beat egg whites until stiff. Set aside.*
⌘ *Beat egg yolks, sugar, and salt until blended.*
⌘ *Mix in flour and add beaten egg whites. Beat in thoroughly.*
⌘ *Drop cookie dough by teaspoonsful—2 inches apart— on greased cookie sheet.*
⌘ *Bake until edges are golden brown, about 10 minutes.*
⌘ *Makes about 3 dozen cookies.*

Potetlefse

Potato Lefse

Preparation

⌘ *Cut potatoes into large chunks and boil in salted water until tender. Drain. When slightly cool, skins will peel away easily.*

⌘ *Mash in cream or milk and butter and salt.*

⌘ *Makes about four cups.*

⌘ *With each cup, mix about 1/2 cup of flour.*

⌘ *Divide each section of dough into four pieces and roll thinly into a circle on liberally floured surface.*

⌘ *Heat non-stick griddle on medium heat (or use vegetable spray).*

⌘ *Cook lefse on griddle, turning often and flattening with spatula when lefse forms bubbles.*

⌘ *As each piece of lefse is cooked to a light brown, set on waxed paper to keep warm until ready to serve all of them.*

⌘ *Serve with softened butter and sugar.*

For crisp lefse

Spread out in single layers on baking sheets. Bake in a 425 degree oven for about 3 minutes. Serve crisp lefse rounds (or irregularly broken pieces) in a basket to eat plain or with butter.

For soft lefse

Stack, wrap in foil, and place in a 350 degree oven for 10 to 15 minutes. Keep warm on an electric warming tray or wrapped in a napkin.

Ingredients

About 2 pounds baking potatoes (3-5 large Russets)
1/2 cup cream or milk
3 tablespoons butter, softened
1 teaspoon salt
4 cups flour

Background

Lefse is good either crisp or soft. Serve with butter, or with cheeses or preserves.

Serving Note

If you plan to serve the lefse right away, stack them as they are cooked, wrap in foil, and place in a 200 degree oven to keep warm. Or, cool completely on a wire rack, stack, and wrap well.

Lefse can be stored, covered or wrapped, in the refrigerator for a week (or frozen for longer storage).

Soft **lefse** can be served: spread with butter and wrapped around slivers of sharp Cheddar cheese or **gjetost** (Norwegian goat cheese); spread with sour cream, sprinkled with brown sugar, then folded to be eaten out of hand; spread with soft butter, sprinkled with cinnamon-sugar, then folded to eat, out of hand; or, spread with sour cream, topped with lingonberry preserves or other fruit preserves and rolled up to eat with a fork.

Pritsar

Vanilla Almond Cookies

Ingredients

1 1/2 cups butter, softened
1 cup sugar
1 egg
1 teaspoon vanilla
1/2 teaspoon almond extract
3 1/2 cups flour
1 teaspoon baking powder
Colored sugar or decorative
   candies (optional)

Preparation

⌘ *In a large mixing bowl, beat butter, sugar and egg until well blended.*
⌘ *Beat in vanilla and almond extracts.*
⌘ *In a separate bowl, mix flour and baking powder together.*
⌘ *Gradually add to butter mixture and mix well.*
⌘ *Refrigerate dough about one hour or until firm enough to use in a cookie press.*
⌘ *Preheat oven to 375º F.*
⌘ *Evenly pack dough into cookie press with design in place.*
⌘ *Make pressed cookie directly onto ungreased cookie sheets, leaving 1-inch between cookies.*
⌘ *Decorate cookies with colored sugar.*
⌘ *Bake for 12-15 minutes. Cookies will be light brown around the edges.*
⌘ *Cool on racks.*
⌘ *Store in airtight containers or plastic bags.*
⌘ *Makes about 5 dozen cookies.*

Gudrun Therese Johansen (Tante Guri) with her sister-in-law Nina and brother Asbjørn Johansen near Selsfossen north of Otta in 1920 during a summer hiking trip in the Rondane Nasjonalpark.

Rømmegrøt

Sour Cream Porridge

Background

Rommegrøt is a Norwegian holiday tradition, especially at wedding feasts. Norwegians also like it topped with blackberry juice or with cinnamon and sugar as a dessert, as a light supper, or even as a breakfast dish. Fruit syrup or stewed fruit are also perfect toppings.

Preparation

⌘ *In a saucepan, bring sour cream to a boil over medium heat. Reduce heat to low.*

⌘ *Sieve the flour into the sour cream mixture gradually, stirring all the while to prevent lumps from forming.*

⌘ *Continue to cook over low heat until the butter begins to separate from the flour.*

⌘ *Turn off heat and pour off the butter or spoon it off into a small bowl.*

⌘ *Gradually add the milk, continuing to stir until porridge is thick and creamy.*

⌘ *Add the salt.*

⌘ *Serve in dessert dishes with sugar and cinnamon, or blackberry juice.*

⌘ *Makes about 4 servings.*

Ingredients

2 cups sour cream
4 cups milk
1 cup flour
1/2 teaspoon salt

Toppings
Melted butter
Cinnamon and sugar
Fruit syrup
or, Cooked fruit.

Jeanne and Chris Willumsen at their hytte near Drammen, Norway.

Tante Jeanne Willumsen once told Faith that Rømmegrøt "is our national dish." It is delicious and creamy, a wonderful addition to a holiday breakfast.

Rømmegrøt

CREAM PUDDING

Ingredients

2 cups heavy cream
1/2 cup water (use to rinse any cream left in carton)
1/2 cup flour
1/2 teaspoon salt
2 cups milk
2 tablespoons sugar

Topping
Sugar and cinnamon (to sprinkle on top)

Serving Note
Half of this recipe makes four small servings in custard cups.

Preparation

⌘ *Premeasure all ingredients. Have at hand: a sieve, a whisk, and a small bowl, gravy ladle.*
⌘ *Bring cream and water to a boil in a large saucepan over medium heat. Stir with a wooden spoon.*
⌘ *Over low heat, gradually sieve the flour into the cream, beating the mixture smooth.*
⌘ *Continue to cook over low heat for about 15 minutes, stirring all the while. Mixture will become thick and smooth. Soon you will see the butter fat begin to separate from the flour.*
⌘ *When you are able to pour off 1/2 cup or nearly that much butter fat, turn off the heat and spoon the butter fat into the small bowl using the gravy ladle.*
⌘ *Over low heat, add milk, salt, and sugar very slowly, stirring continually. Use whisk as needed to smooth out lumps. Continue to cook the mixture until it comes to a boil—thick and smooth.*
⌘ *Pour the hot pudding into individual custard cups.*
⌘ *Serve with cinnamon and sugar, and the butter fat.*

Serving Suggestions

Serve hot, sprinkled with sugar and cinnamon

Rømmebrød

Sour Cream Bread

Ingredients

1 cup sour cream
1 cup butter, melted
4 cups flour
1 tablespoon light corn syrup
2 teaspoons sugar

Notes

This is a very lightly sweetened shortbread cookie, almost a cracker. It makes an ideal "platform" to showcase a special fruit preserve, perhaps homemade strawberry or blackberry preserves.

Preparation

⌘ *Mix sour cream and melted butter.*
⌘ *Gradually beat in flour and corn syrup.*
⌘ *Refrigerate for one hour.*
⌘ *Preheat oven to 400º.*
⌘ *On lightly floured board, roll one quarter of the dough to about 1/4 inch thick.*
⌘ *Sprinkle with 1/2 teaspoon sugar.*
⌘ *Roll sugar into dough with rolling pin.*
⌘ *Cut into 1 1/2 inch squares and place 1/2 inch apart on greased cookie sheet.*
⌘ *Repeat procedure with rest of dough.*
⌘ *Bake for 10-12 minutes or until lightly browned.*
⌘ *Makes 5-6 dozen cookies depending on size.*

Rosett-Bakkels

Norwegian Rosettes

Background

Rosettes, shaped like snowflakes, are made with a special rosette iron. They are a delicate and crispy treat served sprinkled with confectioner's sugar.

Rosette or timbale irons

Used for making fragile fried pastries, rosette irons have fanciful forms, ranging from flowers, butterflies, and stars, to others that create a lacy effect. Timbales are solid forms—rounds, squares, etc., or representational shapes, such as vegetables or trees. The finished pastry forms a small cup.

The two kinds of fried pastry irons are used in the same manner. They are screwed onto a metal rod attached to a heatproof handle; one or two irons may be attached to the same handle. The irons are placed in the cooking oil to heat and then dipped into a thin batter. A light coating of the batter sticks to the iron and is returned to the hot oil and fried quickly until crisp and golden. The procedure is repeated to make each pastry.

Ingredients

4 eggs
2 tablespoons sugar
1 teaspoon salt
2 cups milk
1 teaspoon cardamom
2 cups flour

Preparation

⌘ *Heat oil (1 1/2 inches) in deep electric fry pan to 375º F.*
⌘ *Beat eggs.*
⌘ *Add sugar, salt, milk, cardamom and flour.*
⌘ *Mix thoroughly until batter is smooth.*
⌘ *Place rosette iron in hot oil until hot, approximately one minute.*
⌘ *Use paper towels to absorb excess oil.*
⌘ *Using hot rosette iron, dip into batter to edge of iron.*
⌘ *Dip into deep fat; cover top of iron.*
⌘ *Fry. Best results will be obtained if iron is allowed to stand in hot fat for several seconds.*
⌘ *When rosettes have cooled, sift confectioner's sugar over them.*
⌘ *Makes 72 rosettes.*

Safety Note

For deep fat frying, an electric fry pan or deep fat fryer will allow you to monitor the temperature of the oil. Keep the temperature close to 375º F. by cooking a few doughnuts at a time. Foods cooked at lower temperatures absorb much more oil and result in a heavy, greasy product.

Use great caution when cooking with oil. Hot fat may cause severe burns. Also, it is increasingly flammable at higher temperatures. Be Careful!

Every kitchen should be equipped with a fire extinguisher. Before cooking with oil, ensure your fire extinguisher is in proper working order and is certified for potential use on oil based fires.

Rullekake
Jelly Roll

Ingredients

3 eggs
2/3 cup sugar
3/4 cup flour
1 teaspoon baking powder

Filling

Spread with seedless raspberry jam. Our favorite because of its tart flavor.

Serving Suggestions

Jelly roll is the perfect dessert to serve when unexpected guests arrive. Rullekake is ready so quickly and is most appealing. You can spread jams or preserves on your jelly roll.

Preparation

⌘ *Preheat oven to 450° F.*
⌘ *Beat together eggs and sugar.*
⌘ *Combine flour and baking powder and stir into egg mixture, blending well.*
⌘ *Grease a jelly roll pan, about 12" x 16" x 1".*
⌘ *Spread batter evenly in pan and bake for about 5 minutes.*
⌘ *Sprinkle cake with confectioner's sugar.*
⌘ *Gently loosen cake and turn onto foil or wax paper that has been sprinkled with confectioner's sugar.*
⌘ *Spread jam or preserves on cake and roll up carefully.*
⌘ *Wrap in aluminum foil and keep in refrigerator until ready to serve.*

*The main room or stue from the half-loft house at Maihaugen from Lykre in Skjåk, built about 1750. Its "akershus style" layout may have evolved from the use of fireplaces, as people transitioned from open hearth to fireplaces. This room layout originated in Sweden in the 15th and 16th centuries. With the fireplace or **peis** in the corner, the front door was positoned near the center of the long wall, with direct access to the principal room. The fireplace was diagonally opposite the main seat where the master of the house sat, at the end of the long table or **langbord**. This farmhouse layout was dominant in Gudbrandsdalen and East Norway until well into the 19th century.*

Sandkaker I
Norwegian Vanilla Tarts

Background

Sandkaker are a delicious treat! They are a tart-shaped, crispy, buttery cookie that is easy and fun to make. Norwegians usually serve these cookies plain (often as one of several types of cookie served with coffee). However, when they are completely cool, you can fill them with fresh berries and top with a dollop of whipped cream or ice cream.

Life Cakes or Saint's Hearts were baked on saint's days in early Christian times, and given as gifts. Over time the name became contracted to Sand Tarts.

In Norway, Sandkaker are traditionally baked in **sandkake** forms. We were pleased to find a 15-piece set in a Maryland antiques shop. Our tins have fluted sides and measure about 3-inches across. Smaller fluted tart sets can be purchased in some hardware stores and grocery stores. The ones we found were made in Sweden.

Ingredients

1 1/4 cups butter, softened
3/4 cup sugar
1 egg beaten
2 1/2 cups flour
1 teaspoon almond extract
1/2 cup ground or chopped almonds

Preparation

⌘ *Preheat oven to 350º F.*
⌘ *Cream butter and sugar until fluffy.*
⌘ *Add egg, flour, vanilla, and almonds.*
⌘ *Cover with plastic wrap and chill thoroughly.*
⌘ *Roll dough out into very thin pieces and cut to fit into sandbakkel forms, or pinch off walnut-sized pieces of the dough and press evenly into the bottom and around the sides of Sandbakkel tins.*
⌘ *Bake for 12 to 15 minutes.*
⌘ *When sand cakes are slightly cooled, tap sandbakkel tine against counter top, and they will slip right out.*
⌘ *Makes about 3 1/2 dozen 3-inch tarts.*

Sandkaker, Currant Cake, and Sirupsnippers are seen at left in this painted Norwegian wooden bowl.

Sandkaker II
Sand Tarts or Saint's Hearts

Ingredients

1 pound butter, softened
2 cups sugar
4 cups flour
1 cup finely chopped almonds
1/2 teaspoon cardamom
1/2 teaspoon vanilla
1/2 teaspoon almond extract

Preparation

⌘ *Cream the butter and sugar until light and fluffy.*
⌘ *Mix flour, almonds, cardamom, vanilla, and almond extract.*
⌘ *Press into Sandbakkel tins.*
⌘ *Bake until lightly browned.*
⌘ *When they have cooled a few minutes, tap tin lightly against the counter. They pop right out!*

Marie's Original Manuscript Recipe

Smaa Sandkager
1 mark Mel eltes med 3/4 mark udvasket Smør, 1 Æg, 4 lod Sukker dette udtrilles i en tynd plade skjæres i hvilke fasonger man vil og steges lyse brune.

Sandkaker III
Sand Tarts or Saint's Hearts

Ingredients

1 cup butter, softened
2/3 cup sugar
1 egg
1/4 teaspoon almond extract
1/4 teaspoon vanilla
1/4 teaspoon cardamom
2 3/4 cups flour

Preparation

⌘ *Cream butter and sugar until fluffy.*
⌘ *Add egg, mixing well.*
⌘ *Add almond extract, vanilla, and cardamom.*
⌘ *Stir in flour, mixing to a smooth dough.*
⌘ *Chill dough for one hour.*
⌘ *Preheat oven to 375º F.*
⌘ *Set sandbakkel forms in cupcake pan or on a baking sheet and spray the forms lightly with vegetable cooking spray.*
⌘ *Remove one form at a time and press pieces of dough (slightly smaller than a walnut) thinly against the bottom and sides of the form. Return form to cupcake pan.*
⌘ *Bake for 10-12 minutes, or until Sandkaker are lightly browned on the edges.*
⌘ *Cool for a few minutes. They will pop right out onto a wire rack.*
⌘ *Makes about three dozen tarts.*

Sandkaker IV

Sand Tarts or Saint's Hearts

Preparation

⌘ *Preheat oven to 325º F.*
⌘ *Cream butter and sugar.*
⌘ *Add egg and mix well.*
⌘ *Add almonds, then flour, mixing to a smooth dough.*
⌘ *Chill in refrigerator.*
⌘ *Press pieces of dough into Sandkaker forms. Place forms on a cookie sheet.*
⌘ *Bake for about 12-15 minutes or until golden brown.*
⌘ *Let cool, then turn out of forms by tapping form gently against counter top.*

Ingredients

3/4 cup butter
1/2 cup sugar
1 egg, slightly beaten
1/2 cup grated almonds
1 1/2 cups flour

Sandkake

Sandkake (or Sand Cake), is a type of formkake made with rolled oats that ground to a flour-like consistency, in the blender. It has a coarse, compact texture, and a subtle lemon flavor.

Preparation

⌘ *Preheat oven to 325º F.*
⌘ *Whirl oats in a covered blender until ground to a flour; set aside.*
⌘ *In the large bowl of your electric mixer blend butter with sugar smoothly.*
⌘ *Beat in eggs, one at a time.*
⌘ *Add lemon peel, lemon juice, and vanilla.*
⌘ *Stir to blend in.*
⌘ *Gradually stir in the ground rolled oats and all-purpose flour until well mixed.*
⌘ *Grease and dust with fine dry bread crumbs a 6-cup-sized plain or fluted tube pan or a 5 by 9-inch loaf pan.*
⌘ *Spoon in batter and smooth top.*
⌘ *Bake in 325 degree oven for about 70 minutes or until a wooden skewer, inserted, comes out clean.*
⌘ *Cool in pan 10 minutes.*
⌘ *Invert onto serving dish to cool.*
⌘ *Slice thinly.*
⌘ *Makes 8 to 10 servings.*

Ingredients

1 1/2 cups quick-cooking rolled oats
1 cup butter, softened
1 1/4 cups sugar
4 eggs
1 teaspoon grated lemon peel
2 tablespoons lemon juice
2 teaspoons vanilla
1 1/4 cups all-purpose flour, unsifted
Fine dry bread crumbs

Sandnøtter I
Sand Nuts

Ingredients

1 1/4 cups butter, softened
1 1/4 cups sugar
1 egg
1 2/3 cups flour
2 1/4 cups potato flour
  (potetmel)
2 teaspoons baking powder
1 teaspoon vanilla

Notes

Make this traditional Norwegian favorite, if potato flour (**potetmel**) can be found. This variation has a more crumbly texture than Sandnøtter II. The name ***Sandnøtter*** probably derived from their color before baking and the fact that they are about the size of small nuts.

Preparation

⌘ *Cream butter and sugar.*
⌘ *Mix in egg.*
⌘ *In a separate bowl, mix together the two flours and the baking powder.*
⌘ *Gradually add to the creamed mixture.*
⌘ *Blend in vanilla.*
⌘ *Refrigerate dough for one hour.*
⌘ *Preheat oven to 400º.*
⌘ *Shape into 1-inch balls.*
⌘ *Place 1 1/2 inches apart on greased cookie sheet.*
⌘ *Flatten each ball slightly with a fork.*
⌘ *Bake for 10-12 minutes or until lightly browned.*
⌘ *Makes 7-8 dozen.*

Sandnøtter II

Sand Nuts

Ingredients

1 cup butter, softened
1 1/4 cups sugar
1 egg
3 cups flour
2 teaspoons baking powder
1 teaspoon vanilla

Almonds, whole

Preparation

⌘ *Thoroughly cream butter and sugar.*
⌘ *Mix in egg.*
⌘ *In a separate bowl, mix together the flour and baking powder.*
⌘ *Gradually add to the creamed mixture.*
⌘ *Blend in vanilla.*
⌘ *Refrigerate dough for 1 hour.*
⌘ *Preheat oven to 400.*
⌘ *Shape into 1-inch balls.*
⌘ *Place 1 1/2 inches apart on greased cookie sheet.*
⌘ *Flatten each ball with a fork.*
⌘ *Bake for 10-12 minutes or until lightly browned.*
⌘ *Makes six dozen.*

Note

An almond placed in the center of each cookie before baking is both a decorative and a flavorful touch.

Sitronkake

Lemon Pudding

Background

Taken recipe was taken directly from Marie's manuscript cookbook and included for interest only. This is really an enormous egg pudding. That explains why no flour is called for.

Preparation

⌘ *Preheat oven to 325º.*

⌘ *Beat the 24 egg yolks with the sugar until light.*

⌘ *Add about 1/2 stick of melted butter, beaten until almost white.*

⌘ *Add the stiff, beaten egg whites, plus the juice from 5-6 lemons and 1-2 well grated lemon rinds.*

⌘ *Bake in a big pan ("and we mean big"), or several little ones at low heat until pudding is firm. Serve with whipped cream or fruit.*

Ingredients

24 eggs, separated into yolks and whites

1 cup sugar

Juice from 5-6 lemons (save 1-2 lemon rinds)

1/2 stick butter

Marie's Original Manuscript Recipe

Sitronkake

24 Æggeplommer pidskes godt med 1 mark finstödt Sukker, deri kommer 1/2 mark afklaret Smør, sam er rört hvidt, og de stivslagne hvidder til slut. Saften af 5 a 6 Citroner og skallet af 1 a 2 dette steges it et stort eller helst flere mindre fade ved sagte varme og indtil man ser den er stiv. Serveres med Flødekrem aver.

Sjokoladekuler

Chocolate Balls

Preparation

⌘ *Melt chocolate over very low heat or in double boiler.*

⌘ *In saucepan, mix flour and sugar, then add egg yolk and beat well.*

⌘ *Add 1/4 cup of the scalded milk to the flour mixture, mixing well.*

⌘ *Gradually add remaining milk, and combine with melted chocolate.*

⌘ *Cook on stove until thick.*

⌘ *Put on stove and stir until thick, gradually adding remainder of milk.*

⌘ *Cool.*

⌘ *Roll into small balls, and dust with powdered cocoa.*

⌘ *Makes about two pounds of finished candy.*

Ingredients

1 3/4 pounds hard sweet bakers chocolate, melted

2 tablespoons flour

1/4 cup sugar

1 egg yolk

1 cup milk, scalded

Skillingsboller
Cardamom Buns

Ingredients

Dough

1 package dry yeast
1/4 cup warm water
1 cup milk
1/3 cup butter
1/3 cup sugar
1 teaspoon salt
4 cups flour
1 egg

Filling

2 tablespoons butter, melted
1/3 cup sugar
1 teaspoon ground cardamom

Preparation

⌘ *Dissolve yeast in warm water (105º-110º F).*

⌘ *In a small pan, combine milk, butter, sugar, and salt.*

⌘ *Heat to lukewarm temperature to melt butter and dissolve sugar.*

⌘ *Transfer to a large bowl. Add 1 cup flour and mix well.*

⌘ *Beat in yeast mixture and egg.*

⌘ *Beat in approximately 3 cups of flour to make a soft dough. Dough should be slightly sticky.*

⌘ *Knead dough for 2-3 minutes on a lightly floured board.*

⌘ *Place in greased bowl and turn once to ensure top is greased.*

⌘ *Cover and let rise in warm place until double (about 1½ - 2 hours).*

⌘ *Roll dough out to about 1/3 inch thick and into a rectangle about 10 x 12 inches.*

⌘ *Brush melted butter onto the surface.*

⌘ *Sprinkle liberally with a mixture of 1/3 cup sugar and the cardamom.*

⌘ *Starting from the long side, roll the dough rectangle like a sausage. Crimp edges to seal.*

⌘ *Slice into 3/4 inch slices.*

⌘ *Place in greased muffin cups or on a greased cookie sheet.*

⌘ *Cover and let rise until double in a warm place (about 40 minutes).*

⌘ *Preheat oven to 375º F.*

⌘ *Bake for 12-15 minutes or until brown.*

Smørkranser
Butter Wreath Cookies

Preparation

⌘ *Preheat oven to 350º F.*
⌘ *Cream butter and sugar until light and fluffy.*
⌘ *Add egg and vanilla, beating well.*
⌘ *Stir in flour and almonds.*
⌘ *Use cookie press with a star disc to force out ribbons of dough in wreath shapes onto ungreased cookie sheet. Overlap ends of wreaths about 1/2 inch.*
⌘ *Bake for about 12-15 minutes or until golden brown.*
⌘ *Cool on wire rack.*

Ingredients

3/4 cup butter, softened
1/2 cup sugar
1 egg
1 teaspoon vanilla
1 3/4 cups flour
1/4 cup ground almonds

This hand colored postcard printed in 1893 was found in Marie Fladvad Cottrell's effects. Entitled Fra Karmöen it probably depicts a scene near the "Guthus" she lived in during the year and a half she was away from her husband in Norway in 1907-08. It conveys the compelling charm of the hytte or cabin by the sea, complete with wash on the clothesline flying in the sea breeze.

Smør-Krem
Mocha Butter Cream Frosting

Ingredients

3 tablespoons butter, softened
3 tablespoons cocoa
2 cups confectioner's sugar, sifted
2 teaspoons vanilla
2 tablespoons brewed coffee

Preparation

⌘ *Cream butter and cocoa, add confectioner's sugar, mixing well.*
⌘ *Blend in vanilla and coffee.*
⌘ *Spread on Norsk kake (Norwegian sponge cake).*

Gjærbakst (Sweet Yeast Bread) recipe on p. 171.

Smørpletter
Butter Dots

Ingredients

1/2 cup confectioner's sugar
1 1/2 cups flour
3/4 cup of butter, softened
1 teaspoon almond extract
Almond slices or walnuts for tops

Preparation

⌘ *Mix all ingredients well.*
⌘ *Shape into a sausage about 2 inches thick.*
⌘ *Chill well.*
⌘ *Preheat oven to 350º F.*
⌘ *Slice into 1/4 inch slices.*
⌘ *Arrange on cookie sheet.*
⌘ *Decorate with almond slices or walnuts.*
⌘ *Bake for about 15 minutes.*
⌘ *Makes 36 cookies.*

Smultringer
Norwegian Holiday Doughnuts

Preparation

⌘ *Beat eggs and gradually add sugar.*

⌘ *Mix in sour cream, milk, baking powder, and cardamom.*

⌘ *Add the flour, a little at a time. Dough will be very sticky. Place in clean bowl.*

⌘ *Refrigerate 12 hours or overnight.*

⌘ *Heat about 1 1/2 inches of vegetable oil to 375º F.*

⌘ *On a well floured board, roll out dough to 1/4-inch thickness.*

⌘ *Cut with a floured doughnut cutter or 2 biscuit cutters, one large, one small.*

⌘ *Fry 3-4 doughnuts at a time. Turn when tops are brown, about 2 minutes per side. When done, drain on paper towels.*

⌘ *Sprinkle with sugar when first removed from oil if desired.*

⌘ *Makes about 30 (2 1/2-inch) doughnuts.*

Ingredients

2 eggs
2/3 cup sugar
1 cup sour cream
1/4 cup milk
1 1/2 teaspoons baking powder
1 teaspoon cardamom
3 cups flour
vegetable oil for deep fat frying

*At left, **Smultringer, Hjortetakk or Stag's Antlers, and Fattigman.** Chris Willumsen won the silver tray in a 1928 Oslo snooker tournament. During the German occupation of Norway he buried it with other family valuables at his hytte near Drammen.*

Safety Note

For deep fat frying, an electric fry pan or deep fat fryer will allow you to monitor the temperature of the oil. Keep the temperature close to 375º F by cooking a few doughnuts at a time. Doughnuts cooked at lower temperatures absorb much more oil and result in a heavy, greasy product.

Use great caution when cooking with oil. Hot fat may cause severe burns. Also, it is increasingly flammable at higher temperatures. Be careful!

Every kitchen should be equipped with a fire extinguisher. Before cooking with oil, ensure your fire extinguisher is in proper working order and is certified for potential use on oil based fires.

Sølvkake
Silver Cake

Ingredients

1 cup butter
1 1/2 cups sugar
3 cups sifted cake flour
4 teaspoons baking powder
1/2 teaspoon salt
1 cup milk
1 teaspoon vanilla
8 egg whites
2-3 zwieback for crust, pulverized in food processor

1 or 2 zwieback for crust

Preparation

⌘ *Preheat oven to 375º F.*
⌘ *Cream butter and sugar together until light.*
⌘ *Sift the flour with the baking powder and salt.*
⌘ *Alternately add the flour mixture and the milk to the butter mixture, beating well.*
⌘ *Beat in vanilla.*
⌘ *In a separate bowl, beat the egg whites until stiff. Gently fold them into the cake mixture.*
⌘ *Divide batter between three 8 or 9-inch round cake pans, which have been greased and dusted with zwieback crust.*
⌘ *Bake for 20-25 minutes, or until golden brown and cake tester comes out clean.*
⌘ *Cool and remove from pans.*
⌘ *Makes ten or more servings.*

Note

Zwieback can be omitted. Just grease pans and line bottoms with waxed paper.

Serving Suggestions

As with most Norwegian desserts, this cake is complemented beautifully with fruit, berries or nectarines.

Marie's Original Manuscript Recipe

Sølvkage
1/2 Tekop smelted Smør röres hvidt med 12 lod Sukker, deri kommes 1/2 Thekop Melk, 18 lod Mel, 1 Theske Natron, 1 Krem av tartar tilsist 8 stivslagne Æggehvidder. Formen maa være halv fuld.

Sølvkake

Silver Cake with Coconut and Lemon

Preparation

⌘ *Preheat oven to 375º F.*

⌘ *Cream butter and sugar together until light.*

⌘ *Sift the flour with the baking powder and salt.*

⌘ *Alternately add the flour mixture and the milk to the butter mixture, beating well.*

⌘ *Beat in coconut, lemon peel and lemon extract.*

⌘ *In a separate bowl, beat the egg whites until stiff. Gently fold into the cake mixture.*

⌘ *Divide batter between three 8 or 9-inch round cake pans, which have been greased and dusted with zwieback crust.*

⌘ *Bake for 20-25 minutes, or until golden brown and cake tester comes out clean.*

⌘ *Cool and remove from pans.*

⌘ *Makes ten or more servings.*

Ingredients

1 cup butter
1 1/2 cups sugar
3 cups sifted cake flour
4 teaspoons baking powder
1/2 teaspoon salt
1 cup milk
4 tablespoons grated coconut
1 teaspoon grated lemon peel
1/4 teaspoon lemon extract
8 egg whites
2-3 zwieback for crust, pulverized in food processor

Note

Zwieback can be omitted. Just grease pans and line bottoms with waxed paper.

Marie Theresa Fladvad Cottrell. Her manuscript cookbook is the source for many of the recipes included in this work. Perhaps in 1894, Marie heard from friends who had immigrated to Minnesota. She decided to leave Christiania (Oslo) and go to Minnesota for a visit. Other family records suggest that she planned to continue on to California where she might start a stitchery school. First, she planned to stop and visit a friend in Newport, Rhode Island. She arrived in the United States in 1895, and met the man she was to marry that same year—Charles Middleton Cottrell, a Newport businessman.

Sukkerbrød
Sugar Cake

Ingredients

3 eggs
3/4 cup sugar
1 cup flour
2 teaspoons baking powder
3 oz melted butter

Background

A classic Norwegian cake recipe—a type of **bløtkake** which you can easily modify with vanilla, grated lemon or orange rind and juice, to offer many delicious alternatives. Sugar Cake has a poundcake-like flavor with the lightness of a sponge cake. Makes one layer.

Sliced sugar cake is a great companion with coffee, or with a glass of milk or juice for the children when they get home from school.

Slices can be topped with fruit or whipped cream for a colorful, tasty desert. Or, it can be sliced horizontally and filled with fruit or custard, then topped with whipped cream—an "instant" Norwegian torte.

Preparation

⌘ *Preheat oven to 350º F.*
⌘ *Combine eggs and sugar together, beating well.*
⌘ *Stir together flour and baking powder, then add to egg and sugar mixture.*
⌘ *Add melted butter and beat well.*
⌘ *Pour into greased and floured 8-inch or 9-inch cake pan.*
⌘ *Bake for about 50 minutes or until golden brown.*

Marie's Original Recipe

Sukkerbrøkake
6 Æg, 1/2 mark Sukker pidskes 3/4 time, hvorpaa iblandes 1/2 mark Hvedemel. Det kommes i en form og steges i 1/2 time i stegovn.

Sukkerbrød
Sitron Cognac Pudding

Sugarbread pudding offers a straight forward example of the challenges awaiting those who set out to translate a recipe from the original Norwegian and develop it into a tasty dessert. This recipe is included as an example of an untested recipe in its original form.

Original Preparation

⌘ *To eggs add sugar and French Cognac.*

⌘ *Add flour while beating slowly.*

⌘ *Beat for 1 1/4 hours. [This is far longer than any of us could possibly undertake today. Of course we use our kitchen mixer or food processor. "On my food processor I beat for 9 minutes," Bjørn suggests. The directions for beating a long time were to ensure that plenty of air was whipped up into the batter. Then, when cooking, the trapped air turns to steam and provides the means by which the mixture rises.]*

⌘ *Stir in lemon essence.*

⌘ *Bake for one hour in greased pan.*

Original Ingredients

20 eggs
1 cup Sugar
1 jigger French Cognac
Lemon essence
1 cup flour

Marie's Original Manuscript Recipe

Sukkerbrød

20 Æg, 1 mark Rafinade, 1 fransk dram og den skal slaaes i 5 kvarter saa haves i 6 Citrondraaber, 1 mark mel, steges i 1 Time i en smurt og strøet Form.

Modern alternative recipe
Sugar Bread Cake

The following variation converts the egg-rich pudding into lemon cognac flavored tea cakes.

Preparation

⌘ *Preheat oven to 350º F.*

⌘ *Beat eggs thoroughly with sugar, adding lemon rind, cognac, and vanilla.*

⌘ *Add flour gradually, mixing well. Dough should be thick enough to knead. Add more flour if necessary.*

⌘ *Roll out dough 1/4 to 1/2 inch thick.*

⌘ *Cut into squares and place on greased baking sheet.*

⌘ *Bake until golden brown.*

Ingredients

4 eggs
2 1/2 cups fine granulated sugar
grated rind of 1 lemon
1 tablespoon French Cognac
1 teaspoon vanilla
5 - 5 1/2 cups flour

Tebrød
Tea Bread

Ingredients

1 egg (extra large)
1/2 cup granulated sugar
1/4 cup milk
1 teaspoon almond extract
2 1/2 cups flour
1 teaspoon baking powder
1/2 cup butter, softened

Topping

3 teaspoons chopped nuts (almonds) if desired
1 egg white, beaten
3 teaspoons confectioners or granulated sugar

Background

Nina Johansen, Tove and Bjørn's mother, often baked this recipe. In making tea bread, the method of mixing butter and flour into the dough is called **elte**. It's a very common procedure. This method is used in other recipes, too.

Perhaps this is the Norwegian version of Biscotti. Perfect to serve with coffee.

Original Preparation (pre-electric mixer?)

⌘ *Preheat oven to 350º F.*
⌘ *Combine egg and sugar. Beat until light and fluffy.*
⌘ *Add milk, almond extract, 2 cups of the flour and baking powder.*
⌘ *Mix well. Butter and the remainder of the flour are worked into the dough on the table in this manner:*
⌘ *Shake a generous amount of the flour onto the table.*
⌘ *Place dough on top.*
⌘ *Slice 1/3 of the butter into thin patties and place evenly on top of dough. Sprinkle more flour on top; dough will be sticky.*
⌘ *Knead dough lightly until butter is evenly distributed.*
⌘ *Repeat this until all flour and butter is worked into dough.*
⌘ *Divide dough into three parts. Roll each part into a 'log' approximately 13 inches long.*
⌘ *Arrange on lightly greased cookie sheets.*
⌘ *Brush with beaten egg white and sprinkle with sugar.*
⌘ *Sprinkle nuts on top.*
⌘ *Bake for about 25 minutes or until golden brown.*

Easier Alternative

⌘ *Preheat oven to 350º F.*
⌘ *Combine egg and sugar. Beat until light and fluffy*
⌘ *Add milk, almond extract, flour and baking powder.*
⌘ *Add butter. Beat until dough is well-mixed.*
⌘ *Divide dough into three parts.*
⌘ *On lightly floured surface, roll each part into a "log" aproximately 13-inches long.*
⌘ *Arrange on lightly greased cookie sheet.*
⌘ *Brush "logs" with lightly beaten egg white and sprinkle with sugar and chopped or slivered almonds.*
⌘ *Bake for about 25 minutes or until golden brown.*
⌘ *Remove from oven and cut diagonally with bread knife into 1" pieces while still warm.*

Nina and Asbjørn Johansen on their wedding trip.

Tosca kake I

Tosca Cake

Background

This makes a delicious coffee cake. Drizzled with melted fruit preserves, it becomes a delightful dessert.

Preparation

⌘ *Preheat oven to 350º F.*
⌘ *Beat together eggs, sugar, melted butter, and milk.*
⌘ *Stir flour and baking powder together. Beat into egg mixture.*
⌘ *Pour into greased 8- or 9-inch cake pan.*
⌘ *For topping, cream butter and sugar.*
⌘ *Beat in almonds, milk and flour*
⌘ *Drop topping by spoonfuls on top of batter*
⌘ *Bake for 25-30 minutes or until golden brown.*
⌘ *Cool and remove from pan.*

Serving Suggestions

Serve it warm, right out of the oven with a frosty glass of milk.

Ingredients

Batter
3 eggs
3/4 cup sugar
1/4 butter, melted
3 tablespoons milk
1 1/3 cups flour
2 teaspoons baking powder

Topping
3 tablespoons butter
1/3 cup sugar
1/2 cup chopped almonds
1 1/2 tablespoons milk
1 tablespoon flour

Tosca kake II

Preparation

⌘ *Preheat oven to 325º F.*
⌘ *Beat eggs and sugar until light and foamy.*
⌘ *Stir flour and baking powder together, then add to egg mixture.*
⌘ *Add cream and melted butter.*
⌘ *Pour into greased 8- or 9-inch cake pan.*
⌘ *Prepare topping by combining ingredients in a small pan.*
⌘ *Heat until butter is melted. Scorching will occur if heated too hot.*
⌘ *With a large spoon, spread topping over batter surface.*
⌘ *Bake until lightly brown, about 25 minutes.*
⌘ *Cool and remove from pan.*

Ingredients

Batter
3 eggs
2/3 cup sugar
1 cup flour
2 teaspoons baking powder
2 tablespoons cream (or milk)
1/2 cup butter, melted

Topping
1/4 cup butter
1/4 cup sugar
1/3 cup chopped almonds
1 tablespoon flour
2 tablespoons cream (or milk)

Tyske skiver
German Slices

Ingredients

1 cup butter
2/3 cup sugar
1 egg
2 1/3 cups flour

Background

This is a delicious "refrigerator type" cookie. Dough can be made ahead, then sliced and freshly baked for special company.

Preparation

⌘ *Cream butter and sugar.*
⌘ *Mix in egg.*
⌘ *Gradually add flour and beat well.*
⌘ *Chill dough for 1 hour.*
⌘ *On waxed paper, form a roll of dough approximately 16-inches long and 2-inches in diameter.*
⌘ *Wrap tightly in waxed paper and chill 12 hours or overnight (chilling time can be reduced by placing roll in the freezer).*
⌘ *Preheat oven to 400 F.*
⌘ *Cut dough into 1/4 inch slices.*
⌘ *Place one inch apart on ungreased cookie sheet.*
⌘ *Bake for 10-12 minutes or until lightly browned.*
⌘ *Makes 4 dozen cookies.*

Serving Note

Sprinkle sugar on tops just before baking if desired.

Tyske skiver on a plate hand painted by Olise Fladvad. The diary is the one she kept during her travels to England and France in 1897-98. The photograph of Olise on her bicycle was taken during one of her many rides in and around Bayeux, France. Half a century later thousands of Allied soldiers landed near there at Normandy.

Vanilla Custard Filling

Preparation

⌘ *In the top of a double boiler, mix together 1/4 cup sugar, 1 teaspoon (part of a package) unflavored gelatin, and 2 teaspoons cornstarch.*

⌘ *Stir in 1 1/4 cups milk.*

⌘ *Cook over boiling water, stirring until thickened.*

⌘ *Beat 2 egg yolks and stir into some of the hot milk mixture.*

⌘ *Return to the top of the double boiler and place over simmering water.*

⌘ *Cook, stirring, 2 or 3 minutes longer.*

⌘ *Remove from heat and stir in 1 teaspoon vanilla.*

⌘ *Cool.*

⌘ *Beat until stiff 1/2 cup whipping cream.*

⌘ *Fold into cool, but not set custard.*

⌘ *Chill covered.*

Ingredients

1/4 cup sugar
1 teaspoon unflavored gelatin
2 teaspoons cornstarch
1 1/4 cups milk
2 egg yolks
1 teaspoon vanilla
1/2 cup whipping cream, whipped

Anna Fladvad and Martin Johansen *with their six children in Hamar about 1894. At that time they owned and operated the Victoria Park Hotel in Hamar. Asbjørn (right) was Bjørn and Tove's father. The girl to the right of her father is Gudrun Therese Johansen, born in 1890. She became the beloved Tante Guri to Bjørn and Tove.*

Vaniljeboller
Vanilla Buns

Ingredients

Yeast Buns
1 package dry yeast
1/4 cup lukewarm water
2 tablespoons butter
1/3 cup sugar
2 cups milk
1 egg
1 teaspoon salt
6 cups flour
milk and sugar for tops

Vanilla Cream Filling
3/4 cup light cream
4 egg yolks
1/4 cup sugar
2 teaspoons vanilla extract

Preparation

⌘ *Dissolve yeast in lukewarm water, not hotter than 110º F.*
⌘ *In a small pan, heat butter, sugar and milk. Cool to 110º F (lukewarm).*
⌘ *Using a large mixing bowl, combine the warm milk mixture and the yeast mixture.*
⌘ *Beat in egg and salt.*
⌘ *Gradually add the flour, making a soft dough (it is not necessary to add all the flour). Dough should be slightly sticky.*
⌘ *On a lightly floured board, knead dough for 6-8 minutes. Add a small amount of flour if dough is too sticky to knead.*
⌘ *Place in a greased bowl, turn dough once so top is greased.*
⌘ *Cover and set in a warm place until dough doubles in size (about 1-1 1/2 hours).*
⌘ *While dough is rising, prepare the vanilla cream filling.*

Vanilla Cream Filling Preparation
⌘ *In a medium pan, beat together cream, egg yolks, sugar, and vanilla with a wire whip.*
⌘ *Cook over low heat until thickened, stirring constantly to prevent sticking and scorching.*
⌘ *Refrigerate until dough is ready.*

Back to the Boller
⌘ *When dough is doubled, punch down and divide dough into two portions.*
⌘ *Roll out each piece with a rolling pin to about 1/3 inch thick.*
⌘ *Using a round 2 1/2"-3" biscuit or cookie cutter, cut out rounds.*
⌘ *Place on a greased baking sheet, then spoon about 1 teaspoon of the cooled cream filling onto the middle of each round.*
⌘ *Place another round on top to cover, then pinch the edges together to enclose the filling.*
⌘ *Cover and let rise again for about 30-45 minutes.*
⌘ *Preheat oven to 350º F.*
⌘ *Brush tops lightly with milk and sprinkle with sugar before baking.*
⌘ *Bake for 20 minutes, or until golden brown.*
⌘ *Serve immediately or refrigerate to keep cream filling safe to eat.*

When family photographs were reviewed for the first time in many years some striking similarities became clear. Compare the snapshot above of Marie Theresa Cottrell taken during a Florida vacation in the 1920s to Gudrun Johansen. "They are true cousins," Bjørn Johansen pointed out.

Waffles

Traditionally waffles are served with sour cream and berries, such as cloudberry preserves.

We've never seen cloudberries sold anywhere, however they look like small raspberries. Scandinavian delicacy shops carry them.

Fløtelapper I
Cream Waffles

Preparation

⌘ *Mix flour, cornstarch, sugar, and cardamom in a bowl.*
⌘ *Beat together sour cream, eggs, and melted butter.*
⌘ *Add to flour mixture and blend slowly.*
⌘ *Let batter stand for one hour.*
⌘ *Drop by spoonfulls onto hot, greased griddle or frying pan.*
⌘ *Brown lightly on both sides.*
⌘ *Arrange pancakes on warm platter, sprinkle with confectioner's sugar, and serve with a dollop of raspberry jam or preserves.*

Fløtelapper II
Cream Waffles

Preparation

⌘ *Beat together eggs, buttermilk, and sour cream.*
⌘ *Mix flour, baking powder, and salt.*
⌘ *Combine egg and flour mixture, then stir in melted butter, blending well.*
⌘ *Bake in hot waffle iron according to directions on waffle iron.*

Ingredients

2 tablespoons flour
2 tablespoons corn starch
1 tablespoon sugar
1 1/2 teaspoons cardamom
2 cups sour cream
2 eggs
2 tablespoons melted butter
Raspberry jam
Powdered sugar

Swedish pancake pan or platte panna

A flat frying pan with shallow, round depressions on the surface, usually seven or more, that you fill with a thin batter to make neatly shaped, little round pancakes to serve for dessert or even for breakfast.

Scandinavian or Swedish waffle iron

The waffle grids are a series of hearts joined together; the waffles can be broken apart to make smaller, individual hearts. The iron is either electrified or is placed over direct heat (some have cradle supports). Any waffle batter can be used in it.

Ingredients

4 eggs
1 1/2 cups buttermilk
1 1/2 cups sour cream
2 cups flour
1 1/2 teaspoons baking powder
1 teaspoon salt
2 tablespoons melted butter

Marie's Original Recipe

Vafler

8 Æg, 8 skeer sur fløde, 1 pot melk og mel til det bliver tykt nok. Hviderne stivslåes. Kanel og Kardemomme.

The Diary of

Olise Fladvad

Born in Kristiansund in 1874, Olise, was the seventh child of Tron and Oline Fladvad. [Her Newport nieces pronounced her name "Ah-liss," but it was "O-lise" in Norwegian with a long "o."] She was about ten years old when her family sailed to Oslo in 1884. We know little more about her until the summer of 1897, when she was 23. Her older sister, Marie, had left for the United States in 1895 and had been married there that same year. Olise felt she also had to try her wings. The occasion was Queen Victoria's Jubilee—proclaimed to celebrate her then sixty year reign.

Fortunately for us, Olise decided to keep a diary when she traveled outside Norway. She did so twice for extended periods from 1897 through 1902. Later, in 1920 she was visiting her sister,

Marie in Newport. When she died suddenly from seafood poisoning, her effects passed to Marie, then to her daughter, Theresa, and then to her daughter, Faith. The little black book was unrecognized as Olise' diary until 1994, when it revealed a great deal about her and inferentially, about members of the Fladvad family.

At times her phraseology is somewhat awkward; however, Olise spoke and wrote at least four languages: Norwegian, English, French, and German. Her diary was in English, with brief passages in French and German. Overall, she used her diary entries to practice her writing in English and to keep a growing list of the many plays, orchestral performances, and books she read during her travels. From the Fladvad home in Olso,

In August, 1897 Olise stayed in Sidcup, Kent, southeast of London. She used the location as an "expeditionary base" from which to tour the surrounding countryside by bicycle. She had this postcard photograph taken while she visited Sidcup at the Hugh Colebrook Studio , 5 Grosvenor Terrace, Station Road. The pin she wears at her neck is seen in more detail below.

the Norwegian National Theatre was only a short walk. Surely, Olise had been taken there many times by Marie, who was known for her encyclopedic knowledge of opera. And, when they visited the cafe of Oslo's Grand Hotel on Karl Johan, they would have seen and perhaps met the most famous of Norway's playwrights, Henrik Ibsen. The Fladvad family encouraged education and appreciation of the arts, based on their knowledge of literature and the performing arts.

In the last half of the diary, Olise becomes confident enough to begin critiquing actors and singers, not harshly, but with discerning authority. By 1902-03, Olise was both a seasoned traveler and a veteran devotee of the performing arts.

She herself does not mention personal participation in the performing arts, but we know she

studied painting and language. One charming set of four, hand-painted dessert dishes is inscribed on the reverse with "O.F. 1907."

Queen Victoria's Jubilee

The first entry in the book was for June 22, 1897, the "Jubilee Year in England" she noted. "Her Majesty Queen Victoria is 60 years was a grandiose never seen before and scarcely will be seen in the future."

In England for the Jubilee, Olise noted that there were "assembled from all parts of the world: Emperors, Empresses, Governors, Statesmen, Princes, Princesses, Soldiers, and visitors by the thousands."

"All parts of London were magnificently decorated with flowers, flags, colored lamps, and many of the houses were not to be recognized for their beautiful decorations. Many people paid thousands of pounds for decorating their homes. Some of the streets were quite covered with flower decorations and colored lamps that you seemed to be walking in an avenue of flowers. In the evening the town was illuminated magnificently. The Bank of England and the Mansion House were quite covered with colored lamps. I think the Mansion House had about 35 lamps."

"The weather was in the morning a little doubtful, but turned out lovely and when the Queen was leaving Buckingham Palace, the sun came out and made everything look beautiful. The Queen arrived at St. Paul's Cathedral where the Bishop of London conducted the service. The Queen had chosen a long [route] round to and from the cathedral so that as many people as possible could have the pleasure of seeing their gracious Queen, whom they worship so much and whom worship ought to be given for so many good years reign for her people."

An English Wedding

"On the 27th of July occasion," Olise reported, "which I had the fortune of seeing including the year in England was celebration of Mr. and Mrs. Hodson's eldest daughter's wedding. The wedding was performed at 2 1/2 p.m. The English rule is that they must be married before 3 o'clock p.m. if the marriage counted for lucky."

"The bride wore a very charming dress of cream satin and white chiffon with white flowers in her hair and a tulle veil and carried a shower bouquet of white flowers. She was attended by 6 bridesmaids. The bridesmaids wore dresses of white bengaline silk, trimmed with white and pale pink chiffon. Hats of white satin straw with pink roses and chiffon and look very pretty.

The reception was held in the garden where the guests, a number of about 15 had all sorts of delicious refreshments. The house was everywhere tastily decorated with flowers and looked beautiful. Bride and bridegroom left at 4:30 for their honeymoon to Switzerland and Germany."

To Oxford, England

Olise visited Oxford for three days, a town she described as "one of the most interesting places in England, with its many beautiful colleges . . . all these well built and beautiful buildings, with their peculiar grey, but beautiful color, standing in a meadow and at the back, parks with large trees

grown to perfection. Between each college house generally contains 3 or 4 separate houses which continue one after the other, with beautiful lawns in front of each house...a chapel which is artistical [sic] and carved in wood and stone...dining hall for the students, which is ornamented with historical pictures. Some of the colleges I think can have rooms for 2000 students."

The windows in the chapel are beautifully painted or of stained glass. The niches over the communion table are filled with statues from different times. St. Mary Magdalene College has the loveliest grounds I ever saw. When you have come to the back of the buildings, you see to your right beautiful walks called the Water Walks, entering these delightful walks by a stone bridge over the water which runs the whole way beside the walk. We follow this pathway until we reach another bridge leading to a lovely park, where they keep about 50 deer. From this park you can see an old picturesque water mill... and a few more steps brought me into a delightful avenue known as Addison's Walk. It is a pathway water on each side and shadowed with trees...and is simply delightful.

Bicycle Touring in England

Olise traveled a great deal by bicycle in England and France. She recorded a 36-mile bicycle trip to Seven Oaks [from Sidcup, Kent in southeast London]. "Started about 9 o'clock a.m...arrived in Seven Oaks at 1 o'clock a.m., but we were delayed on the way because of something going wrong with my machine. On the way going we cut our way to a place called Shorum [Shoreham, several miles north of Seven Oaks], which is an old picturesque English village. Started from Shorum 5 p.m. had a nice 5 miles ride down hill, which was delightful and arrived home about 7 o'clock p.m. and enjoyed my arrival and dinner very much after the day's beautiful ride.

A week later, on August 7, 1897, she rode her bicycle to Brighton—56 miles each way. "Started at 5 o'clock p.m.," she reported, "stopped in Croydon the night and continued our way the next day. It was a very hot day and the wind against us the whole way, and certainly very heavy to ride, but we got through it pretty well without getting very tired. There the roads were thoroughly good, but a good deal up hill and with our many rests on the way we did not arrive in Brighton before 6 o'clock p.m."

"Had our dinner and went down to the front, where you have the open sea close to the town and it looked very pretty to see all the lights all around and the pier, which is built rather a good distance out into the sea illuminated."

"The next day we went down to the front again and on the pier. I threw a penny down in the water to be fetched back by boys, as on that way earned their living, and they did it very cleverly. They had only to put their hands down in the water and found it at once.

In the afternoon we drove to a placed Rotterdean [Rottingdean], where we saw the new electric railway, which goes over the sea. Left Brighton the next day at 8 1/2 o'clock a.m. and had a lovely ride home and arrived at 6 o'clock p.m. in Sidcup."

Although her diary does not record it, we know that Olise had her picture taken during her stay in Sidcup, Kent. She sent a copy to her sister, Marie, in Newport, R.I.

Windsor Castle

On August 20, 1897, Olise went by train from Waterloo Station to Windsor which took about an hour. "We arrived there about 12 o'clock, walked about in the town and on our way we had the pleasure of walking close to the river, where I saw any amount of boats, and specially some called house boats, exactly built like a house, where English people for a while in the summer go to live, and very nice it is I should think."

"This proud castle, as our principal attraction, is situated on a hill with a beautiful view over the river and Windsor town and park and look magnificent with its many peculiar and picturesque buildings. It has been the principal seat for British Royalty for

"I got a puncture going through the town and had to stop and get it mended which took about 1/2 hour before we really got started on our ride."

nearly eight centuries," she reported.

"We saw the State Apartments, which were a splendid suite of rooms. The different names of the rooms were Vandyck Room, the Queen's State Drawing Room, the State Anteroom, the Waterloo Chambers, the Grand Reception Room...all were ornamented with beautiful pictures, gobelin tapestry, and the ceilings were exquisitely painted. In the reception room was a magnificent vase presented to the Queen by Nicholas, Emperor of Russia. We were not able to see the Albert Memorial Chapel, which is said to be one of the most beautiful and finished workmanship that there is to be seen."

The Abbey...then Greenwich

Westminster Abbey and Greenwich were the next attractions on her English tourist visit. She visited them on August, 23, 1897.

"In the morning by train to Cannon Street, and by a penny steamer, we came to the Abbey, which is a wonderful and historical place, perhaps one of the most interesting and curious places in England. It can be traced back from the 8th century, but Edward the Confessor was the first to enlarge it and took great pains with the church, as he intended to be buried there himself."

"Rebuilding, enlarging, and decorating by different architects over different periods of time, have made it unique and interesting. I went down the nave to the Poets corner and saw monuments, busts, and statues of so many of England's great Poets... John Milton, Edmund Spen-ser, Samuel William Shakespear [sic], Joseph Addison, and a large number more. After that we went to St. Edward's Chapel where St. Edward's Shrine is standing in the middle and five Kings and six Queens are buried. There are also two coronation chairs, one on the right made for William and Mary's coronation. The ancient one on the left is the chair made for Edward I with a stone underneath the seat, fixed by clamps of iron. Tradition identifies this stone with the one upon which Jacob rested his head."

We continued our way to the right from St. Edwards Chapel to the magnificent Lady Chapel built by Henry the VII and which is lovely worked in stone and woodcarving all round the chapel. The gate at the entrance is made of bronze mounted on a framework of wood and is most beautifully done. All round the Abbey are monument, busts, and statues of all kind of England's great men, in remembrance of their well done work."

"We afterwards went by steamer to Greenwich, where I saw a large place containing many buildings which now are used for a hospital as a part of it, other parts for training officers, and some for training schoolboys. In one of the buildings was a painted hall with a large number of Nelson's picture and many of his remains and curiosities. Another had naval models. This place has in Queen Elizabeth's time been used as her palace. I afterwards saw another hospital called the Trinity Hospital, founded by the Earl of Northhampton in the year 1550. It is now administered by the Merces Co. The institution is meant for old men—invalids without any charge."

"Walking through the beautiful Greenwich park we came to the Observatory, where starting point for maritime measures are taken, accuracy of time and all that kind of thing. It had a beautiful situation on a hill with a view over the river and London."

To Bayeux, France

Olise stayed in England until September 22, 1897 when she and Mrs. Hodson traveled by train and steamer to Bayeux, France.

Olise records that she and Mrs. Hodson "by train from London Bridge to New Haven and by steamer over to Caen where we arrived at 8 o'clock a.m. and from there to Bayeux by train which takes about an hour and we got to the Convent about 11 1/2 and had our dinner. Afterwards, we went to look at the different churches and some peculiar tapestry embroidered by William the Conqueror's wife and very peculiar they were."

Bayeux, in Normandy, is about eight miles from the coast of the English Channel. Forty seven years later it was the site of the greatest amphibious landing in history—the "Longest Day"—which launched the reconquest of Europe then under Nazi occupation and control.

"The 24th of September we went to Caen looked about the town and saw two churches, one of which, Mathilde and the other where William the Conqueror are buried. At 4 o'clock Mrs. Hodson returned to England and I by myself to Bayeux."

On the 25th, Olise notes that she had her "first bicycle ride in Bayeux to a place called Songue, a place near the sea and very pretty lovely country and roads for bicycling."

Olise was piously devout, without being a zealot. She enjoyed her beer and her cigarettes. However, she often stayed in convents and church facilities. Her notes often reflect the services she attended.

On September 26th, she "was in the convent the all day. Wrote some letters. After dinner and the rest of the day spent in the garden."

The next day she began her "first lesson in France and in the afternoon I went out for a ride to Andriett... very nice."

"The 28th only for a ride in the afternoon to a place called Balleroy and the evening playing cards in Miss Denny's room."

Her first painting lesson was undertaken on September 29, 1897, "with Mire du Sacre'-Coeur and a ride in the afternoon to Cranby [La Cambe]."

Bicycling had its challenges. On September 30th, she went "out in the afternoon for a ride to Port en Bessie and the evening I brought my bicycle to a maker to get the pedal put on and which I in the afternoon had ridden with one pedal."

"The 2nd. A ride to Bellepien. It was a lovely day and the air so fresh and cold for riding so nice roads and Miss Gill and I enjoyed it very much."

"October 3rd. Sunday in the morning in church, after dinner out for a walk and in the afternoon Mrs. and Miss Gill for tea and afterwards in the church."

Paris: "I went only out of curiosity"

Olise stayed at the convent in Bayeux until April 21, 1898, when she went to Paris for the first time—by train—a seven hour trip. There she met two Norwegian friends and "we drove to the hotel, Grand Hotel des Capucines where I had only a short time to dress for dinner which we had in the hotel." After dinner, they "went out and saw Paris by night which is really very interesting to see what traffic there is," she wrote.

Olise stayed in convents when possible, but she was not of the Catholic faith. However, she records details of religious services with a viewpoint that clearly indicates she was impressed by the ceremonies and respected the beliefs of others.

"Today, the 1st of November is a day called All the Saints Day and which all the Catholics keep very much to pray to the Saints for help, and that they will pray to God for them. The day after the Catholics pray for the dead ones, which are in the place between Heaven and Hell, that God will forgive them and so they might get into Heaven, which I think is a very nice thing to do." On other occasions, she recorded on a Sunday that she attended as many as seven services in one day—and lists the topics for each sermon.

Although she stayed in convents and attended church services regularly, Olise was not a prude. During her trip to Paris, the lure of seeing the big city overcame her caution. After dinner, she and her Norwegian friends (who were unnamed), "went to see different places, such as the Casino de Paris and in that style but which is not very well for girls to go there, but I went only out of curiosity."

Olise stayed in Paris for ten days "and enjoyed myself immensely and saw all that I possibly could see. There are plenty of Paris to be seen," she concluded, mixing agreement of subject and verb, but leaving a vivid understatement that remains true to this day, nearly a century later.

Olise Meets Her Brother

In Bayeux, Olise lived for many months at the **Benedictines du Tres Saint Sacremen.** *Her bill from September 23, 1897 through December 23, 1897 came to 300 Francs.*

On May 13, 1898 she made a trip to Havre "to see my brother whom I had not seen for 9 years." She went to Caen by train and took the steamer for Havre, where she was met by her brother. "We had a long conversation," she reported, "until we went to bed at 11 o'clock about all what we had seen and got through." They were very pleased to see each other, she reported.

The next day she went with him "to the steamer that he was going back to New York by and it was a lovely boat. He saw me off, back to Bayeux at 3 o'clock and he started at 4 o'clock for New York," she noted. While Olise did not name her brother, our research leads us to conclude that it was Frederick Fladvad.

Life in Bayeux

"My cycle trip to Caen" with two "English ladies" was delayed by the ever present peril for cyclists—a tire puncture. "I got a puncture going through the town and had to stop and get it mended which took about 1/2 hour before we really got started on our ride." The trip must have been beautiful. They went through Creully "where we saw an old chateau and the church which was very old and interesting, and had our chocolate there...and a rest." After reaching Caen and touring four hotels, they completed their sightseeing "just in time for our train which took us back."

On June 8, 1898, Olise described in touching detail a visit with a Mrs. Fawk to the school "where her two boys are about 8 miles from here...on the day they were going to make their first Communion." Five boys were in the group taking Communion, and they "came with lighted candles down to the entrance where there was a little altar." There they "asked their parent's pardon and knelt down before them." The parents then placed their hands on the boy's heads and forgave them all their sins.

"The whole

thing," Olise recorded, "lasted to 10 1/2 (10:30 a.m.) and then the boys had made the first communion. Afterwards they went to another chapel to pray for half an hour before going to dinner." However, Mrs. Fawk could not stay to see the boys after dinner because they had to start back to Bayeux. They did so about eleven, and "had our lunch in the carriage going home that we had brought with us from the convent...and quite enjoyed it."

Mrs. Fawk could not be considered a doting mother.

Bayeux celebrated the Fete of the Saints Sacrement on June 12th, and "there was a procession in the town," Olise recorded.

Olise had this postcard photograph taken during her stay in Bayeux, France at the Leprunier studio at 53 Rue St. Malo. She sent it to her sister, Marie Fladvad Cottrell in Newport, Rhode Island.

"The streets were decorated with flowers and three altars were put up in different places and the streets were very pretty. First came a lot of school children, boys and girls, then a lot of priests and the holy sacrement was carried by a priest underneath a funny covered thing . . . two priests were going in front and throwing essence the whole way before the holy sacrement."

"A lot of ladies and gentlement from Bayeux were following in their best robes as possible and we all had to put on our grand dress for the opportunity." The weather was rainy and cold, she reported, although it was a June day. "But still our summer dresses had to be worn," she notes, "after the nun's opinion."

The remainder of the summer she reports visiting with friends, visits to nearby chateaus for leisurely lunches or dinners. On September 20, 1897 she records a visit to a "very nice chateau" with M. Chabral and her sister Mable," to visit the friends of Madam Sagueau at their country place

called Maury and had a jolly afternoon with Isabelle the daughter and her brother." They took "a photograph of us all dressed up in different costumes, had a nice tea and returned to Limoges after a very joyful day."

They returned to Maury about a week later, but "we had a miserable day as it rained the whole time we were there and could not go out at all but stayed indoors." They amused themselves "with games and at the end had a dance and not so bad after all," she noted.

Attending church services sometimes had a lighter side. On November 1, 1897, Olise records that in Bayeux they celebrated a "big fete called le tous saints and everybody has a holy day." She went to the cathedral in the morning "where the bishop gave the masse." He "made such a lot of ceremonies before the altar that he made us laugh." Madame Chabral became "very cross" over this and called Olise "une moqueuse" [a mocker]. But it was "too funny," Olise explains. The bishop's habit included a "long train on his robe," which required him to give "such funny kicks when he got it [tangled] between his feet so we could not help laughing."

She stayed in France until May 27, 1899, when she reported leaving Limoges with Monsieur Chabral to Paris on my way to visit some of my friends in Chatel called Kellermann. It was a Sunday as I came to Paris. Monsieur Chabral gave a good lunch after in the opera comique where we saw "da vie du Bheme" and left in the evening after a day very well arranged in such a short time." She then traveled by train to visit the Kellermann's in Chatel, "a quiet place where La Moselle runs all along the road with trees on each side." She stayed there five weeks "and during that time did only amuse myself, mostly with bicycle trips in the country" or to Nancy about 60 kilometers from Chatel.

Orient Express to Munich

On July 4, 1899, Olise left Chatel for Nancy to enjoy a final dinner with friends. She then departed "by the train express orient [the Orient Express] and arrived in Munich the next day at 12 o'clock." A Monsieur W. was at the station to meet her and conduct her to the pension. Olise was not very happy with the accommodations offered by the two ladies who owned the pension. It was a "big house...they lived in the top of it and my room not very large." However, she noted soon after that "I have gotten used to it and know more about what I have to be contented with in Germany."

Her stay in Munich is full of visits to exhibitions and galleries. On August 24, 1899 she recorded that she "went for the first time to the state theatre and saw the *Fliegende Hollander* [Flying Dutchman] by Wagner. It was lovely...the music so sad and so powerful."

Two days later she "went out for a walk in the evening and I saw one of the first actors of the state theatre called Passart. He looked very nice...rather a great friend of ladies, I believe. He has been three times married and also twice with the same wives remarried," she noted.

A remembrance for Mama from my girlfriend and Olise.
Datter Olise

On Sunday, August 20th, she recorded that "in the morning had a letter from my brother in law Charles [Cottrell. Marie Cottrell was then expecting a child, Margaret, born May 1, 1900]." She says nothing more about the letter, but it is remarkable that in the late 19th century they were able to arrange their intercontinental mail deliveries to find them even when traveling—even on Sunday.

That evening she went out with Mademoiselle Stademann "to hear the military music and saw many very nice officers." Sadly, today we know that most of these "nice officers" were to go to their deaths in France just a few years later during World War I, along with an entire generation of European youth.

On September 5, 1899, Olise went with Mademoiselle Stademann to Starnberg by the train and from there to Seeshaupt by the steamer which

is on the other side of the Starnberg sea [actually a lake southwest of Munich]. It was rather amusing as there were a great many people at the same time to have their dinner and the service very badly arranged. We called and shouted the best we could to get our eatables so we could be ready to leave with the 2 o'clock boat. And in this way we made a great deal of spectacle." After waiting nearly two hours "we got our last dish just before going to the boat." They had to eat the last dish, an omelet "all in a hurry." They then caught the train back to Munich.

Meeting Fridtjof Nansen

Olise went to see a panorama of Christiania (Oslo) two days later. "I suppose I will see a town very much changed since I left home which is now three years, but much prettier. I suppose," she muses uncharacteristically, "they will not know me again there."

She went to the doctor on September 20th to have her arm looked after. There "was something like a hard button" on it. Someone had opened a door suddenly as she was about to do the same from the other side. The knob had struck her arm.

Later, she "went to the dressmakers who was not at home and as it was just the time to have a promenade, we went up Maximilian Strasse and looked at all the people."

"With a great deal of difficulty," she reported on September 24th, "we got tickets to the lecture of [Fridtjof] Nansen that he gave for the overswimming in Munich." [Nansen crossed Greenland on snowshoes in 1888. In 1893 he made an unsuccessful attempt to reach the North Pole.] He spoke for nearly two hours, she noted, "and not bad German either."

After the lecture, Olise and Mademoiselle Stademann "wanted to see him and went into the room where the Princes and Princesses were to have their interviews with him." Afterwards, "we talked and made our compliments. It was a great pleasure and a good remembrance for me as it was in this month for three years since I left Norway and when Nansen came home from his expedition."

Culture in Munich

She stayed in Munich throughout October attending plays and operas, including Lohengrin by Wagner—"a very long opera...very good and acted by very good performers."

She also took in plays by Bjørnson, Dumas, and Moliere.

"*Das Gluck im Winkel*" by Sudermann was not among her favorites. "I did not find any determination nor much character in the piece; though it has a very good critique."

On November 9, 1899, Olise went with Baroness Zobel to what "is called a weinhouse in German, where she goes every day to drink a glass of wein [wine] with her husband. We met also some of her people...and we had a jolly time of it."

The next day, she took in "Maria Stuart" by Schiller. The actor, Passart, was among the players. "He is the best actor in Munich," Olise noted. "I did not think he played with enough courage, but another called 'Sutzenkirche,' was awfully good. He is quite a young man and so lovely built. It was quite a pleasure to see him," she recorded

with a subtle hint of sensuality. Olise attended an opera or play almost every day throughout November.

Ending the Century and an Era

On December 8, 1899, as the 19th century was about to become history, Olise went with a friend to the theatre to get tickets. They heard some music in the cathedral and tried to go in, however "the church was too full to get in, but the police told us to get up into the big hall where we would be able to see all the nobles when the mass was over.

We did as he told us, and came up into a lovely big hall with a lot of soldiers in gold waiting for the princes to come out of church." At last the service concluded and "they all came in beautiful uniforms...red jackets and weis [white] trousers. They looked about very friendly and I could not help it I had to laugh [because] they stared too much and looked more and more. It was rather nice to see them all and such good looking ones. It was awfully amusing."

In her last entry in the 19th century (and the last entry until 1902 when she left Norway once more), Olise reported attended a recital by Ludwig Wullner—"a well known concertsinger"—with Madame Stademann and another girl. He is a very peculiar man. His voice is not much up to anything, but very sympathetic and himself so very much interesting that I was quite surprised."

The next entry in her travel diary is for September 15, 1902. "From home for my second time going abroad. Had been for 2 1/2 years in our dear country but must get more out. It is a little hard to leave it though. She then went to Berlin via Copenhagen.

Her diary ends in mid visit. The little black book was full and she probably started another book which unfortunately has not survived. However, her notations give us a rare look back in time to the end of an era, to a way of life and living that ended forever in the "guns of August."

For that we are grateful and not a little envious of her endless bicycle excursions down tree shaded lanes to explore the sites and to savor luncheons under the trees with friends. Today we might call that "quality of life."

LETTERS

from
Christian and Jeanne Willumsen
to
Marie Fladvad Cottrell
1940-47

Jeanne and Chris Willumsen at **"Rognlihögda,"** their **"hytte"** in the mountains above Drammen, Norway.

". . . but these are disturbing times."

Christian "Chris" (pron. "Kiss") Willumsen married Jeanne Fladvad, Marie Fladvad Cottrell's younger sister in 1913. She was 31, beautiful and intelligent. He had wanted to marry long before, but she said they must wait until he had made his business successful. He was handsome and entrepreneurial. His businesses were successful— until the German occupation government forced him out of business. They were a devoted couple until his death in 1949. She lived until 1969.

Their life together was rich and full. He built a successful export-import business based in Oslo. The business enabled them to travel widely and to live for extended periods outside Norway. For many years they lived in Brooklyn, New York and in New Jersey. They also lived in Africa for a period. Unfortunately, during their stay in Africa, Chris contracted malaria, a disease he never really overcame

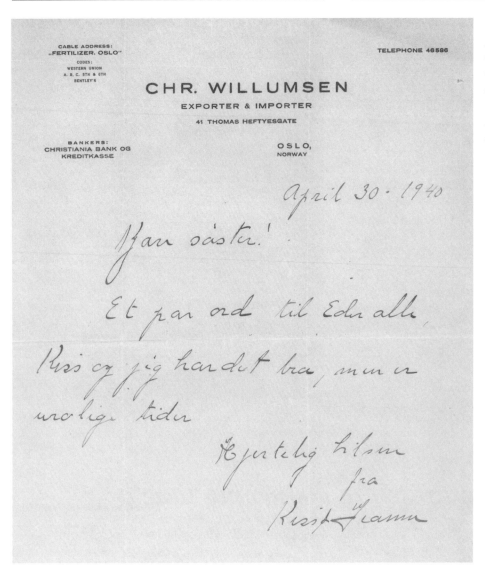

"Dear Sister," Jeanne wrote Marie just days after the German Wehrmacht occupied Oslo, *"a couple of words for you all. Kiss and I are all right, but these are disturbing times. Fondly, Kiss and Jeanne"* She dared not say more.

and which contributed to his relatively early death.

What is clear through the surviving letters and photographs is a remarkable closeness between the couple and her American relatives. There were frequent letters, almost always written by Chris whose English was stronger as a result of his business activities. Few letters from the American relatives have survived, but his letters make it clear that many different relatives were writing and forwarding gifts.

The following letters are included in this work because they provide a unique insight into the affection these families shared and sustained throughout the years, and across the wide gulf of the Atlantic Ocean. In addition, Chris continued to write when he could during and after the German occupation of Norway in April, 1941. His letters offer a poignant insight into the trials suffered by the Norwegian people at the hands of the occupation forces.

The final letter was written by Jeanne herself to her niece, Marie Cottrell Raymond ("Petie") after learning of her sister Marie's death in October, 1947.

The first letter is from Solveig Bull, wife of Ole Bull, Captain of the M/S Oslofjord of the Norwegian-American Line in New York. Marie Cottrell Raymond had written Captain Bull for his advice on how to get in touch with or to assist Jeanne and Kiss Willumsen. Mrs. Bull replied on his behalf since she had most recently returned from occupied Norway and had seen Jeanne and Kiss. She urges caution and patience.

May 2, 1940
The Norwegian-American Line
New York City

Dear Mrs. Raymond:

As I saw Jeanne and Kiss the day before I left Norway 7 weeks ago, my husband thinks it would

Jeanne Fladvad Willumsen, October 3, 1907, age 26.

"Dear Olise," her sister Jeanne wrote on this undated postcard portrait (below), "Otta and I were outside. It gave us a kick to have some pictures taken. Here we are." The portrait was taken in Newport, R.I. at the Rugen Studio, 167 Thames Street, specializing in "photo supplies, electric novelties, and artist materials."

Gunhild Charlette (Jeanne) Fladvad Willumsen, was born in Kristiansund on December 23, 1881. Although 16 years younger than Marie, they were exceptionally close sisters, probably because Marie did not leave Norway until she was about thirty years old. They corresponded frequently throughout their lives and visited whenever possible. The above portrait of Jeanne taken in the Forties was sent "with all good wishes for Christmas and the New Year" to Marie shortly before her death in 1947.

The letter from Chris to Marie *was dated October 3, 1941, almost a year and a half into the German occupation. At no small risk to himself and Jeanne, he decided to try and write Marie using the Luftpost. The envelope (left) survived. The various postmarks indicate that by October 6, 1941 it was in Frankfurt, Germany, where it was opened and read by Nazi postal inspectors. They assigned matching numbers—133014—to the letter and its envelope, reunited them, and forwarded to the United States.*

be better for me to answer the letter you wrote him.

At the present I think it will be difficult for you to get in touch with the Willumsens–and perhaps not very wise to do it either. It might bring them into difficulties, one never knows.

I do believe they are quite safe at the present moment. The Willumsen family has a summer home well hidden in the woods about 1 1/2 hours drive from Oslo and in quite another direction than the Germans have been so far. I am sure they have succeeded in going up there–if they have not been able to get a car they can also reach it by walking–although that, of course, is rather strenuous–but it can be done. There is plenty of space for the whole family.

Besides Wilhelm Willumsen has a big place in Asker and they may be safe out there too. I would not send a telegram so that the Germans who hold the telegraf (sic) station shall have to look them up.

The difficult problem in the future will of course be to get enough food–and later on–as there may be complete disaster–they may want some money. When that will be possible to get through I will let you know how–and if I see any chance of sending a letter, I will also let you know.

If you should not have heard from me by the time matter begin to straighten out in Norway, please remind me. I have my own family there too, and if things get too difficult for us all, I might forget about this.

But I shall always be glad if I can be of any help to Jeanne & Kiss who both are very dear to me.

Sincerely Yours, Solveig Bull.

During all these years Jeanne has been marvelous and never lost her opinion about the outcome of this war. Never flinched for a moment, even when the fortune of the war turned against us.

Thore Bjørke was born January 28, 1815. He became the owner of **Nedre Kvern**—Lower Mill—in December, 1844. The various branches of the Bjørke family lived in and near Furnes, a small farming community approximately five miles Northeast of Hamar on Lake Mjøsa.

The Bjørke house at right sits on a knoll that overlooks Lake Mjøsa to the West, and slopes down to a small valley to the East. Route 222, the "old road" between Hamar and Brumunddal, winds down the valley where wonderfully scenic views of Lake Mjøsa can be seen across the rolling pasture land. The hills of Helgøya Island to the west are often wreathed in low-lying clouds and after the harvest, fall-drenched colors disappear into the grey mists.

The Bjørke farm is flanked by a small apple orchard. To the south of the farm, less than half a mile away is the Furnes Lutheran Church, solidly constructed of white stucco and topped with with a grey slate roof. The Bjørkes and Bakkens rest together in the well-tended church yard next to the cemetery wall. Anders Nielsen Bjørke, born 1792 on Bjørke, married Marie Larsdatter Bakken, who was born 4 April 1804. The Bakken family lived about five miles away, in present day Brumunddal. They made their home at Nedre Kvern. One of their daughters, Oline Bjørke—above—was born April 9, 1837, and married Tron Fladvad.

Christian Willumsen to
Marie Cottrell
November 30, 1940

Dear Marie & Children:

Up to this writing, we have not heard anything from you, although we have heard through Bull [Captain Ole Bull], that you have written us. Outside of this, we know nothing how you and yours are getting along. But hope some day to get news from you.

Your cousin Ole Fladvad died at Namsos August 22nd, 1940, but as we do not correspond with that branch of the family, we have no further news about him.

Another sad death, took place in my family when my dear brother Wilhelm suddenly died, while on his way home on Nov. 12th. He was the head of the family, and has been a great loss to us all.

Last time Jeanne saw your brother Theodore, both he and his wife were doing well.

While time goes and the years tells on us all, I must say that Jeanne keeps up well. We had just taken a photo which we would like to forward to you but must await until another opportunity arises. Jeanne says she feels well, but she suffers from

Bronchitis, particularly during winter times, but so far she has been fairly well. To me she is just the same darling as when we got married and this will continue till the end.

We have a small apartment of 2 rooms, kitchen and bath and feel contented. During these times my business has dwindled, so the future does not look prosperous.

During summer 1939, we had our auto trip up to Nordmøre, and I believe you would be interested to hear about our experience around your father's birthplace [Trond, at Flatvad]. We planned to visit an old friend of ours who lives up there and the entire trip was very successful from beginning to the end. It took us a fortnight. Jeanne had also the opportunity to visit her birthplace Kristiansund and spent a few happy hours there with friends.

On our way back we visited an old

Endre Opdøl took this picture for Chris Willumsen to show him the Flatvad *family farm in Sundallen, near Sundalsøra. He carefully noted the exact house for him with a small "X."*

friend of mine at Sunndalsøra and there we got a lot of information about the family Fladvad.

Jeanne says that one of her aunts married Tore Opdøl who lives on one of the oldest and largest farms in the Sunndalfjorden. The son of this marriage Øystein Opdøl inherited Opdøl, as

> # We have kept up a mental war and in spite of all threats and terror, we kept it up to the last hour. Thank God, with success.

Frankly, I have always admired the consideration that you have shown towards your mother and it has been a great help for her in her daily struggles.

well as Flad-wad and his son again Øystein is now living on the farm Fladvad which is located in Sunndalen. We passed this farm on the way, but Jeanne did not feel inclined to pay a call there which I very much regretted. This later Øystein shall have 3 charming unmarried daughters.

We are of course sorry about the long way that separates us and we are often thinking about you all. As Christmas now is near, we will still be nearer you with our thoughts and are sending you our best wishes for the coming time.

Affectionately yours, Jeanne & Kiss.

Tron Fladvad and Oline Bjørke Fladvad and eight of their nine children taken in about 1874. Jeanne would be born in 1881. In the back row, Ole Fladvad, born in 1863, stands next to his sister, Anna Fladvad Johansen, born in 1861, who rests her hand on her father's shoulder. Second row, left to right, Fredrik Fladvad, born in 1868, died later in Brooklyn, New York. Tron, Oline, and Marie Theresa Fladvad, born in 1865, and her youngest brother, Theodor Fladvad, born in 1872. Gina, Olise, and Otilie ("Otta") Fladvad are in the front row.

I am more in love with her as the years go by. She is a wonderful housewife and manages to get both ends to meet with the small means that we have at our disposal.

Christian Willumsen to Marie Cottrell October 3, 1941

My dear Marie:

It's really too long a time since we have written you and heard anything from you, and I feel inclined to send you a few words, although these are not as complete as we might wish. Your last letter I understand Jeanne has answered, and I wish to thank you most heartily for your good intentions, which we of course at the time cannot make use of.

We are constantly talking about you and understand that you are contented in company with your children and grandchildren. What a pity it is that you must have given up your house in Newport. We have so many nice memories from there and I really hoped that these could be renewed there some day.

We understand that you have changed your residence to Stamford, Connecticut to be with your children, and we are of course very glad to know that you are content in this environment. We have often thought of sending some small enamelled pins to your grandchildren, but this we will have to wait for better times.

As for ourselves, we have to accept the conditions as they are and feel contented. Jeanne, I must say, keeps up well in spite of her bronchitis which bothers her considerably in foggy weather. Otherwise, she looks much the same, and, really, I am more in love with her as the years go by. She is a wonderful housewife and manages to get both ends to meet with the small means that we have at our disposal.

This summer we have been at our log-cabin much of the time, but Jeanne cannot enjoy it as much as I do, on account of weather conditions. Jeanne is under the doctor's care, and I hope that she soon will be all right. Outside of the bronchitis, I do not think that there is anything the matter.

Endre Opdøl's family in a photograph taken at Flatvad in about 1943. *Top, left to right, Ingrid Opdøl, Øystein, and Marit. In the middle are Ingeborg Opdøl, Endre and Liv Gudrun Opdøl. In the foreground are Nils Seljebø, Guro Ester Opdøl Sandbukt, Gudrun Opdøl, and Anna Seljebø Eikestø. Anne Opdøl Arnesen was not pictured, but lives today with her husband, Knut, son Lars, and daughter-in-law, Randi at Flatvad.*

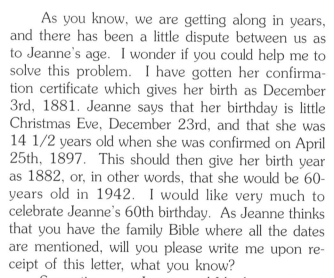

The Willumsens lived at 41 Thomas Heftysgate in downtown Oslo (above and right). He ran an "Exporter & Importer" business from the same building.

As you know, we are getting along in years, and there has been a little dispute between us as to Jeanne's age. I wonder if you could help me to solve this problem. I have gotten her confirmation certificate which gives her birth as December 3rd, 1881. Jeanne says that her birthday is little Christmas Eve, December 23rd, and that she was 14 1/2 years old when she was confirmed on April 25th, 1897. This should then give her birth year as 1882, or, in other words, that she would be 60-years old in 1942. I would like very much to celebrate Jeanne's 60th birthday. As Jeanne thinks that you have the family Bible where all the dates are mentioned, will you please write me upon receipt of this letter, what you know?

Some time ago Jeanne and I had an auto trip up to Nord-More and went through Sunndalen, where your father's family comes from. We learned that the Fladvads still live there, and are very prominent. One of your relatives is today sitting on probably the largest and oldest farms called "Opdøl." She is a widow and I understand her son is sitting on the Flatvad farm. I would have liked to call on them, but Jeanne thought it better not to, so we did not meet any of that family.

As to your Mother's family, I have gone somewhat into this and your grandfather Thore Bjerke was a very hard working and prominent man on Toten in Hedesnarken and lived on the farm called "Nedre Kvern" [lower mill]. He was very energetic, and was a man of large means, and started numerous undertakings, existing even today. I would like to go further into this line of your family, and if you would give me any pointers, please let me know.

Your brother Toddy, Jeanne sees occasionally. And, I would also like to see him at our home, but Jeanne says his wife is nearly deaf, and he seldom goes out. With this I will conclude and ask you to bring our very best regards to all the family, and be assured, that we often are with you in our thoughts and admire the bravery YOU show in the many obstacles that you meet on your way. [Chris was referring to the challenges she faced and overcame when her husband, Charles Cottrell abandoned her and his four daughters in Newport, R.I. in 1916.]

Your affectionate brother-in-law, Kiss.

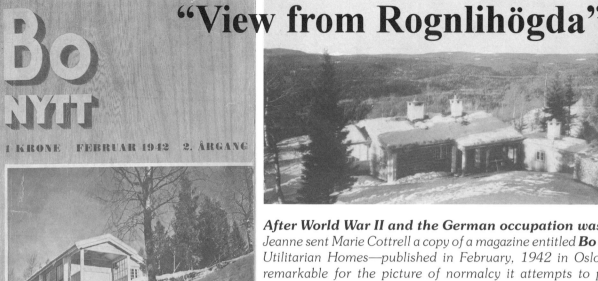

"View from Rognlihögda"

Bo NYTT

1 KRONE   FEBRUAR 1942   2. ÅRGANG

After World War II and the German occupation was over, Jeanne sent Marie Cottrell a copy of a magazine entitled **Bo Nytt**—Utilitarian Homes—published in February, 1942 in Oslo. It is remarkable for the picture of normalcy it attempts to portray during the military occupation. It includes articles on fine glass, bookbinding, and modern art in New York. Jeanne sent it to Marie because one article on vacation homes entitled—"**A Home at Krokskogen**"—included exterior and interior photographs of the "**hytte**" adjacent to theirs which was owned by Chris Willumsen's sister and brother-in-law.

No interior photographs of the Willumsen's vacation house have survived. However, the Bo Nytt article included these interiors of the "house next door." The Willumsen's retreat probably looked somewhat like these comfortable furnishings.

By superimposing adjacent photographs a panoramic view is created of the living and dining room areas. The author pointed out the "**fantasifulle dekorasjoner**," the imaginative decorations. Unbeknownst to the photographer or the readers, the Willumsens had buried all their valuables—including silver serving dishes—somewhere beneath the lawn pictured at upper right. The silver survived. One piece, a silver platter won by Willumsen in a snooker championship in 1928, is one of the author's treasured heirlooms. It is still used to serve delicious Norwegian cookies at Christmas and on other special holidays.

Jeanne and Christian "Chris" (pron. "Kiss") Willumsen owned a **hytte** (summer house) north of Drammen they called **Rognlihögda** (literally: a clearing in a forest of European mountain ash trees). Several snapshots show them enjoying outdoor life there.

In the summer of 1938 *Chris and Jeanne helped Wilhelm Willumsen and his family complete their new hytte at Rognlihögda. They celebrated with a picnic luncheon. Jeanne is seated at lower left and Chris sits across from her. Wilhelm sits at the far end. The Germans marched into Oslo less than two years later, ending forever their way of life. (Photo courtesy Nancy Kaull Budd)*

"We are often talking how you are getting along," Jeanne wrote Marie Cottrell "and children," in 1925 on a winterscape snapshot made into a postcard of **Rognlihögda**. "We are sorry we cannot be together, but are sending you our sincere wishes for Christmas and the New Year." Significantly, the postcard was addressed to Marie at the Newport Bellevue Avenue address, then rerouted by the Post Office to 104 West 13th Street, New York City. Marie had already moved from Newport, five years after Charlie's death.

The Driva River (above) tumbles through the Sunndalen from the Dovrefjell to the Sunndalfjord in west central Norway. Below: the Flatvad farm in the Sunndalen has been owned and operated by family members for over 400 years.

Christian Willumsen to
Marie Fladvad Cottrell
May 24, 1945

My Dear Marie:

First of all, let me congratulate you on behalf of that splendid effort that the United States made in this European war which ended in the liberation of Norway from those beastly tyrants that have occupied our country for 5 long years. What a pity, that the lovable and charming statesman Franklin Roosevelt did not live long enough to see the result of the European war. Your country is only half finished, but all signs tend towards a quick and decisive end to the [problems with the] Japanese in the east. God bless your efforts.

I really did not think that I should live to see two World Wars. What we have experienced here in Norway during the last 5 years, will never leave the minds of the people who have survived this time. We have practically all the time been enclosed in a camp with no opportunity to communicate with foreign countries.

It started as you know on the 9th of April 1940, when German warships with the assistance of our shameful Quisling traitors, tried to force the entrance of the Drøbak Sound, about which there have been many tales. Only recently have we gotten the report from a pensioned artillery captain, who never could give up his old love for the guns, placed on the fortress Oscarsborg. In spite of his retirement, he visited these guns and kept them in good working condition. He was looked upon like an old fool, but people were wrong.

I do not know Marie, if it was in your time that there was a lively discussion concerning the government purchasing two heavy guns to be placed at Oscarsborg. The papers were full of it at the time but they were purchased from Krup and came up here. On the way to the fortress they went overboard to the bottom. They were, however, taken up and put into place. Some witty head baptized them "**Moses**" and "**Aaron**." Ever since, they have been there and nobody expected to hear more from them.

But the Germans did hear from them–when they tried to pass on the 9th of April. The old pensioned artillery captain, had kept cleaning and polishing all the time. When it was reported, that warships approached the fort, not knowing the nationality, the captain took a chance and fired just two shots, one from each gun. The first hit the bridge and smashed it to pieces. The second the after turret, completely destroying it.

The ship proved to be the German pocket battleship "**Blucher**," one of the most modern in the German Navy, carrying many civil persons destined to take over the government here, all dressed in gay uniforms to meet the traitors upon arrival in Oslo where they planned to arrest the King.

After this mishap to the "**Blucher**," she slowed down and came outside one of the torpedo stations. The captain says that when he fired the first torpedo, he was not sure whether it would work, but was happy when he heard it sliding. It hit amidships. The second one hit forward and ended the ships existence then and there–she turned bottom up and sank.

There were about two thousand onboard of which less than one hundred were saved, the others went to the bottom or perished in the flames. This happened at 4 o'clock in the morning, when it was fairly dark. About 9 o'clock the same day, troops came down on our airfields and the rest you know more about than we do, I suppose.

The Germans spread all kinds of rumors, and nobody knew what was what. My sisters had evacu-

Not long after Jeanne enjoyed a formal evening (here with her brother-in-law, Wilhelm Willumsen) she and other Norwegians were forced to wait in food lines. "Jeanne's main business in these years," Chris wrote the family in the United States, "has been to be in line early in the morning to get her ration of whatever there might be—waiting for hours and often being disappointed when her turn came. Yet, we have managed somehow." (Photo courtesy of Nancy Kaull Budd)

ated to our log cabin and my oldest brother came up to us early one morning and asked us to join them. Both Jeanne and I, wanted to stay in town, but as there was no male to protect them, we joined my sisters and stayed there for about one month. Later, others joined us, so there was a full house and we had many experiences.

The Quislings spoiled our war, as the counter orders and no ammunitions came to our troops, so we too soon had to give up our fight. Ever since, however, we have kept up a mental war and in spite of all threats and terror, we kept it up to the last hour. Thank God, with success.

During all these years Jeanne has been marvelous and never lost her opinion about the outcome of this war. Never flinched for a moment, even when the fortune of the war turned against us. We all admire Churchill and Roosevelt for the determined fight. It was a great sorrow to us all, that Roosevelt did not live to see the Germans beaten.

Jeanne's maid and life-long friend, Helga sent this postcard of **Slottet**—*the Palace—in January, 1927. "I must be permitted to thank you so many times for the sweet handkerchief," she said in thanking Marie Cottrell for her Christmas present. "It is so kind of you to remember me. A thousand thank yous. I hope you will soon come to Norway, Mrs. Cottrell. Kindly greetings. Helga."*

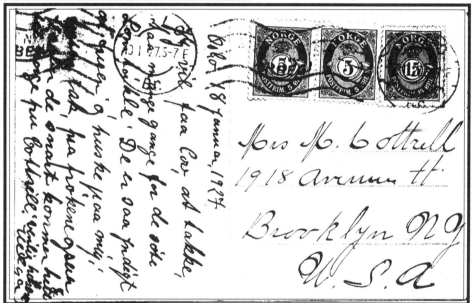

Slottet today *looks much the same. However, many of the stately trees have been taken down to make more room for parades and ceremonies.*

> ## Whatever difficulties there are in the future, we pray, that you will overcome same and find satisfaction and help in your increasing family. After all, there is no better comfort, than you can find in a harmonious family life.

The rest of the war there can be no doubt about, and we hope that it will end soon, without too much loss to your brave nation. That we have got so much to be thankful for.

Jeanne's health is fairly good, although she complains about her back. She is constantly under the doctor's care, so I hope she will be all right when the food condition improves.

Food seems to be the main question here. We have been mostly living on fish, more or less fresh. The Germans have taken the best and such things as mackerel, salmon, lobster, etc. are a dead issue for us. Meat has not been on our table, but we have succeeded in getting some vegetables.

Jeanne's main business in these years, has been to be in line early in the morning to get her ration of whatever there might be–waiting for hours and often being disappointed when her turn came. Yet, we have managed somehow. But it has certainly been a strain on every housewife. Jeanne with her personality has many friends. I have always said to my friends that the best hotel in Oslo is Hotel Willumsen.

Personally, I have had some stomach trouble and

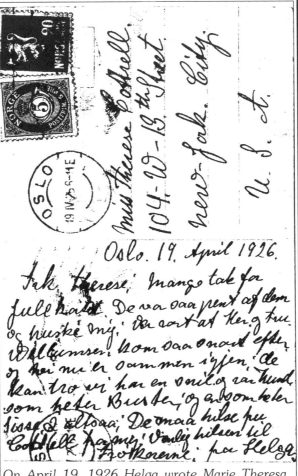

On April 19, 1926 Helga wrote Marie Theresa Cottrell, "Petie," to thank her for her Christmas card. "It was so nice of you to remember me. How sweet that Mr. & Mrs. Willumsen returned so quickly and are now together again. We have a kind and sweet dog whose name is "Buster," and one whose name is "Sisse."

also gone through a minor operation successfully. I am feeling all right today. As the food situation seems to be promising today, I am in hopes that we both will overcome our difficulties in spite of our increasing age.

We have often had you in our thoughts and wondered how you are getting along. As we have not heard from you via the Red Cross, we have taken it for granted that you were all right. Jeanne will write you more fully in a few days and I am looking forward to starting into business again and shall come over as soon as the situation permits. [Sadly, Chris was not able to restart his business and died shortly after the war concluded.]

With our best love to you all from Jeanne and myself, Kiss.

Oslo, Norway
September 13, 1945

My dear Marie:

I have sent you today, as printed matter, a magazine, illustrating the Quisling case and enclosed you will find as well, the history of your father's relatives, compiled back to the year 1542. I am very anxious to know that you receive this and also if you can recollect any of these names.

Your father and his brother, Ole, both went to **Kristiansund** and started

1813-1963 90
CAMILLA COLLETT
NORGE

Residential street view of Oslo in 1926. *This postcard showing her Oslo apartment (with the "X"), was sent to Marie Cottrell Raymond by Helga, Jeanne and Chris Willumsen's beloved maid. She traveled with them to Africa and to America on their many business trips. She lived with them for many years when the Willumsens were living in Bay Ridge, Brooklyn, New York. While carrying her skis by subway from Brooklyn to Bayonne, New Jersey in the Twenties, a frustrated conductor tried to "evict" Helga from the train. In a flash of inspiration, Helga "forgot" her English, and began talking Norwegian and gesturing wildly with the skis. In a similar flash of "inspiration," the conductor decided that she should remain on the train and complete her transit. The story of how Helga carried the skis from Bay Ridge to Bayonne was told many times by the family, always with gales of laughter and merriment. Helga was still alive in 1960, and entertained Faith Raymond who was studying at the University of Oslo.*

Camilla Collett Street was named for the noted Norwegian author and Sufferagete. Today the street looks even better than it did 68 years ago. Only the kiosk is missing. Or is it?

The kiosk has been renovated *and moved to Oslo's Folk Museum where it welcomes thousands of visitors each year.*

there as farmers. Your father's farm, "**Lyshaugen**" [Bright Hill] does not exist today, as the property a long time ago was included in the City of Kristiansund. Ole's farm, which I believe is located in Brunsviken, is still in existence and his family is still located there. Outside of this, I have no further information. If you can recollect anything of interest, please advise me.

As you will see from this, the Flatvad family is related to practically all the most important farms in Sunndalen, and should I try to give you a complete history, it would fill a book.

Another thing of great interest is whether you at any time in the family circle, have heard mentioned that your parents were related to each other?

Just these few lines today. With love and best greetings to you all.

Sincerely yours, Kiss.

Oslo, Norway
August 31, 1945

My Dear Marie:

First you will pardon me the formality of using the machine for practical reasons. Yesterday we received your letter postmarked August the 20th and also Theresa's. We were delighted to have only good news from you. We have also received notice, that a package has arrived at the post office, but have no time to call for same, as yet.

The packages from Theresa and Cecile, we received intact and in good condition. I do not need to tell you, that we have enjoyed the contents, most of which we have not enjoyed for the last 5 years. In the meantime, you will have to bring the donators our most heartfelt and sincerest thanks, until I get the opportunity to write them direct.

Jeanne will also write you, but have no time for this mail. For my own part, you must bring to Jim my best thanks for the splendid Havana cigars, I have been rationing them to 1 a day—whatever was left went into the pipe, so everything was utilized.

Jeanne and I, have just returned from "Rognlihögda," where we have spent a fortnight. We have had a terrible drought here, so the fields were burnt off and very little water. The contents of the packages, came at the right moment. After a good cup of coffee or tea, you can bet your life, that the Havana cigars put me in seventh heaven. What a change to be at Rognlihögda and have freedom, hoisting our three-colored flag and to be yourself again.

During the occupation, we have stayed in our apartment here in town. This consists of only 2 rooms and a bath and kitchen, in an old fashioned house. And, in this we were fortunate, as the Germans found that it was not suitable for such dignified persons. We were therefore lucky not to be bothered by them or their friends.

We are not having any servant girl at present. Helga is employed by an elderly gentleman and likes it very much. From time to time, however, she goes with us to the cabin and is constantly in touch with us.

The servant question is quite a problem and most people are glad to be without them. This of course makes it hard for Jeanne. But in the long run, I believe that this is the best solution. As a whole, I think, that Jeanne today is in fairly good condition. She has difficulty in putting on any weight and to me she looks like a pretty girl in her thirties.

The food question has undoubtedly been bettered, and such things, such that you have sent, are of course, luxuries.

As mentioned to you before, I have been looking into your family tree and have so far come to a result about the family Bjerke. I understand that one of Thore Bjerke's descendants will give out a familybook about this family. Should there be any result, I shall keep you informed.

The results of my findings, I have mailed you

> # The contents of the packages, came at the right moment. After a good cup of coffee or tea, you can bet your life, that the Havana cigars put me in seventh heaven. What a change to be at Rognlihögda and have freedom, hoisting our three-colored flag and to be yourself again.

As Marie was my last sister you can understand that I felt the loss of her so much the more. All the kind memories that I have of her and her home are so dear to me and relieve me much of my sorrow.

under a separate cover, by this mail. I will hope you will receive it in good condition. It contains a list of the families Bjerke-Flatvad, where the most interesting of the Bjerke family is specified. It will be interesting to hear, whether you recognize any of these names.

Enclosed herein you will find a Christmas magazine called "***Juul paa Hedemarken***," where there is a very interesting article about Thore Bjerke and his life. As you probably might be interested to see how we have it on Rognlihögda, I have also included a magazine, that shows the hut that my sister and brother-in-law have built on our property.

In the same post, that we received your letter, I also received a letter from **Endre Opdøl**, who is one of your cousins on your father's side. He is today the proprietor of your homestead "Flatvad" farm in Sunndalen, of which I enclose a photo. In this letter he gives me a complete list of your relatives on your fathers side, and this I shall send you in the next mail. He has also sent me an old photo of your parents with 8 children, the youngest of whom must be Otta, about two years old. This photo, I presume, is taken in Kristiansund about 1874. I am having a copy made and shall send you same.

We understand Marie, that your health is progressing favorably, and we hope that this will continue. I will be sending Jeanne's and my best love to all large and small.

Ever sincerely yours, Kiss.

Oslo
September 20, 1945

My dear Theresa and Bill:

Jeanne was going to write, but she has asked me to do so, and as a dutiful husband, I do so with pleasure.

First of all, let me thank you both for the welcome parcels that we received here some time ago. The coffee, cacao and tea, tasted of course delicious. And, the 10 balls of woolen goods are now in preparation to become a sweater for Jeanne. All arrived here in first class condition and you both please accept our heartfelt thanks, until such time as we can reciprocate.

Really time flies so fast, so it's really difficult to keep tabs on you all. I have the picture of your boy, Bill, before me and I understand that he is bright, handsome, well built and full of pep with his 13 years. We are glad to see that he loves the water and that he has plans of his own. Maybe he can get a chance to find the way across the pond to visit us here. He surely will be more than welcome.

And then you also have a little daughter, Faith. We have no picture of her, but we can readily see her being a good helper in your house.

I hope only it will not take too long a time before I can come over and see you all again. We were a little worried about Marie, but understand now that she is progressing favorably. You say that you have been acting as her secretary, and I have no doubt that you have been a great help for her in these years.

Frankly, I have always admired the consideration that you have shown towards your mother and it has been a great help for her in her daily struggles. We have often wondered how she was able to meet her difficulties in life, but you have all been so considerate and full of lovable thoughts toward her. It's hard to think that she now goes into her 80th year, but she comes from a good stock here in Norway and she really has many years in store yet!

Tante Jeanne *sent this charming, watercolor post card to her niece, Marie Theresa Cottrell in 1912. The Cottrells were living at 104 Mill Street in Newport, R.I. The card shows a little girl putting a small, red doll on the back of a very patient dog. "Dear Theresa," Jeanne wrote shortly after the 1911 Christmas holiday, "Happy New Year! You have gotten a big dog to play with, something very special for you. Hearty greetings from Tante Jeanne."*

As you know, I have gone into your mother's family tree and am wondering, if this interests you? The Fladvad family is really very interesting and may be that at some time, you may find it convenient to spend your holiday on this side. The scenery along the Fladvad farms is one of the show places in this country and I think that a trip would be worth while.

We are very glad to see that you are having a harmonious life together. Certainly, it is a blessing not long for yourself, but also for your environment. When one has gotten that far, life is worth while living. Let me then conclude by again thanking you for your kind thoughts and accept our best love to yourself and children from us both.

Sincerely yours, Kiss–

December 16, 1945
Oslo, Norway

My Dear Marie:

Pardon my using the machine [a typewriter] for convenience sake. This letter is intended to wish you our heartiest congratulations with your 80th birthday, as well as our good wishes for the coming Christmas and the NEW YEAR. Whatever difficulties there are in the future, we pray, that you will overcome same and find satisfaction and help in your increasing family. After all, there is no better comfort, than you can find in a harmonious family life. [The reminder from Christ that she was now eighty years old upset and startled Marie. Realizing that she was now 80 "just about did her in," as her daughter, Petie pointed out later.]

We owe you and your children many thanks for the many packages, that we have received here. It really has been more than welcome and is highly appreciated.

Answering your letter of Nov. 13th, the package containing the shoes for Jeanne was received with its full contents. The shoes fitted her as if they were made for her and she was happy over them in every respect. The pajamas we have also received and I must compliment you on their fine quality. It really was a godsend and I dare not describe, what we had to wear.

Of course nothing of this sort can be obtained here. I realize that there is also a scarcity on your side, so I believe it has put you to a considerable inconvenience.

You mention also, that there is another package on the way, containing knitted dresses, but we have not as yet, received any advice of same. I understand there are thousands of packages coming from the USA, so it takes some time for delivery at this end. Jeanne also says thanks for the hairnet, which was very nice.

In reply to Theresa's question about the relationship between the Bjerke and Flatvad families, I have found what possibly may be a relationship back in 1600. Why I would be much interested to know, whether you Marie, have any knowledge about this. Please let me know and also, if you possess any family Bible with notations therein.

Under separate cover, we have sent you some enamelled buttons, etc. that you possibly can use for the children. I hope, that it will pass through the customs, as it was sent by letter mail.

I have also sent you 6 photos of the Flatvad farm and also of the present owner with his family. I thought you all might be interested in having a picture. I have just received a picture of your parents with their 8 children, taken, I presume in Kristiansund around 1874. I think this very interesting and it is forwarded as printed matter in the first mail. I hope it will arrive in good condition. Kindly advise us, if you have received these things.

We have also received on the 12th instant your letter, telling us that Cecile had two little boys and that all are in good health. We congratulate you all on this occasion and wish every good luck for the newly born.

Ever since Cecile visited us in Brooklyn we

have both had a weak heart for her. We learned to know her charming disposition and understand that she, together with her husband, has created an ideal home.

The maid service seems to be all over the same, as most people here are without them and seem to be glad at that, as their demands are exorbitant.

Our plans for the coming Christmas are that we are going to celebrate 3 days in succession in the family circle and possibly, we may make a trip up to the cabin. Recently, we have gotten snow on the ground, so it looks promising for the younger people.

Jeanne I think is in good shape and is busy as a bee. Her pains in the back seem to be better and most of time is occupied with her duties in the kitchen. We are still living on fish and lately there has been little of that too, so we are looking for a better time in the New Year. Of course, all the shops are still empty and it takes months to have anything repaired–and very expensive.

Jeanne has lots of lady friends and she always shows a willing hand in the dress making way, so she is very popular. At times, I think, it is a little too much, but you know, she has difficulty in saying 'No' when anybody asks for assistance. We have now been married 32 years, without too many scraps and during the last trying years she has been a wonder. I admire her more and more.

As for myself, my back is not so good, so I do not think I dare venture more on skis. I have tried various things, but nothing seems to work on this old body. In business, I have renewed my old connections, but there are many formalities to go through on both sides. For the time being, I am working on a big deal which might put me straight after the five lean years.

I am still doing some hunting, but am handicapped by not having any shotgun. This, together with our two radios, were taken away from us by the German mongrels and nothing has been obtained as yet.

We received a charming letter from Joan and you must in the meantime thank her most heartily, until we get a chance to reply to same. I would also like to send a letter to Eleanor and Ken. We hope they are having a little good luck. The same refers to Theresa and Bill and also Margaret. To all of them we are sending over best wishes for Christmas and the New Year, with thanks for all in the past.

From the correspondence we see, you are in good spirits and that your health is in good shape. You certainly come from good stock and I am sure you have many year in store for you. We pray that these may be happy ones, and that you continue to enjoy the pleasure of your charming children and grandchildren. With love from us both, ever sincerely yours, Jeanne & Kiss.

P.S. In the book *Fra Gauele Dage*, you will find a picture of "Opdól Farm."

Oslo, Norway
October 22, 1947

My dear Theresa!

This morning I received Cecile's telegram informing me that Marie died last night and that a letter will follow. This was of course a great shock to both of us, but some how or other, I had a feeling that Marie's health was not so good anymore. As Marie was my last sister you can understand that I felt the loss of her so much the more. All the kind memories that I have of her and her home are so dear to me and relieve me much of my sorrow. During all the time that I stayed in Marie's home I have only the kindest memories, which I always will carry with me and I know that this is shared by all her children. I am anxiously awaiting further news from you and you must please convey Chris and my own sincere condolences to the rest of the family.

Lots of love to you all, affectionately yours, Chris & Jeanne.

GLOSSARY

OF

NORWEGIAN-ENGLISH FOODS, COOKING, FAMILY LIFE

by

Tove Johansen Halvorsen

Norwegian Americans share a very special legacy in their family ties to a beautiful country, and in the delicious recipes developed over the years. This is especially true of Norwegian Holiday cooking and recipes.

Words, terms, and phrases contained in the Glossary were selected based on their use in cooking, food preparation, household living, and family relationships. We hope they may be of some help to those of you who wish to translate family recipes or letters. While this Glossary will probably not provide the depth needed for serious family research, we do hope it will be helpful. Feel free to recommend additional terms for inclusion in future editions.

To assist readers translating family recipes, we have included various phrases and terms excerpted from Marie Fladvad Cottrell's manuscript cookbook. **These are italicized (in quotes) and retain their original spelling.**

You should keep in mind that although Norway has two official languages, we have been consistent in using only one of them in this Glossary, namely "*rikesmål*." The other official langauge is called "*nynorsk*" (new Norwegian), which is an artificial language created from various dialects spoken in different parts of Norway. There is a strong movement in Norway trying to give this form of Norwegian preference. However, there is an equally strong movement resisting the change. Therefore, both languages are taught in the schools, used in media, and in literature. There is even a special theater in Oslo where all the plays are performed only in "*nynorsk*."

It is not for us to make a judgment regarding these two forms of the language. However, since **rikesmål** is the form the writer is most familiar and comfortable with, this form has been used in this Glossary.

Tove Johansen Halvorsen

NORWEGIAN TERMS ASSOCIATED WITH FOOD, FAMILY, HOME, AND COOKING

A wide variety of traditional Norwegian kitchen equipment is seen in this Oslo **antikvitetshandel** or antiques store.

årfugl
Woodcock.

abbor
Perch.

absint
Absinthe.

aftens
Evening meal.

aftensmat
Evening meal, usually 8-9 p.m.

aquavit
Akavit.

agurk
Cucumber.

agurksalat
Cucumber Salad.

ål
Eel.

alene
Alone or by itself.

alminnelig brød
Light rye bread.

altfor velernært
Overfed.

alun
Alum.

ananas
Pineapple.

ananassaft
Pineapple juice.

and
Duck.

andestek
Roast duck.

ange
Fragrance or smell.

anis
Anise or anise seed.

ansjos
Anchovies.

antikvitetshandel
Antique shop or store.

åpner
Opener.

åpning
Mouth or opening, as in the mouth of a jar.

appelsin
Orange.

appelsinmarmelade
Orange marmalade.

appelsinsaft
Orange Juice.

appelsinskall
Orange peel.

appetitt
Appetite.

appetittvekker
Appetizer.

aprikos
Apricot.

arbeid
Work.

arbeidsrom
Study or workroom.

årestue
Traditional log house with an open hearth. A smoke vent in the roof allowed smoke and bad air to escape.

artisjokk
Artichoke.

artisjokkbunn
Artichoke heart.

arvesølv
Family silver or silver heirlooms.

arvestykke
Heirloom.

aske, oske
Ashes.

asparges
Asparagus.

aspik
Aspic.

att til
Alongside. *Drikke øl att til maten*, drink beer with one's food. *Spise brød att til kjøttet*, eat bread with one's meat.

aure
Trout.

avkjølet
Cooled.

avkjøle
Cool down.

avkokt torsk
Boiled cod.

avlang vannbakkels med vaniljekremfyll og sjokoladeovertrekk
Éclair.

avlange former
Oblong baking form.

avling
Harvest or the crop.

avokado (pære)
Avocado.

avrime
Defrost.

avrunde
Round off.

avta
Decrease or reduce.

avveie
Balance.

bacon og egg
Bacon and eggs.

badstue
Small building or room for hot steam baths (sauna).

bær
Wild berries.

bærskog
Woods or countryside where one goes to pick berries.

bærtur
Berry-picking trip.

bakebrett
Baking sheet.

bakefjel
Bread or pastry board.

bakepulver
Baking powder.

bakeri
Bakery or bakeshop.

bakerovn
Baking oven. *"Varmt som i en bakerovn,"* warm as a baking oven, hot as blazes.

baklengs
Backwards.

bakst
Baking.

bakstehelle
Griddle for flatbrød or lefse.

Bestemor *Marie Fladvad Cottrell whose manuscript cookbook served as the inspiration and basis for* **Flavors of the Fjords***.*

Bestemor *Anna Fladvad Johansen was Marie's older sister. Many of her recipes are included in* **Flavors***. She and her husband, Martin, once owned and operated the Victoria Park Hotel in Hamar.*

bakte poteter
Baked potatoes.

banan
Banana.

bankebiff
Tenderized beef. Served similar to Swiss steak.

barkebrød
Bread made from bark flour and rye.

barnemeny
Children's menu.

bayer
Dark beer.

bekkørret
Brook trout.

belg
Pod.

belønning
Reward.

benløs
Boned or boneless.

benmel
Bone meal.

benytte
Take advantage of.

berberiss
Barberry.

berlinerkrans
Berlin crowns or rings, a type of butter cookie.

besk
Bitter, sharp tasting.

bespise
Feed.

best
Good.

bestefar
Grandfather.

besteforeldre
Grandparents.

bestemor
Grandmother.

bestestue
The "best room," the parlor.

"bestrøes med Sukker og bakes brune"
Sprinkle with sugar and bake until brown.

betasuppe
Meat, marrow, and vegetable soup.

bie
Wait. *"Denne maten er ikke mye å bie på,"* this food won't hold you long.

biff med løk
Beef with onions.

biffstek
Beaf steak.

billig
Inexpensive.

bismak
Off taste, a taste that's not supposed to be present.

bisp
Hot drink made with claret and sugar.

bit
Bite, or a mouthful.

bitter mandel
Bitter almond.

bittersøt
Bitter sweet.

bjørnbær
Blackberry.

blåbær
Blueberry, huckleberry, bilberry. Lit. blue berry. *Det er bare blåbær for ham.* It's as easy as pie for him.

blabærpannekake
Blueberry pancakes.

bladselleri
Celery.

bland i en
Blend in a...

blande
Mix or mixture. *"Olje og vann lar seg ikke blande,"* oil and water don't blend.

blande opp
Mix or dilute.

blandebolle
Mixing bowl.

bland sammen i en kjele
Blend together in a sauce pan.

blanding av oppskårne epler, rosiner
Mincemeat. Lit. a blending or mixture of cut, chopped, sliced apples, raisins.

*Home made **Bløtekake** prepared by Bjørn Fladvad Johansen of Oslo, Norway. For the colorful topping, he used hand picked wild strawberries (**jordbær**) individually frozen. The tart berries made a delicious complement to the sweet whipped cream topping (**krem**). Prior to whipping the cream is **fløte**, after whipping it is **krem**.*

blings
A thick slice or chunk of bread.

blodpudding
Blood pudding.

blomkål
Cauliflower.

blomkålsuppe
Cauliflower soup.

blomsterkrans
Flower wreath.

bløt
Wet or soft.

bløtelegge
Soak. *"Legge i bløt,"* put to soak.

bløtekake
Wet cake or soaked layer cake. Milk is spooned over the layers, then covered with whipped cream.

bløtkokte egg
Soft-boiled egg.

bløtkoke
Soft-boil.

bokk
Strong, dark beer.

bøkling
Type of smoked herring.

bokseåpner
Can opener.

bolle
A sweet bun, roll, or (fish or meat) ball.

bolle med rosiner i
Currant bun.

bønner
Beans.

bord
Table. *"Dekke bordet,"* set the table. *"Ta av bordet,"* clear the table.

bordbønn
Grace.

bordduk
Table cloth.

bordet
The table.

bordkniv
Table knife.

bordkort
Place card.

bordplate
Tabletop.

bordsalt
Table salt.

bordskikk
Table manners. *"Holde bord skikk,"* remain seated at the table until everyone has finished.

bordvin
Table wine.

bort til
Over to, or up to. *"Sette seg bort til bordet,"* sit up to the table.

bøsse
A small container, e.g. for salt. A cellarette.

botsam
Useful, wholesome, or invigorating.

brann
Fire.

breddfull
Brimming full.

brennevin
Spirits in general.

brette
Fold.

brett
Board, as in for rolling out dough. Baking sheet, tray.

bringebær
Raspberry.

brisling
Small herring used to make Sardines.

brød
Bread.

brød med smør på
Bread and butter.

brødbakke
Bread basket.

brødboks
Bread box.

Broderi
Embroidery. Also **prydsøm.**

brødkorn
Food grain or cereals.

brødløs
Out of bread.

brødleiv
A piece of sliced bread.

brødrister
Toaster.

brødskalk
The heel of the loaf.

brødskive
Slice of bread.

brødskorpe
A bread crust.

brødsmuler
Bread crumbs.

brordatter
Niece. Lit. brother's daughter.

brorsønn
Nephew. Lit. brother's son..

brygger
Brewer.

bryllupskake
Wedding cake.

buljong
Bouillon or con-somme'.

bunad
Norwegian national costume.

bunn
Bottom. *"Det er ikke bunn i han,"* he has an unlimited appe-tite.

bunnskrape
Scrape the bottom

*Faith Cottrell Raymond, 17, dressed in her **bunad** from the Hardanger region.*

***These miniature viking sailing ships** are actually sterling silver **bosse** created by the artisans of David Andersen jewelers in Oslo.*

or empty.

bunt
Bundle.

butterdeig
Flaky pastry.

bygg
Barley.

bygg gryn
Pearl barley.

bygning
Farm house, residence. Also, **hus** or **gård**.

da
Then.

dadler
Dates.

dagens suppe
Soup of the Day.

daglig
Daily. *"Gi oss i dag vårt daglige brød,"* give us this day our daily bread.

dagligvareforretning
Grocery store.

dalke
Handle or toy with. *"Sitt ikke og dalk med maten,"* don't dawdle over your food.

dåm
Flavor, taste, or tang.

dampet
Steamed.

datter
Daughter.

datterdatter
Grand daughter.
"de rulles ud til smaa krandse, bestryges med pidskede hvidder og bestrøs med grovstødt Sukker og Mandler"
Then roll out into small rings, coat with beaten egg whites and dip in coarse sugar and almonds.

deig
Dough or doughy mass. *"Slå opp for stor deig,"* make too

much dough, begin on too high a scale.

deigtrau
Kneading trough.

deilig
Delicious.

dekke
Cover, as in cover the rising dough.

dekke bordet
Set the table.

dekketøy
Dishes used to set the table.

dekning
Cover or covering.

del
Part, share, section.

delikat
Delicious or tasty.

delikat anrettet
Arranged in a delicious or tasty way.

delikatere
Enjoy. *"Delikatere seg med et eple,"* enjoy eating an apple.

"den taaler en lang, men ikke for stærk stegning"
Can be baked for a long time, but not at too hot a temperature.

"derpaa haves alt i en gryte og forvælles"
After that everything is poured into a pot and scalded.

dessertbord
Table for desserts.

dessertgaffel
Pastry fork.

dessertskje
Dessert spoon.

det
That.

"det røres i hele tiden til det begynder at blive mykt men må endelig ikke koge, derpaa røres lidt Rugmel og lidt Hvedemel og spiserier"
Stir constantly until soft, but by all means do not let it boil, then add a little whole wheat

*Several different types of apples (**epler**), oranges (**appelsin**), grapes (**druer**) and strawberries (**jordbær**) are seen here in an Oslo market.*

flour and a little white flour and spices.

dill
Dill.

død
Dull, insipid, flat tasting, dead.

dram
Norwegian Snaps, drink, or shot.

drikk
Drink.

drikkehorn
Drinking horn.

drikkekar
Drinking vessel.

drikkelig
Drinkable or fit to drink.

drikkepenger
Tip or gratuity.

drikkevarer
Beverages.

drikkevann
Drinking water.

drivhus
Greenhouse.

druebrennevin
Cognac or grape brandy.

druer
Grape.

druesaft
Grape juice.

druesukker
Grape sugar.

dryppe
Baste.

dryppe steken
Baste the roast.

drysse
To powder or sprinkle. To dust the surface with a powder, e.g. flour. Sprinkle over, as in sifting flour over a wet dough as you're working the dry flour into a wet dough.

drysse over
Drizzle over.

dugurd
Morning meal, a second breakfast.

duke
Set a table, or lay a tablecloth.

dunk
Barrel.

durra
Sorghum.

dypvannsreke
Deep water shrimp.

dyrekjøtt
Reindeer meat.

dyrestek
Reindeer roast.

dyrke
To cultivate.

dyvåt
Soaked or dripping wet, wringing wet.

eddik
Vinegar.

egg
Egg.

egg bløtkokt
Soft boiled/cooked egg.

egg hårdkokt
Hard boiled/cooked egg.

eggedosis
Egg yolks beaten with sugar. Nog.

eggeglass
Egg cup.

Sjokalade and *eplekake med krem* at the Frognerseteren Restaurant near Holmenkollen ski jump. What can beat rich hot chocolate and apple cake while enjoying the spectacular view of Oslo and the fjord?

eggehvite
Egg white.

eggekrem
Soft egg custard used as a topping or filling.

eggeplomme
Egg yolk.

eggerøre
Scrambled eggs.

eggeskal
Egg shell.

einebær
Juniper berry.

ekte
Genuine, real, true.

ektemake
Spouse.

eldbjørg dag
Thirteenth day of Christmas or January 7th. Originally a day of pagan fire worship.

eldhus
Cookhouse separate from the main dwelling used for washing, baking, or brewing.

elektrisk komfyr
Electric cooker or stove.

"ellers"
Otherwise.

eller
or.

elt deigen godt
Knead the dough thoroughly.

elte
Method of mixing butter and flour into the dough. Closest English term would be "cutting" the butter into the flour or kneading.

emner
Material to form, shape, or prepare for further finishing or completion.

en or **et**
A. *"Et stykke kake,"* a piece of cake.

en kopp kaffe
A cup of coffee.

en omelett
An omelett.

ende
End, terminate, or finish.

enebolig
Single family dwelling.

engros pris
The wholesale price.

enkel
Simple or plain, unpretentious.

enkeltvis
Separate.

ensartet
Uniform or homogeneous.

entré
Entry, vestibule, or hall.

eple
Apple. *"Eplet faller ikke langt fra stammen,"* he's a chip off the old block.

eplekake
Apple cake.

eplemos
Apple sauce.

eplepai
Apple pie.

eplesaft
Apple juice. "**Sider**" is the alcoholic variety.

epleterte
Apple turnover or apple cake.

er (aer)
Is.

ernære
Feed, nourish, sustain.

ernærende
Nourishing, nutritious.

erænringsfysiolog
Dietician.

ernæringskjede
Food chain.

ernæringsverdi
Food value.

ert
Pea.
erte skolm
Pea pod.
ertebelg
Pea pod.
erter
Peas.
ertesuppe
Pea soup.
ese
Rise or swell.
eske
Wooden or cardboard box.
estragon
Tarragon.
et forlorent egg
A poached egg.
etappe
A stage or step in a process.
etikett
Label.
etter
After.
etter avkjøling
After cooling.
etterhpå
Afterwards.
etterjuls vinter
That part of winter following Christmas.
etterkommer
Descendant.
ettermiddagste
Afternoon tea.
ettermodne
To ripen after picking.
"etter smag og behag"
According to taste.
etui
Small case for silverware or jewelry.
få
Get, obtain, acquire.
fårestek
Leg of Mutton.
får et oppkok
Is brought to a boil.
fadder
Godparent or sponsor.

faderlig
Fatherly or paternal.
falle
Fall.
farbror
Father's brother, uncle.
fårekjøtt
Mutton or lamb.
fårekotelett
Lamb cutlet or mutton chop.
fårelår
Leg of mutton.

*This **stabur** or raised storage building is located in the Sunndalen where it has protected the crops on the Fladvad **farsgård** or ancestral home for hundreds of years.*

farfar
Father's father, paternal grandfather.
farge
Tine, shade, color or hue.
fårikål
Lamb Stew with Cabbage.
farin
Granulated sugar.
farløs
Fatherless.
farmor
Father's mother, paternal grandmother.
farsgård
Ancestral home (farm) or estate. Also **slektsgård.**
fasan
Pheasant.

fast
Solid, firm, or fixed.
fastelavens bolle
Bun baked and filled with whipped cream to celebrate Shrove-tide.
fastende
Fasting. *"Jeg faster,"* I am not eating.
fatøl
Draft beer.
fatte
Seize or grasp.
fattigman
Fried Cakes, Crullers.
feiebrett
Dust pan.
feire jul
Celebrate Christmas.
felt
Field or space.
fenalår
Cured leg of mutton.
ferdigmat
Convenience foods, fast foods.
ferie
Vacation. *"Feriere ved sjøen,"* go on vacation to the seashore.
fersk
New, fresh, or recent.
fersken
Peach.
ferskvannsfisk
Fresh water fish.
feste
Celebrate.
festlig
Festive.
fett
Fat, lard, or grease. *"Bli stekt i sitt eget fett,"* stew in one's own juice.
fettere
Male first cousins. See **kusiner.**
fettinnhold
Fat content.

fiber I kosten
Dietary fiber.
fiken
Fig.
fin
Excellent, of good
  quality, fine.
inhakk og tilsett
Cut fine and add.
finhakke
Chop up fine, mince.
finbrød
Rye bread.
fisk
Fish.
fiskepudding
Fish pudding.
fiskebolle
Fish ball.
fiskegrateng
Fish souffle'.
fiskekaker
Fish cakes.
fiskemat
Fish products.
fiskesuppe
Fish soup.
fjærfe
Poultry.
fjellørret
Mountain trout.
flå
To skin or flay.
flamme
Flame or blaze.
flaske
Flask, bottle, phial.
flaskeåpner
Bottle opener.
flatbrød
Flat bread, very thin, crisp,
  unleavened bread.
flatbrødsoll
Milk or cream and crumbled flat
  bread.
flekke
Skin or peal.
flekkekniv
Sharp knife.
flenge
Tear, gash, or rip.

Cooking in a 19th century Norwegian kitchen
(kjokken), *complete with Munker pans on the stove* ***(ovn).***
This doll house exhibit can be seen in the Oslo Folk
Museum.

flesk
Pork.
fleskefett
Pork drippings.
flette
Plait or braid.
flink
Clever, able, competent. *"Flink*
  i matlagning," a good cook.
flomme
Flow or stream.
flor
Bloom.
flormelis
Powdered sugar.
fløte
Cream.
fløtegrøt
Cream porridge.

fløtekaramell
Butterscotch.
fløtemugge
Cream pitcher.
fløtesaus
Cream sauce.
fløy
Peeled stick for turning
bread.
flyndre
Flounder.
flyte
Flow or run. *"Flyte*
med melk og
honning," be flowing
with milk and honey.
flytende
Liquid.
fø
Nourish or feed.
fødeby
Hometown.
fødested
Birthplace.
folkeminne
Folklore.
folkevise
Folk song or ballad.
för
Feed or fodder.
forære
Present with, give.
foran
Before or in front of.
forandring
Modification, change, or alter-
ation.
forberede
Prepare or get ready.
fordele
Distribute or apportion.
fordoble
Double.
forevise
Show, exhibit, or present.
forfallsdag
Expiration date.
forfatning
State or condition.
forfriskende
Refreshing or cooling.

The farm Bjørnstad at Maihaugen, the Norwegian folk life museum at Lillehammer. The farm reflects the architecture of the North Gudbrandsdal valley and the older style of Norwegian farm buildings or *gård*.

forkorting
Shortening.

forkulle
Char.

forloren hare
Meat loaf.

forlorent
Poached.

forme
Shape or form.

"formen smøres med smør og stødte kavringer"
Butter the form and sprinkle with zweiback.

"formen smøres godt"
Butter (or grease) the form well/thoroughly.

formkake
Loaf or pound cake.

form kakene
Shape or mold the cake or cookie.

forretning
Business or store.

forretter
Appetizers.

forsiktighet
Discretion, caution, or prudence.

forskjærskniv
Carving knife.

forsluken
Gluttonous or greedy.

forspise seg
Overeat.

forspist
Overfed.

forstå
Understand or comprehend.
"Forstå seg på," be a connoisseur.

forstue
Entrance or lobby. Also **entré.**

forsyne
Supply, furnish, or supply.

forsyning
Supply or stock.

fort
Quickly, fast, rapid.

fortæring
Consumption of drink or food.

fortinne
Tin plate.

fortreffelig
Splendid, excellent.

forvandle
Convert, change, or transform.

forvelle
Bring to a boil.

fossekall
The Norwegian national bird.

fosskoke
Cook at a rolling boil. Lit. foaming cook.

føste nyttårsdag
New Year's Day.

fram
Forward, ahead. Fram: Roald Amundsen's ship in which he explored the antarctic.

framskap
Large farmhouse cupboard, located near the front door.

franskbrød
White bread, long and thin.

frekk
Voracious, greedy.

frese
Sizzle, crackle, sputter (like a fire).

frikassé
Stew.

frilands
Grown outdoors.

frisk
Fresh, well, healthy, hearty, revive, refresh.

frityrsteke
Deep fat fry.

frø
Seed.

frøloff
White bread with seeds.

frokost
Breakfast.

fromasj
Custard or mousse.

frukt
Fruit.

frukt kompott
Stewed and mixed fruit.

fruktkniv
Fruit knife.

fruktsaft
Fruit juice.

fruktgelé
Jelly.

fryse
Freeze.

frysetørret
Freeze dried.

fuglebryst
Breast of a fowl.

fukte
Moisten or dampen.

fuktig
Humid, damp, or moist.

fuktighet
Moisture, wetness, humidity.

fullstappet
Over flowing, chock-a-block.

fylle
Fill.

fylt kålhode
Stuffed cabbage.

fyre
Stoke (a fire).

fyrstekake
Prince's cake. Confectioner's cake with an almond or apple filling.

gaffel
Fork.

gafle
Eat voraciously.

gamlemor
Grandmother, an older lady.

gammel
Old, aged, antique.

*Carrots (**gulrøtter**), tomatoes (**tomater**) from Holland, and iceberg lettuce (**issalat**) are specials offered by this Oslo vegetable market (**grønnsakshandel**).*

gammalost
Fully ripened (pungent) skim milk cheese.

gammeldags mat
Traditional food.

gane
Palate. *"Han har en fin gane når det gjelder vin,"* he has a good palate for wine.

gård
Farm, homestead, manor, estate.

gås
Goose.

gatedør
Front door, entrance door.

gauda
Gouda cheese.

geitost
Goat cheese.

gelé
Jelly or jellied.

gjær
Yeast.

gjære
Rise (dough), ferment .

gjedde
Pike.

gjennomisnet
Iced or chilled.

gjennomstekt
Baked until well done.

gjestebud
Feast, party, banquet.

gjøre
Do or make.

gjøre tykkere
Thicken.

glasshåndkle
Dish towel for glasses.

gløgg
Hot, mulled wine with brandy, raisins, sugar, and almonds.

glovarm
Glowing hot, scorching hot.

god
Good. *"God dag,"* good day. *"God nyttår,"* Happy New Year.

god appetitt
Good appetite.

god jul
Merry Christmas.

godbit
Tid bit.

godgjøre seg
"Stå å godgjøre seg," let stand to ripen, become more flavorful, seasoned, e.g. to marinade.

godt stekt
Well-done.

goro
Wafer baked on a patterned, rectangular iron.

gotterier
Candy, goodies.

granat eple
Pomegranate.

gressløk
Chives.

grateng
Au gratin.

grepfrukt
Grapefruit.

gresskar
Squash, pumpkin.

griljere
Dip in bread crumbs before frying.

grill
Grill or barbecue.

grillet
Grilled.

grille
Broil.

grisesylte
Pickled pork.

grønnlig
Greenish.

grønn
Green or fresh.

grønnkål
Kale.

grønnsak
Vegetable.

grønnsakshandel
Vegetable store.

grønnsakstuing
Creamed vegetables.

grønnsaksuppe
Vegetable soup.

grøt
Mush or hot cereal.

grøtet
Pulpy, mushy, like porridge.

grov
Coarse texture.

grovbrød
Pumperknickle bread. Also, any coarse, dark bread..

grovt mel
Meal or coarse flour.

grunnpris
Basic price. Also, basispris.

gryn
Hulled grain, e.g. pearled barley, grits, groats.

grynsodd
Meat broth with hulled grain.

gryte
Kettle or pot.

grytelokk
Lid to a saucepan.

gryterett
Casserole.

grytidlig
Crack of dawn.

gul
Yellow.

gule erter
Yellow peas.

gulrøtter
Carrots.

gumme
Sweet cheese, a brown cheese made from boiled whole cow's milk.

ha
To have.

ha i
Add or include. "Ha i litt mel," add a little flour.

hagebruk
Horticulture.

hage
Garden or orchard.

hakke
Chop or hack.

halv
Half.

halvfet
Made with skimmed and whole milk.

halvgod
Moderately good, passable.

halvkoke
Parboil.

halvsåle
Sole.

ham
Outer skin.

hammer
Hammer, gavel, mallet.

hams
Hull, husk, or shell, e.g. of a nut.

handel
Trade, commerce, or business.

handling
Action.

hane
Rooster.

hardkokt
Hard-boiled.

hardkokte egg
Hard-boiled eggs.

hare
Hare.

harsk
Rancid or bitter.

hasselnøtter
Hazelnuts.

havregrøt
Oatmeal porridge.

havregryn
Rolled oats.

havrekjeks
Oatmeal bisquits.

havremel
Oatmeal.

havsalt
Sea salt.

helkorn brød
Whole grain or whole wheat bread.

hel
Complete, whole, full, all.

"heldes i en form spises med rød saus"
Pour into a form, eat with red sauce.

helmelk
Whole milk.

helle
Incline or slope.

hellefisk or kveite
Halibut.
helse
Health or vigor.
helsekoststed
Health farm.
helt
Fully, completely, entirely.
hermetikk
Canned food or goods.
herremåltid
Sumptuous meal.
"hertil kommer en smule Vannille som ogsaå kan undværes"
Here comes/hereto add a little/ small amount of Vanilla which may also be excluded.
het
Hot.
hete
Warmth or heat.
heve seg
Rise, as in dough rising.
hjelpe
Assist, help, aid.
hjemmelaget
Homemade.
hjørne
Corner.
hode
The head of something, e.g. a bed, person, lettuce.
hodekål
Cabbage.
hodesalat
Head lettuce.
høne
Chicken, fowl, hen.
honning
Honey.
honningkake
Honey cake, one containing honey as an ingredient.
hønse-egg
Chicken egg.
hønsesuppe
Chicken soup.
horn
Crescent.
høst
Autumn.

hovedbestanddel
Main ingredient.
hovedrett
Entrée or main course.
høytid
Holiday.
hugge
Chop, cut, carve, hew.

*Tante Jeanne and Chris Willumsen at "**Rognlihogda**," their "**hytte**" in the mountains above Drammen, Norway. Christian "Kiss" Willumsen married Jeanne Fladvad, Marie Fladvad Cottrell's younger sister in 1913. She was 31, beautiful and intelligent. He had wanted to marry long before, but she said they must wait until he had made his business successful. He was handsome and entrepreneurial. His export-import businesses were successful--until the German occupation government forced him out of business. They were a devoted couple until his death in 1949. His research into the Fladvad-Bjørke family history was an invaluable resource during preparation of **Flavors of the Fjords.***

huggestabbe
Chopping block.
hummer
Lobster.
hundre
Hundred.
hurtigarbeidende
Fast acting, fast working, quick acting.
hurtigkoker
Pressure cooker.
hus
Building.
husmann
Tenant farmer with a life tenure, cotter, or crofter.
husarbeid
House work.
husflid
Home crafts, folk arts.
husgjest
Boarder.
hustru
Wife.
"hvad man behager kan sættes til"
Whatever you please/put or add whatever pleases you, to one's own taste.
"hvormed formen smøres"
Then butter the pan.
hvem
Who.
hverdag
Weekday, workday.
hvete
Grain, wheat.
hvetebolle
Small wheat bun.
hvetebrød
White bread.
hvetemel
White flour.
"hvidden slaaes til skum"
Beat the egg whites until foamy.
hvit
White.
hvitkål
White cabbage.
hvitløk
Garlic.

hvitting
Whiting.

hvitvin
White wine.

hvor
(from) where, .

hvor mange
How many.

hvor mye
How much.

hvordan
How.

hvorfor
Why.

hyggelig
Comfortable, cheerful, pleasant, nice.

hylle
Shelf or rack.

hyllebær
Elderberry.

hyllebærbusk
Elderberry bush.

hyse
Haddock.

hyssing
Twine or string.

hytte
Summer home, hut, cottage, or cabin.

ikke for krydret
Not too spicy.

ild
Fire or flame.

ildfast
Oven proof.

indre
Inside, inner, interior.

ingefær
Ginger.

ingenting
Nothing.

innbakt eple
Apple dumpling.

innbo
Furniture, household furnishings.

inngang
Entry or entrance.

inngangsdør
Front door.

innmat
Stuffing, giblets, entrails.

innta
Consume.

innunder
Under or below.

invitere
Invite or ask. *"Invitere på kaffe,"* invite for coffee.

is
Ice, sherbet, ice cream.

***Norwegian Christmas Tree** as a centerpiece at the **Julehus** in Drøbak--a tidy little town of some 3,000 people. Hardly a household word--unless you're a child and want to send a Christmas card to Santa Claus. If so, you address the letter to: Mr. Santa Claus, Julenissen N' 1440, Drøbak, Norway. "Julenissen" are Christmas elves or gnomes. In Drøbak however, Christmas does come 365 days a year at the Tregården Julehus ("Three Building Christmas House"). The quaint wooden house is chockful of Christmas presents and ornaments. Many children believe that Santa's workshop is nearby in some secret location. Another surprise: Drøbak is not at the North Pole, but about 20 miles south of Oslo. Over a quarter of a million people visit the Drøbak Christmas House every year.*

isbit
Ice cube.

iskald
Icy cold.

iskrem
Ice cream.

issalat
Iceberg lettuce.

isvann
Ice water.

jafs
Mouthful, gulp.

jarlsbergost
Swiss-style cheese.

jerngryte
Cast iron pot or kettle.

jevne
Flatten or thicken, e.g. soup by adding flour.

jord
Ground or dirt.

jordbær
Strawberry.

jordbruk
Agriculture, farming.

jul
Christmas Day or the Christmas season.

julaften
Christmas Eve.

julegrøt
Rice porridge eaten on Christmas Eve.

julebakst
Christmas baking or Christmas cookies.

juleblot
Old Norse sacrificial feast held about January 12th according to the old pagan (holiday) custom.

julebord
Table arranged with Christmas food.

julebukk
A costumed person who goes from door to door at Christmas to be treated to cookies.

juledag
Christmas day.

juleferie
Christmas holidays.

julegave
Christmas gift.
julehelg
Christmas season.
julehilsen
Christmas greeting.
julehilsener
Christmas greetings.
julekake
Christmas bread.
julekort
Christmas card.
julekost
Christmas food.
julenek
Grain stalks or a sheaf of grain on pole set out for the birds at Christmas.
julenissen
Father Christmas. Lit. Christmas gnome.
juleøl
"Christmas Beer," a strong, dark beer brewed for release just before Christmas.
julesang
Christmas carol.
juletid
Christmas time.
juletravelhet
Rushed Christmas preparations.
juletre
Christmas tree.
juletre pynt
Christmas tree decorations.
jus
Juice.
kafe
Restaurant.
kaffe
Coffee. "Svart kaffe" is black coffee. "Kaffe med fløte" is coffee with cream.
kaffebord
Coffee table.
kaffedokter
Coffee royal, a coffee and brandy drink.
kaffekanne
Coffee pot.

Perhaps no other people in the world love berries as much as Norwegians who use them in many different recipes. Grocery stores like this one in Kristiansund carry a wide variety of berry preserves (**syltetøy**) like these strawberries (**jordbær**) and lingonberries (**tyttebær**).

kaffekvern
Coffee mill or grinder.
kaffepause
Coffee break or pause.
kaffeslabberas
Coffee party.
"kages tilsammen"
Mix together.
kajenne pepper
Cayenne.
kakao
Cocoa.
kakaotre
Cacao tree or bush.
kake
Cake or cookie.
kakeboks
Cookie jar or can.
kakebunn
The bottom layer of a layer cake.
kakedeig
Cake dough or batter.
kakefat
Cake dish or cake plate.
kakeform
Cake pan.
kakene
The pastries.
kaken avkjøles
Allow the cake to cool.
kakespade
Cake knife or cake server.

kakkelovn
Heating oven.
kål
Cabbage.
kalkun
Turkey.
kalori
Calorie.
kalorifattig
Low calorie content.
kaloriinnhold
Calorie content.
kålrabi
Kohlrabi, rutabaga.
kålrulett
Cabbage roll.
kalv
Veal.
kalve filé
Filet of veal.
kalvekjøtt
Veal.
kalvestek
Roast veal.
kameratslig samvær
Friendly gathering.
kamillete
Camomile tea.
kanapé
Canapé.
kandis
Lump of brown sugar, sugar candy.
kandisere
To coat with sugar.
kandisert
Candied.
kanel
Cinnamon.
kanin
Rabbit.
kanne
Container, pot, can, tankard.
kant
Border, edge, rim.
kar
Fully grown man.
karamell
Caramel.
karamell pudding
Caramel custard or creme caramel.

karbonade
Meat patty, hamburger.

kardemomme
Cardamom.

karpe
Carp.

karri
Curry.

karri saus
Curry sauce.

karse
Cress.

kart
Unripe fruit or berry.

karve
Caraway.

kasse
Bin or box.

kasserolle
Sauce pan.

kav
Completely.

kavring
Rusk or hard biscuit, zweiback.

kefir
Soured milk.

kirkebryllup
Church wedding.

kirkebok
Church (book) register.

kirsebær
Cherries.

kirsebærlikør
Cherry brandy.

kjeks
Crackers, cookies, or biscuits.

kjele
Skillet or saucepan.

kjenner
Connoisseur.

kjerne
Churn.

kjerne
Kernel or seed.

kjernemelk
Buttermilk.

kjese
To make cheese aided by rennin, e.g. cheddar.

kjevle
Rolling pin or to roll out.

*This statue of the "Klippfisk woman" (**Klippfiskkjerringa**) of Kristian-sund has now become the symbol of the city. It not only pays tribute to the contributions of the working women of the city (**arbeider-kvinnene**), but represents the enormous importance of dried cod (**klipfisk**) to the city's economy during the 19th century.*

kjøkken
Kitchen or cuisine.

kjøkkenbenk
Kitchen counter.

kjøkkenforkle
Apron used in the kitchen.

kjøkkenhage
Kitchen garden.

kjøkkentøy
Kitchen utensils.

kjøkkenvask
Kitchen sink.

kjøleskap
Refrigerator.

kjøpe
Purchase or buy.

kjøtt
Meat or pulp of fruits.

kjøttboller
Meatballs.

kjøttfull
Meaty, fleshy, fat, succulent.

kjøttgelé
Aspic.

kjøttkaker
Meatballs, only a little larger than **kjøttboller**.

kjøttmat
Meat.

kjøttpålegg
Cooked meats or sandwich meat.

kjøttretter
Meat dishes.

kjøttsuppe
Vegetable soup with meat.

klabbe
Press together, pat.

klar
Clear, transparent.

klede
Cloth, or piece of cloth. *"Dekk den med klede og sett den til heving ca. 1 time,"* cover the mixture with a cloth and set it (the mixture) to rise for about one hour."

klemme
Squeeze or press.

klippe
Cut, clip.

klippfisk
Dried cod--split, salted, and dried in the open air.

klissen
Sticky, gooey, sticking together.

klok
Wise or intelligent.

klump
Dollop or lump.

kna
Knead. *"Godt knadd,"* well

kneaded. *"Kna deigen og elt inn rosinene,"* knead the dough and cut in/add the raisins.

knaske
Munch or chew.
knekkebrød
Rye crispbread, similar to rye

crisp.
kniv
Knife.

*An Oslo **fancy baker** or confectioner (**konditor**) displays a wide variety of delicious bread (**brød**), pastries (**konditorvarer**), and cookies (**kjeks**).*

kniver
Cutlery.

knyte
Tie a knot.

kobberkjele
Copper pot or kettle.

koke
Cook or boil.

kokebok
Cookbook.

koke inn
To evaporate by boiling.

koke kaffe
Make coffee.

kokekar
Cooking pot or pan.

kokekunst
The art of cooking, the culinary arts.

kokende hett
Boiling hot.

koke opp
Bring to a boil, cook to boiling point.

kokken
The cook.

kokosnøtt
Coconut.

kokt
Cooked.

kokt for lenge
Cooked too long.

kokt for lite
Undercooked.

kokt skinke
Boiled ham.

kokte maiskolber
Corn on the cob.

koldtbord
Buffet lunch or supper.

kolesterol
Cholesterol.

kolonialvarer
Groceries.

kompott
Compote.

konditor
Fancy baker, confectioner.

konditori
Confectionery or pastry shop.

konditorvarer
Pastries.

konfekteske
Box of candy, chocolates.

konjakk
Cognac or brandy.

konsument
Consumer.

kopp
Cup. *"En kopp kaffe,"* a cup of coffee.

*A festive **kransekake** is the display window center piece for an Oslo **konditori** on Independence Day (**syttendemai**).*

kopp og skål
Cup and saucer.

koriander
Coriander.

korinter
Currants.

kork
Cork or bottle cap.

korketrekker
Corkscrew.

korn
Grain or cereals.

kornet
Granular.

kornfrokost
Breakfast cereal.

kornslag
Cereal.

kort
Short, brief, concise.

kost
Food.

kosthold
Diet.

kotelett
Cutlet.

krabbe
Crab.

kraftbein
Soupbone. *"Koke kraft på et ben,"* make soup from a bone.

kråketing
Crow convention or caucus, a gathering of people who focus on unimporant matters with a lot of empty talk. Could be called a "raucus caucus."

krakkmandel
Thin-shelled almond.

kramme
Crush, press, or squeeze.

krans
Wreath or garland of flowers, ring or circle.

kransekake
Traditional cake made from almond macaroon rings of decreasing diameter arranged in a cone. Icing is dribbled on the sides, flags are added for decorations, and often a figure is placed on top.

krås
Giblets.

krekling
Crowberry.

krem
Whipped cream.

kremfløte
Whipping cream.
kremmerhus
Paper cornucopia, cone-shaped container for candy.
kreps
Crawfish.
kresen
To be particular or choosy about food, discriminating, picky.
kringle
Pretzel-shaped almond pastry.
Kristiania
Former name for Oslo used from 1624-1924.
krokan
Almond brittle.
krøll
Crinkle.
krone
Crown, tiara, coronet.

krumkake
Crisp, cone-shaped cookie.
kruspersille
Parsley.
krydderier
Condiments, spices, or seasonings.
kryddernellik
Clove(s).
krydderplante
Herb (lit. a seasoning plant).

kryddersild
Marinated or pickled herring.
krydret
Spiced.
kule
Ball.
kulinarisk
Culinary.
kumpe
Potato dumpling. Lit. a lump.

*This **water powered mill** (**kvern**) is located on the banks of the Driva River in the Sunndalen. The Fladvad family used it to grind their wheat (**hvete**), oats (**havre**), and barley (**bygg**) for generations. Today the **kvern** has been restored and is a part of the Leikvin Parish Museum.*

kunne
Can or be able to, was able to.

kunst
Art.

kurv
Basket.

kusiner
Female first cousins. See
 fettere.

kutt
Cut.

kuvertbrikke
Place mat.

kvart
Quarter of something, e.g. an
 apple. *"en kvart ost,"* a
 quarter of a cheese.

kveg
Cattle.

kveld
Evening. *"God kveld,"* good
 evening.

kveldsmat
Late evening meal.

kvern
Mill to grind grain, coffee, nuts,
 pepper, meat.

kverne
Grind.

kvernhus
Building in
 which the
 milling equip-
 ment is
 housed.

kylling
Chicken.

la
Allow or let.

lag en rull
Make a roll or
 shape into a
 roll.

lage
Prepare or
 make.
 "Lage mat,"
 make (or
 prepare)
 food.

lage te
Brew tea.

lager
Storeroom.

lake
Brine.

Lakris
Licorice.

laks
Salmon.

lam
Lamb.

lammekjøtt
Lamb.

lammekotelett
Lamb chop or lamb chop.

lammesteik
Roast lamb.

lapskaus
Beef stew.

lefse
Soft, flat bread. Flat bannock.

legg deigen på bakebordet
Lay or place the dough on the
 baking table.

legge
To place, put, or lay something.

lekker
Pertaining to food, delicious.

Norwegian cooks *use many types of flour (**mel**), including that made
from wheat (**hvetemel**), rice (**rismel**), potatoes (**potetmel**), and oats
(**havremel**).*

lekkerbisken
Tasty morsel, delicacy, delicious
 tidbit.

lekkermunn
Gourmand or epicure.

lett fordøyelig mat
Easily digested food.

**lett frokost med rundstykker
 og kaffe**
Continental breakfast.

lettstekt
Cooked rare.

lever
Liver.

leverpølse
Liver sausage.

leverpostei
Liver paste.

ligge
Lie, be located, situated.

like
To like, enjoy, be comfortable
 with. Also, equal.

linse
Lentil. Also a form of pastry.

linser
Lentils.

**lite kjøttstykke
stekt på spidd**
Kebab.

liten
Small, little.

loff
White bread.

løk
Onion(s).

løksuppe
Onion Soup.

lompe
Soft, flat potato
 bread.

luftig
Light, airy,
 breezy.

lunke
Warm up, take
 the chill off. *"Gi
 kaffekjelen en
 lunk,"* warm up
 the coffee pot.

lute
To treat with lye.

lutefisk
Codfish processed in potash lye (an acquired taste).

mais
Corn.

mais grøpp
Cornmeal mush.

maisgryn
Corn meal.

maisenna
Cornstarch.

maismel
Corn flour or corn starch.

majones
Mayonnaise.

makaroni
Macaroni.

makelig
Slowly, leisurely.

makron
Macaroon.

male
Grind grain, coffee, meat. Also, to paint. *"Male på,"* grind away (at something), repeat again and again.

malm
Metal.

malt
Malt.

måltid
Meal.

mandarin
Mandarin orange.

mandeldeig
Almond (dough) paste.

mandeldråper
Almond extract.

mandelflarn
Almond snaps.

mandelformet
Almond shaped.

mandelmasse
Almond paste.

mandler
Almonds.

mange
Many. *"Mange takk,"* many thanks, thank you very much.

A famous Norwegian "kitchen" (kjokken). The ship's kitchen or galley (bysse) aboard Captain Roald Amundsen's polar ship, Fram (forward).

margben
Marrow bone.

marinert
Marinated.

marmelade
Marmalade.

marsipan
Almond paste.

masse
Substance, or a lot. "Masse mat," a lot of food.

mat
Food, fare. *"Takk for maten,"* thanks for the food (or meal).

matbit
Morsel or bit of food.

mat og drikke
Food and drink.

matbu
Pantry or larder.

mateple
Cooking apple.

matfat
A dish for food.

matfett
Lard.

mathus
A home noted for its good food and cooking.

matlaging
Cooking.

matlukt
Cooking odors.

matolje
Cooking oil.

matvarer
Groceries or food-stuffs.

maule
To consume or eat without any accompanying liquid, i.e. dry, chew, munch.

mave
Stomach.

med
With.

med tenner
Pronged. *"En gaffel med tre tenner,"* a three-pronged fork.

medisterdeig
Mixture of pork lean and minced fat, plus seasonings.

medisterkaker
Pork meat cakes, pork patties.

meget tørr
Extra dry.

meieriprodukter
Dairy produce.

mektig
Powerful.

mel
Flour.

mel tilsatt bakepulver
Self-rising flour.

melbolle
Dumpling.

melete
Flour-covered.

melis
Confectioner's, powdered, or icing sugar.

melisglasur
Icing.

melk
Milk. *"Det nytter ikke å gråte over spilt melk,"* it's no use crying over spilt milk.

melkebutikk
Dairy store.

melkepulver
Powdered milk.

Slottet or palace (below) on May 17, 1994. Queen Sonja, King Harald, and Princess Martha Louise (right) return the cheers and salutes from tens of thousands of children during the annual National Day (**Nasjonal dag**) parade, usually just called **syttendemai tog**. Schools from throughout the Oslo region send their bands (**musik korps**) to march in the parade by the palace, each band followed by students and faculty wearing the national costume (**bunad**) and waving Norwegian flags. Similar parades are held in virtually every other city and village throughout the country.

melkering
Clabbered (slightly curdled) whole milk eaten with sugar and crumbs.

melkespann
Milk pail.

mellom
Between.

melmat
Food made from flour or meal.

melon
Melon, usually muskmelon.

menneske
Person, human being.

merengs
Meringue.

merke
Identifying mark, label, stamp.

mest
Most.

mett
Full of food, satiated, satisfied.

middagsmat
Dinner or food for dinner.

middagsselskap
Dinner party.

Middagsservise
Dinner service.

midten
The middle of.

mikser
Food mixer.

mineralvann
Mineral water (usually carbonated).

miste appetitten
Lose one's appetite.

mjød
Mead, a fermented drink containing honey.

moden
Ripe (apple, grain, cheese).

mokkakopp
Demitasse.

mor
Mother.

mør
Tender.

mørbanke
To tenderize meat by beating.

morbær
Mulberry.

mørbrad
Beef or pork tenderloin.

mørdampe
Steam until tender.

morell
Bing cherry.

morgen
Morning.

mørkt øl
Brown ale.

mormor
Mother's mother, maternal grandmother.

mors folk
Mother's kin, mother's side of the family.

mørt kjøtt
Tender meat.

most
Fermented fruit juice.

muffin
Cup cake.

muggen
Moldy or musty.

multer
Cloudberries.

munn
Mouth.

munnfull
Mouthful.

muskat
Nutmeg.

mussere
Bubble, effervesce, fizz, sparkling water or wine.

musserende/sprudlende vin
Sparkling wine.

myk opp og tilsett
Soften up and add.

mynt
Mint.

mysost
Mild, brown cheese from cow and goat whey.

nåtid
At present, now.

nær
Almost, close, nearly.

næringsfattig
Low in nutritional or food value.

napoleonskake
Vanilla custard cream center between two sweet wafer-like crust layers.

når
When.

nasjonaldag
Independence Day, May 17th.

nasjonaldrakt
National custume. See **bunad.**

natron
Baking soda.

navn
Name.

ned
Down. "Prisene er gått ned," prices have come down.

nederste ribbe
Lower rack (of an oven). *"og stek dem på nederste ribbe,"* and bake them on the lower (oven) rack.

negerkyss
Chocolate-covered cookie.

nellik
Cloves.

nepe
Turnip.

neper
Turnips.

*A Norwegian table set (**opdekning**) for coffee (**kaffe**) and sweet refreshments following the May 17th Independence Day parade (**syttendemai tog**) past the palace (**Slottet**) in Oslo. The red, white, and blue cake in the foreground is a **Syttendemai kake**.*

*A room with a traditional fire place (**peisestue**) located in a corner. This restored farmhouse can be seen at Maihaugen in Lillehammer. The design of this fireplace (**peis**) did not include a mantle (**peishylle**), but the family did use a fireplace stool (**peiskrakk**), kettles (**kjelen**), and a child's cradle (**vogge**).*

nips
Ornament, knick-knack.

niste
Lunch contained in a box or basket.

nok
Enough.

nøkkelost
cheese, spiced with cloves.

nøste
Ball, e.g. of yarn, thread, string.

nøttehams
Husk of a nut.

nøtteknekker
Nut cracker.

nøtteskall
Nutshell.

nudler
Noodle.

null
Zero.

ny
New, modern, recent.

nybakt
Freshly baked.

nybakt brød
Fresh bread.

nybygget
Recently constructed or built.

nydelig
Beautiful, very attractive.

nype
Rosehip.

nyrer
Kidneys.

nyttår
New Year. *Godt nytt år*, Happy New Year.

nyttårsaften
New Year's Eve.

nytte
Use.

ofte
Often.

og
And.

"og naar den er kold"
And when it is cold.

også
Also, too.

okse
Ox.

oksebryst
Brisket of beef.

oksekarbonade
Chopped beef cakes, beef patty.

oksekjøtt
Beef.

øl
Ale or beer.

oldefar
Great grandfather.

oldemor
Great grandmother.

oliven olje
Olive oil.

olje
Oil.

om
If, in case, around.

omfang
Size or dimensions.

omkostning
Expense, cost, or charge.

omkring
About or around.

omsorg
Concern or care.

oppdekning
Table setting, spread.

opp
Upwards motion, up.

oppdisking
Sumptious spread or meal.

oppå
Upon, on top of.

oppbrukt
Consumed, used up.

oppfylle
Fulfill, grant, comply with.

oppkok
Bring to a boil.

oppkvikker
Stimulant, pick me up.

oppnå
Reach, attain, gain.

oppskåret
Cut, sliced.

oppspedd
Thinned or diluted.

oppstille
Place or arrange.

oppstøt
Burp or belch.

oppvarme
Warm up, heat.

oppvask
Washing of dishes and utensils.

oppvaskklut
Dishcloth.

oppvaskmaskin
Dishwasher.

orange
Orange colored.

ord
Word.

ordne
Put in order, organize.

organisk
Organically grown.

ørret
Trout.

This restored 19th century Oslo kitchen (kjokken) in the Oslo City Museum shows the great strides in food preparation and cooking which had taken place since the time of the farm kitchen at left. Oline and Tron Fladvad's kitchen when they lived in Christiania on Holbergsgate might have looked a lot like this.

øse
Dipper, ladle, or scoop. *"Øse opp suppen,"* ladle out the soup.

ost
Cheese. *"Kjøpe en halv ost,"* buy half a cheese.

ostes
Curdle.

ostehøvel
Norwegian cheese slicer which functions much like a plane.

ostemasse
Curds.

østers
Oysters.

oven
Above.

over
Over, across.

overflødighets horn
Cornucopia, or horn of plenty.

over
A little too much.

overøse
To pour upon or over something, to shower or heap.

overskårne
Sliced, cut off, cut through.

overskudd
Surplus or excess.

oversprøyte
Splash, splatter, squirt over.

overstå
Endure or get through something. *"Vel overstått,"* said after a holiday. Equivalent to "welcome back, see you got through (the holidays) in good shape.

ovn
Stove, oven, or furnace. *"Legge i ovnen,"* light the

fire.
"ovnen bør være temmelig varm"
The oven ought to be quite warm.

ovnskrok
Chimney corner.

ovnstekt
Roasted.

på
On or upon.

pærer
Pears.

pai
Pie.

pakke
Package, wrap, pack up.

pålegg
Sandwich fixings.

pålegg
Meat, cheese spread used in sandwiches.

palmesøndag
Palm Sunday.

panert
Breaded.

pannekake
Pancake.

pannekakerøre
Pancake batter.

pappeske
Carton or cardboard box.

pappkartong
Carton.

pappmasjé
Papier-maché.

paprika
Paprika.

paranøtt
Brazil nut.

parmesanost
Parmesan cheese.

påskedag

An Oslo grocer *points out asking prices* **(*prisforlangende*)** *for tasty vegetables, including honey dew melon (**honingmelon**), tomatoes (**tomater**), and red, green, and gold bellpepper (**rød**, **grønn**, and **gul paprika**).*

Easter Sunday.

påskeegg
Easter egg.

påskeferie
Easter vacation.

påsketur
Easter vacation trip.

passe
Suitable.

pasta
Italian pasta.

pastinakk
Parsnips.

Peanutter
Peanuts.

peis
Fireplace or hearth, usually placed in a corner.

peisestue
Room with a fireplace.

peishylle
Mantel.

peiskrakk

Fireplace stool.

pektin
Pectin.

pen
Nice, good-looking.

pensel
Brush.

pensles med
Paint or brush with. *"Pensle dem med egg,"* brush them with egg (white).

pepper
Pepper.

pepperbøsse
Pepper shaker.

pepperkake
Gingersnap or flat rolled spiced (gingerbread) cooky.

pepperkorn
Peppercorn.

pepperkvern
Pepper mill.

peppermynte
Peppermint candy or the peppermint plant.

peppermyntete
Peppermint tea.

pepperrot
Horse radish.

pepre
To season with pepper.

pepret
Peppery.

perlegryn
Pearl barley.

persille
Parsley. *"Pynt steken med persille,"* garnish the roast with parsley.

persilleblad
Parsley leaf. Also, a fragile, delicate person.

persillesmør
Parsley butter.

"pidskes meget godt og til slut haves i de pidskede Hvidder"

A variety of frankfurters (pølser) and meatballs (kjøttboller) in an Oslo meat market display case.

Beat very well and then beat in/ fold in the beaten egg whites.

pikkels
Pickles.

pille
Pluck or pick.

pils
Light lager beer.

pinne
Stick.

pinnekjøtt
Dried mutton steamed in a kettle on a layer of crossed sticks covering the bottom of the kettle. The meat is then placed on the sticks and a litle water is added to make the steam.. West Norwegian delicacy.

piple
Trickle.

pirke
Poke, pick, move ahead with action slowly.

pisk
Whisk.

piskes
Beat.

pisket krem
Whipped cream.

pjolter
Whiskey and soda, highball.

plagg
Piece of clothing.

plante
Seedling or plant.

plantefett
Vegetable oil or fat.

plantesaft
Sap or juice from plants.

plass
Location, place, position.

plass folk
Cotters.

pleieforeldre
Foster parents.

pliktarbeid
A duty, work required by others as a responsibility of occupancy or ownership.

pliktig
Duty bound.

plog
Plow.

plogfår
Furrow.

plomme
Yolk.

plommer
Plums.

plukke
Pick, pluck, gather.

plukkfisk
Fish in a cream sauce.

plum pudding
Plum pudding.

polenta
Cornmeal mush (Italian dish).

polenta grøt
Polenta pudding served with red fruit sauce. A Norwegian adaptation.

polenta gryn
Finely ground cornmeal used for puddings or porridge.

pølse
Sausage or wiener.

pomerans
Bitter tasting orange.

pommes frites
French fries.

pose
Sack, bag, pouch.

postei
Spread, paté.

Potet
Potato.

poteter kokte
Boiled potatoes.

poteter bakte
Baked potatoes.

poteter stekte
Fried potatoes.

potetgull
Potato chips.

The Leikvin Parish Museum *(above) in Sunndal includes an old farm (**gård**) which belonged to Lady Arbuthnott, a Scottish aristocrat who lived there during the latter part of the 19th century. The district lies between the mountain ranges of Snøhetta and Trollheimen with peaks reaching nearly 6,000 feet. The museum contains artifacts from Sunndal and from the first period when English sports fishermen spent their holidays in the Sunndal valley.*

An ancient chest *(left) holds a variety of embroidered (**broderi**) clothing, including items belonging to the national costume (**bunad**) and a fancy apron (**pynteforkle**).*

potetkake
Potato cake, includes grated, raw potatoes in the dough.

potetkjeller
Potato cellar.

potetlumpe
Thick, round pancake of flour and potatoes.

potetmel
Potato flour.

potetmos
Mash potatoes.

potetsalat
Potato salad.

potetskreller
Potato peeler.

potetstappe
Mashed potatoes.

prektig
Beautiful, fine, excellent.

presse
Press, as in to extract, juicer.

prikk
Point or dot.

prim
Soft cheese spread made from whey.

primost
Whey cheese.

pris
Price. *"Til billig pris,"* inexpensive, at a low price.

prisforlangende
Asking price.

prisklasse
Price bracket.

prisliste
Price list.

privatbolig
Private residence.

propp
Cork, stopper, plug. *"Proppe kaker i et barn,"* stuff a child with cookies.

proppfull
Full to the brim.

proppmett
Stuffed with food.

prøve
Try out, test.

prydsøm
Embroidery. Also **broderi**.

pultost
Sharp, soft cheese of soured, skimmed milk used as a spread.

pulver
Powder.

pulverisere
Smash, pulverize.

pulverkaffe
Instant coffee.

punsjebolle
Punch bowl.

pur
Unadulterated, pure, or clean.

purpur
Purple color.

purre
Leek.

purre løk
Leek.

puss
Best outfit, clothes. *"I sin beste puss,"* in one's best clothes.

pusse
Shine or polish.

putre
Simmer or bubble.

putte
Place.

pynte
Decorate, trim, dress up, improve the appearance of. *"Pynte seg,"* dress up.

pynteforkle
Fancy apron.

rå
Raw, e.g. fruits, vegetables, meat, sugar.

rabarbra
Rhubarb.

rabarbra grøt
Rhubarb pudding.

rad
Row, e.g. of flowers.

raffinade
Cube or lump sugar.

rake
Rake or shave.

råkost
Uncooked vegetables.

ramme
Frame or border.

ramsalte
Heavily salted.

rand
Rim or edge.

rangere
Arrange.

rapphøne
Partridge.

raspe
Grate or rasp.

raspeball
Potato dumplings.

råstekt
Underdone food or rare meat.

råsukker
Unrefined sugar.

reddik
Radish.

redskap
Tool, equipment, or appliance.

regnbueørret
Rainbow trout.

reiseskildring
Travelogue, book of travels.

reker
Shrimp.

rekesaus
Shrimp sauce.

rekesmørbrød
Open-faced shrimp sandwich.

rekke
Row of something, e.g. people or to hand something to someone.

remse
Strip, e.g. of cloth, paper, land, dough.

rene
Clean.

renne
A small trench or channel, or liquids running down or through a groove or channel.

rensdyrstek
Roast leg of reindeer.

rense
Clean.

renslighet
Cleanliness.

Various types of antique kitchen equipment on display at the Leikvin Parish Museum in Sunndal.

renvaske
To wash clean.
reol
Book shelves, bookcase.
rest
Remainder, rest, leftovers.
restemiddag
Leftovers for dinner.
rette
Straighten, right, correct.
revet skall av sitron
Grated lemon rind. See **Sitron.**
ribbe
Ribs. Also, to pluck a bird.
riktig
Proper, correct.
ringe
To chime or ring.
ringle
To jingle something, e.g. coins, bells.
rinsk vin
Rhine wine.
rips
White or red currants.
ripsbusk
Currant bush.
ris
Rice.

ris i karri
Rice in curry.
risengrynsgrøt
Rice porridge.
rismel
Rice flour.
riste
Toast, broil, grill, or roast.
ristet
Toasted.
ristet brød (uten smør)
Toast without butter.
ristet brød (og fruktgele)
Toast and jelly.
rive
Grate, shred, grind.
rivjern
Grater.
rød pepper
Red pepper.
rødaktig
Reddish.
rødbete
Red beet.
rødbeter
Red beets, beet root.
røde
Red.

rødgrøt
Fruit pudding.
rødkål
Red cabbage.
rødspette
Flounder.
rødvin
Red wine.
roe
Sugar beet or turnip.
roesukker
Beet sugar.
rogn
Fish roe.
rognebær
Rowanberry.
rognkall
Lumpfish.
røket flesk
Smoke-cured bacon.
røkelaks
Smoked salmon..
røkepølse
Smoked sausage.
røkesild
Kipper. Lit. smoked herring.
røket fisk
Smoked fish.

røkeskinke
Smoke-cured ham.

røket
Smoked.

rom
Place, room, space.

rompudding
Rum pudding.

rompunsj
Rum punch.

rømme
Sour cream.

rømmegrøt
Sour cream porridge, a Norwegian delicacy still offered at **frokost** in most hotels.

rømmekolle
Sour cream sprinkled with sugar and crumbs.

rommmelig
Spacious or roomy.

rør gjæren ut I litt av melken
Stir (to dissolve) the yeast in a little milk.

rør godt sammen
Mix until well blended.

rør i
Add while stirring.

rør sammen over varmen
Mix together while heating.

rør sammen eggene, smøret og sukkeret til det blir en jevn deig
Cream the eggs, butter and sugar to form a smooth batter.

røre
Move, stir, mix, agitate. Batter. *"Rør mel ut i vann,"* mix the flour with the water.

"røres til den bliver kold"
Stir until cold.

"røres godt ind med 8 Aggeblommer"
Mix well with 8 egg yolks.

"røres til det er koldt"
Stir until cooled.

"røres til det koger"
Stir until it starts to boil.

rørsukker
Cane sugar.

rosenkål
Brussels sprouts.

rosettbakkels
Rosette cookies.

rosiner
Raisins.

røske
Shake, tug, or rip, e.g. pick berries off bushes.

rostbiff
Roast beef.

rotfrukt
Edible root crops.

rotstappe
Mashed rutabaga.

røykstue
Historical Norwegian dwelling, usually of logs, having an open fireplace in the center of the room, with a smoke hole directly above.

rugbrød
Rye bread.

rulade
Meat or fish rolled in a dough or a cabbage leaf.

rullekake
Rolled cake, jelly roll.

rullepølse
Collared beef or lamb, pressed, then sliced into cold cuts.

rundbiff
Rump steak.

Norwegian farm houses *were built to withstand extremes in weather and to offer protection from potential enemies. This* **gård** *was restored and moved to Maihaugen in Lillehammer.*

Norwegian farm families were usually large *with many children to help with the endless chores required to ensure self-sufficiency. In addition, several generations often lived together, with the elderly parents turning over operation of the farm to the eldest son and his wife. In return, the son looked after and provided for his parents until they died. With many mouths to feed several times a day, a big table* (**bord**) *complete with a* **langbenk** *and a large cupboard* (**skjenk**) *were required. The candelabra* (**lysestake**) *and drinking bowl* (**bolle**) *provided light and refreshment respectively.*

rundskål
Toast drunk by everyone in attendance.

rundstykker
Hard rolls.

ruskomsnusk
Hodgepodge, dish of leftovers.

rygg
Back of something, a saddle of meat.

ryke
Smoke, steam. *"Ovnen ryker,"* the oven is smoking.

rype
Ptarmigan.

"saa rores lidt Flødekrem i tilsist"
Finally, add a little whipping cream or heavy cream.

saft
Juice.

saft og vann
Fruit punch, mixture of water and berry juice.

safte
Make juice from.

saftig
Succulent, juicy, lush.

saftig grønn
Lush and green.

saftpresse
Juice extractor.

saftsuppe
Soup made from fruit juices, prunes, raisins, and sago.

"så kommer røren deri og steg i ovnen eller koges som anden pudding i 1 1/2 Time, eller til den er stiv"
Add the batter, bake in the oven or boil as pudding for 1

1/2 hours or until stiff.

salat
Lettuce or salad. *"Hvordan er salaten?"* How is the salad?

salatbestikk
Salad set, e.g. fork and spoon.

salat og tomater
Lettuce and tomatoes.

salathode
Head of lettuce.

sallami pølse
Salami.

salongbord
Coffee table.

salt fisk
Salted fish.

salt lake
Brine.

saltmat
Salt preserved or treated foods.

salt sild
Pickled herring.

saltsprengt
Lightly salted.

saltbøsse
Salt cellar, salt shaker.

saltet/lagret/speket
Cured.

saltkar
Salt box.

sammalt hvetemel
Wholewheat flour.

samme
Same.

sammen
Together.

sammenarbeide
Combine into the whole, unify, mix together.

sammenblanding
Blending, mixing, mingling, blended together.

sammensatt
Composed or made up of.

sandkake
Pound cake, or more often, a cookie made of flour, butter, and almonds, baked in small metal forms.

sardiner
Sardines.

saus
Sauce, gravy.

sauseskje
Gravy spoon.

sausenebb
Gravy boat.

scone
Scone.

se
See.

sei
Pollack.

seidel
Mug, beer stein.

seig
Tough, chewy.

selleri
Celery.

selters
Club soda, seltzer water.

semulegryn
Semolina flour, often used to make pudding.

seng
Bed. *"Frokost på sengen,"* breakfast in bed.

sennep
Mustard.

sennepsfrø
Mustard seed.

serviett
Napkin.

sette
Put, place, set.

settebord
Nested tables.

side
Side (of something). *"På denne siden av jul,"* just before Christmas.

sikori
Chicory.

sikt sammen
Sift together.

sikte
Sift.

siktemel
Sifted flour.

sild
Herring.

sildegryn
Thick soup made from barley, vegetables, and pieces of herring.

sile
Pour or strain.

simpel
Plain or coarse.

sinn
Mind.

sirupaktig
Syrupy.

sirupskake
Cookie made from syrup.

sirupssnippers
Treacle gingersnaps. Thin, diamond-shapped cookies made with syrup. *"Snipp"* means a corner, or end (e.g. of a handkerchief or a collar on a man's shirt).

sitron
Lemon. *"Saften av en sitron,"* juice of a lemon.

sitronfromasj
Lemon mousse.

sitronkrem
Lemon cream.

sitronpresse
Lemon press.

sitronsaft
Lemon juice.

sitronskall
Lemon rind or peel.

sitronskive
Lemon slice.

sjallottløk
Shallot.

sjokolade
Chocolate.

sjokoladefromasj
Chocolate mousse.

sjokoladekake
Chocolate cake.

sjokoladekonfekt
Chocolate candy.

sjokoladeselskap
Children's party at which cake and hot chocolate are featured attractions on the menu.

sjø ørret
Sea trout.

sjy
Juice, meat juice served in place of a gravy.

skål
Saucer. Also, "cheers."

skålde
Scald.

skåldvarm
Scalding hot.

skalk
Heel of a loaf of bread or cheese.

skalldyr
Shellfish.

Skape
Make, form, create.

skap
Cupboard.

"skårne Mandler"
Sliced or slivered almonds.

skilpaddesuppe
Turtle soup.

skinke
Ham.

skinke og egg
Ham and eggs.

skinn
Leather, hide, skin.

skjære
Cut, slice, trim.

skje
Spoon.

skjemat
Any food eaten with a spoon.

skjønn
Beautiful.

skjorte
Shirt.

skogsbær
Heathberry.

skorpe
Crust.

skrape
Scrape.

skrell
Peelings.

skrelle
To pare or peel.

skum
Foam.

skummet melk
Skimmed milk.

skyldskap
Family relationship. Also, **slektskap**.

slåes godt
Beat well.

slå
To beat.

slaktekveg
Beef cattle.

slakterbutikk
Butcher shop.

slakterkniv
Cleaver.

slangeagurk
Cucumber.

slekt
Family, kin.

slektskap
Family relationship.

slekts stolthet
Family pride

slektsgård
Ancestral home (farm) or estate. Also **gård.**

slektsnavn
Family name.

slipe
Sharpen, grind, hone.

små
Small, little, inconsequential.

smak
Taste. "Smake til maten," season food to taste.

småkaker
Cookies, pastries, small cakes.

smake av
To have the flavor of.

smakebit
Small taste, sample.

smakfull
Tasteful.

smelt og rør
Melt and mix.

smelte
Melt or liquefy. *"Smelt margarinen,"* melt the margarine.

smeltepunkt
Melting point.

smør
Butter.

smørbrød
Open-faced sandwich. Lit. buttered bread.

smørkopp
Butter dish.

smørform
Butter form.

smørgåsbord
Table set with cold foods.

smørgrøt
Porridge made of milk, flour, and butter.

smørklump
Butter pat.

smørkniv
Butter knife.

smørkrem
Filling made of eggs, butter, and powdered sugar.

smørøye
The melted lump of butter in the middle of a bowl of porridge.

smørpapir
Waxed (grease proof) paper.

smule
Crumb.

smult
Lard.

smultring
Doughnut.

snart
Soon, quickly, or nearly.

snask
Sweets or goodies.

snaske
Chew loudly, noisily.

snerk
Thick coating or crusts, skin on liquids.

snerke
Become covered with a thin coating.

snill
Nice or kind.

snipp
Corner or end, a diamond-shaped cookie, e.g. *sirupsnipper*.

snitt
Cut.

snitte
Cut or slice.

snittebønner
String beans.

snitter
Small, open-faced sandwich.

snøbær
Waxberry.

snøre
Tie or lace.

snurre
Whirl or rotate.

sodavann
Club soda, mineral water.

sodd
Soup (cabbage or grain with meat), broth, or bree (stock remaining from the boiling of meat or fish).

søl
A mess.

solbær
Black currant.

soll
Flatbread crumbled into milk.

soltørke
To dry in the sun.

sølvbrudepar
Couple celebrating their silver anniversary.

sølvbryllup
Silver anniversary.

som
As, like, or which.

"som opløses i en pagel Vand tilsist de pidskede hvidder"
Dissolve in a "pagel" of water, finally add the beaten egg whites.

søndag
Sunday.

sønnedatter
Son's daughter, grandaughter.

sønnesønn
Son's son, grandson.

sønnesønns sønn
Son's son's son, great-grand-son.

sope
Sweep.

sopelime
Broom.

sopp
Mushroom.

sort
Sort or kind. *"En ny sort epler,"* a new kind or variety of apples.

søsken
Brothers and sisters.

søskenbarn
First cousin.

søster
Sister.

søsterdatter
Sister's daughter, niece.

søsterlig
Sisterly.

søstersønn
Sister's son, nephew.

søt
Sweet.

søt mais
Sweet corn.

søt mandel
Sweet almond.

søt melk
Fresh milk.

søt ost
An unspiced cheese made from sweet cow's milk.

søte
Sweeten.

søt kirsebær
Sweet cherry.

søtningsmiddel
Sweetening.

søtsuppe
A fruit soup made with prunes, raisins, etc.

sove
Sleep.

soverom
Bedroom.

soyabønne
Soybean.

soyamjøl
Soy meal.

spann
Pail.

spare
Save.

sparsom
Thin, sparse, scant, or frugal.

sparsomlighet
Thrift or economy.

spe
Water down, dilute, thin.

speilegg
Fried eggs.

speke
Cure.

spekeflesk
Cured bacon.

spekekjøtt
Cured, dried meat.

spekemat
Cured meat.

spekesild
Salted herring.

spekeskinke
Cured ham.

spekk
Pork fat.

spidd
Spit. *"Steke på spidd,"* roast on a spit.

spilkum
Small bowl.

spinat
Spinach.

spise
To eat.

spise frokost
Have breakfast.

spise middag
Dine.

spisebestikk
Flatware.

spisebord
Dining table.

spiseeple
Eating apple.

spisekart
Menu, bill of fare.

spisekrok
Dining alcove or nook.

spiselig
Edible.

spiselig musling
Clam.

spiseskje
Tablespoon.

spisestue
Dining room.

spisetid
Mealtime.

spiskammer
Pantry or larder.

spørre
Inquire or ask.

sprekkefri
Smooth, free of cracks.

sprengt, hermetisk kjøtt
Corned beef.

sprengt okseekjøtt
Corned beef.

sprø
Crisp.

stå
Stand, located.

Stab
Staff.

The Apotek at the Norwegian Folk Museum *stands on the corner of a fully restored city block of 19th century Oslo homes and stores, the* **gamlebyen** *or old city. Inside, the shelves look much as they would have to a shopper looking for chocolate (***sjokolade***), baking powder (***bakepulver***), butter (***smør***), cookies (***kjeks***), cheese (***ost***), and sugar (***sukker***). The folk museum is the largest national museum of cultural history in Norway.*

stabbur
Storehouse on pillars.

stampe
Mash, stamp, pestle.

stappe
Dish of mashed vegetables, e.g. potatoes.

stav
Stick.

"steges langsomt og lyse"
Bake or fry slowly until light.

steke
Roast or bake. *"Steke i ovn."*

stekefett
Cooking fat.

stekeovn
Oven.

stekende varmt
Scorching hot.

stekepanne
Frying pan.

stekeplate
Baking sheet.

stekespidd
Skewer or spit.

"stekes i"
Bake in.

stekt
Fried.

stekte poteter
Fried potatoes.

stell
Work, chores, management.

stelle til
Fix meals.

sten
Stone or pit.

stentøy
Crockery.

sterkt krydret
Heavily spiced.

stikkelsbær
Gooseberry.

stikk
Prick, stick, stab, pierce.

stil
Style, manner.

stille
Set, place, put. Also, quiet.

stivne
Harden, set, stiffen.

stivt
Steep, or stiff. "Stive priser," steep prices.

"stivslagne hvidder"
Stiffly beaten egg whites.

stokkand
Mallard.

stol
Chair.

stoppe
Stop, come to a halt, standstill.

stor
Large, big, great (in quantity). *"En stor middag,"* a dinner party or banquet.

storeter
Glutton.

størkne
Harden, set, congeal.

stor skje
Large spoon.

støv
Pollen, dust.

støyt
Thrust, jab.

stråle
Squirt.

streng
Cord or wire.

strie
Buckram burlap.

strø
Scatter, sprinkle, spread.

stryke
Stroke, brush, pat, smooth, or iron.

strykebord
Ironing table.

strykebrett
Ironing board.

stuemenneske
Homebody.

stuprød
Blood red.

stykke
Piece or bit.

stykker
Pieces of.

sukker
Sugar.

sukkerbit
Lump of sugar.

sukkerbrød
Sponge cake.

sukkerholdig
Sugary.

sukkerkavring
Zwieback, sweet rusk.

sukkerklype
Sugar tongs.

sukkerkulør
Caramel, burnt sugar for taste and coloring.

sukkernepe
Rutabaga, Swedish turnip.

sukkerroe
Sugar beet.

sukkerrør
Sugar cane.

sukkerskål
Sugar bowl.

sukkertopp
Old fashioned cone-shaped sugar loaf.

sukre
Sweeten. *"Sukre ned,"* preserves.

sunn
Healthy, sound, fit.

supe
Suck in, drink in.

suppe
Soup.

suppeøse
Soup ladle.

suppetallerken
Soup plate.

sur
Sour, acid, acidic.

sureple
Crab apple.

surmjølk
Sour milk.

surbrød
Sourdough bread.

surdeig
Sourdough.

surkål
Cabbage cooked with sugar, caraway, vinegar.

surmelk
Buttermilk.

surne
Turn sour.

surost
Sour milk cheese.

surt
Sour.

sval
Cool.

svalgang
Verandah.

svart
Black.

svartelars
Coffee pot.

sveitserost
Swiss cheese.

svelge
Swallow.

svi
Burn, scortch.

svigerdatter
Daughter-in-law.

svigerfar
Father-in-law.

svigerinne
Sister-in-law.

svigermor
Mother-in-law.

svigersønn
Son-in-law.

svinekjøtt
Pork.

svinestek
Pork roast.

svinestek med surkål
Roast pork with sour cabbage.

sviskegrøt
Prune pudding.

svisker
Prunes.

sviskesuppe
Fruit soup with prunes.

svoger
Brother-in-law.

sylte
To can, pickle, or preserve.
    Spiced, pressed pork roll.

syltetøy
Jelly or jam.

syltetøyskål
Jam dish.

synke
Be absorbed, sink into, digest.

syttendemai tog
Independence Day Parade, May
    17th.

ta
Take or grab.

ta med
Take along, bring.

tallerken
Plate, e.g. dinner, lunch, or
    soup.

tallerkenhylle
Dish or plate shelf.

tallerkenrekke
Plate rack.

tante
Aunt or great aunt, sometimes
    a close friend of the family.

te
Tea.

te med sitron
Tea with lemon.

tebord
Tea table, or tea wagon.

tebrød
Tea bread, a dry cake made in
    thin loaves about one-inch
    thick, then cut into diagonal
    slices.

teger kurv
Braided basket made of roots or
    twigs.

tekjøkken
Kitchenette.

tekopp
Teacup.

teppe
Blanket, bed spread, or quilt.

terpe
Plug or cram.

terte
Torte.

tesil
Tea strainer.

teskje
Norwegian teaspoon (smaller
    than American teaspoon).

tevarmer
Tea cosy.

tevann
Tea water.

tid
Time, period.

tidsbesparende
Time saving.

til
Until.

tilbake
Back or left over.

tilbud
Offer or bid.

tilbudspris
Bargain price.

tilsette
Add to.

tilsett vekselvis med fettet
Mix alternately with the fat.

***"til sist de stivslagne
    hvidder"***
Finally, the beaten egg whites.

***"til sist vispes i Flødekrem
    toppen prydes med
    sammenblandet
    Flødekrem, Sukker,
    Sherry, Karamelpulver"***
Finally, add the heavy cream,
    garnish the top with a mix-
    ture of heavy cream, sugar,
    sherry, and caramel powder.

tilsløre
Conceal, veil, cover up.

tilsmurt
Smeared

tipp
Great-great.

tippoldemor
Great-great-grandmother.

tomat
Tomato.

tomatpuré
Tomato puré.

tomatsaft
Tomato juice.

tomatsuppe
Tomato soup.

tømme
Pour, empty, or drain.

tømme kaldt vann på
Pour cold water on...

tomte
Gnome.

tønne
Cask or barrel.

topp sukker
Cone of refined sugar. Pieces

Waffles are a mainstay for Norwegian desserts *and are served with a variety of berry preserves and cream. These waffle irons on sale in Kristiansund are electrically heated. Norwegians take their heirloom waffle irons to their summer cabins (**hytta**) for use on holidays.*

were broken off as needed.

topp
Top.

torg
Market, square.

torghandel
Marketing.

tørr
Dry.

tørrmelk
Dried milk.

torsk
Codfish.

tørst
Thirsty.

tøvær
Thaw.

tøye
Extend, stretch, pull.

tradisjon
Tradition.

trakte
Filter, strain, pour through a

funnel.

tranebær
Cranberry.

tredele
Separate or divide into three parts.

tredje
Third.

tredobbelt
Triple.

trekke ut
Extract.

tremenning
Second cousin.

trenge
Need.

trille
Roll.

trollbær
Baneberry.

trykk-koker
Pressure cooker.

tung
Heavy.

tunge
Tongue.

tungeflyndre
Sole.

tusen
Thousand. *"Tusen takk,"* a thousand thanks, thank you very much.

tuske
Barter.

tygge
Chew, grind away.

tykk biff
Porterhouse steak.

tynn
Thin.

tyttebær
Cowberry (red whortleberry).

u-formet
U-shaped.

"udvasket Smør"
Sweet butter or unsalted butter.

ufordøyelig
Indigestible.

ufyselig
Uninviting, unappetizing.

ul
Spoiled or rancid.

ulme
Smoulder.

umoden
Green, unripe.

urtebrygg
Herb beer.

ute
Out or outside.

utfall
Result, outcome.

utenpå
On the outside of.

utgang
Exit, egress, departure.

utrørt gjær
Dissolved yeast.

vær
Weather.

vaffelhjerte
Heart-shaped waffle.

vafler
Waffles, served with butter and
   jam.

vaktel
Quail.

valnøtter
Walnuts.

valse
Roll or press.

valsemølle
Flour mill using rollers.

vanilje
Vanilla.

vaniljekrem
Vanilla custard.

vaniljepudding
Custard.

vaniljesause
Custard sauce.

vaniljesukker
Sugar to which has been added
   powdered vanilla bean.

våning
Home, dwelling.

vanlig matlag(n)ing
Plain cooking.

vann
Water.

vannet er ikke drikkbart
The water is not fit to drink.

vannkjele
Tea kettle.

vannmelon
Watermelon.

vannmølle
Water mill.

vår
Spring time, ours.

varig
Lasting, durable.

varm
Warm.

varme
To heat.

varm forsiktig
Warm/heat carefully.

varme pølser
Hot dogs or frankfurters.

varsom
Careful.

varsomhet
Caution, cautious.

vaske
Wash.

våt
Damp, moist, or wet.

ved
Near, at, or by. Also, wood.

vedovn
Wood stove.

vegetarkost
Vegetarian food.

vel
Healthy, well.

velsmakende
Tasty, flavorful.

velernært
Well fed or well nourished.

vennlig
Kind, friendly.

vennskap
Kinship or family ties.

verdig
Deserving, worthy, or dignified.

verk
Work, act, or product.

veske
Fluid, liquid or pocketbook.

veslegutt
Little boy.

veslejente
Little girl.

vielsesring
Wedding ring.

vift
Puff, whiff, breath.

vike
Give way, yield.

viktig
Important.

vil ha
Want.

villeple
Crab apple.

vin
Wine.

vinterkarse
Curled cress.

virvle
Swirl, spin.

vise
Exhibit, show, display.

visp
Whisk.

visp stivt
beat stiff.

vispe
Whip or beat (food).

"vispes sammen"
Beat or whip until blended.

"vispes til en dos"
Beaten to the consistency of
   eggedosis.

voksbønne
Wax bean.

vokse
Grow, increase.

vond
Hard, difficult.

vørter
Brewer's wort, a fermenting
   addition of malt.

vørterkake
Sweet, round bread made from
   brewer's wort.

vørterøl
Non-alcoholic beer.

Delicious **(smakfull)** *walnut cake ready to be enjoyed* **med kaffe** *in Steen og Strom's fifth floor cafeteria in Oslo.*

vrang
Reversed, inside out.

wienerbrød
"Vienna bread," or Danish
   pastry.

wienerschnitzel
Veal filet steak.

yndling
Favorite, darling.

ytre
Outer. Also, to express, as to
   express one's opinion.

ytterdør
Front door, main entrance.

Additional Terms

Create your own list of useful Norwegian words and phrases. Don't forget to share it with the author for inclusion in future editions of the Glossary.

Core Values

The following briefly outlines generally accepted definitions for core values.

Integrity Area

Moral courage, conforming to a standard of right behavior honor, dignity, responsibility and accountability.

Doing what has to be done to the point where conflict or even pain may result, still willing to give the effort needed to accomplish whatever it is that must be done.

Making decisions, then living with and implementing them.

Honor, respect, reputation, one whose worth brings respect or fame, a keen sense of ethical conduct, integrity.

Doing what's right, no matter what the consequences.

Dignity, quality or state of being worthy and esteemed, formal reserve of language or conduct.

Pride in action; taking pride in doing one's best.

Fidelity, quality or state of being faithful, accuracy in details, exactness, strict and continuing faithfulness to an obligation, trust or duty.

Truthfulness, sincerity in action, character and utterance, real things, events and facts, in accord with fact or reality;

Accountability, answerable for actions, responsible, subject to retribution for unfulfilled trust or violated obligations;

Accepting the responsibilities of ones job; being accountable for the people and resources one is given to manage.

Being held accountable for your decisions and for the decisions of the people for which one is responsible.

Responsible, able to answer for one's conduct and obligations, trustworthy, able to choose for oneself between right and wrong, holding a specific office, duty or trust;

Trustworthiness, worthy of confidence, dependable, assured reliability in the character, ability, strength and truth of someone or something, charge or duty imposed in faith or confidence or as a condition of some relationship, something committed or entrusted to one to be used or cared for in the interest of another.

Dedication area

Dedication, devoted (set apart for sacred uses with solemn rites), set apart for a specific use, committed to as a goal or a way of life.

Commitment, something pledged, state of being obligated or emotionally impelled, entrusted, delivering into another's charge or the special sense of transferring to a superior power or to a special place of custody.

Doing what is necessary to achieve quality goals.

Physical courage, facing danger, but achieving the objectives--getting the job done.

Not blind courage, but courage to do something right when there is personal risk involved.

Discipline, teaching, learning, training that corrects, molds, or perfect the mental faculties or moral character, orderly prescribed conduct or patterns of behavior, self-control, rules or system of rules governing conduct or activity.

Hard work, doing one's job to the best of one's ability, dedicated stamina to complete tasks moving one toward worthy goals and objectives.

Professionalism, characterized by or conforming to the technical or ethical standards of a profession, the conduct, aims, or qualities that characterize or mark a professional or a professional person.

Perseverance, to take a stand, to go on resolutely or stubbornly in spite of opposition, importunity or warning, existing for a long or longer than usual time or continuously, degraded only slowly by the environment, remaining infective for a relatively long time in a vector after an initial period of incubation, continuing to exist despite interference or treatment.

Diligence, persevering application, characterized by steady, earnest, and energetic application and effort, sticktoitiveness.

Constancy, continuing firmness of emotional attachment without necessarily implying strict obedience to promises or vows.

Purpose, something established as an object or end to be attained. intention, resolution, determination, an aim, full of determination.

Devotion, stresses zeal and service amounting to self-dedication.

Loyalty area

Loyalty, unswerving in allegiance, a faithfulness that is steadfast in the face of any temptation to renounce, desert, or betray, firm resistance to any temptation to desert or betray;

Duty, obligatory tasks, conduct, service or functions that arise from one's position in life or in a group, assigned services, moral or legal obligations, services required.

Feeling the obligation to perform your own job at the best level you can.

Trust, assured reliance on the character, ability, strength or truth of someone or something, one in which confidence is placed, reliance, charge or duty imposed in faith or confidence or as a condition of some relationship.

Respect, to look back, worthy of high regard, esteem.

Confidence that leaders are going to make the right decisions, and that those carrying out actions are going to do so correctly.

Obedience, compliance with the demands or requests of one in authority, will to obey. Adherence to traditions, values and processes.

Faithfulness, unswerving adherence to a person or thing or to the oath or promise by which a tie was contracted.

Tradition area

Tradition, act of handing over, inherited, established, or customary pattern of thought, action or behavior, handing down of information, beliefs, and customs by word of mouth, or by example from one generation to another without written instruction, cultural continuity in social attitudes and institutions.

Appearance, outward aspects, look, in the public view.

Ceremony, formal act or series of acts prescribed by ritual, protocol, or convention, routine action performed with elaborate pomp, observance of established code.

Comraderie, spirit of friendly good fellowship.

Equality, of the same measure, quantity, amount or number as another, like in quality, nature or status, like for each member of a group, class, or society, regarding or affecting all objects in the same way, impartial, free from extremes, not showing variation in appearance, structure or proportion.

Patriotism

Patriotism, love for and devotion to one's country, and contributing to its overall good.

Preparedness, state of adequate preparation in readiness to perform one's mission or job.

Freedom, absence of necessity, coercion, or constraint in choice or action, exempt or released from something onerous, quality of being frank, open, or outspoken, unrestricted use, not unduly hampered or frustrated.

Concerns for People

Concern for people, to sift together, to relate to, involve, engage, occupy, marked interest or regard usually through personal tie or relationship, blended interest, interestedly engaged with and for others.

Caring for others is part of the organization's tradition of taking care of its own, of our sensitivity to the quality of life of our staff and volunteers and their families.

If you are not concerned for those people for whom you are responsible, then you cannot consider yourself an effective leader.

Fairness, marked by impartiality and honesty, free from self-interest, prejudice or favoritism, consonant with merit or importance, free from favor toward either or any side. An elimination of one's own feelings, prejudices and desires so as to achieve a proper balance of conflicting interests.

Justice, leading and managing through the impartial adjustment of conflicting claims or assigning merited rewards or punishments.

Impartiality, unbiased, treating or affecting all equally.

Compassion, sympathetic, conscious of others' distress together with a desire to alleviate it.

Fairness applies honesty, honor, faithfulness, and diligence to all. Everybody.

Excerpted from ***Nonprofit Management Handbook***, 1995 Supplement, Tracy D. Connors (Ed.), John Wiley & Son, New York.

Conversion Table

American and British Weight Measurements

1 ounce (oz)	28 grams
1/2 pound (lb)	225 grams
1 pound (lb)	450 grams
2 sticks butter	225 grams

1 package dry yeast
or
1 cake compressed fresh yeast = 2/3 ounce = 20 grams

American Volume Measurements

1 teaspoon	5 milliliters (ml)		
1 Tablespoon	15 ml		
1 fluid ounce	30 ml		
1/4 cup	1/2 dl		
1/2 cup	1 dl		
2/3 cup	1 1/2 dl		
3/4 cup	2 dl		
1 cup	2.4 dl/284 ml	1/2 pint	8 fluid ounces
1 1/3 cup	3 - 3 1/2 dl		
1 1/2 cup	4 dl		
1 2/3 cup	4 dl		
2 cups	4.7 dl/568 ml	1 pint	16 fluid ounces
4 cups	1 liter (l)	1 quart	32 fluid ounces
5 - 6 cups	1 1/4 - 1 1/2 liters		
1 gallon	3.8 liters		

Oven temperature	Fahrenheit	Celsius
Very slow	250-275	125-135
Slow	300-325	150-175
Moderate	350-375	175-200
Hot	400-425	200-225
Very hot	450-475	225-250
Extremely hot	500-525	250-275

Temperature conversion: when you know degrees Fahrenheit multiply by 5/9 (after subtracting 32) to find Celsius temperature.

Traditional Norwegian Measurements
and
Modern Equivalents

Gamle Norske Mål	English	Metric
Dry Measures		
1 **ort**		0.95 grams
(in money equals 1/4 Daler)		
1 **kvint**		5.0 grams
(a Danish measure)		
1 **lod**	1/32 pund (pound) or 1/2 oz.	15.6 grams
1 **mark**	8 oz.	0.25 kilograms
	approximately 1 (heaping) cup	

(Note: when "lod" was used in connection with "mark" it usually referred to the amount of silver in money.)

1 **pund** or 2 **merker**	1 lb + 1.7 oz	0.498 kilograms
	approximately 2 1/2 cups	
skje or **ske**	spoon	
stang	a stick	
1 **dusin**	12 of anything, a dozen	
1 **snæs**	20, a score	
teskje	"knifepoint" or teaspoon	
plade or **plate**	sheet	

Liquid Measures

*Note: The following liquid measures differed and changed over hundreds of years of use. In addition, they also differed depending on what was being measured, e.g. grain, butter, fish, salt, etc. "**Sætting**," for example, was used for grain and varied widely from locale to locale.*

1 **sætting (halvskjæppe)**	9 quarts or 2.3 gallons	8.7 liters
1 **fjerdingkar**	4 1/2 quarts	4.3 liters
1 **ottingkar**	2 1/3 quarts or 5 pints	2.2 liters
1 **kande**	2 quarts	1.93 liters
1 **pot** or **potte**	1 quart or 4 cups	0.96 liters
	32 fluid ounces	
1 **pægl** or **pagel**	7.7 oz or 1 cup	0.24 liters
	1/2 pint or 8 fluid ounces	

Note:
Ske is the old way of spelling **skje**, and **plade** is now spelled **plate**.

Bibliography

Anderson, Brian. 1981. "Pining for Norway." *Minneapolis-St. Paul* (November): p. 174.

Ayres, Carey. 1989. "The Pancake Boy: An Old Norwegian Folk Tale." *School Library Journal* (January): vol. 35, no. 5, p. 69.

Barwick, JoAnn. 1984. "Norwegian Country" *House Beautiful* (April): vol. 126, p. 73.

Bicha, Karel D. 1987. "Norwegian-American Studies" (book review). *The Journal of American History* (June): p. 186 (2).

Burgess, Anthony. 1985. "Historic Houses: Edvard Grieg's Troldhaugen." *Architectural Digest* (May): vol. 42, p. 248.

Christolon, Blair. 1993. "The Land and People of Norway" (book review). *School Library Journal* (May): vol. 39, no. 5, p. 134.

Culinary Arts Institute. 1970. *The Scandinavian Cookbook*. Chicago, IL.

Cunliffe, Tom. 1991. "Hand-to-Hand, Fjord-to-Fjord." *Sail* (January): vol. 22, no. 1, p. 70.

Dougherty, Margot. 1985. "Dreamboat." *Life* (Chicago)(April): vol. 8, p. 149.

Du Chaillu, Paul. 1882. *The Land of the Midnight Sun*.

Edwards, Linda. 1981. "Summer in Norway." *Cuisine* (July-August): v. 10, p. 28.

Feder, Barnaby J. 1984. "Fjord Country." *The New York Times Magazine* (March 18): v. 133 p. S1.

Forbes, Kathryn. 1943. *Mama's Bank Account*.

Frank, Beryl. 1977. *Scandinavian Cooking*. Barre, MA: Weathervane Books.

Glantz, Shelley. 1992. "Prairie Cabin: A Norwegian Pioneer Woman's Story." *School Library Journal* (April): vol. 38, no. 4, p. 79.

Grogan, David. 1990. "Rosenfole: Medieval Songs from Norway." *People* (March 5): vol. 33, no. 9, p. 22.

Grueninger, Walter F. 1988. "Grieg: Symphonic Dances: Norwegian Dances.: *Consumer's Research Magazine* (May): vol. 71, no. 5, p. 43.

Hale, Frederick. 1984. "Norway's Rendezvous with Modernity." *Current History* (April): vol. 83, p. 173.

Hardwick, Elizabeth. 1983. "Ibsen's Secrets." *The New York Review of Books* (June 30): vol. 30, p. 11.

Harnack, William. 1984. "Norwegian Literature." *The Humanist* (Sept-Oct): v. 44 p. 37.

Hatton, Ragnhild. 1991. "Remembrance of Norway." *History Today* (March): v. 41 p. 5.

Hazel, Julia. 1987. "Our Scandinavian Summer." *Cruising World* (December): vol. 13, no. 12, p. 58.

Hazelton, Nika. 1984. "Arctic Charms." *National Review* (September 21): v. 36 p. 58.

Henriksen, Vera. 1992. *Christmas in Norway.* Oslo: NORINFORM for the Ministry of Foreign Affairs.

Hills, Ann. 1990. "Digging in Norway." *History Today* (March): v. 41 p. 5.

Hofstadter, Dan. 1989. "Midsummer Magic in the Lands of the Midnight Sun." *The New York Times Magazine* (March): v. 138 p. S22.

Holland, Bernard. 1993. "Grieg, the Ideal Cultural Hero." *The New York Times* (January 9): vol. 142, p. 13 (N).

House Beautiful. 1984. "How to Uncover the Hidden Design Treasures of Norway." (April): v. 126 p. 60.

Jenkins, Buck. 1980. "Norway's Stave Churches." *The Saturday Evening Post* (Jan-Feb): v. 252 p. 110.

Jochens, Jenny M. 1987. "The Politics of Reproduction: Medieval Norwegian Kingship." *The American Historical Review* (April): v. 92 p. 327.

Kennan, George F. 1985. "By the Light of the Midnight Sun." *House & Garden* (April): v. 157 p. 178.

Lamb, Lynette. 1990. "Decorah and Spillville: Old World Iowa." *Minneapolis-St. Paul* (May): v. 18 p. 80(3).

Lindgren, Raymond. 1976. "Norway: 1940." *Library Journal* (October 1): vol. 116, no. 16, p. 122.

Luray, Martin. 1986. "Fjords and Flatlands: Scandinavia." *Sail* (March): vol. 17, p. 20.

Manildi, Donald. 1988. "Grieg: Norwegian Folksongs." *American Record Guide* (September-October): vol. 51, no. 5, p. 48.

Martell, Hazell. 1995. *Food & Feasts with the Vikings.* Morristown, NJ: New Discovery Books.

McNulty, Henry. 1983. "A Norwegian Sojourn." *Gourmet* (July): vol. 43, p. 22.

Morris, Jan. 1984. "Snug Little Bergen." *The New York Times Magazine* (March 18):vol. 133.

Munsen, Sylvia. 1982. *Notably Norwegian.* Iowa City, IA: Penfield Press.

Munsen, Sylvia. 1982. *Cooking the Norwegian Way.* Minneapolis: Lerner Publications.

Nelson, Murry. 1992. "Learning from and in Norwegian Schools." *The Education Digest* (March): vol. 57, no. 7, p. 25.

Orwoll, Mark and Martin Rapp. 1992. "Arctic Dreams, Exploring Norway's Coast." *Travel & Leisure* (July): vol. 22, no. 7, p. 104.

Pasternak, Mike. 1992. "Norway, Sailboard Cruising." *Sail* (May): vol. 23, no. 5, p. 60.

Petersen, Peter L. 1988. "Marcus Thrane: A Norwegian Radical in America." *The Journal of American History* (September): vol. 75, no. 2.

Peterson, Edward N. 1991. "Norway and the United States." *The American Historical Review* (June): vol. 96, no. 3.

Polvay, Marina. 1987. *"Oslo." Travel Holiday* (June): vol. 167, p. 68.

Printz, Mike. 1991. "In Their Own Words: Letters for Norwegian Immigrants." *School Library Journal* (August): vol. 37, no. 8, p. 211.

Read, E.C.K. 1994. "Northern Lights: a cruise along Norway's spectacular coastal express route." *The New York Times* (August 21): v. 143 p. 23(N).

Robinson, Bill. 1985. "Ranging the Skagerrak: A Delightful Cruising World." *Yachting* (March): vol. 157, p. 80.

Ryder, Jock. 1983. "Within the Arctic Circle." *Yachting* (March): vol. 153, p. 72.

Schultz, April. 1991. "The Pride of the Race had been touched." *The Journal of American History* (March): v. 77 p. 1265(31).

Sinkler, Rebecca Pepper. 1992. "A House by the Fjords." *The New York Times* (September 6): v. 141, p. XX19(N).

Sjogren, Eric. 1993. "What's Doing in Oslo." *The New York Times* (April 18): vol. 142, p. XX 10.

Sverdrup, Elise. 1968, 1970. *Norway's Delight.* Oslo, Norway: Tanum.

Touchet, Alexia. 1993. "A Norwegian Sojourn." *Gourmet* (June): vol. 53, no. 6, p. 80.

Touchet, Alexis. 1990. "The Norwegian Christmas Kaffebord." *Gourmet* (December): vol. 50, no. 12, p. 112.

Trestrail, Joanne. 1985. "Folklore, Fjords, and Fyrstekake." *Chicago* (October): vol. 34, p. 136.

Undset, Sigrid (1923). *Kristin Lavrinsdatter.* New York: Alfred A. Knopf.

U.S. Department of State. 1992. *Kingdom of Norway* (country profile). (November 16): vol. 3, no. 4.

Walker, Bill. 1987. "Oslo: A Taste of Things to Come." *Travel Holiday* (June): v. 165 p. 62.

Walljasper, Jay. 1981. "All Hail the Norse." *Minneapolis-St. Paul* (November): v. 9 p. 160.

Xan, Erna Oleson. 1990. *Time Honored Norwegian Recipes Adapted to the American Kitchen.* Iowa City, IA: Penfield Press.

Young, Carrie. 1983. "A Scandinavian Thanksgiving in North Dakota." *Gourmet* (November): vol. 43, p. 36.

Index

A

A Doll's House 9, 103
A.T. Stewart & Company 110
Absolutism 66
Ackerman, Sarah Cottrell 109, 124, 157, 156
Advent 32
Aftensmat 36
Akershus 82
Akershus Castle 75
Akershus Festning 47
Akker Bryge 130
Allodial privilege 72
Almond Cake with Cream Topping 194
Almond Krumkake 189
Almond Ring Cake 185
Almond Snaps 193
Almond Sticks 195
Almond Sugar Cake 193
Amalie 88
American Cake 160
Amerikansk kake 160
Amundsen, Roald 4, 6, 96, 98, 128, 131, 132, 136, 152, 156
Andalsnes 86
Andersen, Tore Ørsund 66
Anderson, E.L. 81, 82, 119
Anderson, Hans Christian 40
Apple Balls 198, 199
Apple Cake 167
Apple Custard 167
Aquataine, Eleanor of 113
Aquidneck Island 118
Arbuthnott, Lady Barbara 71
Arendal Cakes 160
Arnold, Governor Benedict 121
Audley Clarke 111, 112
Augusta, Maine 114
Aust-Agder 22
Avalanche 60

B

Bailey's Beach 117
Bakken, Marie Larsdatter 78, 245
Ball-Shaped Spice Cookies 34, 35
Barker, Harriet Cottrell 125, 157, 157
Barker, Ralph Randolph 152, 157, 157
Barker, Samuel 109
Bates' Sanitarium 142, 144
Bates, Dr. W. Lincoln 140, 142
Battle of the Market Square 79
Bayeux, France 235
Bellevue Avenue 105, 118, 120, 139, 141, 146, 156

Benjamin Reynolds 113
Bennett, James Gordon 99, 136
Bergen 47
Bergen Pepper Gingersnaps 38
Bergenske Pebernödder 38
Berlin Crowns 31
Berlin Wreaths 162
Berlinerkranser 28, 31, 161
Biscotti 225
Bishop's Cake 162
Bjerke, Oline 2, 10, 73, 126, 196, 245
Bjerke, Thore 245, 249
Bjørbekk 74
Bjørke 75
Bjørke farm 56
Bjørke, Lars 88
Bjørke, Oline 45, 54, 55, 83, 89, 98, 172
Bjørnhjell 8, 57, 59, 71
Bjørnhjellen 62
Björnson, Björnstjerne 4, 125, 129, 136
Black Death (bubonic plague) 47, 61
Bløtkake 163
Blucher 253
Bo Nytt 250
Bokmål 46
Bolt, Aslak 61
Bonde-novellen 129
Boston, Massachusetts 100
Bouvet Island 19
Brasenenga 93
Breakers, The 120
Brød 171
Brød med Eple 171
Brook, Rupert 148
Brooklyn Bru 53
Brooklyn, New York 241, 256
Broom cakes 188
Brown, Julia 148, 168
Brumunddal 76, 245
Brunsvik 93
Brunsvika, Kristiansund 70, 73, 91
Bryer, Stafford 112
Buckingham Palace 233
Bull, Ole 242
Bull, Solveig 242
Bumerke 57
Bunad 25, 73
Buskerud 22
Butler, Catherine Wallace 113
Butler, Lady Catherine 112, 115
Butter Cream 219
Butter Dots 39, 219
Butter Wreath Cookies 218
Bygdøy 21

C

Cahill, Margaret 114

Campbell, W.C. 151
Cardamom 157, 180
Cardamom Buns 217
Cardamom Krumkake 189
Cardamom Muffins 180
Carl Johan of Sweden 24, 51
Cashman, Will 114
Catherine Street 16, 104, 108
Charles IX 64
Charles X 66
Charles XI 66
Chocolate Balls 216
Christian Frederick, Prince 51, 72
Christian II 49
Christian III 49
Christian IV 49
Christian IV of Denmark 65
Christian, Prince Fredrik 24
Christian VI 67
Christiania
    2, 16, 54, 72, 74, 75, 82, 97, 101, 103, 110, 115,
    116, 119, 120, 128, 130, 152, 222
Christianity 46
Christmas Bread 30
Christmas Cake 177
Churchbook 79
Cincinnati School of Embalming 108
Citronkage 216
City Steam Laundry Company 110, 123, 137
Civic League of Newport 124
Clabbered Cream 165
Cliff Walk 117
Coconut Cookies 195
Coggeshall, David M. 112
Coggeshall, William A. 111
Collett, Camilla 74, 256
Collins, Patrick 114
Conanicut Island 101
Confirmation into the Lutheran Church 68
Connors, Faith Raymond 256
Connors, Tracy 152
Constitution Day 19, 24, 79
Constitution for Norway 72
Conversion Table 305
Cook, Frederick 134
Cookies from the Gudbrands Valley. 172
Copenhagen 75
Core Values 303
Core values 15
Cotter 77
Cotters 50, 51, 66
Cottrell and Bryer 112
Cottrell, Annie Louise 156, 157
Cottrell, Annie Southwick 120, 126, 157
Cottrell Block 99
Cottrell business 138, 141
Cottrell, C.M. & R.C. 109

Cottrell, Catherine Wallace 100, 108, 112, 114, 115, 119,
    138, 141, 142, 143, 156, 157
Cottrell, Cecile Middleton 98
Cottrell, Charles Middleton
    99, 108, 109, 114, 1, 6, 81, 98, 116, 117, 119, 127, 142, 143, 144
Cottrell, Edwin 125
Cottrell, Edwin Angell 156, 157, 158
Cottrell, Eleanor Oline 98, 136
Cottrell, estate of Michael 120
Cottrell, Harriet 114, 115
Cottrell, Harriet Barker 124, 156
Cottrell, Harriet Simes-Nowell 101
Cottrell, Honora Mountain 111
Cottrell, James 110, 111, 112, 116, 119, 144
Cottrell, James Wallace 114
Cottrell, Louise 109, 124, 125
Cottrell, Margaret 98, 121, 122, 123
Cottrell, Marie 1, 6, 98,
    100, 108, 117, 124, 127, 136, 142, 145, 147, 151, 156, 157, 222, 241,
    251
Cottrell, Michael 111, 112, 113, 114, 116, 139, 144
Cottrell, Robert
    99, 107, 108, 113, 114, 116, 125, 135, 141, 144, 147, 156
Cottrell, Samuel 141, 142, 148, 156, 148
Cottrell, Samuel Parker 102, 125, 130
Cottrell store 106, 107, 129
Council of the Realm 75
County Cork, Ireland 111
Cozzens, Charles 111
Cream Porridge 209
Cream Waffles 230
Crooker, Isaiah 111
Customs House 106

D

Daler 54
Danish Kingdom 20
Darien, Connecticut 137, 155
Debt marks 53
Debt øre 53
Denmark 51
Denmark abolished serfdom 77
Doll's House 79
Dombas 12, 13, 85
Dorr revolution 116
Dough Wreaths 173
Doughnuts 220
Dovrefjell 8, 12, 13, 56, 60, 86, 252
Dreyfus, Alfred 116
Driva River 6, 8, 53, 54, 56, 60, 61, 62, 65, 66, 86, 252
Driva River flooding 69
Drøbak Christmas House 177
Drøbak Sound 252

E

Easton, John 99, 136

Easton, Mrs. Gardner C. 154
Eastons Beach 137
Eastons Point 151
Egg Nog 166
Eggedosis 166
Eidsvoll 24, 51, 72, 74, 84
Eidsvoll Constitution 73
Electric Spark 142
Eplekake 167
European Community (EC) 21
European Economic Area (EEA) 21
European Free Trade Association 21
Evangelical Lutheran Church 19, 20

F

Fall River Line 118
Fall River, Massachusetts 114
Får i Kål (lamb and cabbage) 44
Farewell Street 110
Faroe Islands 45
Fattigman 28, 31
Faunce, William Herbert Perry 148
Feire jule 29
Finnmark 22
Fladvad 53, 62
Fladvad, Anna 88, 97, 159
Fladvad, Anna Johansen 89, 247
Fladvad, Bjørn Johansen 4
Fladvad, Endre 72
Fladvad family 32, 231
Fladvad, Fredrik 89, 247
Fladvad, Gunhild Charlotte 65, 124, 241
Fladvad, Lars Ole 93
Fladvad, Marie Theresa Cottrell 9, 14, 54, 55, 65, 73, 81, 89, 96, 97, 98, 115, 116, 117, 119, 132, 155, 200
Fladvad, Marius 11, 92
Fladvad, Ole 89, 91, 246
Fladvad, Oline 10, 11, 231
Fladvad, Olise 92, 119, 120, 126, 128
Fladvad, Otilie 93, 133
Fladvad, Theodor 53, 89, 247
Fladvad, Tron Olesen 3, 45, 54, 73, 87, 89, 98, 102, 123, 196, 245
Flat Bread 169
Flatbrød 169
Flatvad 5, 7, 36, 53, 57, 60, 61, 62, 65, 87
Flatvad, Grøa, Norway 55
Flatvad, Ingrid 73
Flatvad, Lars 10
Flatvad, Lars Olesen 94
Flatvad, Marit 11
Flatvad: Good Earth 67
Flatvaddalen 62
Fløtelapper 230
Fort Adams 110
Fram Museum 130

Franklin, James, Jr. 101
Franklin Street 129
Frederick III 50
Frederik VI 72
Freeholder 50
Freemasoners of Christiania 97
Fried Cookie—"Poor Man's Cake" 31
Frügtkage 167
Frugtkake 169
Furnes 13, 45, 55, 75, 245
Furnes Church 78, 245
Furunaever 77
Fylker 22, 46
Fyrstekake 170

G

Gade, Gerhard 81, 97, 100, 117, 119
Gamelost 12, 95
Gamle Norske Mål 306
Gård 96
Gaufrette iron 188
George III 69
German occupation 11, 93
German occupation government 241
German Slices 227
Ginger Cookies 35
Gingerbread 202
Gingerbread Cookies 34, 203
Gjøa 74, 130
Gjøra, Per 73
Gøja 132
Gorman, Ellen 113
Graham, Mrs. Howard Spencer 151
Grahame, Kenneth 135
Grand Hotel 9, 10, 103
Greason, Sydney 149
Greenwich 235
Grieg, Edvard 172
Grøa 62
Grønsakshandel 23
Guaranty Trust Company 154
Gudbrandsdal 8, 61, 84, 85, 87
Guldkake 173
Gustavus II (Gustavus Adolphus) 64
Gustavus III 77
Guthus 95, 126, 129

H

Haakon Magnus, Crown Prince 19
Haakon VII 20, 98
Håfagre, Harald 13
Hågensen, Tore Bjørnhjell 71
Håkon Håkonson 47
Håkon VI Magnusson 49
Halvorsen, Tove 7
Hamar 45, 75, 78, 81, 84, 245

Hannibal Sehested 75
Hanseatic League 49, 75
Harald, King 24, 27
Harald V 19, 20
Harlem, Gro Brundtland 19
Hebrides 45
Hedemarken 13, 92
Hedesnarken 249
Hedmark 22
Helgøya 76, 84, 85, 245
Helmer, Torvald 103
Henry II 113
Henry VIII 62
High Court of the Realm 20
Hinds, Thomas 93
Hjortetakk 173
Hoås 8, 57, 58, 62
Hoisterett 19
Holbergsgate 10, 95, 97, 103
Homestead law 52
Honningkake 174
Hordaland 22
Hotel Viking 152
Howe, Julia Ward 6, 136
Hubbard, Mrs. John F. 151
Husman 46, 50
Hvitt Peppernøtter 35

I

Ibsen, Henrik 9, 20, 79, 102, 103, 115, 124, 128, 232
Ida Lewis Yacht Club 119
Improved Order of Red Men 120
Innlandet 88
Irving, James Edward 98
Island Cemetery 110
Isle of Man 45
Italian Biscotte 181

J

Ja, Vi elsker dette landet 46, 130
Jacob Fullarton & Company 110
Jagt 88, 92
Jamestown Ferryboat 118
Jamestown, Rhode Island 140, 142
Jan Mayen 19
Joachimstaler 54
Johansen, Bjørn Fladvad 7, 11, 12, 36, 163
Johansen, Martin 88, 97
Johansen, Nina 43
Johansen, Tove Halvorsen 2
John Easton house 99
John Street 110
Johnson, Annie Southwick 110
Johnson, Levi 111
Jordan, Marsh & Company 108
Jordbruger 92

Jotunheimen 60
Joulu 37
Jubilee Year in England 232
Julebukk 37
Julekake 30, 177
Julekost 36
Julenek 32
Julenissen 33, 177
Juleol 28
Juletre 28, 40

K

Kaffestue 94
Kaffevertinne 94
Karamellpudding 179
Kårbø, Marit Fladvad 94
Karl Johan 25, 130
Karl XIII 73
Kaull, Eleanor Cottrell 136
Kaull, Kenneth 157
Kaull, Kenneth Stevens 98
Kennedy, John F. 111
Kielland, Alexander 95
Kilkenny Castle 113
Kilmartin, Ireland 110
King John II of Denmark 75
King of Denmark and Norway 75
King of Norway 72
King's Council 20
Kirkelandet 88
Knutsen, Ole Bjørnhjell 59
Kolvereid 13, 87, 123, 196
Kommerstadbakken 78
Kommuner 46
Konditori 23
Kongeriket Norge 46
Kransekake 23, 184, 185
Kristiansand 56
Kristiansund 10, 11, 13, 67, 73, 88,
    89, 91, 92, 93, 95, 123, 159, 231, 255, 259
Kristiansund Folk Bibliotek 10, 91
Kristiansund harbor 88
Kristiansund's gamle kirke 91
Kristiansund's Longveien 90
Krogh, Christian 20
Krumkake 189
Krumkake iron 188
Kryderkake 190

L

Laagen (Lågen) river 86
Lagting 19
Lake Mjøsa 56, 75, 76, 81, 83, 84, 85, 172, 245
Land register 53
Landskyld 52
Lapps 20

Laup 54
League of Women Voters 142
Lefse 206
Leikvin Bygdemuseum 71
Leikvin Parish Museum 64
Leilendinger 50, 52
Lemon Cardamom Tea Bread 181
Lemon cognac favored tea cakes 224
Lemon Currant Cake 160
Lemon Pudding 216
Lewis, Ida 118
Lie, Trygve 20
Life Cakes 212
Lille Juleaften 29
Lillehamar 84
Lillehammer 45, 48
Lime Rock lighthouse 118
Linser 192
Loennechengården 94
Løken Kirke 58, 59
Louis XVI 72
Løykja 64
Lund, Sweden 47
Lutefisk 33
Lutheran 49
Lutheran Protestant Church 46
Lyhsgården 91, 92
Lyshaugen 257

M

Maihaugen 48, 51
Mandelflarn 193
Mandelkake 193, 194
Maplewood 140, 142
Marie's Manuscript Cookbook 2
Martha Louise, Princess 24
Marzipan 41
Marzipan Pig 37, 40
Mason, George 113
Matrikkel 53
Measures and Currencies 54
Mencken, H. L. 102
Michael Cottrell Estate 141, 142
Middags 27
Middle Ages 54
Middleton, Ireland 110
Middletown, R.I. 137
Mill Street 105
Mjøsa 61, 81
Molasses Diamond Cookies 43
Mølsgraut 44
Moore, Clement 14, 41, 136
Moore, Edward 111
Mor Monsen's Kake 196
Møre og Romsdal 22
Morgan, E.D. 118
Mother Monsen's Cake Cookie Bars 197

Mountain, Honora 110, 112
Muenchinger, Natalie 136
Munch, Edvard 20
Munkerpanner 198
Musik korps 26, 27

N

Namsos 80, 87, 196
Nansen, Fridtjof 115, 132, 240
Napoleansikaker 10
Napoleonic Wars 20, 72
Narragansett Bay 101, 135
National Day 129
National Theater 103
NATO 21
Naval Training Station 138
Nederkverneie 78
Nedre Kvern 249
New York Yacht Club 117, 120
Newport and Fall River Street Railway trolley 114
Newport Artillery 116, 122
Newport Artillery Company 115
Newport Band 120
Newport Chamber of Commerce 6, 11, 151
Newport Chapter of the American Red Cross 143
Newport City Directory 113
Newport County Woman Suffrage Association 142
Newport Gas Light Company 124
Newport Harbor 108
Newport Historical Society 101, 141
Newport Mercury 101, 113, 114, 124, 138, 146
Newport, Rhode Island 1, 12, 55, 94, 99, 159, 168, 234, 243, 248
Newport Savings and Loan Association 147
Newport Yacht Club 118
Newport Yacht Club Regatta 120
Newport's Gilded Age 118
Nidaros 13
Nidaros, Archbishop of 47, 49, 57, 58, 61
Nidaros Cathedral in Trondheim 75
Nisse 32
Nobile, Umberto 134
Nord-More 249
Nord-Trondelag 22
Nordland 22
Nordlandet 88
Nordmøre 56
Norman Bird Sancturary 109
Norsk Folk Museum 82
North Pole 132
Northwest Passage 96, 98, 132
Norway, Kingdom of 19
Norway's first political party 74
Norway's National Day 79
Norway's population 72
Norwegian Antlers 173
Norwegian Cassandra Cookies 181

Norwegian Christmas cookies 28
Norwegian Cones 189
Norwegian Constitution 46, 51
Norwegian Diagonals 166
Norwegian diet 48
Norwegian emigration to America 78
Norwegian Holiday Doughnuts 220
Norwegian National Theatre 231
Norwegian Rosettes 210
Norwegian Royal Crowns 42
Norwegian Sand Tarts 39, 212
Norwegian Sponge Cake 200
Norwegian State Railway System 97
Norwegian-American Line 242
Nowell, Thomas S. 81, 100
Nybakkenn 79
Nynorsk 46

O

Odelsting 19
Olav Engelbrektsson 50
Olav, King 21
Olav, King Haraldsson 46
Olav, Saint 46
Olav V 20
Old Stone Tower 139
Olso 79
Øpdal, Anne Arnesen 8
Opdøl 74
Opdøl, Endre 258
Opdøl, Gudrun Holm 73, 73
Opdøl, Ingrid 10
Oppdal 56, 86
Oppland 22
Orkney Islands 45
Ormond, Duke of 112, 113
Oscarsborg 252
Oscarshall Slott 21
Oslo 22, 23, 47, 101, 116, 152
Oslo Folk Museum 116, 159
Oslo's Grand Hotel 232
Ostfold 22
Oxford, England 233

P

Paper, Woven Hearts 40
Parliamentarians ("Roundheads") 65
Peace of Copenhagen 66
Pear Pudding 169
Peary, Robert E. 133, 134
Pedersen, Ivar 64
Peer Gynt country 172
Pelham Street 6, 101, 121, 130, 134
Pepparkaker 28
Pepperkake 203
Peppernøtter 34, 35, 204

Pinkham, Lydia E. 122
Pinnerudvollen lands 78
Pizzelle iron 188
Plymouth Colony 64
Potato flour 172, 215
Potato Lefse 206
Potatoes 72
Potetlefse 206
Potter, Beatrix 125
Pretzel 186
Pretzel Cinnamon Cookies 186
Pretzel Yeast Bread 186
Primogenitor 50
Prince Carl 20
Prince Carl of Denmark 98
Prince's Cake 170
Purgatory 109

Q

Queen Anne Square 108
Queen Victoria 231
Quisling 252

R

Rafstad in Vang 76
Raspberry jam 186
Raymond, Faith 21, 152
Raymond, Marie Cottrell 1, 115, 145, 146, 147, 148, 157, 201, 256
Raymond, William, III 1, 115
Raymond, William, Jr. 98, 146, 154, 155, 156, 158, 201
Redwood Library 105, 143
Reformation 46, 49, 50
Reynolds, Benjamin 135
Ring Tree Cake 184
Ringsaker 78, 79, 80, 81, 87
River Kvista 92
Rogaland 22
Rogers High School 1, 144, 145, 147
Roman Catholic 19
Romfo 72
Romfo Church 36, 54, 68, 69
Rømmebrød 209
Rommegrøt 208, 209
Romsdal 62, 86, 96
Romsdal valley 11
Rondane 60
Roosevelt, Franklin D. 252
Royal Arcanum 110
Royal Charter 49
Royal Road 13, 86

S

Sail On, Thou Gallant Bark 111
Saint's Hearts 213
Saints' Hearts 212

Sami 20
Sand Nuts 215
Sand Tarts 213
Sandbakkel forms 212
Sandbakkelse 212
Sandkaka 214
Sandkaker 28, 39, 213, 214
Sandnøtter I 215
Sandnøtter II 215
Satbakk-kollen 62
Scott, Robert Falcon 133
Serinakaker 28, 42
Sherman, William 141
Shortbread cookie 181, 209
Sibelius, Jean 117
Sidcup, Kent 233
Silver Cake 221, 222
Simes-Nowell, Ethel 130, 137, 138
Simes-Nowell, Harriett Cottrell 100, 135, 138
Simonsen, Tore Hoås 58
Sirupsnipper 28, 43
Six Weeks in Norway 81, 97, 119
Sjokoladekuler 216
Sjølstad West 88, 196
Skabelsen, Mennesket, og Messiah (Creation, Humani 73
Skibladner 83, 84, 87
Skillingsboller 217
Skillingskaker 12, 95
Skyld 52
Sletta 93
Slottet 24, 25, 129, 254
Smaa Sandkager 213
Smør Kreme 219
Smørkranser 218
Smørpletter 28, 39
Smultringer 220
Snøhetta 56
Soaked Cake 163
Society of the Cincinnati 120
Sogn og Fjordane 22
Solje pin 25
Sonja, Queen 24, 27
Sør-Trøndelag 22
Sour Cream Bread 209
Sour Cream Krumkake 189
Sour Cream Porridge 208
South Pole 134
Spann 52
Spice Cake 190
SS Oscar II 96, 98, 131, 133
St. Canute 37
St. Mary's Roman Catholic Church 111
St. Paul's Cathedral 233
Stamford, Connecticut 1, 98, 127, 154, 248
State Council 19
Sterne, Charles T. 144
Storofsin 61

Storting 19, 24, 46, 51, 72, 73, 74, 98, 101, 103, 127, 152
Sugar Bread Cake 224
Sugar Cake 223
Sugarbread 224
Sukkerbrodkake 223
Sundallen 257
Sunde, Bodil 8
Sunndal Valley 63
Sunndalen 5, 32, 49, 56, 58, 62, 71, 87, 258
Sunndalfjord 56, 252
Sunndalsøra 7, 8, 45, 54, 57, 64
Svalbard 19
Sweden 20, 51
Swedish pancake pan 230
Swinburne, Elizabeth H. 124
Swinburne Hous 121
Swinburne School 124
Symes, George 100
Synnöve Solbakken 4, 129, 136
Syttendemai 24
Syttendemai tog 25, 129

T

Taxation at Flatvad 65, 66
Taxes 54
Taylor, George 111
Tebrod 181
Telemark 22
Tenant farmers 50
Thames Street 106, 107, 110, 112, 113, 122, 123, 129, 141, 142
The King's Fans 182
Thirty Years' War 65
Tompkins, Mary H. 105
Thompson, Frank E. 150
Three Sisters, The 135
Thumbprints 186
Tilslorte Bondepiker 32
Timber trade 66
Timber-boom 80
Ting 46
Tingvoll-fjord 56
Tithe 54
Tithe paid on the Flatvad farm 64, 74
Tolethorpe School 136
Tolethorpe School for Girls 137, 144
Tomter, Nils Jensen 76, 78
Toresen, Bersvend Hoås 58
Toske farm 67
Touro Park 121, 139
Traditional Norwegian Dinner 44
Traditional Norwegian Measurements 306
Treaty of Kiel 73
Tregaarden Julehus 29
Tregården Julehus 177
Trinity Church 101, 108, 110, 111, 114, 126, 128, 137

Trolla 62
Trollheimen 56
Troms 22
Trondheim 13, 57, 61, 67, 87, 119
Trondstua 69
Tyske skiver 227

U

U.S. Congress 52
Ungern-Sternberg, Baron Renaud 141, 141
Union National Bank 116
Union of Kalmar 49
Unity Club 138
University of Oslo 7, 21, 256
Unndalsøra 56
Uterine exhaustion 122

V

Vaniljeboller 229
Vanilla Almond Cookies 207
Vanilla Custard Filling 228
Vanilla Krumkake 189
Vaughan, George 111
Vest-Agder 22
Vestfold 22
Victoria Park Hotel 97
Victoria, Queen 74
Vigeland, Gustav 20
Vigeland Sculpture Park 20
Viking Age 45
Viking burial ground 64
Viking Hotel 11, 94
Voldenga 93

W

Wallace, Eleanor 114
Wallace, Patrick 114, 115
Wallace, Richard 113
Wallace, Thomas 112, 113
War of Calmar 64
Warner Street 111
Washington Square 106
Wergeland, Henrik 73, 74
Wheat Rolls 175
Whiteman, Paul 146, 151, 201
Whitney, Harry Payne 146, 201
Willumsen, Christian 3, 65, 93
Willumsen, Jeanne 7, 40, 208
Willumsen, Wilhelm 244
Woman's Suffrage Amendment 145
World's Best Cake 191
Wreath Cake 185
Wright, Wilbur 125

Y

Yeast Bread with Apples 171
Yellow Cake 173

Notes

> *"...let it be our pride that we ourselves may put meaning into our lives, and sometimes a significance that transcends death. If a man is fortunate he will, before he dies, gather up as much as he can of his civilized heritage and transmit it to his children."*
>
> **—Will and Ariel Durant**

At BelleAire Press we believe the Durants were quite right. Our Vision is to help other families capture and pass along their heritage to all our children. That's why…we're looking for…MORE…Norwegian-American food and heritage!

We're very interested in sharing more tasty Norwegian-American dishes and fascinating stories of the people behind them. The Great Norwegian-American Cookbook (now in preparation) will include a wide variety of traditional recipes.

Each recipe will be accompanied by one or more photographs of the original Norwegian ancestor most closely associated with the recipe, including a brief family history or "thumbnail" biography of the person and the family. Why not ensure your family is represented? Let us hear from you.

We are interested in reviewing your family history manuscripts. Just write or fax us some basic information and we'll be in touch.

 The BelleAire Press, P.O. Box 4284, Crofton, MD 21114-4284, Fax: 301/464-4789, Internet: bap@ix.netcom.com.

YES, please send me:

❏ *Flavors of the Fjords*
  ($39.95+$3.75 P/H, TOTAL: $43.70)

Please register me to receive information about future *Flavors of the Fjords*

❏ *Updates and Supplements*

Please send me more information about:

❏ *The Great Norwegian-American Cookbook*
  (in production). Favorite recipes provided by Norwegian-Americans including family photographs and brief historics. Why not ensure your family is represented?

❏ *The Norwegian-American Experience*
  The newsletter of Norwegian life, travel, food, and culture.

Name _____ Title _____

Address _____

City _____ State/Zip _____

Method of Payment: ❏ Visa ❏ MasterCard ❏ Amex ❏ Discover
                   ❏ Payment Enclosed *(Applicable sales tax will be added.)*

Card No. _____ Expiration Date _____

SIGN HERE _____

Order invalid if not signed. Offer valid in the continental U.S.A., Alaska, Hawaii, and Canada only. (Prices slightly higher in Canada.) Offer expires 12/21/96.

YES, please send information about *Flavors of the Fjords* to:

Name _____ Title _____

Address _____

City _____ State/Zip _____

Mail to: The BelleAire Press, P.O. Box 4284, Crofton, MD 2114-4284, or Fax: 301/464-4789

YES, please send me:

❏ *Flavors of the Fjords*
  ($39.95+$3.75 P/H, TOTAL: $43.70)

Please register me to receive information about future *Flavors of the Fjords*

❏ *Updates and Supplements*

Please send me more information about:

❏ *The Great Norwegian-American Cookbook*
  (in production). Favorite recipes provided by Norwegian-Americans including family photographs and brief historics. Why not ensure your family is represented?

❏ *The Norwegian-American Experience*
  The newsletter of Norwegian life, travel, food, and culture.

Name _____ Title _____

Address _____

City _____ State/Zip _____

Method of Payment: ❏ Visa ❏ MasterCard ❏ Amex ❏ Discover
                   ❏ Payment Enclosed *(Applicable sales tax will be added.)*

Card No. _____ Expiration Date _____

SIGN HERE _____

Order invalid if not signed. Offer valid in the continental U.S.A., Alaska, Hawaii, and Canada only. (Prices slightly higher in Canada.) Offer expires 12/21/96.

YES, please send information about *Flavors of the Fjords* to:

Name _____ Title _____

Address _____

City _____ State/Zip _____

Mail to: The BelleAire Press, P.O. Box 4284, Crofton, MD 2114-4284, or Fax: 301/464-4789

The BelleAire Press

P.O. Box 4284

Crofton, Maryland 21114-4284

The BelleAire Press

P.O. Box 4284

Crofton, Maryland 21114-4284